Reading the New Testament

An Introduction

THIRD EDITION, REVISED AND UPDATED

PHEME PERKINS

PAULIST PRESS
New York / Mahwah, NJ

Cover design by Lynn Else
Illustrations by Frank Sabatté, CSP
Book design by Theresa M. Sparacio and Lynn Else

Library of Congress Cataloging-in-Publication Data

Perkins, Pheme.
    Reading the New Testament : an introduction / Pheme Perkins. — 3rd ed., rev. and updated.
        p. cm.
    Includes bibliographical references (p.   ) and indexes.
    SBN 978-0-8091-4786-1 (alk. paper) — ISBN 978-1-893757-79-0 1. Bible. N.T.—
Introductions. I. Title.
    BS2330.52.P47 2012
    225.6′1—dc23
                                                                        2012014781

Published by Paulist Press
997 Macarthur Boulevard
Mahwah, New Jersey 07430

www.paulistpress.com

Printed and bound in the
United States of America

CONTENTS

PART FOUR: THE GOSPELS: FOUR PORTRAITS OF JESUS

Dedicated to a friend greatly missed
Rev. Lawrence E. Boadt, CSP

Chapter 1

WHY STUDY THE BIBLE?

What Is the New Testament?

Many people would find it difficult to answer the question, "What is the New Testament?" Sometimes students say, "What they read in church," or "the story of Jesus." You will see twenty-seven different writings listed in the table of contents. What holds that group together? They are not twenty-seven chapters in a single book.

Even the phrase "new testament" can be a puzzle. If something is "new," does that mean a major improvement on something that already exists like a new model car? Or does "new" mean something that has never existed before like a new technology? And what about the word *testament*? Most people have heard the expression "last will and testament" for the legal document people prepare to dispose of their property after their death. A "new" testament would suggest that an earlier version was being replaced because something has changed. That's what an ordinary first-century-AD Greek speaker would have thought you were talking about. But a Jew who had grown up outside Syria and Palestine in a community that read its scripture in a Greek translation, not in Hebrew, would recognize that "testament" had a special religious meaning. It was the term used for the covenant that united God and Israel. The expression "new covenant" appears in the prophets referring to a future time when the covenant will be inscribed in the human heart. The cycle of sin and disobedience of God's law, punishment, repentance, and restoration will finally end (see Jer 31:31–34). To our first-century Jewish listener the expression "new covenant" is not about something written down but about the ideal relationship with God.

The most general answer you could give would be to speak of a common belief shared by all the writers: Jesus of Nazareth represents a decisive turning point in God's relationship to humanity. The expression "new covenant" indicates that what the prophets depicted as the ideal relationship

1

between Israel and God has become possible. Of course, there is an element of the ordinary Greek usage of "testament" in the story as well. While the prior covenant focused on Israel as God's people, this new covenant is expanding the definition of *heir* to include anyone who hears and believes the gospel. Or, to put it in the words of Acts 4:12: "There is salvation in no one else, for there is no other name under heaven, given to human beings by which we must be saved."

This common belief in Jesus Christ is expressed in many different ways in the New Testament. We will constantly be asking ourselves how each way of expressing the message speaks to the situation of Christians in the first century. The New Testament provides us with a window into the emergence of Christianity.

The New Testament writings are arranged in groups. The four gospels, which tell the story of Jesus' life and teaching, are grouped together at the beginning. They are the basis for Christian faith and practice. In Christian liturgy, a separate book containing the gospels may receive special treatment: be carried in procession, incensed, and read out only by clergy. In Jewish syn-agogues the scroll containing the Torah of Moses (Genesis through Deuteronomy), which is the foundation of Jewish life, is treated as a sacred object.

Treating the four gospels as a special group meant separating the gospel written by Luke from the second part of his literary work, that is, the Acts of the Apostles. But its stories of the earliest Jerusalem church, of the role of Peter, James, and especially Paul, who is God's instrument to carry the gospel to the nations, provide a framework for reading the next section. It comprises collections of letters written either by or in the name of apostles. First, we have fourteen letters that either were written by Paul or were attributed to his authorship. The last, Hebrews, does not really belong in the group, since it does not claim any connection with the Pauline tradition. The others, whether by Paul or by disciples writing in Paul's name, are divided into two groups, each in descending order of length. The first group comprises letters addressed to churches. The second comprises those addressed to individuals. After the Pauline collection, we have seven letters that were attributed to other apostolic figures: James, Peter, John, and Jude. In the fourth century AD, the church historian Eusebius referred to this group as "catholic" epis-tles. The word *catholic* meant universal. Eusebius explained that even though letters in this group were not quoted very often, they are generally recog-nized in the churches. Finally, the New Testament concludes with a very dif-ferent type of writing, a complex record of visions. Its author is a Christian prophet and teacher in exile on the island of Patmos off the coast of Asia Minor. In keeping with the letter collections that shaped early Christianity, Revelation opens with seven more letters addressed to seven churches in the cities of Asia Minor. This prophetic vision of the struggle against and dramatic end of a world dominated by evil powers with the great victory of Jesus and his "holy ones," celebrated as the Lamb's wedding feast in the new Jerusalem, brings the collection of writings that make up the New Testament to its close.

Dating Books in the New Testament

Unlike modern books, most ancient writings do not carry dates. Clearly, any book must be written after events to which it refers and sometime before it is used by another writer or before the date of our earliest manuscript fragments. Sometimes, like the Book of Daniel, which seems to have been written around 167 BC, a book may "pretend" to be written in an earlier time. Daniel is set in the Babylonian captivity of the sixth century BC. But even distinguishing when a work was composed from the imagined time in which it is set does not tell the whole story. An author may take over older stories or sayings told about someone else, for example, Daniel 1–6 contains a number of stories about Jewish courtiers and their dealings with Babylonian kings. Scholars think that some of these stories actually originated several hundred years before they were used by the author of Daniel.

Even to guess at when a biblical book was written we have to answer a number of questions. First, does the book refer to any historical persons or events for which we can give dates based on other historical information? For example, Daniel 11:40–45 pictures Antiochus IV dying in the final end of the world battle, so the book must have been completed before Antiochus died in Persia in 164 BC. Second, is the book itself used by later writers? Third, how does the date suggested by such clues compare with the setting implied by the narrative? Has the author chosen to write as though living at some other time or place? Fourth, what about the possible dates of stories or traditions being used within a book? Has the author used older traditions or even earlier written materials that we can identify? (Luke 1:1 claims familiarity with a number of earlier accounts, for example.) Fifth, can we isolate possible time and place of origin for any of the traditions being used?

We can only estimate when the New Testament writings were composed. Some of the guesses for a given work are more certain than others. The dates listed here represent a majority opinion of scholars working on the book in question. Any commentary on a given writing will discuss the problems of dating and some of the alternatives.

The Contents of the New Testament

I. Gospels and Acts

(1) *Matthew* (ca. AD 85). This gospel makes use of Mark as well as other traditions about Jesus and collections of Jesus' sayings. It was composed in Greek as the reference to Daniel as "the prophet" in 24:15 implies. (It is only in the Greek translation of the Old Testament that Daniel is included among the prophets.) Matthew also contains special material that suggests a Palestinian origin such as the references to the "towns of Israel" (10:23; 2:20–21, "land of Israel"). Many scholars think that the community that formed the basis of the Matthean church had settled in Syria. Matthew 4:24 has the only reference in the gospels to Jesus' fame spreading "throughout all Syria." The community may have been predominantly Christians of Jewish background, since non-Jews (Gentiles) are referred to as outsiders (5:47; 6:7, 32; 10:5–6, 17–18; 18:17). The community continues to reverence the Jewish law (5:18–19; 23:2), interpreting it in light of Jesus' teaching.

(2) *Mark* (ca. AD 68–70). Our earliest gospel, Mark, has been used by both Matthew and Luke. Mark emphasizes the need for Christians to expect suffering. Mark 13:9–10 speaks of persecution by Jews and "governors and kings." Many scholars think that the crisis of suffering should be linked to Nero's execution of Christians at Rome as scapegoats for the devastating fire in July AD 64, which claimed the lives of both Peter and Paul. Others think that Mark is referring to the sufferings of Christians in Palestine during the Jewish revolt against Rome (AD 66–74). Mark 13 collects a number of prophecies about the coming destruction of the temple and Jerusalem, and Mark 16:7 focuses our attention on Galilee as the place where Jesus' frightened disciples are to see him again. The Marcan community is predominantly Gentile. Explanations for Jewish customs are given (Mark 7:3–4, 11c, 19c). Freedom from Jewish Sabbath rules and purity regulations applies to all Christians (2:27–28; 7:3, 8, 19).

(3) *Luke* (ca. AD 85). When Luke repeats prophecies concerning the destruction of Jerusalem from Mark, Luke makes sure that they reflect details of Titus's siege of Jerusalem (cf. Mark 13:2 and Luke 21:5; Mark 13:14 and Luke 21:10; as well as the sayings about Jerusalem in Luke 13:35a and 19:43–44). Luke 1:2 clearly separates the author from the generation of persons who were "eyewitnesses" to the ministry of Jesus. Uncertainty about Palestinian geography in the narrative suggests that its author was not from that part of the world. The quality of his writing points to education beyond the elementary level. Luke shows familiarity with the Greek Old Testament and with Hellenistic literary techniques. Luke tries to locate the emergence of Christianity within the context of the larger Graeco-Roman world. Some exegetes identify the author Luke with the "fellow worker" in the Pauline

mission (Phlm 24; Col 4:14 [basis for the later story that Luke was a physician] and 2 Tim 4:11).

(4) *John* (ca. AD 90). Johannine traditions about Jesus are different from what we find in the Synoptic Gospels (= Matthew, Mark, and Luke). They do show points of contact with material found in Mark and Luke, which suggests that the Johannine traditions came from an independent line of development of the Jesus tradition. John alludes to expulsion of Christians from Jewish synagogues (John 9:22; 16:2a). The gospel's author is unknown, though its traditions are attributed to an anonymous figure in the narrative, "the beloved disciple." This disciple is not one of the Twelve. He appears only in the story during Jesus' last days in Jerusalem, at the cross (John 19:35), and in the resurrection stories (21:24). He may have been the founder of the Johannine community. John 21:23 hints that, unlike Peter, he did not die a martyr but lived to a considerable age. This anonymous disciple may have been responsible for the unique symbolic language used to identify Jesus with God in the gospel.

(5) *Acts* (ca. AD 95–100). Acts 1:1–5 identifies the book as a continuation of Luke's gospel. This introduction summarizes the gospel story and prepares the reader for the next development that begins with Pentecost. Acts does not present what ancient readers would have seen as a "history" of the earliest years of the church. The events mentioned do not extend beyond Paul's imprisonment at Jerusalem and subsequent removal to Rome for trial (ca. AD 57–60). The story of Peter and the other apostles is dropped when the narrative shifts to Paul's journeys. We never hear about the martyrdom of either of these famous apostles.

II. Pauline Letters

(6) *Romans* (ca. AD 57). Paul wrote this letter to the Christians in Rome as he was winding up his missionary activity in Asia Minor and Greece. After delivering a collection from those churches for the poor in Jerusalem, he hoped to visit Rome and receive aid from Christians there to begin a missionary effort in Spain (Rom 15:22–32). Chapter 16 contains greetings to fellow workers who had been active in Paul's mission in Asia Minor and Greece.

(7) *1 Corinthians* (ca. AD 56). Paul had spent eighteen months working in Corinth (ca. AD 50–52) and had founded the church in this important commercial city. He has received a letter from Christians there as well as various reports about problems at Corinth. He expects that 1 Corinthians will arrive before his associate Timothy comes to Corinth. He urges the Corinthians to give Timothy a warm welcome and to set aside money for the poor in Jerusalem. Paul himself expects to travel through Macedonia to Corinth for a visit (1 Cor 16:1–11).

(8) *2 Corinthians* (ca. AD 56–58). This is a very complex letter, since it appears to be made up of three or four different letters that Paul sent to

Corinth. The visit mentioned in 1 Corinthians had been a disaster. Paul was humiliated by someone in the Corinthian church (2 Cor 2:5–8). His apostleship was being challenged as "weak" and lacking in power by traveling missionaries who had come to Corinth and won a following among the Corinthians (2 Cor 10:10–11; 11:4–6). Paul had apparently canceled another visit to Corinth and had written a very sharp letter of rebuke (2 Cor 1:23—2:4). Second Corinthians 1–7 gives thanks that the rift between Paul and the Corinthians has been healed through the work of Titus. But 2 Corinthians 10–13 is written in such a harsh, sarcastic tone that many think these chapters were not from the earlier "tearful letter" but respond to another outbreak of opposition to Paul due to traveling missionaries. Paul expects to arrive in Corinth shortly (2 Cor 13:10). Second Corinthians 8–9 deals with a different subject entirely, the collection for the poor at Jerusalem. These chapters may be a single letter of appeal or a combination of two letters, one to Corinth and one to the Christians elsewhere in the province of Achaia.

(9) *Galatians* (ca. AD 55). Paul founded this church when he became ill on a journey through Galatia (Gal 4:13). His letter does not mention any plans for a future visit, so some scholars think that Galatians was written toward the end of Paul's missionary work. Paul is confronting a serious problem. When he had converted the Gentiles of this region to Christianity, he did not require that they adopt any Jewish customs. Now others are telling them that they should also adopt Jewish ways. They should show loyalty to the covenant between God and the Jewish people by being circumcised, keeping Jewish holidays, and observing some Jewish dietary rules. Perhaps these teachers alleged that Paul had violated agreements with Peter and James in Jerusalem in not imposing such requirements. Paul is furious. He retells the story of his conversion and his early association with the Jerusalem church (Gal 1:11—2:14). He insists that they all agreed that Gentile converts would be free from the obligations of the Jewish law but that Paul would take up a collection among the Gentiles for the poor believers in Jerusalem.

(10) *Ephesians* (ca. AD 80–90). This letter appears to have been written after Paul's death in Rome using the voice of the apostle as a heroic prisoner (3:1; 4:1; 6:20). Sections echo the Letter to the Colossians. Ephesians develops themes from Paul's letters such as the apostle's insight into God's plan to bring salvation to the Gentiles and the church as the body of Christ. The second half of Ephesians reminds Gentile believers that they must pursue holiness, putting aside all the immorality of the "pagan/Gentile" culture.

(11) *Philippians* (ca. AD 54–55). Paul is writing from one of his earlier imprisonments (2 Cor 1:8–11; 11:23), perhaps in Ephesus (1 Cor 15:32). The letter will be taken back to Philippi by Epaphroditus, who had brought Paul money from the Philippian church and had fallen seriously ill (Phil 2:25–30). Older books sometimes assume that the mention of "Caesar's household" (4:22) means that this letter was written from jail in Rome before his death.

However, Paul really expects to be released (1:25–26), and there is an exchange of news between Paul and the Philippians that would not be possible from Rome. Since there was a cohort of the imperial guard in Ephesus, it seems likely that this letter was written from jail there.

(12) *Colossians* (ca. AD 62–70). Colossae is a hundred miles inland from Ephesus and ten miles from the city of Laodicea, which was devastated by an earthquake in AD 60. Some scholars conclude that Paul composed the letter from an Ephesus jail (Col 4:3, 10, 18) around AD 55. However, there are enough differences in theological expression between this letter and others by Paul to suggest that it must come much later in the series around the time of Paul's death in Rome. Its author is applying Paul's theology to a new religious crisis in the Lycus valley. Whether sent from Rome at the apostle's direction or from the major center of a Pauline school in Ephesus, one cannot tell. The church at Colossae was founded by Epaphras, not Paul (Col 1:6–7). Neither they nor the Christians in Laodicea have ever seen Paul (2:1). These churches are being troubled by false teachings, which seem to combine speculation about the heavenly Christ with elements of Jewish mysticism and perhaps even pagan philosophy. Greetings are sent to Christians in the area from others who have been working in the Pauline mission.

(13) *1 Thessalonians* (ca. AD 51). This appears to be one of the earliest of Paul's letters. Worried about the newly founded church in Thessalonica, Paul sent Timothy to check on the situation. Timothy brought back a glowing report. He also reported that the Thessalonians were troubled by the death of Christians in their church. Paul sends this letter of encouragement.

(14) *2 Thessalonians* (late AD 51? or post AD 70). If Paul wrote the letter, then it must follow 1 Thessalonians. The opening verses (2 Thess 1:1–4) pick up the opening of 1 Thessalonians and its reference to the sufferings endured by believers (1 Thess 1:6–7), But there are elements in the language and theology of 2 Thessalonians that do not seem to fit this stage of Paul's career. People have been confused by teachings about the end of days in letters said to be from Paul (2 Thess 2:1–2). Paul does not use elsewhere the term *mystery* for a scenario imagining the destruction of Satan (2:6–12). Therefore, other scholars suggest a later author, writing to correct false teaching circulating under Paul's authority. God decides when the end will come. Christians should follow the example Paul had set, working hard to earn a living and continuing in love of one another.

(15–17) *1 and 2 Timothy, Titus* (ca. AD 100). Timothy and Titus were Paul's closest associates, who often represented him in the churches (1 Cor 4:17; 2 Cor 8:16–17). These letters reflect a church organization more developed than the one assumed in the Pauline letters of the 50s and 60s. First Timothy and Titus imagine Paul providing final instructions to them as though they were neophytes. Timothy, Titus, and other women and men who had been part of Paul's mission may be passing from the scene themselves.

These letters provide something of a handbook for the next generation, especially those "bishops," "presbyters," and "devout widows" who will lead the local churches and keep them from falling prey to false teaching about Christianity.

(18) *Philemon* (ca. AD 54–55). Another letter from an imprisonment (Ephesus?) that Paul expects will soon be over (v. 22) is addressed to one of Paul's converts and the church that meets in his house. Paul had converted Philemon's runaway slave, Onesimus, to Christianity. In returning the slave to his master, Paul wants Philemon to receive the runaway as a "beloved Christian brother," not as one who deserves harsh punishment.

III. Other "Apostolic Letters"

(19) *Hebrews* (ca. AD 80–90). This writing is an extended speech or exhortation (13:22) to which a letter-style conclusion was attached (13:20–25). The audience have been Christians for some time and are growing lukewarm in their faith or in danger of abandoning it. The elegant Greek and theology of Hebrews do not belong to the Pauline tradition. But because the conclusion mentions Timothy (Heb 13:23), Hebrews was attached to the collection of Paul's letters as early as the second century AD.

(20) *James* (ca. AD 65–85). Although claiming to be a letter from the James who was the leader of Jewish Christians in Jerusalem (Gal 1:19: 2:9, 12) to those living in the diaspora (Jas 1:1), its Greek style makes it unlikely that one of Jesus' Galilean relatives composed the piece. Like Hebrews, James is really not a letter but a speech of exhortation or moral instruction that embodies the ethical wisdom of Jewish believers.

(21) *1 Peter* (ca. AD 75–90). This letter was sent in Peter's name from Christians at Rome (= "Babylon," 1 Pet 5:13) to churches in Asia Minor. The conclusion mentions other well-known figures: Silvanus, an associate of Paul (1 Thess 1:1), and Mark, originally part of Paul's mission (Phlm 24; Col 4:10). Perhaps based on this passage, Christians later credited Mark with writing down Peter's teaching before the apostle's death in Rome (Eusebius, *History of the Church* 2.15). The addressees are suffering harassment and persecution from others because they are Christians. The author encourages them to live in holiness so that nonbelievers will see what God has done in bringing sinners to lives of goodness (1 Pet 2:11–12; 3:14–16; 4:4–5).

(22) *2 Peter* (ca. AD 110). This letter appears to the latest writing in the New Testament. It incorporates material from Jude, assumes readers know a collection of Paul's letters, and refers to the gospel story of the transfiguration (2 Pet 1:16–21). Some people using Paul's letters (3:16) and philosophical argument have been denying that Christ is going to return in judgment.

(23–24) *First and Second John* (ca. AD 100). First John opens as an address to the audience that its author has committed to writing (1 John 2:1,

7–8, 12–14, 21, 26; 5:13). Though 1 John does not quote John's gospel as we know it, the opening (1:1–5) uses language from the gospel, a practice continued throughout the letter (cf. 1 John 4:9 and John 3:16–17). The author encourages those who remain in fellowship with him to stay faithful to that tradition. Other Christians have broken off from the Johannine fellowship to form their own groups (1 John 2:18–23). Second John is a brief note to Johannine Christians in another church warning them not to have anything to do with those who have broken away (2 John v. 9–11).

(25) *Third John* (ca. AD 100). This writing is a personal note from the author of 2 John to an individual, not a community. The leader of a house church in the area was refusing hospitality to missionaries who came from the elder's church. The elder hopes that Gaius provides such hospitality. Third John concludes with a recommendation for Demetrius, who is carrying the letter.

(26) *Jude* (date uncertain). This short letter of exhortation to an unspecified audience is said to be from another of Jesus' "brothers," Jude (Mark 6:3; Matt 13:55). The designation "brother of James" and the reference back to "what the apostles of our Lord Jesus Christ foretold" (Jude v. 17) suggest that it was written after other apostolic letters were in circulation but earlier than 2 Peter, which uses it. Jude includes Jewish legends attached to Moses and Enoch in announcing God's judgment against those who are leading believers astray.

(27) *Revelation* (ca. AD 95). A Christian prophet named John, who had been exiled to the island of Patmos (Rev 1:9–10), presents a striking series of visions for Christians in Asia Minor. The initial letters from the heavenly Son of Man to churches in seven cities offer praise for some and stern warnings for others. Like chapters 7 to 12 in the Book of Daniel, Revelation contains symbolic visions of events leading to the end of the world that describe political powers (the Roman Empire and its rulers) in cryptic symbols. Angelic figures and mythic beasts representing evil powers are behind events on earth. The visions also describe the future glory of those who have remained faithful to God in times of trial. Clues in the visions suggest that the book was written toward the end of the emperor Domitian's reign.

The Bible as Classic and as Canon

You can see that the New Testament contains several different types of writing spread over a period of about sixty years. As the church expanded in the second and third centuries, these writings became a Christian scripture alongside the Jewish scripture that the Christians had from the beginning. Because Christianity took root and spread outside the Aramaic-speaking areas of Palestine and Syria, all of the New Testament writings are in Greek.

The Jewish scriptures used by Christians were not the Hebrew Bible but Greek translations of those works along with additional Jewish works in Greek that are not included in the Jewish canon today. Roman Catholic and Eastern Orthodox Christians retain this form of the Christian Old Testament. The Protestant Reformation reverted to the Hebrew Bible as the Christian Old Testament. Today all translations of the Old Testament into modern languages will employ the best Hebrew texts of the individual books. A Catholic edition will include the additional writings from the Greek Old Testament.

Early Christian writings from the first and second centuries were not limited to those contained in our New Testament. Collections of Jesus' sayings and miracles were in circulation from an early time. The *Gospel of Thomas* is a collection of Jesus' sayings, some of them versions of sayings and parables found in the canonical gospels. Others retold the story of Jesus' life, often filling in the blanks in the four gospels that were to become Christian scripture. The *Protoevangelium of James* from the late second century is an expanded "infancy gospel" that focuses on Mary, introducing her parents Joachim and Ann. Written earlier in the second century, the *Gospel of Peter* depicts Jesus emerging from the tomb on Easter morning to confound a crowd of unbelievers. Both of these gospels include material from the canonical gospels. People also told stories of the various apostles, such as the *Acts of Thomas*, which imagines that apostle's adventures evangelizing India. From the mid-second century on, a whole group of writings sprang up that claimed to give secret teachings transmitted to the apostles by the risen Jesus. The groups that produced these writings claimed to have an apostolic tradition that was not revealed to the Twelve as a group but reserved for those believers who received special spiritual insight, or *gnosis* in Greek. Their writings are often lumped together as "Gnostic gospels" even when they are not "gospels" in the sense of the canonical gospels or other gospels that set out to recount the life and teaching of Jesus. Two of the best known in the popular media are the *Gospel of Mary*, in which Mary Magdalene has Gnostic insights that Jesus' male disciples lack, and the *Gospel of Judas*, first published in 2006.

Doctrinal controversies and confusion over the authority of the various writings being used by different groups played an important role in the move to develop a list of authoritative Christian writings. We call this authoritative collection the canon. Most of the writings in our New Testament were canonical in many churches by the end of the second century AD. Disagreements over the authority of Revelation, Hebrews, and some of the later epistles continued through the fourth century. The Syrian churches continued to use a harmonization of the gospels by Tatian known as the *Diatesseron* until into the fifth century. Thus, what we speak of as the New Testament owes its authority to its acceptance in broad areas of the church. It did not come down from heaven stamped "divine revelation." Nor was it imposed on the faithful from above by fourth-century bishops to check the creativity of Gnostics and other sects. Of course, writings in the canon came to be seen as the work of apostles inspired by God. Moreover, the word *canon* means "rule," so beliefs proposed as Christian that did not measure up to or contradicted the testimony of the canon were rejected.

In addition to its authority as "canon," the Bible has also played an important role in shaping Western culture, in music, art, and literature as well as in the general ethical norms that our culture has taken from its roots in the Jewish and Christian scriptures. Some scholars have described this function of the Bible as that of the "classic." Any work that a culture endows with such authority plays a special role in revealing who we are as a people. Through the classics, we begin to sense the mysteries of the world and of human life that are expressed in the great works of art, music, literature, and philosophy. They challenge us to go beyond the narrow world in which we live and ask about the overall shape of reality. They explore the tragedies of human life that seem beyond our control. In the classics, we discover ways in which the human spirit can reach beyond the boundaries that often seem to limit our possibilities.

Because the Bible is a classic in our culture, its truth is not limited to the religious doctrines and practices that believing Christians derive from it. The Bible belongs to the heritage of everyone in our culture, believer and nonbeliever alike. The Bible's vision of the world, the place of humans in it, and the values and tragedies that shape human life deserve to be set over against the other great visions that have also shaped our tradition.

Of course, study of the Bible as a "classic" will never be enough for the Christian believer. Studying the Bible as a classic that inspired the literature, art, language, and values of various cultures can help believers appreciate its message. However, as scripture in a faith community, the Bible is not a museum piece. Christians have taken upon themselves the obligation to live out the biblical vision in a community with others who are also heirs to the faith expressed in the Bible. As we shall see, the Bible contains a diversity of insights and traditions. The global Christian community is equally pluralistic. Christians do not all agree about how the Bible's insights are to be expressed in the lives of believers today. Different Christian denominations have distinct theological and liturgical traditions. These differences also exercise an important influence on the interpretation of the Bible. Jews read the Torah, the prophets, and the writings in what Christians refer to as the "Old" Testament very differently than Christians. Nevertheless, in our time, one of the unifying factors in Christian experience has been the shared task of historical study of the Bible. We find a source of Christian unity in the faith that we seek to share with our biblical ancestors. Following the example of St. Jerome, the great Latin translator and exegete of the fourth century AD, Christians also learn about the Hebrew scriptures from the Jewish community.

The Qur'an

Today Christians often see copies of the holy book used by Muslim neighbors in homes, on television reports about events in a Muslim country, or in the local bookstore. They may have heard that the Qur'an includes many familiar biblical themes and characters: Adam and Eve, Abraham and his sons, Joseph and his brothers, Moses guiding the children of Israel in the desert, the angels Michael and Gabriel, Mary and Jesus. Both the Hebrew scriptures and the Christian New Testament open with books that narrate the story of God's people. Separate sections are devoted to legal and moral instruction, to the words and visions of prophets, and to religious poetry like the psalms.

When Jews or Christians pick up a translation of the Qur'an expecting it to be like the Bible, they are surprised. It does not tell the story of Muhammad's call to be the final prophet, the transmission of the heavenly teaching by the angel Gabriel, or the struggles to establish Islam. It does not tell the familiar biblical stories as Jews and Christians know them from their scriptures. In fact, it even includes legends that are not in our Bible but were later told among Jews and Christians. The Qur'an knows tales from the later *Infancy Gospel of Thomas* about the precocious child Jesus shaping birds of clay and breathing on them, and the birds flying off (Sura 5:110). Since the Qur'an insists that there is no god but God (Allah), it rejects the Christian view that Christ, the son of Mary, is God (Sura 5:17). Because Muslims are so often depicted in scenes of violence, often against other Muslims, Jews and Christians are often surprised to discover that the Qur'an repeatedly stresses that God is forgiving and compassionate. It contains many references to the great day of God's judgment when all humanity will be judged (Sura 39:72–75). The dead are to be resurrected at the judgment.

Muhammad clearly had contact with some form of both Jewish and Christian scripture. Since references to the biblical stories are woven throughout the 114 suras of the Qur'an, it helps to know the Bible, which has the stories in chronological order. Unlike the Bible, the Qur'an does not collect the ethical commandments in one section like the Ten Commandments or the Sermon on the Mount. It is possible to find many familiar commandments in the Qur'an. The first is to worship no god but God (Allah). Others are to honor parents; not to commit adultery; to care for relatives, the needy, the orphan, and the traveler; not to kill except as justice requires; to be just and fair in dealing with others. The Qur'an also encourages its audience to adopt characteristics that will be familiar to Christians from Jesus' words in the Beatitudes: an attitude of humility and purity of heart (cf. Matt 5:5, 8). So there are many topics for dialogue between Jews, Christians, and Muslims.

Language, Text, and Translation

Sometimes Christians quote the Bible in English as though those were words directly spoken by God, even though the scriptures were written in Hebrew, Aramaic, and Greek. Jews and Muslims retain the original Hebrew or Arabic for their scriptures. Young people must learn to recite long sections of a text in a language they do not speak. However, God's revelation comes to us through human beings seeking to understand God's will within many cultures and languages. Jesus lived in a country in which four different languages could be found: Hebrew, Aramaic, Greek, and Latin. Aramaic was the common language of the people. Dialects of Aramaic were spoken across the Middle East from the Mediterranean to India. But after the conquest of the Near East and Egypt by Alexander the Great in the second half of the fourth century BC, Greek became the dominant official language of government and commerce from Greece to the border of India.

Many Jews continued to learn the Hebrew of their ancestors, and the language developed new dialects and adopted words from the other languages. Two of these Aramaic words are familiar to gospel readers, *abba*, meaning "father" (Mark 14:36), and *mammon*, meaning "wealth" (Matt 6:24). For those Jews who no longer understood Hebrew, we find translations of them into Aramaic. The latter are called targums. Some are almost direct translations. Others are more like paraphrases. Though there is no evidence for use of targums in formal worship, they provide fascinating glimpses into how to understand difficult Hebrew passages and examples of legends associated with the biblical figures.

In 63 BC, the Roman general Pompey marched into Jerusalem, and Roman presence in this area of the world began. The Roman military brought Latin along with it. But since many educated Romans knew Greek and were fond of "things Greek," Latin remained limited to the special concerns of Roman officialdom.

Naturally, the languages used among the people of this region—Hebrew, Aramaic, and Greek—developed like any language spoken over centuries, and they influenced one another. Some odd expressions in the Greek of the New Testament can be identified as peculiarities of Greek from an Aramaic-speaking environment. Jesus' teaching would have been done in Aramaic, since the Jewish population of the towns and villages in Galilee and Judea used that language. All of the New Testament writings were composed in Greek. To that extent, they show us by their very language how rapidly Christianity spread outside its Jewish Palestinian environment to the wider world.

The New Testament has been involved with translation from one language to another since the very beginning. Any single translation into English, Spanish, or another modern language will never be the definitive rendering of the Bible. We constantly learn more about what particular words and phrases meant in biblical times. English also changes constantly so that a good translation of a biblical passage at one time may not make sense a generation later. Some translations seek to put the Bible into English for young teens or a "basic English" spoken around the world as in the new Common English Bible (2010).

Sometimes a passage is so difficult that any translation is really the translator's educated guess about what the author meant to say in the passage. This task is difficult if the writer is using sarcasm or irony. Here is an example. In 2 Corinthians 10:10, Paul is responding to accusations that some people have made against him. A fairly literal translation might be:

> They say, "On the one hand, his letters are weighty and strong; but his bodily presence is weak and his speech contemptuous."

However, Paul is being sarcastic. People have been saying that the Corinthians should not listen to Paul because when he preaches in person, Paul does not put on as good a show as others do. Many modern translations try to capture that tone. Here are two of them:

> "His letters," they say, "are severe and forceful, but when he is here in person, he is unimpressive and his word makes no great impact." [New American Bible]

> Someone said, "He writes powerful and strongly worded letters, but when he is with you, you see only half a man and no preacher at all." [Jerusalem Bible]

Both are easier for people to understand when they hear them. The first is closer to the literal rendering of the sentence, but the second is more successful at capturing the strong irony of Paul's words. The Common English Bible changes the grammar to make the sentence clearer: "I know that some people are saying: 'His letters are severe and powerful, but in person he is weak and his speech is worth nothing.'"

You can see from the example that there is no simple answer to the question of what is the "best" translation of the Bible. Each one has strong points and weak ones. One translation may be more successful with particular sections of the Bible than others. Some translations follow the wording and sentence structure of the text rather slavishly. Others try to find expressions in English that will pack the same emotional punch in our language that the original audience would have felt. We refer to that type of translation as looking for a "functional equivalent." The American Bible Society's Common English Version (1995) is that type. It is important to distinguish between a translation and a "paraphrase" of the Bible. A paraphrase does not preserve the words or sentence structure of the original. Sometimes it is much shorter because it leaves things out. Sometimes it retells the story with things added by the translators that are not there at all. Various forms of *The Living Bible*, a "thought for thought" paraphrase by Kenneth Taylor, have been marketed widely among evangelicals. Paraphrases are not good resources for Bible study. They do not present what the biblical writers said directly.

The most important thing for the beginner is to pick a translation of the Bible that you can read comfortably. Every translation comes in many formats. Study Bibles include introductions, explanatory notes, extra essays, maps, charts, and even illustrations. Devotional Bibles keyed to different audiences incorporate hints for living out the Bible message, often from authors popular with a target audience. Some of the most widely used translations are the New American Bible, revised edition (used in the Roman Catholic lectionary in the United States); the Revised English Bible; the New Jerusalem Bible (another popular Roman Catholic translation); the New International Version (a fairly literal rendering popular with conservative Protestants). The most commonly used translation for study purposes and in mainline Protestant churches (as well as in the Catholic lectionary in Canada) is the New Revised Standard Version. An ecumenical edition of this translation includes the books from the early church's Greek Old Testament that belong to Roman Catholic Bibles, and some additional works that are part of scripture in the Greek Orthodox Church.

The most famous English translation, the King James Version, celebrated its four-hundreth anniversary in 2011. But even that Bible, whose language has shaped so much of English literature, was revised to remove the archaic language, vocabulary, and grammar (1982). The revisers continued to use older forms of the Hebrew and Greek texts than those employed by most scholars today. They insisted upon a literal rendering of the meaning of each Hebrew and Greek word and not adapting idiomatic English expressions.

Entering the New Testament World: Archaeology and History

Though new translations occasionally make news, the most publicized developments are archaeological discoveries connected with the Bible. Sometimes people expect that archaeology proves the truth of the Bible by discovering the remains of cities, roads, and other places mentioned in the biblical narrative. Actually, the relationship between archaeology and the Bible is much more complex. Biblical studies in the past two centuries would have been impossible without the striking growth in archaeological investigation and interpretation of sites in the Near East, Turkey, North Africa, Greece, and Italy.

Archaeological discoveries have included important written remains of the cultures surrounding the Bible. The rich religious and mythological symbolism of the sea peoples of Phoenicia, the Sumerians, the Babylonians, the Assyrians, the Persians, and the Egyptians, to name a few, has taught us a lot about the symbolic and mythic allusions attached to stories, events, and persons in the Bible.

By New Testament times, the symbolic interpretation of figures from the past was quite extensive. We often have to look outside the Bible to other Jewish writings from the period between 300 BC and AD 300 to understand the richness that informed the religious imagination. One of the major finds of the century occurred in caves near the Dead Sea. A whole library of writings that had been used by a Jewish sect was discovered. These scrolls provided our earliest copies of books of the Hebrew Bible, later Jewish writings, as well as writings peculiar to this sect. One of these, *Some of the Works of the Torah,* indicates that members of the group separated themselves from the majority of the people because they disagreed over what the Torah requires. The group followed a solar calendar for determining religious feasts, unlike the lunar one employed. They sought a high degree of purity, especially for the city of Jerusalem. Other documents found in the Qumran caves and from ancient Jewish texts found in Egypt provide rules to be followed by members of the sect. Archaeological remains of buildings below the cliffs probably were occupied by members of that community. It is sometimes referred to by the name of the site, Qumran. You will also find the scrolls referred to as the "Dead Sea Scrolls."

Even though the scrolls were first discovered around 1947, the work of understanding them continues. First-century-AD writers mention a sect called "Essenes" devoted to holiness, living a communal form of life in towns and villages. The Roman author Pliny, who visited Judea in the spring of AD 70, mentions a unique "tribe" (*gens*) that lived off the west bank of the Dead Sea. Some of the peculiar rules that these authors attribute to this sect, such as avoiding oil because it transmits impurity and rules prohibiting spitting, turn up in the sectarian rulebooks. The Qumran site was inhabited from about 100 BC until a devastating fire in 9/8 BC. It was reoccupied at the time of Herod Archelaus (ca. 4 BC) until the Roman legions destroyed it in AD 68.

Discoveries of whole collections of biblical manuscripts, commentaries, and legal and religious writings like these are the most exciting discoveries for those who are primarily interested in interpreting texts. But most archaeology presents us with much less in the way of written material. Inscriptions on stone may preserve an important decree, a list of members in an association, the name of a donor, or some form of dedication. Burial sites may produce inscriptions on tombstones as well as objects from everyday life placed in the tomb. A number of Greek inscriptions show that Jews used Greek as well as Aramaic or Hebrew.

A lengthy inscription that reports a decree of the emperor against desecrating tombs was found in Nazareth. The style of the letters allows archaeologists to date it to the first half of the first century AD. However, since the Romans did not directly rule Galilee until the death of Herod Agrippa in AD 44, the emperor in question was probably Claudius (AD 41–54). The inscription is in Greek:

DECREE OF CAESAR

> It is my pleasure that sepulchres and tombs, which have been erected as solemn memorials of ancestors or children or relatives, shall remain undisturbed in perpetuity. If it be shown that anyone has either destroyed them or otherwise thrown out the bodies which have been buried there or removed them with malicious intent to another place, thus committing a crime against those buried there, or removed the headstones or other stones, I command that against such person the same sentence be passed in respect of solemn memorials of humans as is laid down in respect of the gods. Much rather must one pay respect to those who are buried. Let no one disturb them on any account. Otherwise it is my will that capital sentence be passed upon such person for the crime of tomb-robbery. (from Eric M. Myers and James F. Strange, *Archaeology, the Rabbis, and Early Christianity* [Nashville: Abingdon, 1981], p. 84)

A cemetery in Beth She'arim, a town in Western lower Galilee, contains tombs from the first to the sixth centuries AD. Some of the inscriptions mention resurrection. Others refer to immortality or eternal life. Epitaphs use standardized formulae; it is difficult to know whether they tell us much about what people actually believed about life after death. But since both resurrection of the body and immortality of the soul language could be used by Palestinian Jews, the assumption that one could distinguish Hebrew thought, as oriented toward the person as bodily, from Greek thought, which identified the person with the soul, does not adequately describe the archaeological remains. Most burials were of individuals in troughs of rock-cut tombs or in large stone sarcophagi made from local limestone. Burial caves usually belong to individual families, though a few catacombs contain several elite families. Burial customs among the elite clearly followed trends in the Roman Empire at large during the second and third centuries AD. Common people were not buried in this fashion but rather were wrapped in a shroud and sometimes put in a wooden coffin before being put into a pit or trench.

Even under the best conditions, we cannot always date buildings or determine the use of certain structures. The pious desire to see things exactly as they would have been in the Bible frequently leads to misrepresentations in tourist books. Well-known examples are found in Capernaum. The New Testament mentions a synagogue there in which Jesus taught (Mark 1:21; Luke 4:31). Ruins of a magnificent synagogue have been found there, but they do not come from the first century. A late fourth-century-AD pilgrim, Egeria, mentions seeing a synagogue there. Excavations show that this building was erected on earlier buildings from the first part of the fourth century AD, the period in which the first monumental synagogue buildings appear in Palestine. The synagogue at the time of Jesus would have been considerably smaller, not an ornate worship space but a square or rectangular room with benches around the sides that could serve a variety of community functions.

Another popular Christian tourist site at Capernaum is a house that is alleged to be that of Peter's mother-in-law (Mark 1:29–30). The Christian excavators linked Peter to the remains of a typical first-century house in Capernaum that was used as a Christian "house church" in the fourth century AD and later was converted to a basilica. But, of course, the evidence is never that simple. No one doubts conversion of the structure into a Christian church in the fourth century and the rebuilding to create a basilica-type church in the fifth century. The problem lies in interpreting traces of the occupation of the building prior to that time. The excavators pointed to plastering of the central room toward the end of the first century AD and the graffiti in the plaster as a Christian conversion to public use. Therefore, they insist that the building was continuously venerated as the "house of Peter" from a much earlier period and was, in fact, "Peter's house."

From a more rigorous historical and scientific point of view, we cannot be that confident. We can say that the "house church" at Capernaum is one of our oldest examples of a public building used for Christian worship. We can also say that the type of first-century house represented in excavations from this part of Capernaum gives us some idea of what Peter's house would have been like. It was part of a block of houses built in the first century BC. The blocks of one-story houses were about forty meters by forty meters. Each house consisted of a few rooms around a central courtyard, which contained the oven. Outside stairs led up to the flat roofs. Roofs were normally made of beams, branches, rushes, and mud. They would be relatively cool in the summer and warm in winter. The only windows were small, and high up in the wall. They let light into the house but did not provide a view outside.

Biblical scholars comb the results of archaeological excavations to see what they can learn about places, persons, events, symbols, and language used in the Bible. Sometimes the connections that we are able to make help us to understand things that were obscure in the Bible. Sometimes the biblical text provides a key hint to interpreting the physical remains at a given site or leads us to look for things there that we might otherwise ignore. One of the most important developments in modern archaeology and biblical studies has been emphasis on reconstructing the lives of ordinary people. Archaeology used to focus on the "big figures and monuments," the palaces, temples, and city gates. Now we are asking about the evidence for houses, streets, diet, burials, ages, and beliefs of the population as a whole.

The New Testament and Christian Life

Even those who are not Christians participate in the study of New Testament times as archaeologists and historians. The New Testament reflects the origins and earliest development of a religious movement that would shape the course of Western civilization and through it the history of the world. Everyone comes into contact with Christianity in some way whether directly or indirectly through values in Western culture that have their roots in Christianity. Similarly, anyone who wishes to understand much of Western literature, art, or music has to have some familiarity with the Bible and basic Christian beliefs.

When most people think of studying the New Testament, they don't think about its cultural significance. They think about the role that the Bible plays in the lives of believing Christians. There is no Christian group, Protestant or Catholic, that does not give the Bible, and especially the New Testament, a central role in its faith and worship. Because the Bible is shared by all Christians, it plays an important role today in bringing Christians together. Many churches have Bible study groups for laypeople that include Christians from different denominations.

We will see that there were different types of Christians in New Testament times. Some Christians of Jewish origin continued to follow the customs of Judaism and to worship in the synagogue and temple. Other Christians of Gentile origin focused their whole religious experience around belief in Jesus. What they took from Judaism was their scripture, the Greek translation of the Old Testament, a firm belief in one God over against the pagan gods and goddesses, and general ethical principles about justice, charity, and sexual morality.

We will also find in the New Testament that there are different lines of Christian tradition that are linked with important apostles. James, the leader of the church in Jerusalem, became the focal point for Jewish Christianity. Peter, who apparently left Jerusalem for missionary activity in the Antioch region, became the sponsor for a Christianity that retained its ties with Judaism through the Old Testament symbolism. Antioch became an important center of Petrine tradition. After Peter's death in Rome, letters in that tradition were sent from Rome to churches in Asia Minor. Paul, the most famous missionary to the Gentiles, established churches in the cities of Asia Minor and Greece. Finally, the churches of the Johannine tradition developed a unique symbolic

**Jewish communities of the diaspora
in the eastern part of the Roman Empire**

language and a clear perception of the divinity of Jesus. The New Testament was entirely written in Greek and reflects the churches of the Greek-speaking part of the empire. Further to the east, in eastern Syria and part of India, an equally strong Christian tradition grew up around the memory of the apostle Thomas. Its writings were composed in an eastern dialect of Aramaic, called Syriac.

If you remember the basic fact that the New Testament permits some differences in Christian traditions and practice, then you will understand that it is possible for different Christian churches to consider themselves faithful to the Bible. In some churches, everything depends upon the Bible. The sermon is the focus of the service surrounded with readings from the Bible, responsive readings of the psalms, prayers formulated in biblical language, and the singing of hymns. Members may spend time in private Bible reading and often bring their Bibles to church with them. They may have memorized large portions of the Bible in summer camps as kids. Whenever they run up against a problem, they will look for a solution or for words of comfort in the Bible. Sometimes Christians in these churches accuse other Christians of not following the Bible because they don't use the Bible in the same way.

The Catholic Church is a good example of a church that is often attacked as "not biblical" by other Christian groups. This charge has a long history. Part of it is true. For Catholics, the Bible is not the only way to approach God. Nor is the Bible the only source of church teaching and practice. Catholics insist that sacraments, especially the weekly (or daily) celebration of the Lord's Supper (Eucharist, Mass), bring a person into God's presence and are sources of God's grace for a person's life. The reading of the Bible and preaching form the first part of the service. They call believers to remember Christ and the Christian life that they have promised to lead in baptism and confirmation. But, to a Catholic, it would seem strange to stop with the prayers and service of the word. The Catholic wants to respond with a "yes" to God's word and the affirming presence of God's grace by participating in the meal that Christ left to his followers. As St. Paul told the Corinthians, the Supper commemorates the sacrificial death of Christ for us until Christ comes again (1 Cor 11:23–26).

The Bible also plays another role in the religious lives of those Catholics who belong to religious orders. From very early times the monks developed services of prayer based on reciting the psalms. These prayers marked the key turning points of the day and came to be known as the "Divine Office." Some religious groups are devoted to chanting the entire Office each day, which along with the daily celebration of the Eucharist can mean several hours of community prayer. Naturally, priests and members of religious orders who are working in schools, hospitals, and the like cannot drop everything for such extensive prayers. Shorter versions of the Office have been developed for them to use. Sometimes Catholic laypeople will also use shorter versions as their private prayer. The evening service known as Vespers has inspired many famous musical settings.

Since Vatican II, Catholics have been studying the Bible through courses, workshops, and parish Bible-study and faith-sharing groups. They find that Bible study enriches their faith in a number of ways. The Bible readings that are part of the liturgy become more meaningful. Psalms and other passages from the Bible become the focal points for private prayer and reflection. Study of the Bible also puts some of our modern problems in better perspective. It teaches us that faith is never "finished" or simple. It has a story. It develops. The first Christians often had to struggle to figure things out just as we do. Because they were successful, they established a tradition of faith that has continued for two thousand years. We have to preserve that tradition and hand it on in the twenty-first century.

Summary

You can see that there is a lot to studying the Bible. There are many different reasons that a person might have for doing so. Those who are interested in the history of Western culture need to know what the most important themes, symbols, and images in the Bible are so that they can recognize them in Western literature and art. They also need to know the major "ideas" found in the biblical writers. Those ideas have played a role in shaping Western thought and values. And they continue to play an important role in our understanding of what makes a just society.

Others may come to study the Bible because they are interested in the history involved. Or they may be interested in comparative religions. They may want to know how such a powerful religious movement as Christianity started and developed. They want to compare Christianity's story with that of other religions, such as Islam or Buddhism, that emerged as a kind of "protest" within an existing religious environment and that continue to guide the lives of large numbers of people around the world.

Still others come to study the Bible because they are Christians. For some Christians, Bible study is a way of getting back in touch with a faith they might have experienced as children but then had lost contact with. For other Christians, Bible study is part of their personal reading of the Bible. They realize that you can only go so far by just memorizing Bible verses. Eventually it is necessary to imagine what the world of the Bible was like. What did the various words, images, and symbols mean to an audience in their time? What was the challenge being presented? How did people respond to that challenge? Believing Christians will then try to apply insights gained from the biblical stories of faith to their lives.

These are all important reasons for studying the Bible today. A person may share all of these goals or only some of them. This book is written from the perspective of a person who shares all of these goals. But as an introduction to reading the New Testament, the emphasis lies on becoming familiar with basic information about the history, language, religion, and culture of New Testament times. It is not about how to translate the ideas and images of the New Testament into Christian life or theology today, since students use this book in many parts of the English-speaking world. When you have finished your introduction to the New Testament, you may want to pursue further study in one of these directions.

STUDY QUESTIONS

Facts You Should Know

1. How many "books" are in the New Testament? What are the main types of writing found in the New Testament?
2. What do we mean when we speak of the Bible as canon? What do we mean when we speak of the Bible as a classic?
3. What languages were spoken in Palestine during Jesus' lifetime? What language was the New Testament written in?
4. How does archaeology help us understand the Bible? Describe each of the following archaeological discoveries: (a) Qumran; (b) Capernaum; (c) cemetery at Beth She'arim.

Things to Think About

1. If someone asked you to tell a favorite story from the New Testament, what story would you tell? Do you know where to find it in the New Testament?
2. What approach to the Bible is the most interesting to you? Learning about the people and their times? Learning the Bible as a source for personal inspiration and guidance?
3. When was the last time you heard, read, or studied any passage from the Bible? What do you remember about that passage?

Chapter 2

THE WORLD OF JESUS

Galilee, Samaria, and Judea

We have all watched the embarrassment of TV commentators when a crisis breaks out in some part of the world with which they are not familiar. Lessons learned years ago in geography class fail as names of countries, boundaries, and alliances shift with the turmoil of world events. If we can barely keep up with the world we live in, it is hardly surprising to find confusion about the world in which Jesus lived.

Some of the political realities of the first century AD were determined by the geographical location of the Jewish states. The region of Syria-Palestine either found itself dominated by a greater power, which left some autonomy to the local inhabitants, or, when the major powers were weak, it managed to enjoy independence under a local dynasty that expanded its rule over the surrounding territory. Some periods of independence, such as the kingship of David and Solomon in the tenth century BC or the century of rule by Hasmonean kings from the mid-second century BC until Pompey's (Roman) conquest in 63 BC were often idealized. People looked on them as models for a future liberation from foreign domination.

In 198 BC, the Seleucid king Antiochus III seized control from the Egyptian Ptolemies. His Syrian empire stretched from the Persian Gulf to the Aegean. Samaria was the center of an administrative district that included Galilee, Judea, and Perea. His successor, Antiochus IV, provoked rebellion by outlawing the Jewish religion. In the 160s BC, Judea again became an independent district. Other districts were created along the coastal plain and east of the Jordan River. The Seleucid rulers also established independent Greek cities, since they found their most loyal supporters in the aristocracy of such cities. A number of cities took the name "Antioch" in honor of the ruling dynasty. For the history of Christianity, the most important "Antioch" was a beautiful city in Syria. St. Paul began his missionary work in the church there, and it was the place where believers first got the name "Christians" (Acts 11:19–26).

Some Jews in Jerusalem also wanted to create a "Greek city," "Antioch," there, located on the western of the two hills that made up the ancient city. It contained a marketplace and a fortress known as Acra. During the revolt, Jerusalem was divided. The Jews were established on the temple mount, called "Mount Zion," while the Syrians and their Jewish sympathizers, were entrenched around the Acra.

The Jews had established control over most of the city by 162 BC, but the struggle for complete independence from Syria would continue for several decades. In 152 BC, the Syrians appointed Jonathan high priest and de facto ruler of Judea. He enlarged the territory over which he held control. However, it was not until 141 BC that his brother Simeon, the last of the Maccabee brothers, was able to capture Acra and reunite Jerusalem. His successor, John Hyrcanus, set about gaining a foothold on the "king's highway," which lay east of the Jordan, and then the other international highway through Palestine, the Via Maris. After that, he turned to conquer Samaria. The Samaritan temple and the city that surrounded it on Mount Gerezim were destroyed. But the Samaritans continued to maintain a distinctive national and religious identity, venerating Moses and their version of the Torah, as the Samaritan woman tells Jesus in John's gospel (John 4:7–26). Samaritans continue to worship God on this mountain and celebrate Passover by sacrificing, roasting, and eating the lamb as commanded in Exodus 12.

Fresh from clearing the Mediterranean of pirates, the Roman general Pompey took Jerusalem in 63 BC. He returned the Greek cities to their former Gentile inhabitants. The Jews lost Joppa on the coast and the rich agricultural land in the Jezreel valley. In addition, Pompey created a league of ten cities east of the Jordan, the "Decapolis." Pompey seems to have intended that these cities would form a buffer zone between the Roman Empire and the Arabian steppe. These ten cities were thoroughly Greek in their outlook. In Roman times, there was considerable traffic between Galilee and this area of the Transjordan. Matthew 4:23–25 includes people from the Decapolis among those who listened to Jesus. Mark 5:1–20 and 7:31 even presume that Jesus went there to minister.

Herod and His Kingdom

Herod the Great was named "king" of the region by the Romans in 40 BC, though he needed Roman help to assume the throne in 37 BC. The emperor Augustus expanded his kingdom by giving Herod the coastal cities from Gaza to the Tower of Straton (except Ascalon), the city of Samaria, and the cities of Gadara and Hippos. In order to show his gratitude, Herod rebuilt and expanded the cities of Caesarea on the coast (known as Caesarea

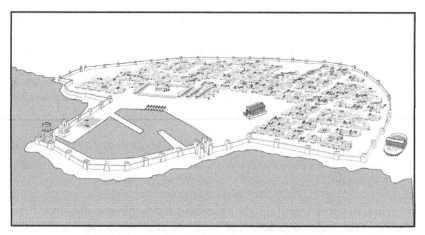

Reconstruction of the ancient city of Caesarea Maritima

Maritima to distinguish it from Caesarea Philippi) and Samaria, which he renamed Sebaste, Greek for Augustus. In Caesarea, Herod built a great temple to Augustus pictured on coins minted by Herod's son Philip. Caesarea was also provided with a deep-water harbor, which provided the only secure anchorage between Joppa and Accho. Sebaste was given new city walls, a forum, a theater, and a temple of Augustus on a platform facing the harbor. Because Caesarea lay outside the boundaries of Galilee proper, it did not have much influence on the lives of Galilean peasants, but it became the residence of the Roman governor of Judea in AD 6. Archaeologists found an inscription bearing the name Pontius Pilate from a temple dedicated to the emperor Tiberius. Games held there every four years included musical, athletic, and gladiatorial competitions along with horseracing.

The city of Tiberias was founded by Herod's son, Herod Antipas, in AD 13. It was on the Sea of Galilee in a fertile area and was noted for hot springs said to cure skin diseases. However, the city was also built over an ancient cemetery, rendering it unclean according to the rabbis. It appears that the Jewish inhabitants of this city belonged to the aristocratic circles associated with the Herodian court. Antipas also populated the new city by giving houses and plots of land to poorer residents. Fishing was their main occupation.

Herod's kingdom comprised quite a mixed population: a Jewish element (Judea and Galilee), Idumeans (Herod was an Idumean), Samaritans (who already had a long history of friction with the Jews), and the non-Jewish population of the Greek towns. Herod's fears of an uprising led him to strengthen the existing fortresses of Alexandrium, Hyrcania, Machaerus, and Masada; and to build a new one at Herodium, the site of the royal tomb. Part of his rebuilding in Jerusalem included a fortified palace protected on the north by three towers. Phasael, the tallest, was equivalent to a fifteen-story building. The lower part of one tower can still be seen today. Another fortress, Antonia, dominated the northwest corner of the temple mount. Herod initiated an expansive rebuilding of the temple complex, which continued well into the first century. The temple mount was one of the largest temple precincts in the Greco-Roman world, covering some thirty-five acres. Unlike the usual temple complex that was approached along a single sacred way, Herod's design provided access from all points in the city through gates in the walls.

When Herod died (4 BC), the kingdom was divided between his three sons. Archelaus, the eldest, received Judea, which had the bulk of the Jewish population, Idumea, and Samaria (including the cities of Caesarea and Sebaste). He was given the title *ethnarch*, "ruler of a people," not his father's title "king." The other sons received the title *tetrarch*, "ruler of a quarter." Herod Antipas, the second son, ruled over two widely separated areas, Galilee and Perea. The third, Philip, received the lands east of the Jordan. Herod's sister, Salome, received the towns of Jamnia and Azotus and the domain of Phasaelis in the Jordan valley.

Archelaus was deposed in AD 6 after a short, turbulent reign. His region came under direct Roman rule. It was administered by a "prefect" of equestrian rank responsible to the legate of Syria. When Philip died in AD 34, his land was provisionally taken over by the imperial administration. The emperor Caligula, with whom he had grown up in Rome, gave Herod Agrippa (Agrippa I), the tetrarchy of Philip together with the region of Chalcis and the title "king" in AD 37. In AD 39, Caligula exiled Herod Antipas and gave Agrippa his territory as well. Then the emperor Claudius gave Agrippa I Judea and Samaria. Thus, he regained almost all of the territory once ruled by his grandfather, Herod the Great. Agrippa I ruled this domain for only three years (AD 41–44). His son Agrippa II received Chalcis from Claudius in AD 53, and two-thirds of Perea and half of lower Galilee

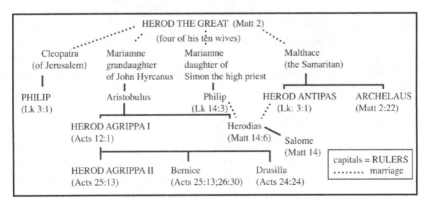

Abridged genealogy of the Herodian family

(Tiberias and Tarichaeae) from Nero in AD 54. After his death (c. AD 95), the Herodian dynasty ended.

Jesus grew up in Nazareth, a small agricultural village (pop. ca. 500), which had been occupied since the third century BC. It lay a couple of miles off a main road through lower Galilee. Sepphoris, the next large town five miles to the northwest, was the geographic center and administrative headquarters of the region. Three important localities mentioned in the New Testament lie along the Sea of Galilee—Tiberias, Tarichaeae, or, as it is called in Aramaic, "Migdal Nunaiyya" (home of Mary Magdalene), and Capernaum. Upper Galilee consisted of highlands. In this region, there are peaks of over 3,000 feet. Mount Meron, the highest, is 3,963 feet. It is an area of rugged peaks, valleys, basins, and gorges. Traffic passed through the area destined for the port of Tyre along a road that ran from Damascus over Paneas, and through the Dishon valley. It is a region of independent village life and strongly attached to ancestral custom. The principal city in this area was Gishala. Josephus complains that during the revolt against Rome, the peasants of Upper Galilee were more interested in farming than in defending the city (*War* 4.84).

Although it is possible to establish boundaries between various territories and administrative regions, it is more difficult to describe the ethnic make-up of a particular area or city. From Hasmonean times, we find a desire to establish Jewish areas especially in Judea proper. However, in Jamnia and Azotus their status as imperial estates would suggest a mix of Gentile and Jewish residents, since the higher administrative ranks would probably have been filled by non-Jews. Similarly, Gentiles administered the royal estates in the Jezreel valley. The two large Galilean cities, Tiberias and Sepphoris, were Jewish municipalities. Yet Herod Antipas is reported to have settled Gentiles in Tiberias when he founded the city. Even Capernaum, which sat on the border of two regions as is evident by the presence of a customs collector there, appears to have had some Gentiles. Herod had settled colonies of veterans at Geba, and mercenaries may have stayed on after their discharge. The centurions mentioned in the gospels may have been former legionary officers in charge of drilling native auxiliary troops (Matt 8:5–13; Luke 7:2–10). The Jewish population of Jerusalem was constantly increased by an influx of Jews from other countries. A third of the funerary inscriptions are either completely or partially in Greek.

Jerusalem: A Pilgrimage City

Jews from outside Palestine, called "the diaspora," regularly made pilgrimages to Jerusalem to celebrate the great feasts. Synagogues in the city appear to have been established to accommodate them. Excavations uncovered a large complex that had been donated by a person whose name clearly shows Roman origins:

Theodotus, the son of Vettneus, priest and archisynagogos (ruler of the synagogue), son of the archisynagogos, grandson of the archisynagogos, built this synagogue for the reading of the Torah and the study of the commandments, and the hostel and the rooms and the water installations for needy travellers from foreign lands. The foundations of the synagogue were laid by his fathers and the elders and Simonides.

The combination of synagogue and lodging facilities would have made it easy for persons from a particular region to meet others who spoke the same language and to obtain help.

The Old Testament law commanded that adult males make the pilgrimage to Jerusalem three times a year, for the feasts of Passover (Pesah) and Unleavened Bread, the Festival of Weeks (Shavuot) or First Fruits, known as Pentecost among Greek-speaking Jews, and the festival that followed the autumn harvest, Booths or Tabernacles (Sukkot; Exod 23:17; Deut 16:13–16). Persons from the diaspora could not fulfill that obligation literally. Some form of festive meal and assembly for prayer, singing, and Torah reading may have been observed in local communities. Jews from the diaspora sent representatives with the annual half-shekel tax for support of the temple that was required of Jewish males. Roman edicts protected that offering as "sacred money" and mandated harsh penalties against any who might attempt to seize it.

Although only men were bound by the law, women and children took part in pilgrimages and ceremonies. They are mentioned in inscriptions referring to Jews from the diaspora. Although the Passover was once eaten in the temple courtyard (Deut 16:7), by the first century Passover was a family celebration eaten in private homes within Jerusalem. In the diaspora itself, some wealthy women seem to have built synagogues and are honored with inscriptions conferring on them the same title as Theodotus, archisynagogos. Other foreigners who came for the great festivals were proselytes, Gentiles who had converted to Judaism. Herod's rebuilding of the temple complex encouraged participation by Jewish women and children as well as outsiders. It incorporated two new courtyard areas, the outermost for Gentiles and beyond its barrier, a courtyard for women. The Jewish historian Josephus acknowledges the significance of the latter: "This court was thrown open for worship to all Jewish women alike whether natives of the country or visitors from abroad" (*Jewish War* 5.199).

The great pilgrimages and offerings strengthened the ties between Jerusalem and Jewish communities outside Palestine. Envoys and letters might then be sent back from Jerusalem to the communities in the diaspora. The very early spread of Christianity from Jerusalem outward into the Roman world followed the patterns already established in Jerusalem's relationships to diaspora Judaism. The first converts at Pentecost are Jews visit-

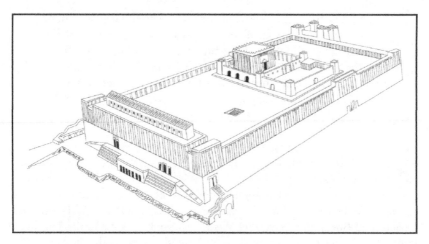

Reconstruction of the temple built by Herod the Great in Jerusalem

ing in Jerusalem for the feast (Acts 2:5–11). St. Paul brings converts from churches he founded in Greece at Passover to deliver a collection to aid poor Christians in Jerusalem (Rom 15:25–27).

The Political and Social World

Our survey of the shifting boundaries, provinces, cities, and rulers has already shown something of the "large-scale" realities of political and social life in Jesus' time. The destiny of the country was in the hands of others far removed from most people. Excavations in Jerusalem's Upper City have revealed the luxurious villas and palaces of the high priests and other wealthy persons. But not even the Herodian rulers and the wealthy elite could claim to be independent. They owed their position to personal ties and loyalty to Rome and even to personal relationships with members of the imperial family.

Under this arrangement, Palestine was relatively peaceful and prosperous. The Jewish revolt of AD 66 to 70 was quickly extinguished in Galilee. Diaspora Jews made no move to join in an uprising, which they may have considered more a local struggle for power than the overthrow of a power hostile to God's people; Roman edicts protected certain Jewish practices. The temple tax was treated as "sacred money" and exempted from prohibitions against the export of gold and silver. The sacred Torah scrolls were also protected. Any Gentile who stole the temple offering or Torah scrolls could be prosecuted for a sacrilegious act. The penalty was confiscation of one's property. Roman edicts also stipulated that Jews could not be issued a summons to appear in court on the Sabbath, since failure to appear would cost them the case. Jews were exempt from certain "civic liturgies," that is, obligations to pay for various public works projects—often enough with religious associations—and from compulsory service in the military. We find repeated complaints against local officials in the eastern part of the empire, which required Roman intervention to protect these rights.

Loyalty to a demanding set of religious beliefs contributed to the cultural vitality of Judaism and provided a common bond between those who might otherwise have been sharply divided. Even considerable diversity between Jewish groups like the Pharisees and the Sadducees over religious observance and observance of the law did not shake the common core of devotion to the temple and to the religious practices of Judaism. Sectarian groups did oppose the Jerusalem priesthood and argued against common interpretations of the law. In the mid-twentieth century, the library of a movement that claimed to restore an Israel faithful to God's covenant was discovered near the Dead Sea at Qumran. The finds provided our earliest biblical manuscripts, commentaries on various prophets, noncanonical books on biblical themes, liturgical books, and several editions of the rulebooks employed by members of the sect, called the Essenes or the new Covenanters.

The movement took various forms. Some rules provide for marriage and family while others presume a tight communal structure of adult males. They turn over all their possessions to the group, eat a ritual meal, and study the Torah night and day. Some passages suggest that members thought of themselves as a temple of holiness. No history of the sect is found among the scrolls. Scholars continue to piece a story together from archaeology and bits of information found in other contexts. The founder, known to us only by the "code name" used in the sect, "Teacher of Righteousness," emerged in the second half of the second century. Some cryptic interpretations of prophecies by Habbakuk reflect episodes from the early years of the group. A certain "Wicked Priest" is said to have come and attacked the Teacher on the Day of Atonement. Since the sect followed a solar calendar different from the lunar calendar of the Jerusalem temple, its high Holy Days did not correspond to those observed by other Jews. Whatever the political events surrounding the sect's founding, the sectarian piety that isolated Essenes from fellow Jews means that we never meet them in the New Testament.

Although the region of Syro-Palestine was relatively peaceful, that does not mean that the Herodian kings and Roman prefects were always model rulers. When John the Baptist spoke out against Herod Antipas's marriage to his brother's wife, he had John imprisoned and then killed. Some of Antipas's attempts to ingratiate himself with the emperor Tiberius behind the back of the Syrian legate Vitellius only netted him an angry ally. When the Nabatean king, father of Herod's first wife, attacked, the Roman legate left Herod to suffer a stinging defeat. The Marcan picture of village leaders, Herodian nobles, and Roman military commanders gathered to celebrate Herod's

ures the political unity of powerful men in the region (Mark
nperor Caligula exiled Herod Antipas in AD 37 in order to make
his friend Herod Agrippa king.

Scholars are cautious about overdramatizing the economic divisions
mentioned in the gospels. No one doubts that the wealthy, especially the
absentee landlords in Jerusalem, engaged in conspicuous consumption well
beyond anything that the temple functionaries, petty traders, merchants,
laborers, and the like could ever imagine. But in the Galilean villages, the
divisions were between rich and poor peasants. Some of the best lands had
come under royal and imperial control by the first century; there is no
archaeological evidence for major disruptions in village land ownership.
Jesus' parables show us two types of landowner. There is the Herodian noble
with slaves to act as stewards and peasants beset by their debts to such
landowners. But there are also stories of small family holdings passed from
father to son. In the Parable of the Prodigal Son, the father, his sons, and a

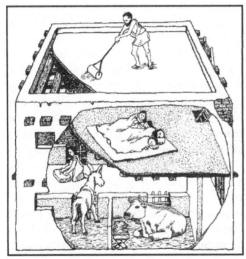

Reconstruction of a Galilean house

few servants work the land
(Luke 15:11–31). A father and
two sons are involved in culti-
vating a family vineyard (Matt
21:28–31). Zebedee, his sons,
and his hired servants are
working the fishing boats
(Mark 1:16–20). Security or
poverty for these small opera-
tions resulted from uncontrol-
lable natural phenomena such
as drought, agricultural pests,
or a bad catch.

It is difficult to measure
the burden of taxation in this
period. Taxes were levied on
the produce of the land, men,
property, sale of animals, and
all transport of goods across boundaries. In addition, Jewish males paid a
half-shekel for support of the Jerusalem temple. Religious law also commanded that people pay "tithes," a portion of the fruits of a person's labor, to
the priests and Levites. What was subject to tithing, the strictness with which
it was observed, and whether tithes were paid to priests living in the local
area or were paid in Jerusalem were all questions of some dispute in Jesus'
day. The rules of the Qumran sect objected to the annual temple tax, which
had to be paid in Tyrian silver coins. The Covenanters insisted that Torah
only required a one-time payment upon reaching the age of twenty. Some
scholars think that Jesus may have protested the hardship imposed upon

villagers when he overturned the moneychangers' tables (Mark 11:15–17). Coming up with coins to exchange for the silver shekel would have been difficult.

The "tax collectors" who are scorned by the people in the gospels are those, like Levi, who collected the customs tolls and other fees connected with transporting goods across borders. They were generally suspected of becoming wealthy by various forms of fraud in collecting such taxes (see the story of Zacchaeus in Luke 19:1–10).

Taxes on the produce of the soil were supplemented by a "head tax." This tax applied to all who were subject to the Romans directly. Persons had to be registered on the tax rolls of the town or city in which they lived. When the Roman governor took over Judea in AD 6, a census was taken for tax purposes. Luke 2:1–2 thinks that Jesus' birth in Judea occurred when his parents went to Bethlehem for the census. However, they would not have done so for that reason. Taxes were collected according to place of residence, which was clearly in Herod's Galilee, not in Judea. By linking the two events together, Luke is able to present Jesus' parents as loyal Jewish subjects in the larger Roman Empire.

The wealthy, Hellenized Jews of the Herodian court and the high priestly families in Jerusalem served as intermediaries between Roman officials and the people. Herod Agrippa even complained to the emperor that Pilate was a cruel man who took bribes and executed people without trial. Why the Jews rebelled against Rome in AD 66 to 70 is difficult to say. Evidently, the Jewish upper class, which tended to be moderate, was no longer able to mediate potential conflicts. Josephus insists that the rebels were worse tyrants than the Romans had ever been. In August of 70, Roman legions stormed the temple and fortress of Jerusalem, looting and burning the city. The capture of Jerusalem is commemorated on the arch set up in Rome by the victor, Titus. There you can see the great seven-branched candlestick from the temple being carried off in triumphal procession.

Religious Parties and Sects

The Various Religious Parties within the First Century AD. Judaism emerged from the religious and political developments of the previous two centuries. Since the temple at Jerusalem was the center of Jewish life, the high priestly families in the city formed a wealthy, aristocratic elite. Archaeologists have found the elaborate Roman-style houses in the Upper City. These multistory dwellings around a central courtyard with frescoes and mosaic floors included imported glassware, wine, and other luxury goods. Enjoyment of the luxuries typical of wealthy Romans did not mean disloyalty to the law. They avoided paintings of living creatures and included facilities for the ritual purification required by the Torah.

Of course, the elaborate services and sacrifices of the temple required other priests, Levites, and temple servants to carry out the daily rounds of offerings and oversee the wealth stored in the temple treasuries. The hereditary priestly families from the different regions had appointed times to come up to Jerusalem and serve. Priests were expected to observe special rules of purity. No one could be a priest who had any physical imperfection. There is a story that when Antigonus, a contender for the Jewish throne, was given the high priest Hyrcanus as a prisoner, "Antigonus mutilated his ears with his own teeth so that never again could he resume the high priesthood" (Josephus, *War* 1.270).

The high priest would appear on the Sabbath, on special festivals, and on the annual day of repentance, Yom Kippur, when he alone entered the most holy sanctuary of the temple. Here is the description that Josephus gives of the splendid garments that the high priest wore for that occasion:

> When ministering, he wore breeches which covered his thighs up to the loins, a linen undergarment, and over that a blue robe reaching to his feet, full and tasseled; to the tassels were attached alternately golden bells and pomegranates, the bells signifying thunder and the pomegranates lightning. The embroidered sash that bound the robe to the breast was adorned by five bands in different colors—gold, purple, scarlet, linen and blue, with which the curtains of the sanctuary were also woven. The same combination appeared in the high priest's ephod [possibly a cape to which the breastplate was attached], gold being predominant. Shaped like an ordinary breastplate, it was held by two golden brooches set with very large and beautiful sardonyxes [an unknown gem] engraved with the names of the twelve tribes. On the other side were twelve more stones in four groups of three—sardius, topaz and emerald; carbuncle, jasper and sapphire; agate, amethyst and jacinth; onyx, beryl and chrysolite—and on each of these was the name of one of the heads of the tribes. On his head the high priest wore a tiara of fine linen wreathed with blue and circled by another crown of gold on which were embossed the four sacred letters [of the name Yahweh]. (Josephus, *War* 5.231–35)

The temple area was divided into a number of chambers and courtyards. Only the officiating priests entered the court immediately in front of the temple where the great altar and the places for slaughtering the sacrificial animals were located. Only Israelite males were permitted beyond the walls that separated the temple area from the court of the women. Israelite men who were not in a state of ritual purity were confined to the court of the women. Herod the Great added an additional court outside that for Jewish women, a courtyard for non-Jews. These two additional courts encouraged participation by women, children, and even Gentiles. Persons suffering from leprosy or related diseases were barred from the holy city of Jerusalem altogether. The Pool of Siloam, to which Jesus sent the blind man in John 9:7, was an enormous immersion pool, which hundreds of pilgrims could have used to purify themselves before going to the temple.

A group generally known as "the scribes" emerged as interpreters of the law in the period after the exile. It is the group known as the Pharisees who had the widest influence on the interpretation of the law in the time of Jesus. They originated sometime in the second century BC out of the various groups known as "the pious."

Both priests and laypeople might belong to the party of the Pharisees. The aim of Pharisaic interpretation of the law was to make every sphere of life holy. Essene writings appear to be attacking Pharisaic interpretations of the law when they claim that many are being led astray by the "seekers of smooth things." This objection shows that the Pharisees were not always the rigid conservatives they appear to be in the gospels. Their goal was to find an application of the law that both respected its importance and could be lived out in ordinary life. One of their innovations was to promote eating ordinary food as though it were food that had been offered in sacrifice. That re-

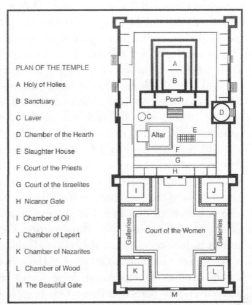

PLAN OF THE TEMPLE

A Holy of Holies
B Sanctuary
C Laver
D Chamber of the Hearth
E Slaughter House
F Court of the Priests
G Court of the Israelites
H Nicanor Gate
I Chamber of Oil
J Chamber of Lepert
K Chamber of Nazarites
L Chamber of Wood
M The Beautiful Gate

Floor plan of the temple

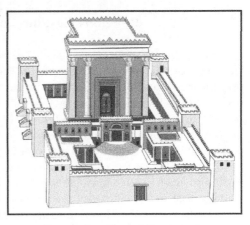

Reconstruction of the temple

quired ritual handwashing. Jesus objects to that teaching of the scribes and
Pharisees (Mark 7:1–15). He insisted that holiness is found in a person's
heart. But the Jewish custom of "handwashing" before eating became so well
known that it even turns up in Roman satire depicting Jews (Petronius,
Satyricon 34.4).

The name "Pharisee" comes from the Hebrew *p'rushim*, "separated
ones." What this designation meant was that the Pharisees tried to separate
themselves from all that was impure. They were also careful to pay tithes on
everything that might possibly be subject to tithing. Although the Christian
parable holds him up as a figure of scorn, the Pharisee in the Parable of the
Pharisee and the Tax Collector (Luke 18:10–13) expresses the serious devotion
to God felt by members of this sect. The Pharisees were able to restructure
Judaism after the destruction of the temple and its cult. The oral law was cod-
ified in a work known as the Mishnah around AD 200. Thus, the Pharisees, not
the high priests, were the ancestors of rabbinic Judaism and, through the rabbinic traditions, of the various forms of Judaism that we know today.

In the first century BC, the Pharisees had been engaged in political
struggles for influence with another party known as the Sadducees. The
Sadducees represented the wealthy aristocracy and the priestly families.
They opposed the "oral law" of the Pharisees along with other innovations in
Jewish belief such as belief in resurrection or an afterlife. However, they
shared similar concerns for ritual purity. The rubbish heaps of aristocratic
houses in Jerusalem prove that point. Unlike stoneware, pottery dishes and
cooking pots could become impure. Leviticus 11:33 required that such ves-
sels be broken. Archaeologists have found piles of cooking pots in cisterns
that have holes pierced in them. One large house yielded thirty-five of them.
The holes make use of an impure vessel impossible.

Religious Customs and Beliefs

A Covenant People Living by God's Torah. The law, given by God, provided the basic framework for Jewish life. The different groups might argue
over the interpretation of the law, but no one would think that a person who
lived "outside" the law would enjoy God's blessing. In Galilee and Judea, the
law was also the basis for all legal relationships. It was not just a set of religious rules. Jews living as minority communities in the diaspora were allowed
to conduct their own internal affairs according to the law as well.

We may have a hard time understanding why challenges to the law
excited so much controversy. The law is not an arbitrary set of statutes that
could be changed by king or citizen assembly at any time. It was understood
to be God's revelation to Moses on Sinai. Israel had entered into a covenant,
a solemn pact, with God to abide by the law and to honor no other gods. In

return, the people of Israel would enjoy a special place as God's chosen people. God would protect, guide, and bless them throughout their history.

When things did not go well, many people sought the cause in Israel's failure to remain faithful to the law. The Covenanters saw most of the history of Israel as infidelity. When new members were accepted into the sect they were said to be entering into a "covenant before God." This "new covenant" replaces the disobedience of the old covenant.

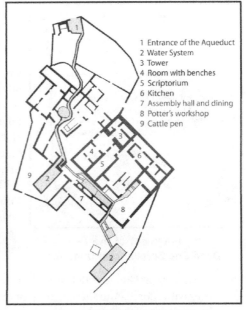

1 Entrance of the Aqueduct
2 Water System
3 Tower
4 Room with benches
5 Scriptorium
6 Kitchen
7 Assembly hall and dining
8 Potter's workshop
9 Cattle pen

Plan of Qumran

Everyone who joins the community must enter into a covenant before God to do everything He has commanded and not to turn away from Him through fear or through any trial to which one may be subjected by Belial [= Satan]...then the priests are to recount the bounteous acts of God and to recite His tender mercies toward Israel. The Levites are to recite all the sins and transgressions that the children of Israel have committed as a result of the dominion of Satan. Everyone who enters should make a confession saying: "We have acted wickedly; we have transgressed; we have sinned and done wickedly, we and our fathers before us by going against the Truth. God has been right to bring His judgment on us and on our fathers before us. But from ancient times, He has been merciful to us and always will be." Then the priests are to bless all those who cast their lot with God...and the Levites to curse all who have cast their lot with Belial.

The Essenes believed that God's mercies to Israel would be given to faithful members of the sect. Christians would insist that they had entered a new covenant with God through Jesus' death on their behalf. "This is my blood of the covenant" (Matt 26:28).

Most Jews would not have drawn such sharp divisions between "the holy ones" and the wicked that sectarian groups did. They might agree that the

**Fragment of the
Dead Sea Scrolls from Qumran**

people as a whole had sinned against God through disobedience but expected God to raise up a new king and to bring the nation out of sinfulness to righteousness. Here is an example of that expectation from one of the "Psalms of Solomon." They are a collection of eighteen psalms apparently written in the middle of the first century BC. *Psalms of Solomon* 2.30–35 alludes to the death of Pompey in 48 BC. *Psalms of Solomon* 17.23–51 describes an "anointed" king like David who will come to restore God's people:

> ...we hope in God, our deliverer. For the might of our God is forever with mercy. And the kingdom of our God is over the nations in judgment forever. You, O Lord, chose David as king over Israel, and swore that his kingdom would never fail before you. But, because of our sins, sinners rose up against us...They did not glorify your name...They destroyed the throne of David in tumultuous arrogance...Look on their plight and raise up for them, their king, the son of David...and gird him with strength so that he can destroy the unrighteous rulers, and throw out of Jerusalem the nations that trample her to destruction...and he shall gather a holy people and lead them in righteousness...and he shall force the pagan nations to serve under his yoke; and he shall purify Jerusalem, making it holy as of old; so that nations will come from the ends of the earth to see His glory.

This righteous king from the Davidic line will cast out foreign rulers and their sinful Jewish allies, restore the ten lost tribes, and rule God's holy people forever.

God's New Order to Destroy Evil. Another writing from the very end of the first century BC, the *Assumption of Moses*, proposes a somewhat different version of this hope for a nation free from evil. The *Assumption of Moses* 6.2–6 lashes out against Herod the Great:

> An insolent king will succeed them [the Hasmoneans], who will not be of the race of the priests, a man bold and shameless, and he will judge them as they shall deserve. And he will cut off their

chief men with the sword, and will destroy them in secret places, so that no one may know where their bodies are. He will slay the young and the old, and he will not spare anyone. And fear of him will be bitter…for thirty-four years.

The *Assumption of Moses* describes a bitter period of persecution suffered by the righteous. This persecution originally reflected the death of faithful Jews under Antiochus IV. But the author sees these events as the final case of bloodshed that will demand God's response:

His [= God's] Kingdom will appear throughout creation.
     And then Satan will no longer exist, and sorrow will depart with him.
     And the hands of the angel appointed chief will be filled, and he will avenge them against their enemies.
     For the Heavenly One will arise from His royal throne, and He will go forth from His holy dwelling, with indignation and wrath on account of His children.
     The earth will tremble and be shaken to its depths.
     The high mountains will be leveled and the hills be shaken and fall.
     And the horns of the sun be broken and it will turn dark; the moon will not give her light and be turned to blood….
     For the Most High, the only Eternal God, will arise, and He will appear to punish the Gentiles, and He will destroy all their idols. Then you, O Israel, will be happy…and God will exalt you, and bring you near to the stars. And you will look down from above and see your enemies in hell. And you will recognize them and rejoice. And you will give thanks and praise to your creator. (*Ass. Mos.* 10)

This vision breaks the boundaries of a historical succession of earthly rulers. God arises from the heavenly throne to create the new order. This action follows directly upon the death of a martyr, Taxo, and his sons. Taxo, a righteous person, chooses death so that God will come to deliver the people. This understanding of the martyr's death originates with the promise of Deuteronomy 32:43 that God will avenge the "blood of his children." The same promise is invoked in the story of the heroic mother and her sons in 2 Maccabees 7. Sinful Israelites deserve any death at the hand of enemy powers. But when the innocent righteous suffer persecution and death, God must become their defender. Christians used this model to understand the death of Jesus as the offering of an innocent, righteous person to free a sinful humanity from the punishment due its sins against God (Rom 3:24–26).

Human sinfulness is not the only reason given for evil in these passages. Perhaps you were not surprised to find references to Belial (or Satan) as the source of evil. But Satan does not play that role in the Old Testament. There "the Satan" operates as an agent of God (Num 22; Job 1–2; Zech 3; 1 Chron 21). Evil is human doing pure and simple. Sometime in the second century BC, the idea that there was a demonic principle of evil working to corrupt God's creation by leading human beings astray appears in Jewish sources (*Jub.* 1.20, "spirit of wickedness"; 23.29). The writings of the new Covenanters give dramatic expression to this view. They speak of human beings as divided into two types. Some are guided by the "angel of light," others by the Satanic "angel of darkness":

> Now God created man to rule the world and appointed two spirits whose direction he would follow until the final Judgment: the spirits of Truth and of Falsehood. All who practice righteousness are under the domination of the Prince of Light and walk in light; all who practice evil are under the Angel of Darkness and walk in darkness. Through the Angel of Darkness, however, even those who practice righteousness are made prone to error. All their sins and transgressions are the result of his domination, which is permitted by God's inscrutable design until the time He has appointed. But the God of Israel and His Angel of Truth are always there to help the sons of light. God created these spirits of light and darkness and made them the instigators of every action and thought.

New Ideas and Symbols

These selections show us that a number of new ideas had come into circulation in the two centuries prior to the time of Jesus. They were ways of understanding the significance of what was happening in Israel's history. First, the direct links to the Davidic kingship and to the Zadokite priesthood had been ruptured. The existing kings and high priests were no longer in that line of descent. Had God broken the promise to sustain the Davidic line forever? Some people might have been political pragmatists arguing that Israel simply had to get along in the world as it was. But other people, observing the abuses of the present rulers, answered that God was always faithful and merciful. God would soon raise up a righteous king of David's line. Groups with a strong attachment to the priesthood like the new Covenanters held that God would restore the true priesthood. The Dead Sea Scrolls discoveries included remains of several copies of what is called the *Temple Scroll* that speaks of (1) an entirely new temple complex; (2) a festival calendar based on a solar year of 364 days; (3) special rules of purity for the temple, the holy city of Jerusalem, and the cities of the land; (4) a section of legal materials based on Deuteronomy.

Second, there were disagreements over the relationship between human effort and divine action in bringing about this new order. Some writings speak as though the new leaders, king (and priest), would emerge in the ordinary course of historical events. Others rejected that view. Only divine intervention, sometimes through a heavenly figure, could destroy the wicked and break the power of Satan. The following passage, presented as a revelation from the dying Levi to his sons, describes the coming of a priestly figure:

> Then the Lord will raise up a new priest. And all the words of the Lord will be revealed to him, and he will judge the earth righteously for many days. His star will arise in heaven like that of a king, and light the light of knowledge as the sun does the day. He will be magnified in the world, and shine forth on the earth like the sun, and remove all darkness from under heaven. There will be peace in all the earth, and the heavens will exult in his day, and the earth will be glad. And the glorious angels of the Lord's presence will be glad in him. The heavens will be opened and sanctification will come upon him from the temple of glory, with the Father's voice as from Abraham to Isaac. The glory of the Most High will be uttered over him, and the spirit of understanding and holiness will rest upon him. And no one shall ever succeed him. In his priesthood the Gentiles will increase in knowledge [= religious devotion to God] and be enlightened through the graciousness of the Lord. In his priesthood sin will come to an end, and the lawless will stop doing evil. He will open the gates of paradise, remove the threatening sword against Adam, and give the holy ones the tree of life to eat, and the spirit of holiness will be upon them. He will bind Beliar, and give his children power to tread on evil spirits. And the Lord will rejoice in his children, and be pleased with his beloved ones forever. Then Abraham and Isaac and Jacob will exult, and I [= Levi] will be glad, and all the holy ones will clothe themselves with joy.

Various signs indicate his coming. (Some of them are familiar from the Christmas stories in the gospels.) This high priest is not limited by human knowledge since "all the words of the Lord will be revealed to him." His appearance will bring about an era of peace when even the Gentiles will come to acknowledge God.

Sin will come to an end and a redeemed humanity will enjoy the fruits of paradise. However, only those who are found righteous at the judgment inaugurated by this high priest will participate in the glorious future.

Third, the concept of a universal judgment at the end of history is another of the "new ideas" that had developed in this period. The patterns of "salvation history" in the Old Testament left the nation as a whole to suffer divine judgment through natural disasters or at the hands of enemy nations as punishment for evils attributed to its leaders. Balancing punishment and rewards with the holiness or sin of each person was not an issue. The persecution and suffering of righteous persons sparked reflection on how God's "justice" was present in individual lives as well as the corporate life of the nation in the postexilic period. An end-time judgment scene was one way of answering questions about God's care for individuals.

A fourth "new idea" appears in the dualism connected with the figure of Satan and of angelic (demonic) forces at work behind the evils of the world. Such dualism could never become absolute, since Jews believed in God's sovereign power as Creator of all things. Therefore, the judgment not only rewards and punishes individuals, it demonstrates God's rule over all of human history. Some writings of this period introduce the idea of set periods of history. God knows the evils that are to come in each. God also controls their unfolding. Usually, most of the ages are said to have passed. The author thinks that the end will occur soon.

Global wars, famines, persecution of the righteous, and an increase in evil are commonly presented as signs of the "end-time." One of the most influential "historical surveys" appears in the second half of the Book of Daniel (Dan 7–12). It employs a traditional scheme of four successive world empires. This scheme is combined with mythic images of four beasts coming out of the sea. The myth of the god defeating the dragon monster of the watery chaos in order to establish order is a very ancient one in the Near East. Yahweh slays the dragon in creating the world (Job 26:7–13), or with the exodus (Isa 51:9–10). Daniel uses these images to convey the terror and chaos of the mid-second century BC.

"One Like a Son of Man"

Such dramatic visions are not intended to frighten the faithful. They provide hope by showing that God's power will be victorious over evil. For example, Daniel 7 imagines a scene of heavenly victory that employs ancient mythic symbols. Four vicious beasts caused havoc on the earth, waging war against the holy ones (Dan 7:1–12, 15–22). The destruction of the last enemy is signaled when "one like a son of man" (also translated, "one like a human being"; Dan 7:13) ascends to the throne of God, the Ancient of Days on the clouds of heaven. Israelite imagery describes Yahweh as the one who rides on clouds. But the image is taken from the Canaanite myths of Baal, the divine figure who conquers the sea monster symbolic of evil and chaos. In the myth, Baal is a younger god, subordinate to 'El, the father of gods and human

beings. Daniel is using archaic imagery to assure readers that their persecution under Antiochus IV (167–164 BC) is the culmination of demonic evils.
It will come to an end with a glorious divine victory. Instead of analyzing the
historical situation in human terms, Daniel sees it as a reflection of the cosmic drama in which God's reign replaces the forces of evil.

The New Testament presents Jesus as that "Son of Man." The heavenly
origins of the "Son of Man" figure are evident in his association with angels
(Matt 13:41; 16:27; 24:31; 25:31; Mark 8:38; 13:27, 41; Luke 9:26) and his
role in the final judgment. Here is a description from another Jewish visionary work (first century AD) that pictures the "Son of Man" enthroned in judgment. Notice that the righteous and elect have been raised up from the earth
to a joyous fellowship with the Son of Man:

> And the Lord of Spirits seated him on his glorious throne and the
> spirit of righteousness was poured out upon him and the word of
> his mouth slays all the sinners…and they shall be downcast. Panic
> will seize them when they see the Son of Man sitting on his glo-
> rious throne. The kings, the mighty, and all who possess the earth
> will glorify and praise the one who rules over all and who was hid-
> den, for the Son of Man was hidden from the beginning; the Most
> High preserved him in his mighty presence and revealed him to
> the elect…And the righteous and the elect will have risen from
> the earth and cease to be downcast. And they will be clothed with
> glorious garments. (*1 Enoch* 62, 2–15)

This example shows that in Jesus' day Daniel 7 was understood as a scene of
universal judgment by a figure enthroned in heaven. Therefore, when "Son
of Man" is used as a title or symbolic expression for Jesus, images should
come to mind of a heavenly savior figure whose enthronement represents the
establishment of God's kingdom. "Son of Man" was not used for Jesus'
humanity in contrast to the expression "Son of God." For a first-century
Jewish audience the phrase "Son of God" was used in reference to such
human figures as the king (Ps 2:7; Isa 9:6), Israel as God's people (Exod 4:22;
Hos 11:1), or of persons who were particularly wise or righteous (Wis 2:13,
16). Angels may also be referred to as "sons of God" (Ps 89:7; Dan 3:25).

Writings like Daniel are often called "apocalyptic," from the Greek
word *apocalypsis* ("revelation"), because they claim to contain the secrets of
God's plan for this world and the heavenly world. The recipient is always a
famous figure from the past like Daniel or Enoch whose symbolic dreams or
visions are often decoded by an angel revealer. Apocalypses frequently repeat
the same sequence of events in parallel visions using different symbols.
Daniel 8 and 10–12 form such a parallel. Daniel 9 interprets the prophecies
of Jeremiah 25:11–12 and 29:10 that seventy years after the Jews were taken

into captivity by the Babylonians (587 BC) they would be restored to their land. The focus of the interpretation is on the last "week of years," the time in which Daniel is being written. During that time there was an "anointed one" (Onias III, reported in 2 Macc 4:3) and the temple was profaned. However, these evil days were coming to an end. Daniel 10–11 explains that there is a great conflict of heavenly powers behind the historical struggles that the sage Daniel faced during the Babylonian period and that the faithful in the author's own time confront under Antiochus IV. Daniel 11:32 predicts that Antiochus will "seduce with flattery those who violate the covenant," that is, those Hellenizing Jews who supported the Syrian king's policies. But the people who "know God" will be led by "the wise" to stand firm.

Resurrection of the Righteous

Daniel 12:1–3 introduces what was another new theme in this period: the resurrection of the righteous. Here that destiny is a special reward for the "wise." "Shining like stars" means that they become companions of the angels in heaven. This image of the resurrection of the righteous appears in *1 Enoch* 39:5: "the dwelling places of the righteous are with the holy angels." Jesus uses it in Mark 12:25 to answer the Sadducees' objection that resurrection is a foolish idea. The writings found at Qumran do not contain explicit references to resurrection from death to a new form of heavenly life, but that idea could have been presupposed in passages that describe members of the sect as purified and given a place with the angelic host. This selection from a collection of hymns uses that language to describe the transformation of those who join the community of the new Covenanters:

> You [= God] have taken a spirit distorted by sin, and purged it of the stain of transgression and given it a place in the host of the holy ones, and brought it into communion with the sons of heaven. You have made mere humans to share the lots of the spirits of knowledge; to praise your name in their chorus. (1 QH 3.19–21)

Many other images of exaltation in God's presence or resurrection to new life or new creation can be found from the second century BC on. The mother and her seven sons confess their faith in God's power to give them new bodies in the resurrection in 2 Maccabees 7. *First Enoch* 92–105 promises that in the judgment sinners responsible for oppressing the righteous will be thrown into the dark, fiery regions of Sheol, while the righteous will come to life and join the angels in glory.

Because Christians refer to Jesus as the messiah (the word simply means "anointed"), they sometimes imagine that these earlier Jewish writers had a fixed concept of "the messiah," one who would inaugurate God's kingdom. Instead, we find many different pictures of how the present age would end. Some people thought that God would deliver the people from their present evils by restoring a king from the descendants of David to rule over Israel. Others thought that the corrupt high priesthood would be replaced with a true one. Others believed that God would raise up two "anointed" figures, a king and a righteous high priest. Still other people thought that salvation would be brought through a heavenly figure—for example, the angel Michael might defeat the evil angels, or, perhaps, the mysterious, heavenly "Son of Man" would come in judgment and defeat the enemies of God's people. Still other writers say nothing about an agent, anointed or otherwise. They speak of God acting directly in human history.

The Religious Life of the People

Apocalyptic visions and their prophecies contributed much of the religious symbolism used in the New Testament. But Jesus' audience was usually the general populace, not members of one of the groups devoted to the study of the law or to interpreting such visions. For them, religious life was part of the daily routine of the home and the local synagogue.

Synagogue. We do not have any ritual texts describing the order of worship in a first-century-AD synagogue. However, the New Testament accounts of synagogue worship (Luke 4:16–17; Acts 13:14–15; 15:21) agree with the comments made by Jewish writers of the period. Unlike other peoples who heard their law only on special, ceremonial occasions, Jews assembled in their synagogues, or "prayer houses," once a week to study the law of Moses (Josephus, *Against Apion* 2.174; Philo, *Embassy to Gaius* 156). Reading from the prophets and some form of exposition or sermon must have accompanied Torah reading.

The religious center of Judaism in the first century AD was the Jerusalem temple. Synagogues were not "sacred places" like the temple, which was the place in which God dwelt. Most Jews lived in the diaspora, outside Judea and Galilee. Those who referred to the communal buildings in which they gathered as *prosuch* ("prayer place") may have sought to give the local synagogue something of the sacred character attached to a temple. They could not make the three yearly pilgrimages to Jerusalem called for in the law. So Jews adopted a practice of praying at the times when sacrifices would have been offered to God in the temple (Dan 6:10–13). The first-century Jewish historian Josephus retells the story of Moses so that it includes the command to pray three times a day (*Antiquities* 4.212).

First-century-AD synagogues in Judea were square or rectangular buildings with columns and benches, capable of supporting a range of communal

**Mosaic floor of the third- to fourth-century synagogue at
Hamat Tiberias depicting at the center the ark that houses the Torah,
two menorahs, ram's horns, and incense shovels**

activities. Later synagogues from the third to the seventh centuries AD were
more ornate, with mosaic floors and small shrine-like structures that constitute a Torah shrine. Among the hundreds of inscriptions that refer to synagogues, synagogue officials, and benefactors, a number indicate that
non-Jews could be honored for their contributions to a local community (see
Luke 7:6). It is impossible to determine whether such persons regularly
joined the Jewish community for Sabbath services or not.

Great Festivals. Pilgrimages to the temple in Jerusalem were linked with
the agricultural seasons. Villagers probably associated God's faithfulness with
fruitful harvest as well as with the events of salvation that were remembered
at each feast.

Passover (pesah) and the festival of unleavened bread *(masot)* is best
known to Christians because Jesus' death and resurrection occurred during this
feast. However, because they are remembering Jesus' last meal with his followers, Christians often forget that Passover is a time of great rejoicing. It commemorates the fact that God brought the Israelites out of slavery in Egypt.
They are told to remember (Exod 6:7; Num 15:41) what God has done forever.
We do not know exactly how the Passover meal was celebrated in Jesus' time.
Meals occurred in private homes, not the temple precincts. There appear to
have been debates over when the lambs were to be sacrificed, before or after
the daily burnt offering, and whether or not a family group could act as "priest,"
slaughtering their own lamb. The basic rules for Passover observance derived
from Exodus: (1) remember annually (Exod 13:3); (2) eat unleavened bread
(Exod 12:18); (3) cleanse all leaven out of one's house.

Traditions that go back to Jesus' time claimed that the leaven represented the "evil inclination" that leads people away from God. A first-century
Jewish philosopher from Alexandria, Philo, explained that leaven "puffs up"
bread. Therefore, it symbolized the arrogance of the pharaoh who would not
let the people go. The negative associations of "leaven" should be remembered when reading Jesus' Parable of the Leaven in Matthew 13:33.

Notice how important remembering is in the Passover context.
Christians speak of the Eucharist as "remembering" the death of Jesus (see
1 Cor 11:24–25). Remembering is not just thinking about the past. It is a call
to recognize that those events are also about us. The Mishnah tractate on
Passover gives us an example of what is meant:

> Rabbi Gamaliel used to say: "Whoever has not said the verses
> concerning these three things at Passover has not fulfilled his
> obligation. They are Passover, unleavened bread, and bitter
> herbs. "Passover" because God passed over the houses of our
> ancestors in Egypt; "unleavened bread" because our ancestors
> were redeemed from Egypt; "bitter herbs" because the Egyptians
> embittered the lives of our ancestors in Egypt. In every genera-
> tion a person must regard himself as if he, himself, came forth
> from Egypt, for it is written, "And you shall tell your son on that
> day, It is because of what the Lord did for me when I came out
> of Egypt" (m. Pesahim 10.5).

Pentecost, or the Festival of Weeks (*shavuot*), drew more pilgrims to
Jerusalem than Passover according to Josephus even though it is the least
important of the three festivals in the Torah. Leviticus 23:9–22 prescribes
that an offering be brought fifty days after the omer offering. The omer was
a barley offering that marked the beginning of the spring grain harvest.
Exactly when that was to occur was a matter of debate, though many sources
thought it should be the second day of Passover. The Festival of Weeks is to
occur seven weeks later. Two loaves of leavened bread made from newly har-
vested wheat were presented in the temple. At some point this festival was
linked to the giving of the law at Sinai and God's covenant with the people by
some Jews. Others continued to treat it solely as an agricultural festival. A
fragment of legislation from the Qumran scrolls indicates that the new
Covenanters did not eat wheat from the new harvest until the loaves representing the first fruits had been offered up. This festival lost its significance
after the Jerusalem temple was destroyed in AD 70.

Tabernacles (*sukkot*) was the most important agricultural festival. It celebrated the end of the fall harvest and the beginning of sowing (Exod 23:16).
Some passages refer to it simply as "the festival of the Lord" (Lev 23:39; Hos
9:5). Leviticus 23:39–43 prescribes a seven-day festival like Passover. The

people are to dwell in huts as a reminder of the journey in the wilderness and are to come to the temple waving branches of citron, palm, myrtle, and willow, while singing praises to God. Philo reports that in first-century Alexandria people erected booths and gathered in synagogues for prayer and songs of praise (*Flaccus* 116–24). Zechariah 14:16–19 prophesied that when God judged the world all the nations would annually go to Jerusalem at Tabernacles. Any nation that failed to do so would not receive rain for its crops. The Gospel of John has Jesus deliver two discourses in the temple during the feast (7:14–39; 8:12–20). Today, whenever they can, Jews build booths for Tabernacles. People will eat in them, especially on the first day of the feast, and sometimes discuss Torah there.

New Year. All cultures celebrate the New Year. Judaism marks it with solemn holy days, referred to as the "high holy days." They begin with the first day of the year, Rosh Ha-Shanah, and end ten days later with the Day of Atonement, Yom Kippur. This is a period of serious reflection on the ways in which one has failed to be faithful to God during the past year. The people are to devote Yom Kippur to fasting and repentance before God (Lev 23: 23–32). While the Jerusalem temple was standing, the day was marked by special sacrifices. A "scapegoat" bearing the sins of the people was driven out into the desert and killed. The Day of Atonement was the only day on which the high priest entered the most sacred part of the temple, the Holy of Holies. Jews throughout the world spent the entire day in fasting, penitential prayers, and praise of God. Yom Kippur was one of the best-known Jewish holy days (Philo, *Moses* 2.23).

In the New Testament, the Letter to the Hebrews uses the symbolism of the Day of Atonement for Christ. He is the High Priest who has entered the heavenly sanctuary by offering an atonement sacrifice that will never need to be repeated (Heb 9:1–22).

Hanukkah. The festival of Hanukkah originated in the second century BC under the Maccabees. It commemorates the rededication of the temple and is an eight-day holiday modeled after Sukkot, which the people had been unable to celebrate while the temple was in pagan hands (2 Macc 1; 1–2; 18; 10:6–7). Hanukkah is a minor feast in the Jewish calendar except in countries like the United States, where it competes with the Christian celebration of Christmas. On each day of the feast, another candle in the eight-branched candlestick, the menorah, is lit. A legend claimed that although there had been only one flask of oil left in the temple, it kept the lamps burning for eight days. Or, according to another legend, when the victorious Maccabees entered the temple, they found eight iron spears there and lit lamps on each of them. In the New Testament the Gospel of John has Jesus appear in the temple area during this feast (John 10:22).

Summary

Worship at the local synagogue, daily prayers, Sabbath meals, the great pilgrimage feasts, and other holy days of the Jewish calendar reminded people of their special relationship to God. They did not worship the gods and goddesses of their pagan neighbors. Although it sometimes seemed that God had left the people at the mercy of the great powers, the Jewish people continued to look forward to the day when God would send them salvation.

Of course, people had different visions of what salvation would be like. Some thought that a new king like David would make Israel a great nation. Others imagined that the complete renewal of the temple and its priesthood would inaugurate a new age of holiness. Still others thought that evil had a grip on all nations and human institutions. The wicked would be judged and condemned to eternal suffering in a dark, fiery region. Salvation would be a heavenly, angel-like existence for those who had remained faithful to God. Some people felt that they should show their devotion to God by joining a sect that had a stricter interpretation of the law than that followed by most people. They might become Pharisees or members of the community of the new Covenanters (Essenes). Crowds responded to John the Baptist's call to repent because the time of judgment was at hand. The gospels show us that those who followed Jesus were not members of pious sects but ordinary people who had been farmers, fishermen, collectors of taxes, and the like.

STUDY QUESTIONS

Facts You Should Know

1. How were Galilee, Samaria, and Judea governed in the first century AD?
2. What were the three pilgrimage festivals? What did each one celebrate?
3. What was the "temple tax"?
4. What were the special Jewish privileges that Roman edicts protected?
5. What were the distinguishing characteristics of the following groups within Judaism: (a) priests and Levites; (b) scribes; (c) Sadducees; (d) Pharisees; (e) community of the new covenant (Essenes)?
6. What expectations for the future did groups of Jews associate with each of the following: (a) "anointed king," like David; (b) "anointed priest"; (c) new covenant; (d) God's rule or kingdom; (e) judgment of the world; (f) "Son of Man"?
7. What was a synagogue? How is it different from the temple?

Things to Do

1. Read Daniel 7–12. Pick out the mythic images of battle between heavenly powers and demonic beasts. How do they describe the political situation of God's faithful people? Pick out the prayers uttered by the visionary and the words of consolation spoken by the angel. What message do they give the pious?

2. Read the story of the mother and her seven sons in 2 Maccabees 7. Pick out the words that the mother and sons say against the tyrant. What does the hope of resurrection mean for the martyrs in this story?

Things to Think About

1. The three Jewish pilgrimage festivals connect the agricultural cycle with events in God's salvation and creation of a people. How do the great Christian festivals link "nature" and events of salvation?

2. What modern symbols are used to give an "apocalyptic" picture of a world in which evil has the "upper hand" and which will soon end in a great catastrophe or war? Do those images carry with them pictures of divine salvation and hope for a new order like the apocalyptic visions of Jesus' day? What do people put their hope in today?

Chapter 3

THE LIFE OF JESUS

Seeking Jesus of Nazareth

Almost as soon as anyone becomes famous in our culture, whether that person is a political leader, a rock star, or a professional athlete, books about that person start appearing. There will be TV, radio, and Web media to satisfy our curiosity. It seems hard to imagine how the early Christians spread the message about Jesus for thirty to fifty years before there were any written accounts of Jesus' life and teaching. The gospel writers could not engage in the sort of interviewing and research that biographers do today. Each gospel tells the story of Jesus differently. The special point of view reflected in a gospel often provides clues about the audience of Christians that the writer had in mind. Literary critics refer to the sense of its intended readers that a written text projects as the "implied" audience.

Now you may be wondering whether the gospels tell us anything at all about Jesus of Nazareth. Some people have even written books claiming that they do not. They insist that all the gospels tell us is what the authors thought Jesus was like derived from sayings and stories available in a particular region. What Christians believe about Jesus is really based on the four gospel images of Jesus that have been accepted as authentic sources for faith and worship by believers across the Christian world by the end of the second century AD. Even so, one could argue that it is not necessary to ask what Jesus' life would look like if one could record him on video in Galilee.

We cannot simply describe what the earliest Christians believed about Jesus without asking how they came to that belief. "Jesus" was not a figure of the distant, mythical past. He was an individual known by some of the first generation of Christians, as were his disciples, many followers, and relatives who started the Christian movement after Jesus had been crucified by the Roman governor. Of course, we know from our own experience that the same persons and events are not remembered in the same way by all of the participants even within families. We also know that our understanding of something a person said or did changes radically when we get a larger perspective, perhaps learning something else about the person or seeing how an individual's life turned out in the end.

Scholars can also use the growing body of information about first-century Syro-Palestine and about the various forms Jewish life and practice took at the time to fit stories and sayings of Jesus into that world. They use such information to paint a picture of what Jesus was like. They ask how those who first heard Jesus' words might have understood them. We are constantly building up a more detailed picture of Jesus as a figure in first-century Galilee and Judea. Parts of the picture remain unclear, debated, or even blank because we do not have enough information to fill in needed details. Critics of "historical Jesus" studies protest that the finished portraits reflect the biases of twenty-first-century believers more than Jesus himself. But with patient study of literary materials, inscriptions, archaeological remains, and the traditions preserved about Jesus in the gospels, we can learn a great deal about Jesus of Nazareth.

How the Stories Are Preserved

Jesus' disciples did not sit there writing down what Jesus said and did. They traveled about with him, heard him teaching the crowds, asked him questions, and witnessed miraculous cures. Stories and sayings were then repeated to others. Many of the stories about Jesus follow a set pattern that matches stories told about other famous figures. The sayings of Jesus also fall into familiar patterns. Using a basic pattern meant that a person had to remember only enough detail about a particular episode or saying to fill in the pattern. Scholars use the generic term *forms* for the patterns into which these short, easily remembered units of tradition fall. Analysis of the various types is called "form criticism." Early in the twentieth century, scholars anticipated that if one could identify the form of a given unit, one could attach that form to a particular setting or use within early Christian groups. As we have collected many more examples of the forms from ancient sources, that hypothesis has been dropped.

Miracle Stories. One of the easiest types of story to recognize is the miracle story. People are always interested in miraculous cures. Here is a story about a Syrian (non-Jewish) healer from Palestine:

> Everyone has heard of the Syrian from Palestine, an expert at such things. Whatever moonstruck—rolling their eyes and filling their mouths with foam—people come, they arise and he dispatches

them away healthy, when they are free from the terror [= a demon, thought to be possessing the person] and for a large fee. When he stands by them as they are lying there he asks from whence they came into the body. The sick man is silent, but the demon answers in Greek or some other barbarian tongue. The Syrian levels oaths at him, but if the demon is not persuaded, he threatens and expels the demon.

This healing belongs to the subtype called an "exorcism," which involved curing a person thought to be possessed by a demon. A number of such stories were told about Jesus. Here is one from Mark 1:23–26:

And immediately, there was in their synagogue a man with an unclean spirit; and he cried out, "What have you to do with us, Jesus of Nazareth? Have you come to destroy us? I know who you are, the Holy One of God." But Jesus rebuked him, saying, "Be silent, and come out of him!" And the unclean spirit, convulsing him and crying with a loud voice, came out of him.

This story is told in a much more dramatic way than the report about the Syrian exorcist. But you can see that it has the basic features of an exorcism: (1) demonstration of the symptoms of the illness; (2) verbal conflict between the demon and the exorcist; (3) violent departure of the demon from the person. Miracle stories conclude with proof that the person has really been healed. In Mark 1:27, for example, the people talk among themselves about the event:

And they were all amazed so that they questioned among themselves saying, "What is this? A new teaching! With authority he commands even the unclean spirits and they obey him."

In the story about the Syrian exorcist, the healer was out to get money from the people he cured. In antiquity people were suspicious of those who seemed to have magical powers. They thought that such people, using the demons, were "getting rich" with fake cures. You can see that the second charge does not apply to Jesus. He was teaching in the synagogue when he was interrupted by the possessed man. Jesus is never paid for a miracle. As the miracle story was told among Christians, it had a double purpose. For those who didn't yet believe in Jesus, it might persuade them that he was "from God." For those who did believe, the demon's reaction to Jesus is almost a confession of faith in Jesus' true identity. Jesus' ministry is going to break up the power of demons. Therefore the first suspicion is also false. Jesus is not working with demons but against them.

The earliest Christians may have made collections of miracle stories about Jesus to use in missionary preaching. Some scholars suggest that Mark used such a collection in composing his gospel. For example, we even find two versions of some miracles. Jesus feeds a large number of people (Mark 6:30–44 [5,000 people]; 8:1–10 [4,000 people]) and he calms severe storms at sea (Mark 4:35–41; 6:45–50). You might think that Jesus simply did the same thing more than once. But if you look closely at each of the double stories you will notice that the disciples are just as bewildered the second time around as they were the first. They would not seem to have learned anything. That is why it makes better sense to think that the double stories are two different versions of a single episode. The Gospel of John, which does not seem to have used the Gospel of Mark, has its own versions of the feeding and storm stories (John 6:1–13; 6:16–21).

Mark may have known two different versions of these stories which had been circulated in some form of notebook collection of miracles. John seems to know a similar miracle collection. Matthew and Luke each had Mark's gospel available when writing their gospels. But Luke leaves out the section of Mark that contains the duplications. Matthew, on the other hand, takes the second storm story, in which Jesus rescues the disciples by walking on water, and adds another scene to it. Peter asks Jesus if he can walk on water too, but as Peter begins to do so, his faith in Jesus wavers. Jesus must rescue him from sinking. At the end of the expanded story, Jesus' disciples worship him as "truly, Son of God" (Matt 14:28–33).

Matthew's version tells you something important about how the gospel writers treated their material. They did not simply copy. They expanded stories and added new ones, providing readers with new insights into the story of Jesus. In Matthew's gospel, Peter is the foundation of the church (Matt 16:18). Matthew's narrative shows Peter being prepared for this role. Here Peter learns an important lesson about faith. Perhaps Matthew's church was shaken by the turmoil in Syro-Palestine that followed the Roman destruction of Jerusalem. In that setting, Christians would have read this story as reassuring them that God would guard and protect the church.

Pronouncement Stories. Other stories told about Jesus' focus on teaching. A popular type often told about famous teachers in antiquity was the "pronouncement story." These stories begin with some form of "tension," perhaps a question by disciples, a paradox posed by opponents, or a problematic situation. The wisdom of the hero is demonstrated when he or she resolves the situation using an appropriate saying or pronouncement. Often the saying that forms the resolution of a story could just as well be independent of the setting. Sometimes such sayings are proverbs that can be used in any number of contexts.

Here is one of many such stories about the Cynic philosopher Diogenes. Cynic philosophers wandered from city to city in a coarse cloak with few possessions. They often chastised their hosts and audiences for concern with luxury, bodily pleasures, and all the cares that make life difficult for people. A philosopher, who lives without possessions and worldly concerns, is truly "free." Here Diogenes has suffered a fate feared by many in antiquity. He has been captured by pirates and is about to be sold into slavery:

> [Speaking to his fellow captives]…then he [= Diogenes] said this in sport and ridicule: "Stop pretending ignorance and crying over your imminent slavery, as if you were really free before you fell into the hands of pirates and were not slaves to even worse masters. Now perhaps you will get moderate masters who will cut out of you the luxury by which you were ruined, and who will instill in you perseverance and self-control, the most honored of good things." As he went through these things, the buyers stood and listened, amazed at his freedom from emotion. Some also asked him whether he was skilled at anything. And he said that he was skilled at ruling men. "So, if any of you needs a master, let him come forward and strike a bargain with the sellers." But they laughed at him and said, "What free man needs a master?" "All," he said, "who are base and who honor pleasure and despise toil, the greatest incitements to evil."

You can see that the story is meant to demonstrate the superiority of the Cynic teaching. Like the pronouncement stories in the gospels, this one is part of a longer narrative account of Diogenes' adventures.

Often pronouncement stories in the gospels preserve teaching that had become critical for the later development of the community. Here is one in which the "hero" is a pagan woman, who asks Jesus to perform a miracle for her:

THE SYRO-PHOENICIAN WOMAN   **[3–1]**

Mark 7:24–30:	**Matthew 15:21–28:**
And from there he arose and went away to the region of Tyre and Sidon.	And Jesus went away from there and withdrew to the district of Tyre and Sidon.
And he entered a house and would not have anyone know it; yet he could not be hid.	
But immediately a woman whose little daughter was	And behold a Canaanite woman

Continued

Continued

Mark 7:24–30:	Matthew 15:21–28:
possessed by an unclean spirit, heard of him, and came and fell down at his feet. Now the woman was a Greek, a Syro-Phoenician by birth. And she begged him to cast the demon out of her daughter.	from that region came out and cried, "Have mercy on me, O Lord, Son of David; my daughter is severely possessed by a demon." But he did not answer her a word. And his disciples came and begged him saying, "Send her away for she is crying after us." He answered, "I was sent only to the lost sheep of the house of Israel." But she came and knelt before him, saying, "Lord, help me!"
And he said to her, "Let the children first be fed, for it is not right to take the bread of children and give it to the dogs."	And he answered, "It is not fair to take the children's bread and throw it to the dogs."
But she answered him, "Yes, Lord; yet even the dogs under the table eat the children's crumbs."	She said, "Yes, Lord; yet even the dogs eat the crumbs that fall from their master's table."
And he said to her, "For this saying, you may go your way; the demon has left your daughter." And she went home and found the child lying in bed and the demon gone.	Then Jesus answered her, "O woman, great is your faith! Be it done as you desire." And her daughter was healed instantly.

Make a careful comparison of the two versions of this story. In Mark's version, the woman's clever response wins her case. Matthew shifts the reason that

Jesus grants her request to her faith. Look back at Matthew 14:31. Jesus chides Peter for being a person of "little faith." By praising the woman's faith, Matthew turns her into an example for all Christians. You will also notice that Matthew has heightened the drama. She has to overcome more obstacles than in Mark. Jesus ignores her. The disciples want to get rid of her. And Jesus insists that his mission is only to the Jewish people, "the lost sheep of the house of Israel."

The expansion in Matthew suggests that this story spoke to an important question in the earliest churches. Jesus' mission had been to Israel. But the early apostles quickly found converts among non-Jews as well. When we study Paul's letters, we will see early communities struggling with the question of whether Gentile converts should also become Jews. Eventually, most of the leaders agreed that Gentiles could be part of the community without becoming Jews, "children of Israel." In the context of a church still struggling to integrate non-Jewish believers, the story of Jesus healing the daughter of a Gentile takes on new life. It shows that even a Gentile was capable of a faith in Jesus that would lead to salvation. Some scholars suggest that Matthew wrote for a church in transition from evangelizing Jews to preaching among the Gentiles. (See the strong affirmation of that mission in Matt 28:16–20.) This story would support that mission.

Sayings and Parables. While some of Jesus' teaching is preserved in stories about him, much of it appears in sayings and stories that are reported as direct instruction either to the crowds or to disciples. Here too we find different types of saying. We also find allusions to the Old Testament, to common folklore themes and familiar proverbs.

Stories and sayings often come down to us in different versions. There are even sayings of Jesus that are reported in other early writers that are not found in the four gospels. For example, Acts 20:35b; 1 Corinthians 9:14 (indirectly), and 1 Thessalonians 4:15 all refer to words of the Lord that are not in the gospels. Luke 1:1–4 and John 20:30 both indicate that the evangelists consciously selected their material from a larger pool of available traditions about Jesus. These traditions may have circulated in both oral and written forms.

Parables

The most popular form of Jesus' teaching remains the parable. Jesus' parables range from very short, "one-liner" comparisons and analogies to miniature stories in which one or more characters take part. One of the best-known short parables is that of the shepherd who goes in search of a lost sheep:

PARABLE OF THE LOST SHEEP   [3–2]

Matthew 18:12–14:

What do you think? If a man has a hundred sheep, and one of them has gone astray, does he not leave the ninety-nine on the mountains and go in search of the one that went astray?

And if he finds it, truly I say to you, he rejoices over it more than over the ninety-nine that never went astray.

Luke 15:3–7:

So he told them this parable, What man of you, having a hundred sheep, if he has lost one of them, does not leave the ninety-nine in the wilderness and go after the one which is lost until he finds it? And when he has found it, he lays it on his shoulders, rejoicing.

And when he comes home, he calls together his friends and his neighbors, saying to them, "Rejoice with me, for I have found my sheep which was lost."

So it is not the will of my Father in heaven that one of these little ones should perish.

Just so, I tell you, there will be more joy in heaven over one sinner who repents than over ninety-nine righteous who have no need of repentance.

Gospel of Thomas 107:

Jesus said, "The Kingdom is like a shepherd who had a hundred sheep. One of them, the largest, went astray. He left the ninety-nine and looked for that one until he found it. When he had gone to such trouble, he said to the sheep, "I love you more than the ninety-nine."

We have two versions of the parable in the Synoptic Gospels. If you look up the context of the parable in each of the gospels you will see that Matthew has Jesus address the parable to disciples, especially to those who are going to be leaders of the church. They must care for all members of the community and not despise the "little ones." Luke has Jesus address the parable to hostile Pharisees who were critical of his associations with sinners. They thought that the messiah should be sent to the "righteous of Israel," those who were really looking for God's salvation.

You will also notice that Luke's version of the parable has an additional scene. The shepherd collects his friends for a celebration. Luke 15 contains three parables about things that are "lost": a sheep, a coin, and a son (the prodigal son). Each one ends with a celebration and rejoicing. The feast of celebration is critical to the action in the final story of the prodigal son. Therefore, it looks as though Luke has used that theme to structure the whole chapter. Go to the beginning of the chapter. There we find a meal as the context in which the criticism of Jesus has been raised. One can consider that meal the reverse of the "celebration" of repentance and forgiveness being called for in the stories.

We can also use nongospel tradition to show that the story of the lost sheep circulated in the oral tradition without Luke's second part. A version of this parable has come down to us in a second-century collection of sayings of Jesus, the *Gospel of Thomas*. Its version lacks some of the urgency conveyed by Matthew and Luke. By not referring to mountains or the wilderness it also avoids the troubling problem of whether the shepherd was so concerned about the lost one that he left the other sheep exposed. And the *Gospel of Thomas* explains the special relationship between the shepherd and the lost sheep by making it the best one in the flock. Such shifts easily can occur in a story as it is handed on from one teller to the next. The *Gospel of Thomas* version follows the simple structure of such a story: seeking the sheep, finding it, and reaction. The Lucan expansion calling in neighbors to celebrate applies the lesson to the audience.

Instructions for Disciples

Other sayings take the form of "rules" or instructions about the life of discipleship. These were often gathered into collections on related topics. Naturally, instruction on prayer plays an important role in the life of the community. Matthew and Luke each contain a section of Jesus' teaching on prayer, which includes the Lord's Prayer. Matthew's explains how Christian piety differs from that of Jews and pagans (Matt 6:1–18). Luke has teaching on prayer result from the disciples' observation of Jesus praying and their desire to learn about prayer (Luke 11:1–13). Compare the two versions of the Lord's Prayer. You can see that Matthew's has been "filled out" to provide the parallel phrasing that would make it appropriate for communal worship:

THE LORD'S PRAYER [3–3]

Matthew 6:9–13:
Our Father who art in heaven, hallowed be thy name. Thy kingdom come; thy will be done, on earth as it is in heaven.
Give us this day our daily bread;
And forgive us our debts, as we also have forgiven our debtors;

And lead us not into temptation, but deliver us from evil.

Luke 11:2–4:
Father, who art in heaven, hallowed be thy name. Thy kingdom come.

Give us each day our daily bread;
And forgive us our sins, for we ourselves forgive everyone who is indebted to us.
And lead us not into temptation.

Continued

Continued

Jewish Kaddish Prayer:
Magnified and sanctified be His great name in the world that He created according to His will. May He establish His Kingdom in your lifetime; in your days; and in the lifetime of the house of Israel, even speedily at a near time.

Mark 11:25:
And whenever you stand praying, forgive, if you have anything against anyone; so that your Father also, who is in heaven, may forgive you your trespasses.

The first part of Jesus' prayer focuses on the coming of the kingdom of God. It reflects a Jewish prayer (the Kaddish prayer). The second half speaks of the needs of those who are to be Jesus' disciples. They must be preserved from "temptation," that is, from the "testing" that might lead them astray from God's will. The bread petition reflects Jesus' more general teaching against anxiety (cf. Matt 6:25–34; Luke 12:22–34; 16:10–13). Jesus links God's forgiveness with our treatment of others. This point is emphasized in Matthew 6:14–15. Although the Gospel of Mark does not contain the Lord's Prayer, it does contain another saying of Jesus that makes the same point about forgiveness (Mark 11:25). The addition that is made in Christian liturgies, "for thine is the kingdom and the power and the glory forever and ever," appears in an early Christian writing from the end of the first century, the *Didache*, as "for thine is the power and the glory forever." The *Didache* instructs Christians to recite the Lord's Prayer three times a day. Matthew includes the prayer in a triad of pious practices: almsgiving, prayer, and fasting. The *Gospel of Thomas* preserves a saying on true piety that takes this triad and adds to it the question of dietary laws:

> And his disciples questioned him and said, "Do you want us to fast? How shall we pray? Shall we give alms? What diet shall we observe?" Jesus said, "Do not tell lies, and do not do what you hate, for all things are plain in the sight of Heaven. For nothing hidden will not become manifest and nothing covered will remain without being uncovered." (*Gos. Thom.* 6)

Jesus' rejection of Jewish concerns about kosher food is preserved in the synoptic tradition in Mark 7:14–23 (cf. Matt 15:10–20).

The *Gospel of Thomas* 6 uses a form of saying that is sometimes referred to as a judgment saying. The passive verb represents God as the author of the action. Whatever is hidden now will be revealed in the judgment. Mark 4:21–23 combines that saying with a saying about a lamp, which occurs in many forms in both the canonical gospels and in the traditions outside the gospels:

And he said to them, "Is a lamp brought in to be put under a bushel, or under a bed, and not on a stand? For there is nothing hid, except to be made manifest; nor is anything secret, except to come to light. Let him who has ears to hear, hear."

The saying about the lamp probably existed in a proverbial form such as we find in Matthew 5:15a, Luke 8:16, or 11:33, to the effect that no one lights a lamp and puts it under a vessel or a basket. The gospels use this proverb to warn the disciples not to hide what they have received. The element of warning is intensified by incorporating the proverb into a context of judgment sayings.

In addition to proverbs and judgment sayings, there are sayings that are called "legal sayings." Although most of these sayings are not "laws" in our sense of the word, they set forth the way in which Jesus' disciples are to live their lives. The one that has been most frequently embodied in the legal system of Christian countries has been Jesus' saying against divorce (e.g., Matt 5:31–32; 19:3–9, in the context of a debate with the Pharisees). Jesus rejected the rather liberal standards for divorce in antiquity as contrary to the intention of God in creation, though the law of Moses does allow for divorce so long as the husband follows proper legal procedures by giving his wife a divorce decree. Some Christians take other sayings from the Sermon on the Mount as strict rules of conduct. The prohibition against swearing oaths in Matthew 5:33–37 they take to mean that they cannot swear an oath of allegiance or an oath in court. Of course, if people always told the truth directly as Jesus commands, then the use of oaths to back up a person's word would not be necessary.

Jesus' legal sayings do not form a legal code to replace the law of Moses by which Jews lived and governed themselves. Rather, Jesus' legal sayings represent a challenge to the type of person who thinks that the will of God is perfectly embodied in the law. Such a person might presume that as long as "it's legal" in the Mosaic law, it represents the will of God. But Jesus keeps insisting that the law cannot come close to the real perfection of God or the change of heart required to live for God alone.

Collections of Sayings. Naturally, as the early Christians handed down sayings and parables of Jesus, they made collections of them just as they did of stories about Jesus. The *Gospel of Thomas*, which in its present form comes from the second century, seems to be based on just such a collection of sayings. It's not a gospel like the four canonical gospels because it does not narrate the ministry of Jesus in Galilee, the concluding days in Jerusalem, and the death and resurrection as they do. The *Gospel of Thomas* appears to be based on a collection of sayings that circulated in the eastern part of Syria, which was an area of strong Christian churches in the early centuries.

Almost a century before the *Gospel of Thomas* was discovered in 1945, German scholars had concluded Matthew and Luke had used a collection of Jesus' sayings and parables to supplement the teaching material found in Mark. This source was called "Q" from the German word for source, *Quelle*. They concluded that Q had to have been a written collection because of the close verbal overlap between the material common to the two writers as you can see in the Parable of the Lost Sheep and in the Lord's Prayer. At the same time, differences between versions and in the order of material make it unlikely that Matthew copied the material out of Luke or vice versa.

In general, the Lucan form of the Q material is less elaborately reworked than that in Matthew, so we will give the passages commonly assigned to Q in their Lucan version. Jesus is pictured in the Q sayings as the Son of Man who comes to bring the end-time salvation. Satan will be defeated, judgment is coming, and the faithful perseverance of the disciples of Jesus will win them salvation.

Many scholars imagine that Q was shaped by the earliest Jesus follow- ers in Palestine and Syria. Their way of life was much like that of Jesus him- self. They traveled from village to village announcing that the kingdom of God was at hand. Jesus, the Son of Man, who is about to come in judgment, had demonstrated the defeat of Satan's kingdom in his exorcisms. His disci- ples were continuing Jesus' summons to Israel to repent.

You can also see that all of our reports about what Jesus said and did have been handed down within the context of a believing community. Neither the gospel writers nor their sources were engaged in "investigative reporting." The stories about Jesus, the collections of his miracles and of his sayings are all intended to awaken and nourish faith in Jesus as the one sent by God to bring salvation.

Jesus as Teacher and Miracle-Worker

The traditions about Jesus emphasize two aspects of his ministry: teach- ing and healing. Mark 1:21–28 combines these two features in an opening scene at the synagogue in Capernaum. While Jesus is teaching the people, a possessed man begins to cry out, "What have you to do with us, Jesus of Nazareth? Have you come to destroy us? I know who you are, the Holy One of God" (v. 24). That is quite a theological insight for a demon. The crowd reacts in amazement at Jesus' teaching and his authority over the demons. Mark suggests that Jesus' reputation as a healer drew people to him from all over the region.

MATERIAL ASSIGNED TO Q   [3–4]

Narrative:
Centurion's Slave (Luke 7:2,6b–10)

Ethical Exhortation:
Serving Two Masters (16:13)
Light/Darkness Within (11:34–36)
Faith and Forgiveness (17:3b–4,6)

Eschatological Warning:
Judgment Preached (3:7–9)
Baptism with Spirit and Fire (3:16–17)
Judging and Eschatological Judgment (6:37–42)
Woes on the Cities (10:13–15)
Woes on Scribes and Pharisees (11:39–52)
Fire, Baptism, Sword, and Division (12:49–53)
Signs of the Time (12:54–56)
Repent (12:57f)
Prepare for the Crisis (13:24–29)
Lament: Doom of Jerusalem (13:34–35)
Judgment: Careless and Preoccupied (17:24, 26f, 33–37)

Eschatological Conflict:
With the Devil (4:2–12)
Defeat the Prince of Demons (11:14–22)
Dispel Unclean Spirits (11:23–26)

Eschatological Promise:
Beatitudes (6:20b–23)
Love Enemies (6:27–36)
Lord's Prayer (11:2–4)
What God Will Give (11:9–13)
Seek the Kingdom (12:22–31)
Treasure in Heaven (12:33f)
Role in the Kingdom (22:28–30)

Eschatological Discipleship:
Gratitude for Knowledge Revealed by God (10:21–24)
Fitness for Kingdom (9:57–60)
Kingdom Near (10:2–12)
Fearless Confession (12:2–12)
Bearing the Cross (14:26f)

Continued

Continued

Eschatological Parables:
Watchfulness (12:39–40, 42–46)
Leaven (13:20f)
Great Supper (14:16–23)
Lost Sheep (15:4–7)
Talents (19:11–27)
House Built on Sand/Rock (6:47–49)

Jesus Brings Eschatological Salvation:
Fulfills scripture (7:18–23)
Brings the Kingdom (7:24–35)
Fulfills the law and the Prophets (16:16–17)
To Receive Jesus Is to Receive God (10:16)
Sign of Jonah (11:29b–32)
Jesus' Table in the Kingdom (14:15; 22:28–30)
Messiah Coming to Jerusalem (13:34–35; 19:41–44)

Of course Jesus was not the only person reputed to work miracles (see Matt 12:27). Sometimes, as in the case of the Syrian miracle-worker that we quoted earlier, such persons were accused of being in the business to make money from those who were gullible. Neither Jesus, nor his disciples, are ever accused of profiting from the power to heal. People often sought to be healed at temples devoted to the healing god Asclepius. In the reports from famous shrines, we sometimes find the motif of doubt and conversion to belief in the god. Here is such a story:

> A man who could move only one finger of his hand came to the god as a supplicant. When he saw the votive tablets in the sanctuary he did not believe the cures and made fun of the inscriptions. In his sleep [in the sanctuary] he had a vision. It seemed to him that as he was playing dice in the room under the temple and was about to throw, the god appeared, jumped on his hand and stretched out his fingers. When he had stepped off, he saw himself bend his hand and stretch out each finger on its own; when he had stretched them all out straight, the god asked him whether he still did not believe the votive tablets, and he said no. "Because you had no faith in them, though they were worthy of belief your name in the future shall be Apistos [= 'without faith']," said the god. When day came he emerged from the sanctuary cured.

This story illustrates the theme of faith, which plays an important role in Jesus' miracles. Jesus, too, is able to cure persons who are paralyzed (Mark 2:1–12; 3:1–6). In the gospels, we frequently find faith at a different point in the narrative. Instead of using the miracle to convince someone who does not believe, Jesus performs the miracle only after he or the disciples (by trying to push the person aside) have challenged the person's faith (Mark 2:5; 5:34; 5:36; 7:27–29; 10:48–52).

The emphasis on faith was one way in which the tradition could make it clear that Jesus was not some sort of "magician" or "money-seeking wonder worker." Even so Jesus had to reject two different types of "crowd reaction" to his healing abilities. One was the desire to set him up as some sort of mass leader and wonder-worker (John 6:15). The other was to credit Jesus' miracles to some clever manipulation of demonic or at least dubious powers (Mark 3:20–22; 5:17). Even in our own day, versions of these views show up in attempts to discredit Christian belief. Certainly, Jesus' miracles did bring him popular attention as Mark suggests. But the gospels also show a certain reserve in their narration of the miracles and resistance to popular adulation that is unlike other accounts of miracle-working in antiquity.

Because miracles are ambiguous, they have to be viewed within a larger context. Jesus sees his exorcisms as signs of liberation and hope. Casting out demons shows that God's kingdom is present (Matt 12:28). Other sayings speak of a vision in which he sees Satan falling from heaven (Luke 10:18), his kingdom falling apart (Mark 3:24–26), and his house being robbed (Mark 3:27). Another way of connecting the miracles and Jesus' coming to bring salvation is to connect them with the promises in Isaiah 35:5–6 that the blind shall see, the deaf hear, the lame walk, and the dumb speak. Matthew 15:30–31 uses this Isaiah passage as a summary of Jesus' healing activity. All of these themes are represented in the miracles of Jesus (dumb, Matt 9:32–34; deaf and dumb, Mark 7:32–35; blind, Mark 8:22–26; 10:46–52; Matt 9:27–31; John 9:1–11; lame, Mark 2:1–12; John 5:1–9).

Of course, Jesus' miracles are not limited to those associated with Old Testament prophecies. But by making the connection to prophetic images of salvation, it was possible to show that the time of salvation had come. The limitations and evils that held people in bondage were no longer insurmountable. They are not "trapped" in a world dominated by evil. People could experience the saving power of God in their lives. As the early Christians retold these stories about Jesus' miracles, they showed that the miracles pointed to Jesus as the one who embodies God's power just as the demon in the Marcan story hailed Jesus as the "Holy One of God."

Jesus as Teacher

Jesus announced that God's reign was at hand. Hearers should recognize that God is inaugurating a new time of salvation. Some people may have thought that, like one of the scribes, Jesus was going to engage in interpreting the law. But instead Jesus breaks with established traditions of interpreting the law by proclaiming that salvation and healing and even human need take priority over such obligations as observing the Sabbath (Mark 2:23–28; 3:1–6). Some expected Jesus to be like the Pharisees or other pious laymen who went beyond what was required of the law in their personal lives. Jesus is criticized for not observing ritual washings before meals (Mark 7:2) and for not teaching his disciples to fast (Mark 2:18). Neither practice is required by the law. Nor were Jews, in general, required to avoid contact with fellow Jews who were sinners, but Jesus was criticized for associating with sinners (Mark 2:15–17; Luke 7:34). Mark 7:15 preserves a saying of Jesus that shifts the focus away from external purity rules to the inner dispositions of a person: "There is nothing outside a person, which by going in can defile, but the things which come out of a person are what defile." Such debates present Jesus as a teacher who sought to expand the sphere of personal holiness and devotion to God. Yet his teaching and conduct sometimes conflicted with what people expected from such teachers.

In other respects, Jesus may have appeared to be closer to the prophets. He often spoke directly of the will of God for the people. Some of his puzzling actions and sayings have also been compared to those of the prophets—for example, this saying in Matthew 8:22 (Luke 9:60): "Let the dead bury their dead." Such disregard of filial piety would have been shocking to anyone, Jewish or pagan, in antiquity. If we look back at the Old Testament, however, we find two examples in which the prophet is commanded to break with burial rites. Jeremiah is told not to take part in mourning because an age is coming in which burial will be neglected (Jer 16:5–7). Ezekiel is told not to observe the usual rites when his wife dies (Ezek 24:15–18), as a sign of how the people will behave when Yahweh brings judgment on them by destroying the temple and permitting the death of many of the young. Jesus' command to a would-be disciple makes sense as a prophetic sign that the kingdom is at hand. The usual conventions of piety and behavior are broken because God's salvation and judgment are coming into the experience of Jesus and his generation.

The idea that Jesus' presence and actions show people that they are living in an "exceptional time" also shows up in the responses given to the charges of breaking the Sabbath, "so the Son of Man is Lord even of the sabbath" (Mark 2:28). It is used in the collection of sayings that defend Jesus and his followers for not fasting (Mark 2:19, 21–22). Other "prophetic" elements in Jesus' teaching have been recast in the gospels to reflect later events. Jesus made predictions about the impending destruction of the temple in Jerusalem (Mark 13:2; 14:58). He may also have predicted his own suffering and death, linking his fate with the death of John the Baptist (Mark 9:12–13).

The radical character of some of Jesus' sayings can be understood only when we recognize that they do not stem from a world that "goes on as usual." They are not calculated to assure success in an ongoing pattern of human relationships. Instead, Jesus speaks of a "new age" that reverses the values of the old one. This reversal is evident in the activities of healing and liberation for the sick, poor, and oppressed, which are associated with the Old Testament (as in Luke 4:18–21). Other reversal sayings speak of changing common evaluations of persons and status, "becoming like a child" (Mark 10:15) or the "first" as servant of all (Mark 10:43). The biggest transformation is evident in the call for a radically different way of relating to others as in the sayings about nonretaliation and love of enemies (e.g., Luke 6:27–36). We cannot simply take Jesus' sayings as though they describe the way in which people are likely to act. They are a summons to changing our hearts in light of the coming kingdom of God.

Jesus and His Followers

Everyone knows that Jesus was accompanied by a group of disciples. The gospels preserve stories about how some of them came to follow Jesus: Mark 1:16–18 (Simon Peter and Andrew), and 1:19–20 (James and John, sons of Zebedee). Matthew 4:18–20, 21–22 and Luke 5:1–11 combine the call of Peter with that of James and John but omit Andrew; Mark 2:14//Matthew 9:9//Luke 5:27–28 (Levi, in Mark/Luke, Matthew, in Matt); John 1:35–50 has another set of five: an unnamed person, Andrew, Simon Peter, Philip, and Nathanael. Most people know that Jesus had a core group of twelve disciples. Mark 3:16–19 lists their names as Simon Peter, James and John the sons of Zebedee, Andrew, Philip, Bartholomew, Matthew, Thomas, James son of Alphaeus, Thaddaeus, Simon the Canaanite, and Judas Iscariot. But the gospels mention other persons who followed Jesus as well. Mark 4:10 speaks of "those who were about him with the Twelve." Luke 8:1–3 speaks of Jesus accompanied by the Twelve and women whom he had healed and who provided financial support. John mentions other disciples of Jesus not in lists of the Twelve, the unnamed follower of the Baptist, Nathanael, and a disciple called the "Beloved Disciple," who was the source of the gospel's tradition (John 1:35–36, 45; 13:23; 18:15; 19:26–27, 35; 21:2, 7, 20, 24). The circle of Jesus' followers was larger than the special list of "twelve."

The number "twelve" symbolizes the twelve tribes of Israel. A saying in Matthew 19:28/Luke 22:30 presents the Twelve judging the twelve tribes of Israel in the new age. Psalm 122:4–5 speaks of the tribes going up to Jerusalem, where thrones have been set up in judgment. Luke, conscious of Judas's impending betrayal, omits the number "twelve" from his version of the saying. Acts 1:23–26 describes the followers of Jesus at Jerusalem choosing someone to replace Judas who had been among them from the beginning. Once the number "twelve" had been restored it was not necessary to continue to appoint persons to the circle of the Twelve.

However, the Twelve quickly become confused with another group in early Christianity, "apostles." Luke uses the term *apostles* for the Twelve (e.g., Luke 6:13; Acts 1:26). But the term *apostle* referred to persons who were missionaries sent to preach the gospel and has its background in the Jewish idea of specially commissioned emissaries. You can see how the two terms differ if you read 1 Corinthians 15:5–9. Paul, who is himself an "apostle," speaks of Jesus appearing to Peter and then to the "Twelve" separately from appearances to James, the brother of the Lord and not the son of Zebedee, other apostles, other believers, and finally to himself. The confusion between the Twelve and the larger group of apostles is rooted in the fact that the gospels also describe the Twelve as being sent out by Jesus to engage in a mission of preaching and healing (Mark 6:7–13; Matt 10:1–15; Luke 9:1–6; Luke 10:1–16). Read one of those passages. You will notice a number of rules that the disciples are to follow in their preaching. These rules make them radically dependent upon the hospitality that they receive from others along the way, since they are not to take money or provisions.

There are a number of situations in antiquity in which a person might leave family and occupation to become the "disciple" of a popular leader. The most familiar would be persons who went to become students of a particular teacher. Some popular philosophers, especially from the Cynic school, also led a wandering lifestyle, warning the crowds of humanity about the blindness of their ways. A person might also join a gang of robbers, preying on travelers or resisting the Roman occupation. Barabbas and the two "thieves" with whom Jesus was crucified may have been rebels of this sort. Or one might join a group of disciples surrounding a prophetic figure. John the Baptist gathered a group of disciples distinct from the crowds who came to hear him and be baptized as a sign of their repentance.

The Baptist was executed by Herod Antipas because of his popularity (Josephus, *Antiquities* 18.118–19) and the fears that his preaching might cause an uprising. Similar fears may have motivated the Jewish officials who handed Jesus over to Pilate as a potential rebel. But in neither case does their condemnation imply that the Baptist or Jesus was actually devoted to the violent overthrow of a corrupt political regime. Both Jesus and John preached a message of God's impending judgment and called upon people to repent. Jesus insisted that the time of God's rule was already becoming present in his ministry. The general picture of Galilee in the time of Jesus suggests a fairly peaceful region. Even when the Jews did revolt against Rome in AD 66 to 70, the resistance in Galilee was quickly extinguished.

Jesus' teaching sometimes overlaps with that of the Pharisees and others devoted to interpreting the law. But he does not pursue the kind of detailed interpretation and exegesis of the letter of the law that we find among the Pharisees or the new Covenanters. Therefore, his followers may have considered him a popular religious teacher but not a scribe or rabbi. In

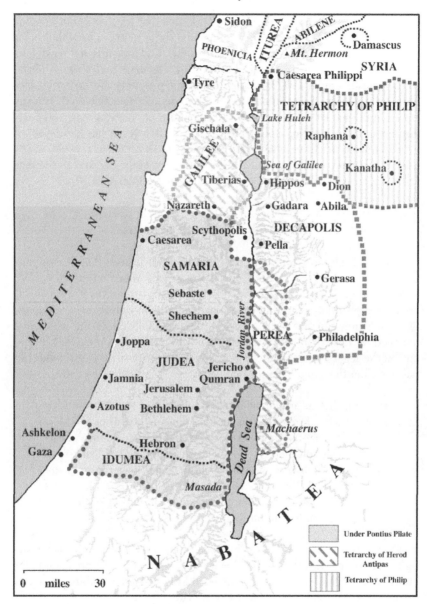

Palestine under early Roman procurators

addition to teaching, Jesus' ministry also incorporated prophetic sayings and actions as well as nature miracles, healings, and exorcisms. Charges that Jesus' miracles were enabled by demons (Mark 3:22–27; Matt 12:22–30; Luke 11:14–23) led to accusations that Jesus was a magician and deceiver of the people. Justin Martyr (ca. AD 150) indicates that Jews drew this conclusion: "Yet though they [= the Jews] witnessed these miracles with their own eyes, they attributed them to magic; indeed they had the audacity to call him a magician, a deceiver of the people" (Justin, *Dialogue with Trypho* 69.7). Josephus uses similar language about messianic prophets and Zealot leaders during the Jewish revolt against Rome (Josephus, *War* 2.259; 6.288). If Jesus comes in the name of God, then his teaching, prophetic warnings, and healings must all be signs of God's activity. If not, then Jesus can be identified with any of the negative images for a popular leader: deceiver, rebel, magician. We will never know what led Judas to betray Jesus, but we can see that Jesus was a problematic figure even for his own disciples.

The Trial and Death of Jesus

One of the most certain historical facts about Jesus is that he was condemned to be crucified by the Roman prefect of Judea, Pontius Pilate. We know from the references to crucifixion in literary sources that it was considered the appropriate punishment for slaves and the most hardened criminals. St. Paul comments that Jesus' death on the cross falls under the curse pronounced by Deuteronomy 21:22–23 (Gal 3:13). His interpretation is borne out by the legal rulings of the new Covenanters sect such as the following passage from the *Temple Scroll*:

> If a man has informed against his people and has delivered his people up to a foreign nation and has done evil to his people, you shall hang him on a tree and he shall die. On the evidence of two witnesses and on the evidence of three witnesses, he shall be put to death....Their bodies shall not pass the night on the tree, you shall bury them that very day, for what is hanged on the tree is accursed by God and humanity and you shall not defile the land I am giving you for an inheritance.

You can see from the tone of this passage that many of those who saw Jesus on the cross or heard that he had been crucified would have presumed him guilty of a terrible crime. The cross would be a major stumbling block to belief just as St. Paul says it is in 1 Corinthians 1:18–25.

Archaeologists have discovered the skeleton of a young Jewish man, Yehohanan, who had been crucified in the first century. He was buried in his family tomb. One of its members was a potter. Another had been active in the building of Herod's temple. Since it seems unlikely that someone from that family would be a common robber (and certainly not a slave), we can only guess that he had engaged in activity that the Romans found suspect.

Whatever his crime, the family was able to obtain possession of the body and to bury it in their own tomb.

Our only evidence for the charges against Jesus comes from gospel accounts that were written decades after the event. We do not have anything resembling a contemporary court record. In addition, we are in the dark about critical legal issues. Some historians agree with the assertion in John 18:31 that a Jewish court could not have put Jesus to death so that even if they had found Jesus guilty on the religious charge of leading God's people astray (Deut 13:2–6; 18:20–22), they would have had to get the Roman governor to execute Jesus. Others insist that the Sanhedrin could have still exercised the death penalty in any case where the offense was clearly a religious one.

While the gospels all agree that Jesus was handed over to Pilate by Jewish authorities, the nature of the Jewish proceedings against him is unclear. It was possible for a private party to bring someone up on charges before the governor. Then it was up to him to decide how to deal with the case. No more than two or three persons were needed to act as accusers. Thus, you should not imagine that Jesus was handed over by the entire Jewish people or even the entire Sanhedrin. Mark 14:55–65 (and Matt 26:59–68) presumes a trial in which conflicting testimony was brought forward, and Jesus was finally condemned as a blasphemer. Luke implies that no verdict was reached (Luke 22:71; Acts 13:27–28). John presumes that the decision to have Jesus executed had been made before Jesus was arrested (11:45–53). Charges of blasphemy are leveled at Jesus throughout John's gospel (John 5:18; 8:59; 10:31). Prior to being turned over to Pilate, Jesus is interrogated by the former high priest Annas (John 18:19–24). Luke 23:6–12 has an additional episode in which Pilate sends Jesus off to Herod. That scene has no legal basis, since offenses were tried where they occurred. Some scholars think that Luke's expansion reflects a tradition that Herod had the extraordinary privilege of extraditing offenders who fled his jurisdiction for other parts of the empire. On the other hand, it could be a literary addition to the passion narrative that cements all political and religious authorities together in their hostility toward Jesus. Acts 4:26–27 identifies Herod Antipas as one of the "kings of the earth" arrayed against Jesus.

It is possible that Jesus was never legally condemned by a Jewish court. With its members from differing parties and traditions of interpreting the law, it may have been very difficult to obtain a verdict in the Sanhedrin. Josephus (War 6.300–305) tells the story of a prophet, Ananias (ca. AD 62), who upset the authorities by predicting the destruction of the temple. He was turned over to Roman authorities who let him go as a "lunatic." It is also possible that the Sanhedrin session with Jesus was merely a hearing to determine grounds on which he might be turned over to Pilate. Thus, while it is clear that some of the Jewish leaders had decided that Jesus' words and actions were potentially dangerous, it is far from clear that there was any consensus that Jesus had committed a capital offense. Jesus should not be presented as hostile to the whole religious tradition of his people, Israel.

Pilate was free to handle the case in any way that he chose. The formulation of the charge "king of the Jews" reflects a Roman viewpoint: the condemned is a rebel leader trying to stir up the people. The expression "king of the Jews" had been employed by Herod the Great as a self-aggrandizing attempt to represent himself to Rome as the ruler of Jews everywhere, not simply of the territory that Rome permitted him to govern. What we know of Pilate does not suggest a person overly concerned with the niceties of Jewish feelings or the guilt or innocence of those he condemned for seditious behavior (cf. Luke 13:1–2). In AD 35, Pilate sent soldiers to Samaria to prevent the Samaritans from following one of their prophets up Mount Gerezim. Some of the people were killed, and the aftermath led to Pilate's recall (Josephus, *Antiquities* 18.86–87). Since the high priest Caiaphas lost his office soon after Pilate was removed, historians presume that Pilate and Caiaphas had some sort of political understanding. Whatever their relationship, the ten-year period of Pilate's administration in Judea (AD 26–36) was unusually stable. In 1961, archaeologists discovered an inscription that links Pilate to the erection of a building in Caesarea (ca. AD 31) that honored the emperor Tiberius. Thus, a person handed over as an evildoer by Caiaphas would hardly have caused Pilate much concern. Of course, we have only looked at the trial and death of Jesus through the eyes of a historian trying to figure out the legal facts of the case. From that perspective, it appears to be an example of human evil, the thoughtless destruction of an innocent person. But the early Christians were able to look at Jesus' own acceptance of that death through the image of the Suffering Servant from Isaiah 53:6–12. They saw that Jesus suffered for the sins of humanity to bring us back into a living relationship with God (e.g., Mark 10:45b; Rom 4:25; 2 Cor 5:21). They used the language of sacrifice, of the expiation for sin on the Day of Atonement, to describe it (Heb 9:11–15; Rom 3:25–26). And they saw in Jesus' death the supreme manifestation of God's love (Gal 2:20; Rom 5:8; John 3:16). For Christians, then, the death of Jesus also demonstrates a power of love that goes beyond the worst of human evil and sin.

Summary

We have seen that the New Testament does not provide us with the kind of information that would be found in a modern historical biography of a famous person. One of the most critical events in Jesus' story, his trial and death, poses a number of historical questions that we cannot resolve. As they were handed on, Jesus' deeds and teachings were reshaped to address the problems faced by later groups of Christians. Sometimes it is easy to detect the concerns that led to new emphases, as in the link between the story of the Syro-Phoenician woman and the mission to the Gentiles in Matthew. Or we may see the fuller and more balanced expressions in Matthew's version of the Lord's Prayer as representative of the use of that prayer in Christian worship. But in other cases it is difficult to decide how a particular tradition may have developed.

We have also seen that as Jesus healed and preached among the people, he gathered around him a diverse group of followers. A special group of "twelve" represented the renewal of Israel through Jesus' ministry. But there were other disciples, women and men, who followed Jesus as well. Then there were persons drawn to him in the hope of being healed or out of curiosity about his preaching. Some may have become disciples. Some may have thought of Jesus as just another healer, prophetic preacher of repentance, or interpreter of the law. And at least some persons among the Jewish leaders in Jerusalem were so offended or concerned about the impact of Jesus' activities that they initiated the events that led to his execution by the Roman prefect in Judea, Pontius Pilate.

We have also seen that it is not easy to fit Jesus into any of the established categories for popular, religious, or political leaders. Jesus was not an authority in one of the Jewish groups of the time like the Pharisees or new Covenanters. His family did not belong to a priestly tribe, so he was not a Jewish priest or Levite. The infancy narratives in Luke 1–2 and Matthew 1–2 claim a relationship to the "house of David." But that relationship is clearly indirect. Jesus' family was not recognized as "heirs to the throne of David." If some people thought of Jesus in political terms as "messiah" or "anointed" leader of the people, they might have thought that he would establish a new dynasty or that he might bring about the final judgment of God. For those in the crowds, Jesus' leadership did not stem from any established role but rather was based on his popular appeal as healer or prophetic figure. You can also see that for many of these people Jesus' death would be the end of the story, since both political leaders and healers have to be alive to draw a following. Prophets and teachers may continue to influence others through disciples who preserve their teaching. We will see that Jesus' disciples do far more than preserve his teaching. They claim that God has raised Jesus from death and that Jesus is the decisive turning point in salvation for all of humanity.

STUDY QUESTIONS

Facts You Should Know

1. Name the two basic types of stories about Jesus and give the characteristics of each type.
2. Name three different types of sayings by Jesus and give the characteristics of each type.
3. Why do we find different versions of the same parable, saying, or incident in the gospel traditions?
4. What is the *Gospel of Thomas*? The "Q" source?
5. What other miracle-workers were active in the first century AD? How do the stories of Jesus' miracles compare with stories told about others?
6. Give two examples of "radical" or "shocking" elements in the teaching of Jesus. What do these examples tell Jesus' audience about the "time" in which they live?
7. What is the significance of the "Twelve"? How is that group distinguished from "disciples of Jesus" and from "apostles"?
8. Why would the crucifixion of Jesus by the Romans have led some people to conclude that he could not have been God's spokesperson?
9. Describe unresolved historical questions about the trial of Jesus.

Things to Do

1. Study the stories of the Syro-Phoenician woman (3–1) and the lost sheep (3–2). Make a list of the common details and of everything that is special to each version. Pick out the special features that a particular author might be directing at the later situation of Christians. Can you find any similarities between Matthew's versions of the two stories?
2. Read the stories of Jesus' trial(s) in Mark 14:53—15:20 and Luke 22:54—23:25. First, make a list of the common elements in the two accounts. Then find the differences between them. What reasons can you think of for some of the differences?
3. Take a concordance and look under the word *faith* to find all of the times in which *faith* is used in connection with a miracle of Jesus in one of the gospels. Compare the use of *faith* by the gospel writers with the use of faith in the story of the healing by the god Asclepius.

Things to Think About

1. What significance do the miracles of Jesus have for today's Christian? What do Christians need to remember when they pray to Jesus for healing?

2. What kind of popular leader(s) might Jesus be confused with today? What parts of his ministry or teaching might make him such a threat some people would want him jailed or killed? What kind of "follower" of Jesus do you think you would have been?

Chapter 4

THE PREACHING OF JESUS

Proclaiming the Kingdom of God

The expression "kingdom (or 'reign') of God" introduces Jesus' message (e.g., Mark 1:15). It would evoke images of God ruling over the people, as in the Lord's Prayer, "thy kingdom come, thy will be done." Some people would have said that experience of God's rule could come only in a new age when evil had been destroyed. Familiar passages from Isaiah anticipated a time when Jerusalem would be such a beacon that all nations would acknowledge the Lord's presence there (Isa 62:1–3). In Jesus' preaching, the "kingdom" is not just a reference to some distant event. Its presence makes itself felt in persons whose lives are changed. But the kingdom is not identical with changes in this world. There is still the future coming in which its promise of salvation is completed. Jesus says to his disciples at the Last Supper, "I will no longer drink of the fruit of the vine with you until that day when I drink it new in the reign of God" (Mark 14:25). Drinking "new wine" at a banquet with the Lord is a symbol of rejoicing in the new age.

Another saying of Jesus points to the presence of the reign of God:

> Once Jesus was asked by the Pharisees when the reign of God would come, and he answered, "It is not by observation that the reign of God comes; people will not even say, 'Look, here it is, or there!' For the reign of God is among you." (Luke 17:20–21)

This saying captured the imagination of early Christians. Several versions of it found their way into the *Gospel of Thomas*:

> His disciples said to him, "On what day will the kingdom come?" [Jesus said,] "It does not come with the expectation of it. People will not say, 'Look, here or Look, there!' Rather the Kingdom of

the Father is spread out on the earth and human beings do not see it." (*Gos. Thom.* 113)

Jesus said, "If those who draw you on say to you, 'Look, the Kingdom is in heaven,' then the birds of heaven will be there before you. If they say to you, 'It is in the sea,' then the fish will be there before you. But the kingdom is within you and outside you." (*Gos. Thom.* 3)

Though the Lord's Prayer asks for God's kingdom to come, Jesus rejected speculation about the time and place of its arrival. Disciples should learn to discern the presence of the kingdom in their midst. Jesus points to his exorcisms as one sign that the kingdom is present (Luke 11:20). There is even a very puzzling passage in which Jesus says that some of those present "will not taste death until they see the kingdom of God" (Luke 9:27; Mark 9:1). Jesus' contemporaries might have assumed that the final judgment and new creation were right around the corner.

Jesus also proclaims the "reign of God" in the parables that point toward what it means to experience the kingdom. Mark 4:11 speaks of the parables as revealing the "mystery of the kingdom." Those who fail to grasp it are cut off from the kingdom. Some parables like the Parable of the Seed Growing Secretly (Mark 4:26–29) and the Parable of the Mustard Seed (Mark 4:30–32) compare the kingdom of God to a small, almost unnoticed seed. But when the seed is fully grown then there is a harvest or a nesting place for the birds. In this way, Jesus shows us that the kingdom is not something that arrives with a dramatic, cosmic gesture as the myths of the end of the world have it. The kingdom may begin in a way that is almost invisible.

Jesus also spoke about the kinds of persons who would "enter the kingdom." Mark 12:28–34 contains a pronouncement story in which a scribe asks Jesus what the greatest commandment is. Jesus summarizes the law by speaking of the obligation to love God with our whole heart and to love our neighbor. The scribe approves and repeats what Jesus has said. Then Jesus says to the scribe, "You are not far from the kingdom of God." So we can see one type of person who is close to the kingdom, someone who perceives the essentials of a religious life in terms of the love of God and neighbor. This scribe is not like others in the gospel who try to trap Jesus or who take offense at Jesus healing on the Sabbath. Another very famous saying of Jesus compares persons who would enter the kingdom of God to children (Mark 10:13–16). This saying was also widely repeated:

Truly I say to you, whoever does not receive the kingdom of God like a child shall not enter it. (Mark 10:15)

Truly, I say to you, unless you turn and become like children you will never enter the kingdom of heaven. (Matt 18:3)

Truly, truly I say to you, unless a person is born anew, that person cannot see the kingdom of God. (John 3:3)

Jesus saw infants nursing. He said to his disciples, "These nursing infants are like those who enter the kingdom." (*Gos. Thom.* 22)

A major change is required in those who become part of the kingdom. The versions in John and the *Gospel of Thomas* even think of that change as beginning all over again like a newborn infant. John 3:5 links this new beginning with the ritual of baptism when one is born of "water and the Spirit."

Parables as a Language of Faith

Jesus showed what he meant by faith through the parables. Some of the parables show us people doing surprising things. They suggest that the kingdom can radically change a person's life. For example, Matthew 13:44–46 preserves two parables in which the characters take quick action. A day laborer digging in a field finds a treasure. He quickly buys the field for himself. A pearl merchant finds a very valuable pearl so he sells everything else in order to get it. We can understand both of these acts as something that people might do in extraordinary situations. Jesus is telling us that the kingdom creates that type of situation.

Other parables challenge us to evaluate the actions of particular characters in the stories. Their actions and success or failure indicate how persons should live in the presence of the kingdom. Sometimes the parable may have been given an introduction by the gospel writer that links it to the kingdom. A striking example of the link between the kingdom and unusual human behavior occurs in the Parable of the Workers in the Vineyard in Matthew 20:1–15. Matthew has added a proverbial expression—"The last shall be first and the first last"—which was often used of the reversal to take place in the new age (v. 16). The parable reflects a situation common in the agricultural economy of the time: when it was necessary to harvest the grapes, a vineyard owner would have to hire day laborers. Roman books on agriculture advise people to plant grapes that ripen at different times so that they would not have to hire too many people or work for too many days to pick them. Since the grape harvest was one of the busiest times, the story presumes a situation of serious unemployment. If day laborers could go all day without work at this time of year, things must have been much worse at other times.

You can see from reading the story that the experience of the persons in the story depended upon which group one belonged to. The people who worked all day, even though they may have been happy to accept the work when they started, go away unhappy. We don't hear from the other workers, but we would guess that those who had waited all day without work and then found themselves with a day's pay at the last minute were rejoicing. The owner does have to face the complaints of the first group. He may claim that he is "good," but the first group no longer experience his behavior as good even though he has honored their original contract and has also followed the law that required owners to pay the workers their wages on the same day (Lev 19:13; Deut 24:15). If this parable is about the coming of God's reign, then it turns out that the reign of God does not create universal peace and harmony. This parable is a good example of how we may have to change our lives and our presuppositions about what is fair and just if we are to experience the reign of God.

Another parable in which a "good" or generous action by the central character creates tension is the Parable of the Prodigal Son in Luke 15:11–32. The younger son, like the figure of Joseph in the Old Testament, finds himself among pagans at a time of famine. But instead of lifting the whole country to prosperity and becoming second only to the ruler as Joseph had done, the younger son is a starving pig-herder (Jews do not eat pork). So he decides it would be better to return home and beg his father for mercy. The father surprises the younger son by throwing a party in his honor. The older son, who has remained at home working with his father, becomes angry. He says what many people feel in similar situations. His younger brother has done nothing to deserve such treatment, while he has worked hard and never been given anything like the welcome his brother is getting. Notice that the father does not reject the elder. He reminds him that everything the father has will be his. But the father does say that it is wrong to be angry and resentful. He insists that it is right to celebrate the return of the younger.

The story reminds us that God extends forgiveness to those who seek to change their lives no matter what they may have done. The younger son agreed with his older brother that he did not "deserve" a banquet. He wasn't even planning to ask his father to take him back as though he were a "son"—just to treat him like a hired hand. But the father does not want the younger son back living in disgrace. He wants him back as the son he should be. The banquet is a dramatic way to make the point. Other parables of Jesus have this pattern of finding what is lost. Luke puts two of them just before the Parable of the Prodigal Son: the Lost Sheep (Luke 15:3–7; cf. Matt 18:12–14) and the Lost Coin (Luke 15:8–10). Luke 15:1–2 provides an important clue as to why Jesus emphasized parables of this sort. Luke says that Jesus was severely criticized by the Pharisees for associating with sinners. They thought that a good or righteous person would gather people just as holy. In that way, a group of righteous persons would be built up that might encourage others to be just as devoted to

God. Jesus claimed that his message was not just for the righteous. He came to seek out those who were "lost" and who might even have given up on any hope of salvation. Instead, Jesus teaches that God is something like a shepherd finding a lost sheep, a woman finding a lost coin, or the father in the story of the "prodigal" (= lost) son. God is overjoyed when what has been lost returns.

Wisdom in the Sayings of Jesus

Another very common form of teaching in Jesus' time was the collection of "wise sayings," or proverbs. Sayings of this sort do not have any special situation in mind. They are general pieces of wise advice. A wisdom saying can apply to a number of different situations. Proverbs do not claim to be new insights. Since proverbial wisdom is often aimed at the young, sayings may give advice about how to be successful in friendship, family, work, and so on. They often draw a sharp contrast between the "wise" and the "foolish." Most people, it appears, fall into the latter category.

Proverbs and Ecclesiasticus (or Ben Sirach) contain wisdom sayings of this sort. Here is an example from Ben Sirach about lending money:

> Lend to your neighbor in the time of his need; and in turn, repay your neighbor promptly. Confirm your word and keep faith with him, and on every occasion you will find what you need. Many persons regard a loan as a windfall, and cause trouble to those who help them. A man will kiss another's hands until he gets a loan, and will lower his voice in speaking of his neighbor's money; but at the time for repayment he will delay, and will pay in words of unconcern, and will find fault with the time. If the lender exerts pressure, he will hardly get back half, and will regard that as a windfall. If he does not, the borrower has robbed him of his money and he has needlessly made him his enemy; he will repay him with curses and reproaches, and instead of glory will repay him with dishonor. Because of such wickedness therefore many have refused to lend; they have been afraid of being defrauded needlessly. (Sir 29:2–7)

You can see that the sage expects his audience to lend to those in need. But he also recognizes the rather dismal record of human relationships when such loans are at stake. Experiences like that might cause people to refuse to make loans altogether. Those who borrow are to keep their word and repay the loan as they promised.

We also find Jesus speaking about lending to others and about keeping one's word. Here are some of the sayings attributed to him:

Again you have heard it said to your ancestors, "You shall not swear falsely, but shall perform to the Lord what you have sworn." But I say to you, "Do not swear at all, either by heaven, for it is the throne of God, or by the earth, for it is his footstool, or by Jerusalem, for it is the city of the great King. And do not swear by your head, for you cannot make one hair white or black. Let what you say be simply 'Yes' or 'No'; anything more than this comes from evil." (Matt 5:33–37)

Give to him who begs from you, and do not refuse him who would borrow from you. (Matt 5:42)

You can see that Jesus agrees that people should give and keep their word. He even goes so far as to reject the "oaths" that people swear to prove their honesty. He also agrees that they should be generous in lending to those who wish to borrow. But you may notice something different in Jesus' tone. He does not engage in pessimistic reflection on the fact that most persons will abuse that privilege. This omission does not mean that Jesus was blind to the kind of human failings treated in Ben Sirach. We have already seen parables in which he uses such examples very vividly. But Jesus' teaching springs from the presence of God's reign. It is not simply good advice about how to maintain one's integrity in a world of fools and dishonest people.

Sirach also tells his audience that the pursuit of God's commandments is more important than the pursuit of wealth:

Lay up your treasure according to the commandments of the Most High, and it will profit you more than gold. Store up almsgiving in your treasury and it will rescue you from all affliction. (Sir 29:11–12)

Jesus reminds his followers that service to God cannot be combined with service to money:

Do not lay up for yourselves treasures on earth where moth and rust consume and where thieves break in and steal, but lay up for yourselves treasure in heaven, where neither moth nor rust consumes and where thieves do not break in and steal. For where your treasure is, there your heart will be also. (Matt 6:19–21)

No one can serve two masters; for either he will hate the one and love the other, or he will be devoted to the one and despise the other. You cannot serve God and mammon. (Matt 6:24)

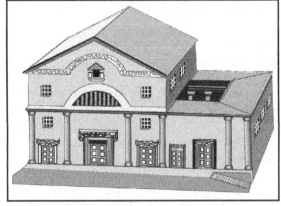

Jesus was clearly able to use the wisdom traditions of Israel to shape his own instruction.

Summons to Discipleship

You can see that Jesus' teaching that the reign of God is present and his use of the wisdom sayings both presume that his followers will begin to live in a new way. Sometimes people think that Jesus' words are just a vision of how things "ought to be" or will be when there is a new age in which God's rule is firmly established, not "hidden" like the seeds in Jesus' parables (see Mark 4:3–8, 26–29, 31–32). However, Jesus is represented as speaking directly to his audience about their life and behavior, not about some future ideal. On the other hand, you will see that the explicit sayings and deeds of Jesus do not play a major role in the ethical teaching of the letters of Paul. Clearly, the first Christians did not treat Jesus as a lawgiver who was setting up a "sect" within Judaism that had its own special rulebooks to follow as the Teacher of Righteousness had done. So we would also be making a big mistake if we thought of Jesus' preaching as a "new" or a special interpretation of the Mosaic law such as we find it among the Pharisees or the new Covenanters.

The Lord's Prayer

Although Jesus did not set up legal requirements for Christian behavior, his preaching does give clear examples of how Christians should act. The Lord's Prayer combines the future expectation of the rule of God and our present life as Christians. Look at Matthew's version of the prayer (Chart 3–3). Each section has a conclusion to balance out the petition to which it is attached. These petitions also make the future side of the reign of God evident. The first petition, that the name of God be "sanctified" or made holy, can be related to the prophecy of Ezekiel 36:22–28. Yahweh is about to "vindicate the holiness" of his name, which had been "profaned among the nations" because of the sinfulness of the people. **Reconstruction of the synagogue at Capernaum**

You can see that this image does not simply refer to praising God as holy. It means that the people of God show that God is holy in their lives. The addition that Matthew makes to this section of the prayer emphasizes that point. God's rule, already a reality in heaven, still has to become a reality on earth. But God, not merely some form of human moral or legal renewal, brings about the coming of the kingdom in the "heaven-like" obedience to God's will on earth.

The second half of the prayer addresses petitions to God from the community of believing disciples. These petitions express their own desire to live in a way that does manifest the holiness of God. The conclusion that Matthew gives to the third petition makes the eschatological character of "temptation" evident. Just as the new Covenanters spoke of the danger of the "evil inclination" and the "Angel of Darkness" leading righteous persons away from following the law, so Matthew understands "temptation" to mean falling under the power of "the evil one." (The tendency to translate the Greek as though it were an abstract noun ["evil"] gives the impression that this phrase is simply a variant of the previous petition.) The Christian community acknowledges the power of evil to lead people away from devotion to the will of God and that it must rely on God's aid to maintain its holiness.

The petition for bread, which Luke's version has generalized from "today" to "every day," contains an unusual word to describe the bread— *epiousion*. English speakers use the word *daily* as a guess about the meaning of that word. Some church fathers thought that the bread being referred to was the bread of the Eucharist. However, if you read through Matthew 6, you will notice that much of the rest of the chapter concerns anxiety about material things and the basic necessities of life (vv. 19–21, 24, 25–34). It would seem that Matthew understands the petition to be related to these anxieties. The symbolism attached to the bread might then be that of the "manna" which God had given the Israelites to keep them from starving in the wilderness. Proverbs 30:8 has the wise person ask God to provide only the food that the person needs. Therefore, the best guess about the meaning of the word *epiousion* is to follow the church fathers who thought that it meant the bread "of our need" or "for our sustenance." This understanding means that Jesus' disciples are to have a particular relationship to material things. They are not to hoard or rely on them, but are to rely on what God provides.

The petition about forgiveness appears to have been altered by Luke from "debts" to "sins," from "debtors" to "persons who have done wrong to us," and from "have forgiven" to "forgive." These shifts are understandable within a Gentile context that did not know the religious significance of forgiveness of debts in the Old Testament tradition. The most dramatic examples of this tradition are found in the legislation about the "jubilee year," which is a time of "release" for the poor. Special times, the "Sabbath" and jubilee years, required Israel to recall her own bondage and liberation by

God. Slaves were to be freed and the land allowed to lie fallow (e.g., Exod 21:2–6; 23:10–11; Deut 15:1–18; Lev 25). Jesus' Parable of the Seed Growing Secretly (Mark 4:26–29) draws upon the image of the land producing food "of itself," what persons were allowed to harvest during the sabbatical year, to describe how fruitful the kingdom is. Within this context, to speak of Christians as "having forgiven debtors" makes life in light of the kingdom a continual enactment of the redemption and liberation of the jubilee year.

God's Forgiveness

Other passages in the teaching of Jesus also emphasize the radical nature of the forgiveness that is part of Jesus' understanding of God. Matthew 18:21–35 links the Parable of the Unforgiving Servant to Peter's request for a ruling on how often we have to forgive others. Both Jesus' answer to the question and the parable make it clear that there are no limits on forgiveness. Matthew 7:1–5 contains a sharp warning against judging others, while Matthew 6:14–15 adds a reminder that the forgiveness we receive from God requires that we forgive others. Various formulations of the "love command" expand beyond the love of neighbor to love of enemies, as in Matthew 5:43–48. You will notice that Matthew uses that passage to conclude a collection of sayings against retaliation for specific wrongs, including "debt," that is, Christians are to lend without demanding repayment. Thus, one of the most important parts of Jesus' ethical teaching is the "love command." Jesus expects his disciples to make the experiences of redemption and forgiveness a reality of their lives. He tells them stories in which the characters do extraordinary things in order to demonstrate what forgiveness, generosity, and mercy mean. In the Parable of the Unforgiving Servant, the king was willing to wipe out a debt that was much bigger than the annual revenue of Herod's whole kingdom (Matt 18:24–27). Unfortunately, the servant didn't learn anything from that experience. He went out and threatened a fellow servant over a small debt (vv. 28–34).

Jesus did more than talk about mercy and forgiveness. He also scandalized some people by welcoming sinners and eating with them himself. Luke 7:36–50 contains a dramatic story in which Jesus is a guest of one of the local Pharisees. A woman known to be a sinner suddenly comes in weeping and anoints Jesus' feet. When the Pharisee is puzzled because Jesus permits a sinner near him, Jesus replies with another tale about debtors. He asks who will love the lender more, the one who is freed of a large debt or of a small one? When the Pharisee agrees that the person forgiven a large debt will love the lender more, Jesus applies the case to the sinful woman. Her love has already been shown in what she has done for Jesus. Therefore, her many sins are forgiven. Other passages in the gospels show that people who wished to attack Jesus spoke of him as a friend of tax collectors and sinners (Matt 11:16–19).

Levi, a tax collector, became a disciple of Jesus (Matt 9:9–13; Mark 2:13–17; Luke 5:27–32).

We sometimes forget how amazing Jesus' behavior toward sinners was because we think of a "sinner" as someone like us, a person who is trying to live a good life but who falls short and has to ask God's forgiveness. In Judaism, a person like that is not a "sinner." That person can use the rituals of atonement to receive forgiveness for the failings in his or her efforts to follow God. A "sinner," on the other hand, is a person who deliberately turns against God. That person is leading a life that he or she knows is contrary to the law. The "wicked" scorn righteousness, justice, and piety to pursue their own desires. Tax collectors were considered to be engaged in an occupation that excluded them from the "people of God" because they were working for the Romans in collecting taxes and other fees. Tax collectors also had a reputation for defrauding people by demanding more than was owed and pocketing the difference and for using violence in collecting fees. So you can see that it was the kind of occupation in which a person could hardly claim to be "just" and "merciful." When the prodigal son squandered his father's money in sexual immorality and then wound up working as a pig-herder for a pagan (pigs were considered "unclean" by Jews, who do not eat pork), he was acting like one of the "wicked."

Most people thought that when God brought salvation to the people, only the righteous, who were trying hard to follow God's will, would be saved. The "wicked" would be condemned for their evil ways. Jesus, on the other hand, insists that God reaches out to the wicked as well. He told a parable about a shepherd leaving the flock to find a lost sheep (Luke 15:1–7; Matt 18:10–14) to demonstrate the attitude of God toward the wicked. The "righteous" are all right. Jesus has come to seek out those who are lost. People like that do not even think that they have a chance of being accepted by God. Matthew's version of this parable makes it clear that Jesus' disciples are expected to continue that concern for those who are "lost." Matthew realizes that there is a danger of Christianity becoming a group just for the pious, the good people. So he surrounds Jesus' parable with a warning that the angels of the "little ones" stand before God. Church leaders must seek out the wandering and lost. They must never take an attitude of self-righteousness and "despise" such persons.

Summary

When Jesus preached about the "reign of God," he was not only speaking about God's power in the future. He was also calling his disciples to experience what God's power could do to change their lives now. We are expected to live in a way that depends upon the power of God and not upon our human prejudices, divisions, cares, and anxieties. Otherwise, we will not experience the joy of salvation when the reign of God is completely manifest.

The central feature of the new life of disciples can be found in Jesus' vision of the mercy, love, and forgiveness of God. This love also has to govern the relationships that Christians have with one another. They cannot judge or condemn others. They must be looking for ways in which they can show what love, mercy, and forgiveness mean in their lives by extending them to others. And they must also be willing to seek out persons who are not part of their own group of pious or righteous people. They must be willing to help the poor and suffering. They must go even further and seek the "lost sheep," people who are so marginal to society and to religion that they would not even think of approaching God or a church.

STUDY QUESTIONS

Facts You Should Know

1. Give examples from the teaching of Jesus that point to the kingdom both as "present" in the experience of disciples and as "future expectation."
2. What do the sayings about "becoming like a child" tell disciples about entering the kingdom?
3. Describe the objections raised to the behavior of the central character in the Parable of the Workers in the Vineyard and the Parable of the Prodigal Son.
4. How do Jesus' sayings about lending and wealth differ from similar sayings in the wisdom traditions of Israel?
5. What does each petition of the Lord's Prayer tell us about the kingdom and discipleship?
6. Why was Jesus' behavior toward "sinners" a scandal to his contemporaries?

Things to Do

1. Read Luke 15. Compare Luke's version of the Parable of the Lost Sheep with the other versions (Chart 3–2). What elements in Luke's version fit in with themes in the rest of the chapter?
2. Use a concordance to find the passages in Matthew that warn disciples that they must show forgiveness to others if they are to expect it from God. Read the Parable of the Unforgiving Servant. How does the parable illustrate this teaching?
3. Read Mark 4. Find all the allusions to "secrecy" and "hiddenness" in the chapter. How is this theme related to the seed images used in the parable?

Things to Think About

1. Make yourself a list of the characteristics of discipleship in the Lord's Prayer. How would you make them part of your life?
2. How do you think the conflicts that are left hanging at the end of the Parable of the Workers in the Vineyard and the Parable of the Prodigal Son might have been resolved?
3. What situations today call for forgiveness and reconciliation? How might Jesus' parables be applied to those situations? Could you write such a parable for today?

Chapter 5

THE RESURRECTION
OF JESUS

Images of Death and Life in Judaism

Christians celebrate Jesus' return from death to life at Easter. Jesus' disciples announced that he had been raised up by God to heavenly glory and honor. We have seen that images of bodily resurrection and the exaltation of the righteous were among the new symbols of hope that God would restore life to a suffering people used by some Jews in the two centuries before the time of Jesus. Or as Wisdom 3:1–4 puts it: "The souls of the righteous are in the hand of God, and no torment will ever touch them. In the eyes of the foolish they seemed to have died....For though in the sight of others they were punished, their hope is full of immortality." But many Jews, like the Sadducees (Mark 12:18), held on to the common view of death in the Old Testament that it is the end of all relationships, whether with other humans or with God. Only God lives forever (Ps 90:1–6).

People like the Sadducees argued that the idea of God restoring the dead such as one finds in the martyr stories of 2 Maccabees—"One cannot but choose to die at the hands of mortals and to cherish the hope that God gives of being raised again" (2 Macc 7:14)—was absurd. Not only was that promise missing from the law of Moses, it led to bizarre consequences if God returned the dead to a bodily type of existence (Mark 12:18–27; Acts 23:6–9). Jesus is shown to be on the side of the Pharisees in this dispute. He points out that the Sadducees are too materialistic in asking "whose wife" a woman will be in the resurrection. They should think of resurrection as being a spiritual existence like that of the angels. St. Paul makes a similar point against an overly materialistic interpretation of resurrection in 1 Corinthians 15:35–55.

Martyrs and Suffering Righteous Ones

When we first begin to hear about resurrection some two hundred years before Jesus, we find that these images of hope respond to a serious religious crisis. Those people who were most faithful to God's commandments were being persecuted and martyred. Daniel 12:1–3 promises that those who have suffered will be delivered and those who have done evil punished, even if God has to bring them out of the grave to do so. It also has a special promise for those who have led the people in righteousness during these evil times. They will shine like stars.

The story of the mother and her seven sons who were martyred under Antiochus IV found in 2 Maccabees 7 also contains promises of resurrection. The second brother tells his torturer, "You accursed wretch, you dismiss us from this present life, but the King of the universe will raise us up to an everlasting renewal of life because we have died for his laws" (7:9). The fourth brother proclaims that while there is hope of being raised for those who die because they are faithful to God, there is no "resurrection to life" for the wicked (7:14). Second Maccabees does not expect Antiochus and his associates to be raised for judgment. They will experience God's judgment when God drives them out of the land (7:37). The author sees this punishment in a legend about the horrible death of the tyrant in anguish, his body rotting with worms. With his last breath, the king attempts to gain God's favor by renouncing his own divine pretensions, claiming he would build a sanctuary for God and even become a Jew. Naturally, such promises were too late to spare Antiochus an agonizing death (9:5–28).

Another promise of eternal life for the righteous who have suffered at the hands of the wicked occurs in Wisdom 2–5. Its author is familiar with Greek philosophical thought and so speaks of the "souls of the righteous" resting at peace with God (Wis 3:1–3). Wisdom 2 contains a dialogue among the evil people, who argue that there is nothing to stop them from oppressing the poor and doing anything else they can get away with: "Let our might be our law of right" (Wis 2:11). Since this life is all there is, they may as well enjoy it. However, the existence of righteous people angers them, so they claim that they will "test" the righteous person's claim to being a "child of God" by killing him. The wicked get their answer only when they die. Then they discover that they are condemned to vanish into oblivion, but that the righteous person lives in the presence of God, among the angels forever (Wis 5:1–16).

Resurrection, Vindication, and Judgment

You can see that the idea of resurrection is connected with a central point in the biblical tradition: human beings are to live by the order that God has established. If they do so, then they are blessed by God. If they rebel and try to create their own justice apart from God, then they will be condemned. Israel was to create a society in which God's justice and mercy were expressed. Exile and captivity were seen by the prophets as God's punishment. One of the martyred brothers in 2 Maccabees prays that God will accept their deaths as an atonement for the sins of the nation and lift the curse against the land (2 Macc 7:32–33). The author of 2 Maccabees wants the reader to understand that without the faithful sufferings of the martyrs, the military victories that the Jews won against Antiochus IV would never have happened. God did accept those sufferings as an atonement for the sins of the people.

This example reminds us that the resurrection of the martyrs, which is predicted in 2 Maccabees, was more than a personal reward for the individual. It was a statement that their deaths had not been "in vain." Though Antiochus IV killed them, the martyrs were proved right in the end. God's justice triumphed. Thus, resurrection is frequently associated with scenes of divine judgment. In this world, we often do not see that goodness and faithfulness to God are victorious. Sometimes the idea of resurrection included a cosmic scene in which all people would be gathered in front of God's throne and would be judged either by God or by a heavenly figure referred to as the "Son of Man." This figure appears in Daniel 7:13–14. He ascends to God's throne and is given an everlasting rule over all the nations of the earth. Early Christians anticipated that Jesus would judge the nations as Son of Man (Matt 25:31–33).

Here is a passage from a Jewish apocalyptic writing, *1 Enoch*. It describes God, the Lord of Spirits, judging the nations through the Son of Man. The powerful rulers of the earth, who have persecuted the righteous, "the holy and elect ones," are being judged:

> On the day of judgment, all the kings, the governors, the high officials, and the landlords shall see and recognize him—how he sits on his throne of glory, and righteousness is judged before him, and no nonsensical talk shall be uttered in his presence. Then pain shall come upon them as on a woman in travail with birth pangs—...and pain shall seize them when they see the Son of Man sitting on the throne of his glory....For the Son of Man was concealed from the beginning, and the Most High One preserved him in the presence of his power; then he revealed him to the holy and the elect ones. On that day, all the kings and governors, and high officials, and those who rule the earth shall fall down before him on their faces and worship and raise their hopes

in that Son of Man; they shall beg and plead for mercy at his feet....He will deliver them to the angels for punishments in order that vengeance shall be executed upon them—oppressors of his children and his elect ones....The righteous and elect ones shall be saved on that day; the Lord of the Spirits will abide over them; they shall eat and rest and rise with that Son of Man forever. They shall wear the garments of glory. These garments of yours shall become the garments of life from the Lord of Spirits. Neither shall your garments wear out, nor your glory come to an end before the Lord of Spirits. (*1 Enoch* 62)

In this passage, the righteous receive "eternal garments" and life in the presence of God forever as the reward for their righteousness and suffering. You can also see that while the wicked are condemned and punished, the primary focus of resurrection language is positive. It refers to the vindication of the righteous. They will live forever with God and experience the salvation for which they had been hoping.

The Resurrection of Jesus

In these Jewish traditions, we see people expressing their faith that God's power to save and God's concern with justice extends beyond this life. Those who condemned Jesus to death passed a negative judgment on his relationship to God (compare Wis 2:16–20). Jesus' own disciples were confused and afraid when Jesus was arrested and executed. They probably expected that God would vindicate Jesus at the judgment along with the other righteous people who had suffered persecution.

However, the story of Jesus' resurrection is not just a reaffirmation of this Jewish hope, as Martha says about her brother Lazarus: "I know that he will rise again in the resurrection on the last day" (John 11:24). The disciples did not simply remember that Jesus had believed in resurrection, get their courage back, and pick up preaching where Jesus had left off. Instead, their experiences persuaded them that God had already raised Jesus up from the dead. God had already enthroned Jesus in heaven like the Son of Man. Jesus is alive with God and will be the one to judge the world.

Our earliest evidence for Christian belief in Jesus' resurrection comes from the letters of St. Paul. Paul had been persecuting the early Christian movement when God revealed Jesus to him. This vision of the risen Lord changed Paul from being a bitter opponent of Christianity to being one of its most important missionaries (Gal 1:15–16). In 1 Corinthians 15:3–5, Paul repeats an early creed, which he said all Christians were taught:

> For I delivered to you as of first importance what I also received,
> that Christ died for our sins in accordance with the scriptures,
> that he was buried, that he was raised on the third day in accor-
> dance with the scriptures, and that he appeared to Cephas
> [Peter], then to the Twelve.

He goes on to mention others who had seen the risen Lord, concluding with
his own experience (vv. 6–8). Unlike the gospel writers, who belong to the
next generation of Christians, Paul is speaking about people who belonged to
Jesus' generation. The Twelve, including Peter and James, had all known
Jesus intimately. Neither they nor Paul left us any firsthand descriptions of
what their visions of the Lord were like. But they made it clear that they were
not claiming simply that Jesus had an immortal soul that was now resting
peacefully in heaven. They claimed that God had taken Jesus of Nazareth, a
man whom they knew, and done something that had not been done to any
other person. God had raised Jesus from the dead and exalted him to the
heavenly throne.

No one actually saw Jesus being raised. The gospels contain stories
about an Easter morning visit to Jesus' tomb. When it is found to be empty,
the women are confused and frightened. John 20:1–2, 11–15 describes Mary
Magdalene as thinking that someone had either stolen or moved Jesus' body.
In the earliest version of the tomb story (Mark 16:1–8a), an angel announces
that Jesus has been raised. Originally, Mark's gospel ended with the women
fleeing from the tomb. Later, additional material was put at the end of Mark
(Mark 16:9–20) to conclude the story with an appearance of the risen Lord
as in the other gospels.

As you can tell from the Jewish images of resurrection and judgment, resurrection was described as coming out of the tomb. The righteous would either
become like angels or have new "eternal, glorious garments" to put on. No one
thought that resurrection would simply mean the physical body coming back to
life. But the most obvious explanation for a body missing from a tomb was that
the tomb had been robbed or the body moved. At first, Jesus' disciples could
hardly imagine that Jesus had actually been raised. That took the revelations by
the angel and by Jesus himself before they could believe it. Only after they
were convinced that Jesus lived exalted in heaven could the disciples link Jesus'
resurrection with the fact that his body was missing from the tomb.

Summary

The earliest creed quoted by St. Paul focuses on two points, Jesus'
death and Jesus' resurrection. Jesus' death is proclaimed as the source of forgiveness for all people. It is not limited to atoning for the sins of the nation

of Israel at a specific time like the death of the Maccabean martyrs. Jesus' resurrection also goes beyond what people expected based on the martyr traditions or the stories of the suffering righteous in Wisdom. Jesus' resurrection is a present reality. Jesus is proclaimed as alive with God. Death has not cut Jesus off from his disciples. Instead, he remains present with them though in a new way.

Without the Easter message, Jesus might be remembered as a righteous person who healed people and taught about the kingdom of God. He might have been the founder of a small Jewish sect as John the Baptist or the Teacher of Righteousness had been. But the message of Jesus' resurrection claims much more than that. It claims that Jesus has been exalted and vindicated in a way that no human being ever has been. Jesus lives in a special relationship with God. Naturally, it is not possible to prove that what Christians believe about Jesus' resurrection is true by some sort of historical investigation. We can talk about Jesus' teaching in that way, and we can compare Jesus' teaching with that of other famous teachers. We can even talk about Jesus' death from a historical point of view. We can compare it with the deaths of other martyrs and servants of God in his own time and even in our time.

When we come to resurrection, however, we are speaking about the center of Christian faith. People today often find it difficult to imagine how resurrection could be true in our scientific and technological world of astronauts and space shuttles, cosmological distances and times. People in Jesus' day found it difficult to believe for other reasons. As we have seen, many Jews did not believe in resurrection at all because it was an innovation. It wasn't part of their oldest tradition. Even Pharisees who did believe in resurrection would find it difficult to believe that God had raised up someone of their own generation, especially since God had not yet judged the world. And those who heard that Jesus died on a cross would find it particularly difficult to believe that God had raised Jesus, since they would think that such a death implied God's curse, not salvation. First Corinthians 15 shows that Paul's Gentile converts in Corinth also have difficulty believing in resurrection. Paul has to insist that it is at the heart of the Christian faith. He also insists that what God has done in raising Jesus is the beginning of a resurrection that will encompass all Christians. Therefore, Paul tells them that if they do not believe in resurrection, their whole Christian faith is in vain.

STUDY QUESTIONS

Facts You Should Know

1. Give two arguments that a Jewish person who heard Jesus' disciples preaching that God had raised from the dead Jesus of Nazareth—a person crucified by Pontius Pilate—might give against the Christian claims.

2.   Based on the images and resurrection of the righteous that were circu-
      lating in Jesus' time, what would the claim that a person had been raised
      say about that person's relationship to God?
3.   What was the first reaction to the announcement that Jesus' tomb was
      empty?

Things to Do

1.   Read the stories of the finding of Jesus' tomb empty in Mark 16:1–8a,
      Matthew 27:26—28:15, and Luke 24:1–11. First, list the common fea-
      tures. Then list the differences between the versions. How do the vari-
      ants in Matthew and Luke seek to answer objections that outsiders may
      have made against Christian preaching of the resurrection?
2.   Read the stories of encounters between the risen Jesus and disciples in
      Matthew 28:16–20 and Luke 24:13–49. List all the examples of doubt
      and uncertainty in these stories. What do these examples tell the reader
      about the process by which the followers of Jesus came to believe in res-
      urrection?

Things to Think About

1.   What do you think of when you recite the words about resurrection in
      the creed? Which of the stories about Jesus' resurrection comes closest
      to expressing your feelings about resurrection?
2.   Imagine yourself in Jerusalem hearing Jesus' followers talking about
      Jesus' resurrection. How would you react? Would you raise objections?
      If so, which ones?

Chapter 6

THE BEGINNINGS
OF CHRISTOLOGY

Asking "Who Is This Jesus?"

Even Jesus' own disciples found it difficult to answer the question of "who" Jesus was. The gospels tell stories of disbelief among Jesus' relatives and fellow townspeople (e.g., Mark 3:21, 31–35; 6:1–6; John 7:2–8). Enemies looked at Jesus' miracles and presumed that he was a magician in league with Satan (Mark 3:22–27). They suggested that his association with tax collectors and sinners, people who turned against the commandments of God, made any claim to speak for God dubious (e.g., Matt 11:19; Luke 15:1–2). Comments about his origins were used to discredit him (e.g., Mark 6:3; John 6:42). In the end, one of Jesus' own disciples, Judas Iscariot, turned him over to authorities.

Historians have suggested a number of answers to the question of "who" Jesus was. Some emphasize the importance of his miracle working and exorcisms in drawing a crowd. Early Christian art represented Jesus with a wand like Moses, raising Lazarus from the dead (John 11:38–44), turning water into wine (John 2:1–11), or multiplying loaves and fishes (Mark 6:33–44). In other scenes of healing the sick, Jesus either lays his hands on the sufferer or makes a gesture indicating speech by pointing to the individual. This difference suggests that perhaps the artists of the third to fifth centuries distinguished between Jesus as healer and Jesus as endowed with magical powers represented by the wand.

Other historians study resistance movements that sprung up at the death of Herod the Great (4 BC) and again in the AD 60s. They suggest that Jesus appealed to the peasantry of Galilee with his message concerning God's kingdom as the reversal of all social hierarchies. Perhaps the Galileans saw Jesus as an anointed leader or "king" of Israel, chosen directly by God as David had been, not some local dynast supported by Rome like the Herodians.

A variant of this view emphasizes the impoverishment and the outcast status of many of Jesus' followers. Such had little hope of improving their lot or profiting from the new Roman order. Jesus proclaimed that these persons were the beloved children of God who would soon experience salvation. Still other scholars picture Jesus in the mold of earlier prophets. Jesus' word unmasked the injustice and evils of his day, warned of the judgment against those who did not repent, and promised salvation to the faithful.

All of these views can claim some support in the New Testament and in what we know of Palestine in Jesus' time. Jesus was an extraordinary healer. He did appeal to the crowds of ordinary people and come into conflict with the powerful. People did think he might be a prophet from God. In the Qur'an the infant Jesus speaks to defend his mother's honor: "I am the servant of God. He brought me the Book and made me a prophet and made me blessed....He did not make me wicked. Peace be upon me the day I was born, the day I die, and the day I am resurrected alive!" (Sura 19:33). So Muslims know Jesus as son of Mary, a pious, miracle-working prophet, who ascended to heaven upon his death. However, Jesus' disciples and Christians ever since ask the question "Who is Jesus?" in another way. They are convinced that, in Jesus, God's saving power has come to humanity in a unique way that could never be repeated or improved upon. The question "Who is this Jesus?" is tied to the question of Jesus' role as an agent of salvation.

Resurrection, Jesus, and God

Belief in Jesus' resurrection points out some answers to the question of who Jesus is. Not only does resurrection imply that Jesus' mission was from God as in the Qur'an account, in the Christian gospels it also places a special stamp on Jesus' life. Jesus is more than the righteous martyr or persecuted prophet, since God has exalted Jesus to the heavenly throne. As Lord, Jesus has a special place in God's rule over the world (Phil 2:6–11). One might say that Jesus' mission did not end with death. It took on a new dimension with his exaltation to heavenly rule.

Motifs of vindication and judgment were closely linked to resurrection symbols in Judaism. Not surprisingly, Christians understood Jesus as the one who would come in the future to exercise God's judgment (1 Thess 1:9–10).

You can see another example of the exalted Jesus as the focus of Christian hope in Mark 13:11 and Luke 21:15. When Luke recasts the Marcan promise of divine help for Christians who must testify about their belief, he speaks of Jesus rather than the Holy Spirit. This shift does not reflect any neglect of the Spirit's role on Luke's part, since the Spirit plays a critical role in guiding the young community in Acts. It does show that the

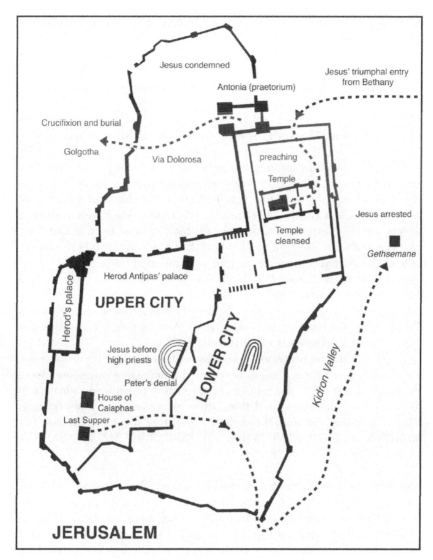

Plan of Jerusalem at the time of Jesus

exalted Jesus was felt to exercise divine functions in guiding and protecting the community (also see Matt 28:20).

The exaltation of the risen Jesus led Christians to give him divine functions. This development may have been eased by the fact that some Jewish groups pictured angelic beings acting with divine power and authority. The mysterious "one like a Son of Man," that is, "an angelic figure in human likeness," ascends to the divine throne in Daniel 7:14–15. Daniel 12:1 speaks of

Michael, the angelic prince of the people, coming at the time of judgment to deliver the righteous. The exalted Jesus could be seen to play the role of such heavenly figures. Hebrews 1:4–14 contains an argument based on a number of Old Testament quotations that shows that Jesus, the exalted Son, is higher than any angel. Thus a special relationship exists between Jesus and God.

Jesus as Messiah, Son of God, Son of Man, Lord

Another way of capturing the significance of "who Jesus is" is to use titles that point to various aspects of Jesus' role in salvation. There are a number of these expressions in the New Testament, but the most frequent are "messiah," "Son of God," "Son of Man," and "Lord." When New Testament writers use these expressions, they already have in mind the fact that Jesus has been exalted to the right hand of God. Hebrews 1:4 says that the superiority of the exalted Jesus to the angels is grounded in the superiority of his name to theirs. The "name" that the author has in mind is "Son." God has not called any of the angels "Son" (Heb 1:5). Romans 1:3–4 is an old confessional formula in which the earthly Jesus is described as a descendant (= son) of David, while the risen Jesus is designated "Son of God." The expression "Lord" is also used to speak of Jesus (Rom 1:4, 7).

We will not be concerned with how each of the four expressions was used by different writers. For our purposes, it is enough to have some idea of what they meant within the context of first-century Judaism and what it tells us when Jesus' followers used these titles to explain who Jesus is. Early Christians summed up what they believed to be true about Jesus in short formulas such as we find in Paul's letters (e.g., Rom 1:3–4; 1 Thess 1:9–10; 1 Cor 15:3–5).

Messiah. The word *messiah* is derived from the Hebrew *masiah*, "anointed one." It is translated into Greek as *christos* and so becomes the basis of the "Christ," which we often think of as part of Jesus' name. Anointing of a king or a prophet indicated that that person had been chosen by God to protect or rule the people. Some Jewish writings in Jesus' time look for anointed figures, a king, a priest, or a prophet, to come as a leader of the people in the last days. Such expectations might be attached to the Davidic kingship (2 Sam 6:21). David is also described as "anointed" of God in 2 Samuel 23:1–17 and in Psalms 18:51; 89:39, 52; 123:10, 17. In Jesus' time, the kings were not descended from David. The prophet Jeremiah had predicted the end of the pre-exilic Davidic line and the coming of an ideal king, a new David (Jer 33:15; Ezek 37:23–24). He does not speak of that king as "anointed," but we do find such expectations for an anointed king in Daniel 9:25 and *Psalms of Solomon* 17.23, 36. Writings found at Qumran speak of several anointed figures coming in the last days. Luke 3:15 describes the people as wondering whether John the Baptist was such an "anointed" person.

You can see from these examples that the expression *messiah* does not convey much information about a person. It merely indicates those who had a special role from God. The expectation of "anointed" figures in the last days did not specify whether such persons would be political leaders like the Davidic king, prophetic leaders like the Baptist, or anointed priests like someone from the expected renewed high priesthood that we have seen existed in this period.

Because *messiah* could be applied to different types of leaders, people might have easily referred to Jesus as "anointed" during his lifetime. He did preach that the rule of God was being realized in his own ministry. And if he had a role in bringing people to the rule of God, then one can easily see that Jesus would become the focus of such expectations. In addition, the crucifixion of Jesus as "king of the Jews" suggests that such speculation led to the charge that he was a political danger to the state. Mark 8:30–31 portrays Jesus himself as critical of the "messianic" expectations attached to him because they do not embody the element of suffering that is central to his mission. Indeed, none of the "anointed" figures mentioned in first-century Jewish texts were expected to die. The coming of the "anointed" was to bring an end to the evil and corrupt rulers who caused righteous persons to suffer. The "anointed" was to gather the righteous of Israel and to bring about the "new covenant" with God, the people as God had intended it to be.

You can see that crucifying Jesus as one who claimed to be "anointed king" was a way in which his enemies could deny any claims that Jesus was God's agent for the last days. Without the resurrection, that strategy would have succeeded. Jesus' followers might have been able to continue following some of his teachings, they might have continued their fellowship with one another and outsiders, they might have spoken of Jesus as a righteous martyr, and they might even have hoped for a future manifestation of God's rule. But they could never have claimed that the crucified Jesus was God's "anointed one," sent to lead the people in the last days. With Jesus' resurrection, they not only spoke of Jesus whose life ended in crucifixion as "messiah," but they also expected that Jesus would play a role in the salvation of the "last days" when he appeared as judge (cf. Acts 3:20–21). Luke 24:26, 46 shows that Christians still felt compelled to explain how the "messiah" came to suffer. These verses suggest that they had to reread the scriptures to show that, contrary to what people had thought, suffering had been part of the destiny of the messiah in God's plan.

Son of Man. The expression "Son of Man" is one of the most puzzling expressions in the gospels. We have seen that in Daniel 7:14–15 a mythic story of "one like a Son of Man" pictures the heavenly defender of righteous Israel ascending to God's throne. In a section of *1 Enoch* that may postdate the earliest use of "Son of Man" for Jesus, we see God seating the "Son of Man" on the throne at the time of judgment. Sinners are condemned and the righteous are exalted into heavenly glory. Some of the images of Jesus as "Son of Man" in the gospels clearly allude to the scenario of heavenly judgment (e.g., Mark 8:38; Matt 19:28; 25:31–32). To speak of Jesus as "Son of Man" in such a context is to attribute to him the role of God's heavenly agent in judgment.

Unlike the expression "anointed," "Son of Man" does not appear to have been common in either Judaism or early Christianity. Daniel 7 does not speak of the angelic figure as the Son of Man but as one *like* a "Son of Man." In other words, the visionary claims to have seen a heavenly being that had human form, ascending to God's throne. The passages in *1 Enoch* are metaphoric expansions on the Daniel image. They do not suppose that the reader already expects a "Son of Man" to be the agent of divine judgment. The mysterious figure of judgment is referred to in a number of other ways in this section of *1 Enoch*, such as "righteous and elect one" (*1 Enoch* 49.2–4) and "Lord's anointed" (48.10). *First Enoch* 71.14 identifies this figure with Enoch himself. However, this section of *1 Enoch* was apparently composed in the second half of the first century, too late to be evidence that "Son of Man" was being used among Jews generally as a designation for the expected messianic leader of the people. Some scholars even think that the concluding identification of the Son of Man with Enoch was a direct response to Christian claims about Jesus.

We also find that the expression "Son of Man" is almost entirely limited to the gospels, where it is placed on the lips of Jesus. The only exceptions are in passages that draw upon the imagery of Daniel to describe the exalted Jesus (Acts 7:56; Rev 1:13; 14:14). In some of the sayings of Jesus, there seems to be a distinction between Jesus and the "Son of Man" as a heavenly judge who will vindicate Jesus' own mission (e.g., Mark 8:38; 13:26; 14:62). Matthew 16:28 identifies the "kingdom of God" (from Mark 9:1) as the kingdom of the Son of Man, who comes "with his angels in the glory of his Father" (16:27). This description apparently presumes that the reader will make the necessary identification of Jesus with the coming Son of Man.

Although it is possible to trace the images of a heavenly "Son of Man" back to the interpretation of Daniel 7, we have not discovered any evidence that the expression referred to an individual, whether heavenly or human, in a way that would make it an intelligible identification for people to have used to describe Jesus. Scholars have turned to the Aramaic that Jesus spoke to see what else the expression might have meant. In the Aramaic of the first century, *bar 'enas* can be used either as a generic, "a human being, a mortal," or as an indefinite expression, "someone." Some of the sayings of Jesus appear to have used this generic expression (e.g., Mark 2:10). We also find the expression used in passion predictions, where it may have been put on the lips of Jesus by the evangelist (Luke 9:22; contrast Matt 16:21, "he"). Luke 17:24–25 contrasts the heavenly drama of the coming of the "Son of Man" in judgment with the suffering that he must endure.

As you can see from the imagery surrounding the expression "Son of Man," the combination of "Son of Man" with suffering (Mark 8:31; Luke 9:22) is every bit as strange as speaking of a "suffering messiah." Some scholars have tried to link use of the expression "Son of Man" in connection with vindication for the suffering righteous of Daniel 7:19 to Jesus' own interpretation of the Suffering Servant theme found in passages such as Isaiah 42:1; 43:10; 49:6; 52:13; 53:11. They suggest that Jesus used the Daniel metaphor. The combination of these motifs is evident in the sayings about the suffering Son of Man, but it is difficult to show that that interpretation was already part of Jesus' teaching. It may have been part of the process of reinterpreting the scriptures to explain the "messianic suffering" of Jesus after the resurrection. Other scholars, admitting that we do not have enough evidence to fill in the links that would account for Christian use of this expression, suggest that we view the interpretations of Jesus as "Son of Man" as developments that were attached to Jesus' use of the generic expression *bar 'enas* in his sayings.

Son of God. Mindful of the monotheistic context of Judaism, we are not surprised to find that the expression "Son of God" is not necessarily a direct affirmation of Jesus' divinity. Within Judaism the expression "son(s) of God" might mean angels (e.g., Gen 6:2; Job 1:6; Ps 29:1; Dan 3:25). It might mean Israel as "God's son" (Exod 4:22; Deut 14:1; Hos 11:1; Wis 18:13). It might be a title of adoption for the king (Ps 2:7; 2 Sam 7:14). Or it can even be used for the righteous individual (Sir 4:10; Wis 2:18).

However, we do not find the expression in Palestinian Judaism for a "messianic" king, that is, for a person whom God will send to lead the people in the last days. The expression does appear in some Qumran texts for a Davidic king (e.g., 4QFlor 1–2.1.10), but the text does not speak of that king as "anointed" and could refer to any Jewish king. But we do know from the formulas that Paul quotes in 1 Thessalonians 1:10 and Romans 1:3–4 that the expression "Son of God" had been used to express belief in Jesus' exaltation with God from a very early period. The imagery of Psalm 2:7 played a role in the conviction that God had designated Jesus "Son" as we can see from Hebrews 1:5. The gospel narratives picture God naming Jesus "Son" at the baptism (e.g., Mark 1:11) and the transfiguration (e.g., Mark 9:7).

The expression "Son of God" played an important role in early Christianity. It could describe Jesus' special obedience to God's will by using "Son of God" in the sense of the righteous one who suffers. It could express Jesus' exaltation in heaven by using "Son of God" in the sense of the king "adopted" by God to rule over the people. It could express the special character of Jesus' relationship with God by using "Son of God" to express the idea of being chosen as it had been used for the special relationship between God and Israel. And because "son(s) of God" could also refer to the chosen people, the expression was used for Christians too. Jesus is "God's own Son," but through baptism, every Christian is adopted as a "son of God" (e.g., Rom 8:14–17).

Lord. One of the most common titles for Jesus in the New Testament is "Lord." Where "son of God" could express the new relationship of the Christian to God, "Lord" could be used to express the relationship between the Christian and the exalted Jesus. Christians are all "servants" of the one Lord. The ethical consequences of this expression were very important in the Christian communities. Not only was the Christian obedient to the "Lord," the Christian was also told that being servants of the one Lord meant that no one could claim to be superior to others. Paul describes Christians as those who call on the name of "our Lord Jesus Christ" in every place (1 Cor 1:2). Although men and women are different, "in the Lord" they are dependent upon each other (1 Cor 11:11–12). People in the church have to use different talents in serving the Lord (1 Cor 12:4–11). Christian masters are told to be just in their treatment of slaves, since they know that they have a "Lord" and master in heaven (Eph 6:9).

Of course, the expression "the Lord" does not always refer to human beings who have power over others. If it did, it would hardly have come to be such an important title for Jesus. In the Old Testament, "the Lord" is used to refer to God. The New Testament continues to use "the Lord" to mean God as well as to refer to Jesus. There are some passages in which we cannot tell which is meant. A very early hymn, which Paul quotes in Philippians 2:6–11, speaks of the exalted Christ receiving the name "Lord." Since all the powers of heaven and earth are subject to Christ as Lord, it clearly means that Christ has divine authority. We can trace the use of "Lord" as a title back to the earliest Aramaic-speaking Christians. One of their prayers or confessions of faith was *marana tha*, meaning "Our Lord, come!" Paul preserves this prayer in 1 Corinthians 16:22.

Gentile Christians were also familiar with the use of the Greek word for "Lord," *kyrios*, as a title used to address a god or goddess. Paul reflects this practice when he refers to the "so-called gods and lords" in 1 Corinthians 8:5. He contrasts this view with the confession that there is one God, the Father and source of all things, and one Lord, Jesus Christ (v. 6). In both Jewish and Gentile environments, then, calling Jesus "Lord" indicated divine status. You can see that the passage in 1 Corinthians 8:6 preserves the monotheistic character of Judaism by making clear that the Jesus whom Christians confess as "Lord" is an agent of God, not a separate divinity like the many "gods and lords" that the Corinthians had worshiped before they became Christians. The language of "Father" and "Son" was also used to preserve the distinction between Jesus and God. It would take several more centuries for Christians to find a way of expressing the divinity of Jesus in a way that preserved belief in one God. Greek philosophical terms would be used for the task, but the New Testament language of Father, Son, and Spirit maintains the links between the earliest Christian beliefs and the doctrines of the incarnation and the Trinity in these later formulations.

Jesus in Worship: Acclamation and Hymn

We are familiar with the titles for Jesus from the gospels and the letters of Paul. But before the gospels or the letters were written, Christians were using these titles to express their faith. Paul's letters make it very clear that Christian worship was the place where such expressions were used. Remember the expression *marana tha*, "Our Lord, come!" You can see that that is an exclamation or a prayer for the coming of the Lord. Paul mentions it in 1 Corinthians 16:22. When we look at Paul's description of the Lord's Supper, or Eucharist, in 1 Corinthians 11, we find Paul telling the Corinthians that the Supper is a memorial of Christ's death until he comes (1 Cor 11:26). Therefore, many scholars think that the prayer for the return of the Lord was also part of that service along with the "holy kiss" between members of the church that is mentioned in 1 Corinthians 16:20.

First Corinthians 12:3, which is also trying to explain how worship of Christ is different from the idol worship that the Corinthians had known, refers to saying "Christ is Lord" in the Spirit. An acclamation that Christ is Lord may have occurred in other contexts of worship. The Spirit also inspires the newly baptized Christians to call on God as Abba, Father. When they do so, they are expressing their new status as adopted children of God (e.g., Rom 8:15–16; Gal 4:6). Of course, they are also recognizing that Jesus, the Son of God, made that new reality possible. Many of the short formulas that Paul uses in his letters (e.g., 1 Cor 8:6; Rom 1:3–4; 1 Thess 1:9–10) were probably also familiar to his readers from their use in worship.

Early Christian Hymns

We also find in the New Testament longer passages that we designate as "hymns," though we do not know whether they were sung or recited. Their language and form set them apart from the surrounding material even though the New Testament authors are using these hymns to illustrate points about Jesus. They have not copied them simply to provide information about hymns that should be used. In these hymns, we see early Christians finding new ways of expressing the uniqueness of Jesus.

Our earliest example of such a hymn, Philippians 2:6–11, stresses Jesus' willingness to abandon divine status in order to be obedient to God. If you

remember the story of Adam in Genesis, you can see that this hymn makes
Christ the opposite of Adam. He doesn't try to "be like God," which Adam
and Eve thought they could do by eating of the tree of "knowledge of good
and evil." Christ is not disobedient at all. Instead, Christ is even willing to
give up "being like God" and suffer the humiliating death on the cross:

[Christ Jesus], who, though he was in the form of God, did not
think being equal to God something to be grasped but emptied
himself,

taking the form of a slave,
born in human likeness.
And being found in human likeness,
he humbled himself,
becoming obedient to death,
[even death on a cross].
Therefore God has highly exalted him,
and given him the name above every other name, that at the
    name
of Jesus every knee should bend,
[in heaven and on earth and under the earth],
and every tongue confess that Jesus Christ is Lord,
to the glory of God, the Father.

Unlike Adam and Adam's descendants, Jesus is the one "without sin" (2 Cor
5:21). There is no reason for him to suffer the death he does, which is the
penalty for human sin. But, the hymn asserts, because Jesus showed such
obedience, he is entitled to exaltation. He can be worshiped as "Lord."

The short formula in 1 Corinthians 8:6 hinted that the Lord Jesus was
somehow identified with the power through which God brought all things
into being. Other New Testament hymns use this idea that Jesus embodies
God's wisdom or word, the power by which God created all things, to fill out
the hint that Jesus had surrendered "being like God" in order to save humanity through his obedient death. The pattern of these hymns often shifts from
the humiliation/exaltation of Jesus, to speaking of Jesus as an "image," "radi-
ance," or "likeness" of God (words used to describe God's creative wisdom or
word in some Jewish philosophers of the first century). Hebrews 1:2b–4 has
all the elements of this type of hymn: (a) the Son is God's creative wisdom,
which is of divine nature and which upholds the world; (b) the Son died for
the sins of humanity; (c) the Son is exalted at the right hand of God above all
the angels, with a "greater name" than any other powers in the universe.

The hymns in Colossians 1:15–20 and in John 1:1, 3–4, (5?), 9(?), 10–
12, 14a, c, 16 omit the exaltation. They focus on the identification of Christ

with God's eternal wisdom and on the redemption that Christ has brought to humanity. Redemption involves descent into the world in John's hymn. However, that coming is already prepared by the fact that God's word/wisdom is active in the world as its light and life. Redemption is pictured as revelation, accepting the "light" visible in the incarnate Son. Colossians 1:15–20 focuses almost entirely on the heavenly reality of Christ. Verses 15 to 17 describe the "first-born" of God as the agent of creation. Verses 18 to 20 speak of the reconciliation of all things to God in Christ's body, the church. Only the final verse mentions Christ's death on the cross as the means by which reconciliation takes place.

While the various titles used of Jesus have been shaped by the conviction that Jesus is exalted at God's right hand, the acclamations and hymns make it even clearer that the early Christians found Jesus to be more than just a holy person or righteous teacher or great healer or martyr. Jesus is not just "with God" as a reward for his righteous suffering like the martyrs or the suffering righteous person of Wisdom 2. Instead, Jesus embodies God's own power in creating and maintaining the world, and in ruling over the world as "Lord" and as Savior and Judge of humanity. The community's experiences of the Spirit drawing persons into a new relationship with God that was expressed in their calling upon God as *Abba* or hailing Jesus as Lord played an important role in shaping these beliefs.

Jesus and God

Though the risen Jesus is imagined as an exalted, heavenly figure and worshiped as a manifestation of God, the early Christians would have insisted that Jesus was not "God" in the sense in which the Father is God. They knew that Jesus was also a human being who really experienced suffering and death. Neither God in the Jewish tradition nor the gods of the pagan cults could be said to "die." Archaic myths sometimes spoke of a god or goddess being held captive by death and later liberated, often only for a time. Such myths explained the apparent death of nature in winter and its return to life in the spring. But these myths were not part of the early understanding of Jesus' death and resurrection/exaltation. (Later Christians sometimes appealed to the ancient myths to prove that God had also prepared the pagans to receive the truth of Christianity.) Some of the hymns and formulas antedate the letters of Paul. They must have been used among persons who were also contemporaries of Jesus. Paul himself had met Peter, James, and probably others who had known Jesus during his lifetime. He knew that the Jesus whom Christians worship as "Lord" was a real human person just as surely as he knew that God is the invisible, eternal Creator of everything that exists (cf. Rom 1:20).

If you read the New Testament carefully, you will notice that Jesus is rarely spoken of as "God." The most direct example, John 20:28, occurs as an acclamation or gesture of worship. The Fourth Gospel is acutely aware of charges made against Christians for blasphemy because they made Jesus, a human being, God (e.g., John 5:18). The author uses the imagery of Father/Son to explain that Jesus is not a rival god but the faithful emissary of the Father. What Jesus does is what God does. Jesus' powers to judge and give life have been given him by the Father (John 5:19–30). The Philippians' hymn makes a similar point by emphasizing the contrast between Jesus' obedience and Adam's disobedience. Jesus did not consider "being divine" something to be "grabbed," "held on to," or "exploited for his own advantage" (the Greek word *harpagmos* in Philippians 2:6 can carry all of these connotations).

Christology as a special topic in Christian theology emerges when Christians began to work out explanations for who Jesus is and what Jesus' relationship to God is in a systematic fashion. The New Testament authors do not engage in such explanations. They present us with their emerging convictions about Jesus in a number of different images and literary forms. Often, as we have seen, these images have their roots in different Jewish traditions. Some are based on beliefs about God's agents of salvation, both human and angelic. Others, like the identification of Jesus with God's word/wisdom active in creation, come from more philosophical reflection on how God can be said to be active in the world when God is so far above that world and so different from anything in it. Many of these Jewish traditions had to be given a new meaning when applied to Jesus. It was not easy to see how the "messiah" could be identified with a crucified person. Nor was it easy to see how a human being who had recently lived and died could be said to be God's creative wisdom. Often the various images occur in different places in the New Testament traditions. They are not put together in a single account of who Jesus is.

Stories and the Identity of Jesus

Some time ago, one of my students was interviewing me for the school paper. She said that the editors of the paper had told her that they wanted "stories," idiosyncrasies, and other such things as part of the articles on different faculty members. I referred her to some former students. The editors of the paper recognized something important about how we identify people. We don't always look for titles, lists of accomplishments, social position, family, and so on. Often we are most interested in people when someone else tells us a story about them.

You already know that much of our material about Jesus is preserved in stories and sayings that people repeated to one another. Miracle stories identify Jesus as a sort of "divine man." He is able to heal and exercise exceptional powers over demons and the forces of nature. Many of the stories carry an additional message about Jesus' healing. A person is said to be healed because of his or her faith in Jesus. Or a miracle is presented as a sign of forgiveness of sins. Jesus' treatment of the demons shows their power over human life, but Jesus is greater than they are.

Jesus' sayings and parables not only show us Jesus as a teacher, they also ask us to compare Jesus with other teachers. The sayings, which are often part of a verbal debate, contrast Jesus' answers with the false views or even inability to answer of his opponents. Sometimes Jesus' teaching invites comparison with similar themes in the Old Testament. Jesus may affirm what is in the Old Testament, he may present it in an intensified form, or he may consider it insufficient or subordinate to some other expression of the will of God. The evangelists frequently remind their readers that Jesus' teaching was different from that of others. Mark 1:27 mentions Jesus' teaching in the context of an exorcism. The reader is to see the same power in Jesus' words as in his deeds. Matthew 7:28–29 concludes the Sermon on the Mount with the observation that Jesus' teaching caused amazement because it had an authority different from that of the scribes. Luke 4:22 has the people praise Jesus' teaching and wonder at the "gracious words which came from his mouth." Since the scripture about which Jesus taught begins with the prophet saying the Spirit of God rests upon him (v. 18), Luke's reader is to understand that Jesus has spoken in the power of the Spirit.

These brief examples show how stories carry important messages about who Jesus is that are not easily represented in titles, creeds, or hymns. We have concentrated on the shorter stories that people repeated to one another. However, each of the evangelists has also told the story about Jesus from a unique perspective. Study of how each gospel is structured and which themes about Jesus it develops helps us to present the picture of Jesus that is given in each of the gospels. Just as you may find that two people disagree about the way in which a particular character is presented in a book or a movie, so scholars have different views of what the Christology of each of the gospel writers is.

Often a gospel presents us with a number of puzzles that we have to fit together. Mark, for example, begins with an emphasis on Jesus' powerful miracles but also has Jesus tell both demons and humans that they are to be silent. The second half of Mark emphasizes the necessity for the Son of Man to suffer. The disciples in Mark become almost as hostile to this teaching as Jesus' enemies in the gospel are to other parts of his teaching. At the end of the gospel, the women run away from the tomb frightened and don't tell anyone. No one doubts that an important part of Mark's Christology is that Jesus is the "suffering Son of Man." But how are the powerful miracles to be fitted in? Some scholars have argued that Mark wanted to oppose the image of Jesus that would come from emphasis on the miracles, that of a "divine man," because it did not make room for the necessity of suffering. Others see the miracles as reassurance to a suffering community. Even though Jesus had to suffer and even though Christians have to follow Jesus in suffering, Jesus does have the power to save us.

We have a hint that that is how Matthew understood the story of Jesus calming the sea. Matthew 14:22–27 is based on the story in Mark 6:45–52. But Mark's story ends with the disciples not understanding anything about Jesus. The miracle did not increase their faith. Matthew substitutes a story about Peter walking on water for the Marcan ending (Matt 14:28–32). When Peter's faith in Jesus wavers, he begins to sink. Jesus rescues Peter and reprimands him for his "little faith." Then when Jesus enters the boat the disciples worship him as "Son of God." Matthew's version of the story is clearly aimed at teaching Christians that they must have faith in Jesus to save them from whatever trials they suffer. They should not be persons of "little faith," since the Jesus they worship is really "Son of God."

You can see that Matthew has used one of the titles for Jesus in a gesture of worship. This gesture also links the miracle story to the confession that Jesus is "Son of God." Matthew has shifted the ending of the story that he found in Mark in order to make it clear that these beliefs in Jesus should also have a message for the church of his day. They will be saved if they continue to trust in Jesus.

Summary

We have explored a number of ways in which the early Christians began to express their belief that Jesus has a special relationship with God that no other human being can have. In theological terms, the word *Christology* is used to refer to an explanation of who Jesus is in relationship to God. The New Testament does not use the abstract categories of the theologians. It uses the titles and images of its Jewish background. It also tells stories about Jesus that identify who he is. Jesus is not confused with God the Father. But Jesus is "next to God." Not even the angels are as close to God.

The New Testament insists that Jesus shares the powers of God in a special way. But the whole point of Jesus' divine power is to make salvation possible. Jesus can forgive sin, can give life, and can act as judge. Therefore those who believe in Jesus are to be confident that they will be saved. In many different ways, the New Testament tells its readers that Jesus is much more than a good, loving, and wise human being. Jesus is God coming to save humanity.

STUDY QUESTIONS

Facts You Should Know

1. How does the New Testament distinguish the sense in which Jesus is spoken of as divine from the "one God" of its monotheistic creed?
2. Explain the meaning of the four titles "messiah," "Son of Man," "Son of God," and "Lord" within the context of first-century Judaism.
3. How is belief in Jesus' resurrection as exaltation tied to the use of the titles "Son of Man" and "Lord"?
4. Give examples of how the title "Lord" was used in early Christian worship.
5. How did early Christian hymns associate Jesus with divine powers?

Things to Do

1. Look up the short formulas that express Christian belief in some of Paul's letters (e.g., Rom 1:3–4; 1 Thess 1:9–10; 1 Cor 15:3–5). List the beliefs about Jesus and God that are found in those formulas.
2. Look up the "hymns" about Jesus in Philippians 2:6–11; Hebrews 1:1–4; Colossians 1:15–20; and John 1:1, 3–5, 9–12, 14ac, 16. How does each hymn express the "before" of Jesus' existence, the turning point of obedient death, and the final exaltation of Jesus?
3. Use a concordance to find examples of the three uses of "Son of Man" in Mark: (a) heavenly figure, coming judge; (b) suffering Son of Man; (c) "son of man" as an indefinite expression for any human being.

Things to Think About

1. Try writing your own "Christological hymn." What are the crucial elements in the "before," obedience, and exaltation of Jesus for you?
2. If you had to make up short prayers or formulas for Christian worship, what titles or phrases would you use to express the reality of who Jesus is? (Do not limit yourself to those found in the New Testament.)

Chapter 7

THE WORLD OF PAUL

Christianity in an Urban Environment

Jesus and his disciples came from the rural world of villages, farmers, fishermen, and the like. But the spread of Christianity occurred in the cities. Paul himself had been brought up in one such city, Tarsus. It was a prosperous commercial city on the southeastern coast of Asia Minor. It was also the Roman capital of its region, Cilicia. Major roads led to Asia Minor and to Syria in the East. Its university rivaled schools in Athens and Alexandria. The Jewish community of this city would have spoken Greek rather than Hebrew or Aramaic. They would have read a Greek translation of the Jewish scriptures. Elements of popular Greek philosophy, especially concepts from Stoic thought, and some familiar techniques of Greek rhetoric found in Paul's letters suggest that he had assimilated some of the prevailing culture of Tarsus.

Thessalonica. Some of the cities in which Paul established churches were important Roman centers. One of his earliest letters is to Thessalonica, a city in Macedonia. It had been founded in 316 BC by one of Alexander the Great's generals. Like Tarsus, it was the Roman capital of the province. Cicero spent part of his exile there in 58 BC and the city had supported Octavian (Augustus) and Anthony in their war against Brutus, which had ended with the battle of Philippi in 42 BC. It was a prosperous city since it lay on a major Roman road, the Via Egnatia. Archaeologists have found a number of remains that attest to the religious life of the ancient city. Not only was there a Jewish community, there was also a synagogue of Samaritans. In addition to the favorite Greek gods Zeus, Dionysus, and Demeter, people worshiped the Egyptian gods Serapis and Isis, and some gods of Phrygian origin, the Cabiri, who were very popular with sailors as well as with farmers. They were confused with the twins Castor and Pollux and a huge carving of them guarded the western gate of the city. The city also maintained civic cults in honor of its

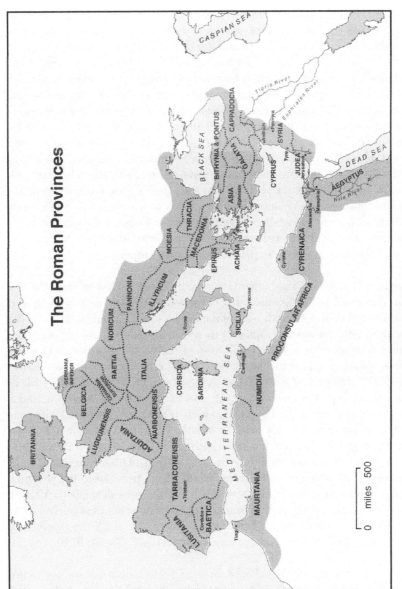

The Roman provinces in AD 70

Roman benefactors. Divine honors were paid to the goddess Roma, to emperors like Julius Caesar and Augustus, and to other benefactors.

Philippi. Philippi lies in northeastern Greece and is another major stopping place on the Via Egnatia. It was the most thoroughly Roman of all the cities in which Paul established churches. After defeating Brutus on the plains west of the city in 42 BC, Anthony settled many of the veterans of his army here and established it as a Roman colony. Augustus sent more colonists after he defeated Anthony and Cleopatra in 31 BC, refounding the city as Colonia Iulia Augusta Philippensis. These Roman settlers along with a few of the original inhabitants were the "citizens" of the city. The city was governed by "Italian law," rather than local codes. However, the religious life of the city was much more diversified than its Roman origins might suggest. In addition to the Greek and Roman deities, there were sanctuaries to the Thracian goddess Bendis, to Phrygian Cybele, and to gods from Egypt. Excavations in the ancient forum area have uncovered temples as well as rock reliefs of various divinities. Since no synagogue remains have been found, some scholars think that there may not have been a large Jewish presence in the city. Not surprisingly, cultic honors were also paid to the Roman emperor.

Corinth. Corinth was the "newest" city among those in Greece, since the city that flourished in the classical Greek period had been destroyed by the Romans in 147 BC. Corinth was refounded by Julius Caesar in 44 BC. Like the other cities, it was the capital of its province. The city was populated by Italian freedmen, though by Paul's time in the mid-first century AD many Greek-speaking settlers had also arrived in the city. Excavations have uncovered an inscription that refers to the "synagogue of the Hebrews," the numerous pagan temples, a sanctuary devoted to the healing god Asclepius, and a temple area honoring the Egyptian goddess Isis. At least some of Paul's converts were not entirely ready to break with the vibrant religious life of the city, participating in banquets to honor the gods (cf. 1 Cor 8:10; 10:14–22) and purchasing meat from sacrificed animals (1 Cor 10:25). Other excavations have uncovered the platform in the forum where Paul's trial before the governor Gallio could have taken place (Acts 18:12, 17), the rows of small, dark shops like the leatherworking shop of Aquila and Prisca in which Paul worked (Acts 18:1–3; 1 Cor 9:3–6, 12), and the type of houses in which the community would have gathered for its meetings (1 Cor 11:17–22, 33–34; 16:19).

Ephesus. This city, which had been founded by Ionian Greeks, was one of the largest in the Roman world. Its famed temple of the goddess Artemis forms the backdrop for a dramatic tale of the riot caused by Christianity's introduction into that city (Acts 19:1–40). It was the capital of the Roman province of Asia and a major crossroad between Asia Minor and the rest of the Roman world. A road system extending into Persia began in the city. Ephesus appears to have served as a base for the Pauline missionary efforts in Asia Minor (Acts 19:10). Paul may even have suffered imprisonment there (1 Cor 15:32).

Ephesus was known throughout the Roman world. A popular romance novel, *An Ephesian Tale,* from the second century AD opens with a handsome young man despising all other beauty, even the god Eros. At a festival in honor of Artemis, he meets his match in a beautiful young woman and their adventures are the subject of a long narrative. Shakespeare used Ephesus as a setting in *The Comedy of Errors.*

Antioch. A number of other cities are also mentioned in the Pauline mission. Paul began his activities as part of a missionary team sent by the church at Antioch (Acts 11:25–26; 13:1–3) on the Orontes river, which was the capital of the Roman province of Syria (now in Turkey). Founded in 300 BC, Antioch had been the capital of the Seleucid kingdom. After Rome and Alexandria, this city at the juncture of Asia Minor and Syria was the third most important in the Roman Empire. Among the many elegant Roman-period buildings, the city had one of the earliest amphitheaters in the Roman world. Herod the Great paid for the paving of a two-mile colonnaded street. Its "Olympic games" became famous throughout the Roman world. Christianity had come to the Jewish community of that city when the Hellenists associated with St. Stephen were driven from Jerusalem circa AD 40 (Acts 11:19–20). There Jesus' followers were first called "Christians" (Acts 11:26). That church began to accept Gentiles into its fellowship without requiring that they become Jews first. This decision caused such controversy that a meeting in Jerusalem was convened to settle the question (Acts 15:1–19; Gal 2:1–10). It was agreed that Gentile Christians did not have to adopt the customs of Judaism, nor did they have to submit to circumcision. Many scholars think Matthew's gospel was written in Antioch. We hear more of Antioch in the beginning of the second century. Its bishop Ignatius (died ca. AD 117) wrote a series of letters to churches in Asia Minor as he traveled to his martyrdom in Rome.

Rome. Rome had all the features of the other cities magnified. It was a flourishing melting pot of commerce and trade. Slaves and merchants from the East brought their gods and goddesses with them to the capital. Rome also had a large Jewish community, partly descendants of prisoners brought back from Roman campaigns in the East during the second century BC. Sometime around AD 40, unknown Christian missionaries had brought the message about Christ to that city. Riots over the "name of Chrestus" [= Christ] led the emperor Claudius to expel some Jews from the city circa AD 49; Paul's friends Prisca and Aquila had been forced out of the city at that time (Acts 18:1–3). Of course, other Jews and Christians remained in the city and eventually those expelled from Rome returned. Paul and Peter were both among the Christians martyred at Rome when the great fire under the emperor Nero (July AD 64) was blamed on Christians.

Competing Religions and Philosophies

One of the things any traveler would notice about these cities was their diversity. People came from all over the empire and along with them came gods, goddesses, and competing philosophies—not to mention the magicians, astrologers, and street preachers. Cities had public festivals honoring important local gods along with honoring the "good fortune" of Rome and the imperial family. Such festivals would be celebrated with elaborate processions, the slaughtering of animals in the appropriate temples, and often feasting. The Jews were known for refusing to engage in such religious celebrations. Since these festivals were civic occasions, not matters of personal conviction, Jews were scorned as "haters of humanity." However, outsiders admired the strict monotheism and the ethical code of Judaism. Inscriptions show that wealthy civic leaders sometimes paid for building or decorating a synagogue and may even have attended without necessarily converting to Judaism. To do so, a person would have to break with family, friends, and social customs, not to mention any public office that required one to function as priest or priestess in one of the city's religious cults.

Astrology and Magic. Naturally, as people found their world being uprooted when they moved from their native country to cities in which they did not enjoy the status of being citizens, they also became worried about controlling their lives. Both astrology and magic were widely practiced among all classes. Fate was sometimes pictured as a stern goddess. Astrology would tell you your destiny. If you were lucky, the magician might help you get control over some part of it. Magic spells sought victory at the track or the love of another, not to mention disaster for enemies. This pagan love spell includes names of the Jewish God:

> I abjure you, demonic spirit, who rests here, by the sacred names Aoth, Abaoth; by the god of Abraam and the Iao of Jahu… hearken to the glorious and fearful and great name, and hasten to Urbanus son of Urbana and bring him Domitiana, daughter of Candida, so that he, loving, frantic, sleepless with love and desire for her, may beg her to return to his house and become his wife…. Make it so that he, loving, shall obey her like a slave and desire no other wife or maiden but have Domitiana alone, daughter of Candida, as his wife for the whole of their life, at once, at once, quick, quick!

Isis Cult. Magic was not the only way to deal with fate. The Egyptian goddess Isis was widely known as a powerful ruler over fate. Frescos from the Roman houses at Pompeii show ceremonies in her honor with the sacred jug of Nile water, priests with their shaved heads dressed in white, and Egyptian plants. A temple to Isis built in Rome (ca. AD 38) is represented on coins. A large granite carving of Isis's husband, Osiris, had been imported from Egypt for the temple. A complex in honor of Isis was found near the harbor warehouses at Corinth. She was thought to aid sailors.

The elaborate list of praises of Isis that could be found in carvings, as well as in some writings, showed that she was the origin of all human culture. Here is part of such an inscription from Asia Minor:

> I am Isis, mistress of every land.
> I gave and established laws for humans which no one can change.
> I am the one who finds fruit for humans.
> I am the one who rises in the Dog Star.
> I am the one called goddess by women.
> I divided earth from the heavens.
> I showed the paths of the stars.
> I set up the course of the sun and moon.
> I devised business in the sea.
> I made justice strong.
> I brought women and men together.
> I established that women should bear children after nine months.
> I ordained that parents should be loved by their children.
> I and my brother Osiris put an end to cannibalism.
> I revealed mysteries to humans.
> I taught them to honor images of the gods.
> I consecrated the temples of the gods.
> I broke down governments of tyrants.
> I put an end to murders.
> I caused men to love women.
> I made justice stronger than gold and silver.
> I established marriage contracts.
> I assigned languages to Greeks and barbarians.
> I ordained that nothing should be more feared than an oath.
> I deliver the person who plots evil against others into the hands of
> those he plots against.
> I established penalties for the unjust.
> Justice prevails with me.
> I am the Queen of rivers, winds, and sea.
> No one is honored without me.
> I am Queen of War.

I am Queen of the thunderbolt.
I stir up the sea, and I calm it.
I am in the rays of the sun.
I free captives.
I created walled cities.
I am called the Lawgiver.
I overcome fate.
Fate listens to me.
Hail, O Egypt, that nourished me.

Priestess of Isis

Isis was the mistress of everything humans needed for civilization. She was in charge of the stars and the weather, of trading and founding cities. She established languages, laws, and religions. She saw to justice, and she could also free her worshipers from captivity and fate.

In addition to public processions, temples, inscriptions, wall paintings, and myths about Isis, there were also secret rituals. These rituals, which are associated with a number of different gods and goddesses, are called "mystery religions." Areas in the sanctuaries that were partly underground may have been the places in which the person initiated into the "mysteries" saw visions of the sacred myth or of items linked with the god or goddess. Strict prohibitions against describing what went on in these cults were so well honored in antiquity that we know little about them.

An account of Isis's initiation does survive in a second-century novel, *The Golden Ass*. Its author, Apuleius, appears to be drawing upon his own experience in the Isis temples of Corinth and Rome. The novel concerns the adventures of a young man whose fascination with magic (in the service of love) leads to his being turned into an ass. Finally, the goddess appears to him and tells him that she can save him from the fate he is suffering. When he goes to a public procession of the goddess, Lucius is restored to human shape. The priest tells him that he should be grateful to his powerful protector:

O Lucius, after enduring so many labors and escaping so many storms of Fate, you have finally reached the safe port of rest and mercy! Neither your noble birth, nor your high rank, nor your great learning did anything for you because you turned to slavish pleasures; by youthful stupidity, you won the grim reward of your unfortunate curiosity. And yet though Fate's blindness tortured you, she has brought you to this religious blessedness. Let Fate go elsewhere and rage in her wild fury. Let her find someone else to torment. For Fate has no power over those who have devoted themselves to serving the majesty of our goddess....Now you are safe and protected by a "Fate" who is not blind but who can see and who by her light enlightens other gods. Therefore rejoice, put on a happy expression matching your white robe and follow the procession of this savior goddess with happy steps.

When it was time for him to be initiated into the mysteries, Lucius had to abstain from meat and wine for ten days. Then he had to purify himself with a ritual washing. The ceremony took place at night in the innermost part of the temple. Though he does not describe the ceremony itself, he claims to have descended to the gates of hell and returned reborn. The new initiate was then shown to other worshipers almost like a god himself:

Hear then and believe, for I tell you the truth. I drew near the confines of death....I was carried again through the elements and returned to earth. At the dead of night I saw the sun shining brightly. I approached the gods above and the gods below, and worshiped them face to face....As soon as it was morning and the solemn rites had been completed, I came forth in the twelve gowns worn by the initiate....For in the middle of the holy shrine, before the statue of the goddess, I was directed to stand on a wooden platform, arrayed in a linen robe so richly embroidered that I was something to see. The precious cape which hung from my shoulders down to the ground was adorned wherever you looked with the figures of animals in various colors....The cape the initiates call Olympian. In my right hand, I carried a flaming torch, and my head was decorated with a crown made of white palm leaves, spread out to stand up like rays. After I had been adorned like the sun and set up like an image of a god, the curtains were suddenly drawn and people crowded around to gaze at me.

Lucius goes on to describe his daily devotions to the goddess in her temple and further initiations. He claims to have spoken to her husband, Osiris, god of the underworld, in a dream. He also credits Osiris with helping him gain a flourishing legal practice in Rome.

The story of Lucius and Isis gives you some idea of the emotional heights of ancient paganism. Though Jewish and Christian writers often speak of the pagans as worshiping the lifeless statues of the gods and goddesses, some people, at least, claimed to have a special relationship with particular gods and goddesses. You can also see something of the practical side of religion. The mystery cults were not primarily concerned with the afterlife, though someone who had been to the underworld had little to fear there. They were about finding the right powers to help a person be successful in all the troubles of this life: Lucius was now under the personal care of a powerful divine being. You can then see why belief that Jesus had been exalted to be Lord over all the powers of the cosmos might appeal to people who were looking for salvation from the powers of fate. Paul reminds the Galatians that before they became Christians, they were subject to the powers of the universe and to beings who were not gods (Gal 4:8–9). Christianity also had two things the pagan cults did not. It had an ethical code that sought to establish justice, love, and peace among believers. Moreover, it created a new community, which embodied these values and in which one would be welcomed wherever one went.

Philosophical Schools. Philosophers also promised that people who followed their teachings could find happiness. They offered a rational account of the place of humans in the cosmos, and insisted that reason could get control over the passions and false ideas that led humans astray and made them unhappy. Philosophers traveled from city to city. Young men might go to famous schools like those at Athens or Tarsus to study philosophy. Philosophic literature was not confined to the great books read in the universities. It included anecdotes about the lives of famous philosophers, letters, and handbooks that summarized philosophic teaching. New Testament authors employ such popular philosophic teaching. The image of the divine as something that pervades the universe and is not captured in religious cults is used in Acts 17:23–28, for example. The idea that humans should make moral and intellectual progress from being "children" driven by ignorance and passions to being adults guided by the maturity that comes with wisdom and virtue is exploited effectively in Paul's warning to the Corinthians against priding themselves on a wisdom that they do not have. They are still in need of "baby food" (1 Cor 3:1–3).

Since Christianity emphasized the necessity to live a moral life, it naturally came into dialogue with ethics taught in philosophical schools. Here is a sketch of three leading schools of philosophy in the New Testament world:

(a) *Epicureanism*. You might have read in a science book that the Epicureans held that the whole world was made up of different-shaped atoms and empty space. They thought that if we humans would just remember that fact, we could overcome our three main fears. First, we should never be afraid of death. All we are is a composite of different types of atoms (including those for the mind or soul). When we die, these atoms all come untangled and go off to become parts of something else. There is nothing left to experience death or to live afterward. Second, we should not fear the gods. Epicureans believed that gods did exist. People had seen them and people all over the world believed in them. But like everything else, the gods have to be made up of atoms too, even if theirs don't come apart the way ours do. Epicurus argued that the main attribute of the gods is "blessedness." But if the gods are blessed, they are not going to worry themselves about what human beings, destined to be dissolved into atoms anyway, might do. Third, we should not worry about misfortune or fate. We cannot do anything about that. But we should attempt to arrange everything that we can in our life so that it will give as little pain and as much pleasure as possible. This meant withdrawing from politics or public affairs where one was likely to have enemies and troubles to a private, tranquil life. Epicureans often fostered small circles of "friends" devoted to these ideals.

(b) *Platonism*. The philosophic teaching developed by followers of Plato challenged the materialism of other philosophic schools. The material world is a mere shadow or image of the divine realities that are associated with the Good and are often described as "ideas" in the mind of the divine. Human beings reach out to the divine through the mind when they turn away from the world of sense impressions to the world of reason, often represented as embodied in mathematical forms. Since the "mind" is not material, it cannot "die" as the body does. Instead, some Platonists held out the image of the soul of the philosopher fleeing its bodily prison for its true home among the stars. Souls that remained captives of the material world and its senses were often thought to be reincarnated in human or animal bodies. However, this view of reincarnation was not correlated with a strict system of punishment and reward for the deeds of a past life as in some doctrines of karma. A soul that has not been freed from its attachment to this world through philosophic contemplation will choose a life in keeping with the state it had upon dying.

(c) *Stoicism*. The first two philosophies were named after their founders. Stoicism was named after the painted Stoa in Athens, the place where its founder, Zeno, used to teach. Like Epicureanism, Stoicism insisted on a materialistic account of the world. However, the Stoics claimed that everything came into existence through the condensations of an original fire, or divine spirit. This spirit is also rational. The comprehensive order of the universe is due to the fact that the divine spirit penetrates everything that has come to be in it. Periodically the cosmos would return to its original fiery state and the process would start over again. Stoic philosophy was often accused of being the most fatalistic of all, since everything in the universe was connected and happened according to the laws that governed the "tensions" in the divine spirit. Sometimes the Stoics also spoke of the spirit as the divine word pervading all things.

The main attraction of Stoic ethics is its ideal of "passionlessness." Passions, after all, are merely movements or "tension" in one's soul. The wise person will gain control over the passions and be able to face both good and bad fortune with peaceful detachment. There is no point in being worried about what we cannot change, the external things that happen to us in life.

But we can be concerned about what really is under our control, that is, our reactions to external things. They cause most of our misery anyway. We are like dogs tied to a cart. If we resist the motion of the cart by lying down when it starts to move, we will be injured. But if we get up and run along with the cart, we will arrive at the same place as the dog who is dragged but without pain and injury.

Here is a passage from this time from the famous Stoic philosopher Epictetus (b. ca. AD 50). Epictetus had spent part of his life as a slave:

> Keep this thought ready for use at dawn, by day and night. There is but one way to calm, and that is to give up all claim to things that lie outside the sphere of moral purpose; to regard nothing as your own; to surrender everything to the deity, to Fortune; to yield everything to those whom Zeus had made supervisors; and to devote yourself to one thing only, that which is your own.... That is why I cannot yet say that someone is industrious until I know for what reason...for I would not have you praise or blame a person for things that may be either good or bad, but only for judgments, because they are a person's own possessions, which make one's actions either base or noble....If you have gotten rid of or reduced a malignant disposition...If you are not moved by the things that once moved you, at least not to the same degree, then you can celebrate day after day....How much greater cause for thanksgiving is this than a consulship or governorship.

The language and ideas of Stoicism were very popular. They would come to play an important part in the formation of Christian ascetic traditions. Since Stoics held that all people were citizens of the cosmos, which is a living organism, some scholars detect Stoic ideas in Paul's descriptions of the church as body of Christ.

Social Status of Pauline Christians

What we see of the early communities in Paul's letters suggests that Christians came from diverse backgrounds. Yet they did claim to distinguish themselves from others by their way of life. When Paul speaks of himself as laboring not to be a burden to his converts whom he treats the way a father or even a nurse would gently care for children (1 Thess 2:7–11), he reminds the reader of the philosopher's claim to be sent as a healer for a sick humanity. When he tells the Thessalonians to live in love for one another, to mind their own affairs, to live by the work of their hands and not be dependent upon anyone (1 Thess 4:9–12), he reminds them of the Epicurean ideal of quiet withdrawal. Paul's harsh words against those who confused Christianity with "wisdom" and "rhetorical preaching" at Corinth (1 Cor 1:4) show that there were believers who identified Christianity with the ideals expounded by philosophy. These believers seem to have concluded that Christianity endowed them with a certain status and superiority to others. Paul castigates them for forgetting the true paradox of the cross. God's wisdom is not the same as human wisdom. They have also forgotten the example of patient suffering and humility set for them by apostles like Paul and Apollos.

We are better able to understand some of the conflicts that broke out in Corinth when we consider the kinds of persons who made up the first churches. We have already seen that in other cases difficulties arose between Christians of Jewish and Christians of Gentile backgrounds. Those who were confusing Christian holiness with the ideals of popular philosophy probably had some education beyond the rudiments taught by the grammarians. Such persons may have considered themselves better than other believers who were craftsmen, traders, and even slaves. Paul learned about some of the problems at Corinth from "Chloe's people," presumably the household slaves of this woman who was traveling on other business. He writes a letter of recommendation for Phoebe, the patron or deaconess of the church in one of Corinth's ports, so that Christians in Rome will assist her in whatever venture brings her to the city (Rom 16:1–2).

Since only the wealthy minority had houses that could accommodate a number of people, in large cities like Corinth or Rome Christians were probably divided up into a number of "house churches." When Paul reprimands the Corinthians for their divisions at the Lord's Supper, he speaks of some members of the church eating and drinking lavishly, while the poor go hungry and are dishonored (1 Cor 11:17–34). Probably the person who owned the house provided a special banquet at the Lord's Supper for a few friends, leaving only the ritual bread and wine for the rest. Such behavior imitated the kind of sharp social divisions that we find in ancient society. Inscriptions giving the banqueting rules for private associations often stipulate either the monetary contribution each member is to make or the amount and type of food to be provided for participants. Paul expects to address the situation by instilling a Christ-like concern for others, not by erecting similar laws.

One of the most intriguing discoveries at ancient Corinth was a paving stone marked with the name Erastus. The paving was donated in return for holding the civic office of *aedile*, one of the highest in the city. Paul mentions a man by the name of Erastus in Romans 16:23 as someone who held an office of *oikonomos* in the city. The title suggests a person in charge of civic funds. If the same man is the donor of the pavement, then he went on to the office of *aedile*. Some scholars have noticed that the inscription does not have enough room for an indication of the name of Erastus's father. Therefore, Erastus was probably a wealthy freedman. Christianity may have appealed to

**The Erastus Inscription, discovered in ancient Corinth in 1929
with the abbreviated words: ERASTUS. PRO. AED. S. P. STRAVIT.
Its translation is: "Erastus, in return for his aedileship,
laid this pavement at his own expense."**

persons like Erastus, since it insisted that in Christ there was no distinction
between slave and free (cf. 1 Cor 12:13).

Women as Converts

Paul mentions by name as associates or patrons of the Christian movement a number of women. The economic and social position of women was
much less restricted in the Roman city than in classical Athens. Stoic philosophers had claimed that women and men must practice virtue in the same way.
Women should be educated in philosophy so that they will be better managers
of their households. Female slaves were often freed to marry their patrons.
Women were also active in trade and manufacture. Some lent money to finance
such ventures. Like men, though not as frequently, wealthy women might
donate buildings to their community. At Pompeii, a woman who had made her
money in brick making donated a building to a workman's association and was
rewarded with the title *sacerdos publica* ("public priest," though this does not
mean that she exercised any particular cultic functions). Another woman built
the temple to the "genius of Augustus." Women appeared in lawsuits as independent litigants. A few women are named on coins and in inscriptions as
benefactors of cities and even officials.

Though not as frequently, women also joined the cultic groups that
were linked to particular crafts. They also show up in inscriptions as patrons
and founders of groups whose membership was primarily male. A patron
might provide her home for meetings, build a separate building, or pay the
expenses for sacrifices, festivals, and the like. A rough estimate suggests that
between 5 and 10 percent of the private associations had women as patrons.
Women also played roles in both private and civic cults. Some religious cults
were exclusively for women, but others had a mixed membership. The
philosopher Plutarch thought that a husband ought to teach his wife philosophy so that she would not be prone to joining foreign cults. He commented:

> It is becoming for a wife to worship and to know only the gods
> that her husband believes in, and to shut the door tight upon all
> queer rituals and outlandish superstitions. For with no god do
> stealthy and secret rites performed by a woman find any favor.

The wives and mother of King Izates of Adiabene played an important role
in his conversion to Judaism. Some women among the Roman aristocracy
were accused of Jewish sympathies. The cult of the goddess Isis was particularly popular with women. Isis was, among other things, the goddess who protected marriage and chastity. There is no evidence that women were
particularly responsible for religious innovation. Nevertheless, they did play
a more substantial role in the newer religious cults than in the more established traditional ones. Their position in Christian churches seems to follow
the same pattern.

The Church and the Forms of Association

The early churches had several models around which they might shape
their association. For Jesus' disciples and their Jewish converts, the synagogue,
the home, and even the temple in Jerusalem continued to be the focus of religious devotion. Synagogues in the Hellenistic cities appear to have been private
homes that were converted for community use. Certain elements of early
Christian worship such as reading and interpretation of scripture, prayers,
psalms, and ethical exhortation were doubtless taken from the Jewish synagogue. Jewish communities also provided "courts" to settle disputes between
their members. In 1 Corinthians 6:1–8, Paul chastises the Corinthians for their
lawsuits. He acknowledges that the "love command" should make a Christian
willing to suffer wrong rather than to drag another into court (v. 7). But he
clearly does not think that the community as a whole will live by that principle.
Therefore he encourages them to find someone wise enough to settle disputes
between Christians rather than take such cases to outside courts (vv. 4–5).

There was a wide variety of voluntary associations in Greco-Roman
cities. These served persons in a similar trade and provided important forms
of mutual assistance such as burial for members while promoting the worship
of a particular god or goddess. We do not know anything about burial practices among Christians at this early stage. First Corinthians 15:29 contains an
enigmatic reference to "baptism for the dead" and the Thessalonians were
concerned about the fate of Christians who died before the second coming
of the Lord (1 Thess 4:13—5:11). Therefore, it seems probable that Christian
churches functioned as "burial associations" for their members. Voluntary
associations often depended upon wealthy patrons to provide for sacrifices,
feasts, and a place of worship, though some assessed dues from members.

Patrons played an important role in the Pauline churches as well. However, there are some striking differences. The voluntary associations, though they did cross some social and gender boundaries, were much more limited in scope than the early Christian communities, which sought to convert anyone who would believe in Christ. Voluntary associations did not recruit by propagating their cult deity as the sole source of salvation. Nor do we find among early Christians the elaborate offices and titles that are characteristic of the officials of cult associations.

Still other possibilities for associations were provided by the philosophical schools, particularly the groups of "friends" who followed the teachings of Epicurus. We have seen that the emphasis on the moral conduct of one's life was an important part of popular philosophical teaching at this time. These groups stressed friendship among members and may have followed the practice of their founder by exchanging philosophic letters between groups. In the second century, pagans would lump Christians and Epicureans together as "atheists," since both groups challenged the accepted beliefs about the gods.

The fourth institution that contributed to shaping the early Christian community was the "household." Christians met in private houses, not public buildings or temples. They also adopted the language of family relationships: all are children of God, brothers and sisters of one another and of Christ. The ancient "household" was considerably more complex than what we think of as a "family." Roman law held that all persons, male and female, were ultimately under the authority of the oldest male head of their family. (Women remained part of their paternal family while their children belonged to the father's family.) In addition, slaves and others dependent upon a wealthy person would be considered part of the latter's household. Even a peasant farmer or a craftsman in the city might have a number of persons living in his or her household who were not "family" in the sense in which we use the term.

Ethical writers emphasized the necessity for a hierarchy to ensure good order within the household. Such advice, called "household codes," found their way into early Christian preaching. They emphasized the fact that not only should wives, children, and slaves show appropriate respect and obedience to husbands, parents, and masters, but the superior parties also had an obligation to treat those under their care with love and concern. Husbands had to love their wives. Parents had to take care not to overburden their children. Masters had to treat their slaves justly. They should not exercise the absolute domination and cruelty that the law permitted (e.g., Col 3:18—4:1; Eph 5:21—6:9; 1 Pet 2:13—3:7). When the Pauline churches came to establish a list of qualities for "bishops," they insisted that such a person had to be able to manage his own household well (e.g., 1 Tim 3:4–5). Proper behavior also insisted that wives should defer to their husbands and should not speak in public. These rules too found their way into the Pauline churches (e.g., 1 Cor 14:33b–35; 1 Tim 2:11–12).

Today many of these rules seem peculiar, since our households are much different. We forget that even fathers were subject to obedience and deference to the oldest male in their families, that women were much younger than their husbands and usually not as well educated, and that children were not considered to be real persons at all. St. Paul speaks of the child as being a "slave," indeed assigned a slave to look after it, until coming of age (Gal 4:1–2). While a wealthy convert to Christianity might bring his or her whole household into the community, this was not true for many converts, especially women and slaves. Their conversion to Christianity might arouse suspicion. First Peter suggests that suspicions often led to ridicule and punishment of Christians. The church was something like a new "household community." However, its members also had to continue to live in the households to which they belonged, which were not usually Christian. The Christian churches sought to show others that their "household" contained what was best in human life. It did not try to destroy the non-Christian "households" in which its members lived.

None of the four models—synagogue, cult association, philosophical school, or household—quite captures the shape of the early Christian communities. Perhaps one of the most important things is captured by the special sense of belonging to a "church." It was not just the group that met in a particular household; nor was it just the group of households that represented the Christians of a specific city; nor was it just all the Christians in churches that belonged to Paul's mission. From the beginning, the church also had a universal model. It was the "new Israel." That meant that everyone in the world who worshiped Christ belonged to "the church" (e.g,. 1 Cor 1:2), just as all Jews anywhere in the world belonged to "Israel." The Greek word for church, *ekklesia*, stood for the assembly of citizens. However, the expression for the church, "church of God" (cf. 1 Cor 10:32), has its roots in a biblical phrase, "assembly of the Lord," which referred to all the tribes of Israel gathered together. One of the ways in which the sense of a universal church was maintained was through the constant traveling by Christians. They were able to find hospitality among Christians in the cities through which they passed and were able to share news of other churches. Apostles and missionaries were not the only ones involved in this process. Often ordinary Christians involved in trade sought hospitality with other believers.

The Workshop and Paul's Missionary Practice

We usually think of Paul's mission as comprised of stirring sermons given in synagogues, the public places, or private homes of people in the cities. Certainly he did use all of these places. However, there is one other element of Paul's missionary activity that we forget—he worked at the trade of "tent-making." This trade probably involved all kinds of leather working. Paul easily could have carried the tools of his trade with him. Having his tools made it possible for the apostle to scratch out a living on his long journeys by repairing leather goods for other travelers.

Paul set himself up as an example for the Thessalonians. He worked to support himself and not be a burden to anyone (1 Thess 2:9; 4:11–12). Paul linked this work with his preaching and with his "fatherly care" for his converts. However, others sometimes looked at it differently. Some philosophers may have praised a life in which one was dependent on no one. A person who could adopt the poverty and hardships of the tradesperson proved that he was not preaching in order to gain wealth and popularity. Nevertheless, most people felt that the only truly respectable life was led by those not compelled to engage in physical labor for a living. A philosopher should live from his teaching if he was not wealthy enough to live off the produce of estates. The great Stoic philosopher Epictetus even managed to go from being a slave to being a person of wealth and importance.

You can already imagine what persons who held this view must have thought of Paul. Paul's letters to Corinth show that a number of people criticized Paul for continuing to live such a "slavish" life (e.g., 1 Cor 9; 2 Cor 10–13). They knew that other apostles like Peter not only received support for themselves but also for their wives (and presumably their families). They knew that Jesus had told his disciples to get their support from preaching the gospel (1 Cor 9:4–5, 14). Paul admits all that. But he insists that he is freely giving up the right to support so as to make the gospel available "for free."

If you have ever been in the Middle East or lived in an area of this country with craftsmen and small shops, you know that "doing business" is not the same as it is in most of our cities. You may sit and chat, even have a coffee or make general suggestions. The shopkeeper or tradesman may know your family. Often those relationships will go back several generations. Since he traveled, Paul would not be able to build up such longstanding relationships. He would have to work in someone else's shop. But he still would have had plenty of time to talk with the people who came into the shop. Such conversation would not be confined to arranging and paying for the job as it is in an impersonal society. By using the workshop as part of his mission, Paul made it possible for persons to hear him who would not have met him in the homes of wealthier Christians at Corinth. He said that as much as possible he wanted all people to hear about Christ so he was willing to "make myself a slave to all, that I might win the more" (1 Cor 9:19).

Summary

The diversity of these cities seems a long way from the small, stable Galilean villages, where most of life was set in traditional patterns and where travel was usually limited to the five or so miles that were required to go to market. People sought others from their own country or trade to form smaller communities within the cities. They brought gods and goddesses from their homelands into the Graeco-Roman cities. At the same time, each city had its own religious cults and festivals. And many of the Pauline cities, which owed either their origins or their prosperity to Rome, might have temples in honor of Rome, its gods, and its emperor.

The Jewish community had learned to live in such cities by separating itself from others. Protected by Roman edict, Jews were not compelled to join in any civic religious activities. Jews could not be summoned to court on the Sabbath. They had their own food laws, which also limited contacts with outsiders. Marriage to a non-Jew was severely discouraged. The earliest Christian missionaries were part of that Jewish environment. But St. Paul insists that God called him to preach to the Gentiles (Gal 1:16). He was not the only Christian missionary to recognize that the gospel had to be preached beyond the boundaries of the Jewish community.

The task of preaching Christ in the cities of the ancient world was as great as any that has ever faced Christians. Apostles like Paul had to find a way to relate the gospel message to those who had not grown up with the Jewish faith and its scripture. They had to relate Christ to the religious and philosophical movements that were competing for people's attention in the ancient city. Moreover, they had to come up with some form of community structure that could embrace all persons. Christ could not be limited to a particular group, class, or gender. People had to learn to call each other "brother" and "sister" across every possible boundary that might divide them. People had to care for others, even for churches they had never seen. As you read the letters of Paul, you will see that the first churches were not perfect. People did not understand what Paul had taught them. They quarreled with each other. Sometimes they even did things that were clearly wrong. We shouldn't be surprised. What family or organization of human beings doesn't have such problems? We should be amazed that Christianity managed at all. The gospel message had to touch the depths of the human spirit for it to have shaped a new form of human belonging in the Roman world. Only the tiny minority of Christians ever would have predicted that those who followed the Lord would outlast the greatness of Rome.

STUDY QUESTIONS

Facts You Should Know

1. Give a brief description of each of the following cities: (a) Thessalonica; (b) Philippi; (c) Corinth; (d) Antioch; (e) Rome.
2. Describe the Isis cult. How was the universal rule of the goddess expressed in the cult?
3. Describe the following philosophic views: (a) Epicureanism; (b) Platonism; (c) Stoicism.
4. Describe the diverse social origins of persons in the Pauline churches.
5. Give the characteristics of each of the following forms of association and indicate how that type of association contributed to the structuring of early Christian communities: (a) synagogues; (b) trade associations; (c) philosophical schools; (d) the Graeco-Roman household.

Things to Do

1. Locate on a map all of the cities mentioned in the chapter and the provinces to which they belonged.
2. Read 1 Corinthians and find all of the phrases that refer to "social status" among the Corinthians. Then make a list of the "status" language that Paul uses for himself. What does Paul think about the Corinthian views of social status?
3. Look up maps for the ancient cities of Rome, Corinth, and Antioch (e.g., in the *Harper's Bible Dictionary*) and identify areas and buildings common to ancient cities.

Things to Think About

1. How diverse are the backgrounds of people in your church? What does diversity contribute to the life of the community?
2. If you had to make a list of social institutions in modern society that are "like churches" or that have influenced the way churches are run and the way Christians understand themselves as a community, what would they be?

Chapter 8

THE LIFE OF PAUL

Sources for Paul's Life

Paul's own letters are our main source for information about his life. Paul was not one of the original disciples and had not known Jesus personally. He had been a zealous Pharisee and was persecuting the Christians vigorously when God suddenly revealed the risen Lord to him (Gal 1:11–28). Paul says that his first response was to preach in Roman Arabia and then in the region of Damascus. After three years, he spent two weeks in Jerusalem with Peter and James. Then he returned to Syria and his home region of Cilicia. Fourteen years later Paul was part of the delegation from the church at Antioch in Syria that met with leaders in Jerusalem to discuss the position of non-Jewish converts. They accepted the principle of Paul's Gentile mission that Gentiles could be Christians without converting to Judaism (2:1–10). Shortly after that meeting, Paul began his own mission in Asia Minor and Greece. Paul's letters are written to the churches founded during this period (ca. AD 50–57). When he wrote to a church he did not found at Rome, Paul was winding up that phase of his life. At some risk to himself, he was going to deliver a collection for the poor at Jerusalem. He then hoped to journey to Rome and after a visit with the churches there go on to go a new mission in Spain (Rom 15:22–32).

We also learn from Paul's letters that he often had to change or interrupt his travel plans. He suffered from illness, which he says taught him that God's power could work through weakness (2 Cor 12:7–10). Paul preached in Galatia when stranded there by illness (Gal 4:13). He also mentions other forms of suffering, the hardships at work, being driven out of cities, the hardships of journeys (including shipwreck), being beaten, and even imprisoned (e.g., 1 Thess 2:2; 1 Cor 4:9–13; 15:32; 2 Cor 11:23–27). In jail Paul often did not know if he would live or die or when his case might be resolved (e.g., Phil 1:19–26; Phlm 22–23).

Detail of a fifth-century mosaic from the Capella Arcivescovile in Ravena, Italy, depicting a portrait of Paul probably based on the description provided in the Acts of Thecla

None of Paul's letters are dated. The various journeys he mentions and the hints at time intervals in Galatians provide clues for relating the letters to one another. Acts, written several decades after Paul's death, fills out the story of the apostle by expanding upon other material that the community had preserved. Although Acts is written by a "Luke," one of Paul's associates in Philemon 23 and Colossians 4:14, Luke is not one of Paul's assistants. Many of the problems referred to in Paul's letters never appear in Acts. Acts 15 reports a very different agreement about the Gentiles than Paul does in Galatians 2. Paul says the only requirement was that a collection be taken up for the poor of Jerusalem. Acts says nothing about the collection. It claims that Gentiles who become Christians should avoid food that has been strangled, food that has been used in a sacrifice to idols, and sexual immorality (Acts 15:28–29). Paul permits eating meat from an animal used in sacrifices as long as the meat came from the market or was served in a private home (1 Cor 8). Some scholars think that Luke found a copy of the decree by James and presumed that it came from the Jerusalem Council. They suggest that it might have been formulated after the break between Paul and Peter reported in Galatians 2:11–14. It is not always easy to fit the information in Acts together with what Paul says in his letters.

Pauline Chronology

Scholars attempt to patch together references to events that we can date approximately in Paul's letters and in Acts, Paul's movements as reflected in his letters, and Paul's journeys in Acts, where they can be correlated with the clues within the letters to arrive at a chronology for Paul's life and letters. Naturally, this process is open to numerous difficulties, for example, it is not easy to tell when the periods of three and fourteen years mentioned in Galatians are to begin. Paul says that his missionary work in Damascus occurred under the ethnarch king Aretas (2 Cor 11:31–32). The political relationships between Aretas and Rome suggest a time between the late summer of AD 37 and the death of Aretas in AD 39. Fourteen years later would place the Council at Jerusalem in AD 51. Other scholars date the council in AD 49.

Acts 18:12–17 says that Paul was brought before the proconsul Gallio in Corinth. An inscription at Delphi contains a letter from the emperor Claudius, which opens by saying that the emperor had been acclaimed for the twenty-sixth time and that Gallio had reported a serious problem of depopulation in Delphi. The instructions to Gallio's successor propose recruiting "well-born" persons from elsewhere to settle at Delphi with the privileges of citizens. Gallio did not serve his entire term because he became ill. He left the province by sea. Therefore, he must have left before the dangers of winter travel (see Acts 27:9; 28:11). It seems that during the year he served as proconsul, Gallio was in Corinth only between June and October.

It is difficult to determine when the twenty-sixth and twenty-seventh acclamations of Claudius took place. If the twenty-sixth acclamation took place after the first significant victory in the spring campaign of AD 52, then Claudius must have written the letter in the spring or early summer. It would seem likely that Gallio's term was 51/52, which would narrow the encounter with Paul down to July to October of AD 51. Other scholars think that Gallio's appointment was in the year AD 50/51. The end of Paul's life presents another problem of Roman dating. Paul's arrest and imprisonment at Jerusalem took place under the procurator Felix. Paul's departure for trial in Rome occurred after Festus had replaced Felix (Acts 25:1—26:32). Felix was an imperial freedman, known for his cruelty. One of his wives was the Jewish princess Drusilla, daughter of King Agrippa I. The date of his recall is uncertain, probably around AD 60. However, some argue for an earlier date, since his brother Pallas still had enough influence to protect Felix from the charges he faced in Rome. If one accepts a date around AD 60, then Paul was imprisoned in AD 57. Paul's trial in Rome, whose outcome Acts does not report, would probably have condemned him to death circa AD 62.

The seven letters that Paul wrote himself—Romans, 1 and 2 Corinthians, Galatians, Philippians, Philemon, and 1 Thessalonians—belong to the period before Paul's departure for Jerusalem. Romans, the last of these, was written from Corinth in AD 55/58. First and Second Corinthians follow upon at least one earlier letter after Paul's expulsion from Corinth. These letters stem from the period between AD 51 and Paul's return sometime in AD 55/56. Philippians and Philemon were both written from prison. People used to think that that must have been Paul's final imprisonment at Rome, but Paul had been in prison because of his preaching on earlier occasions (2 Cor 11:23). In addition, the Philippians sent Paul aid and were well informed about his circumstances. Philemon was the head of a house church that met in Colossae (Col 4:9, 17). Paul expected to visit there upon his release from prison (Phlm 22). First Corinthians 15:32 speaks of Paul "fighting with the beasts at Ephesus." This allusion became the basis of stories of Paul's encounter with a lion he had baptized in the arena. Some scholars think it may be a gloss by a scribe who knew that legend. These clues suggest that Ephesus was the place in which the imprisonment of Philippians and Philemon occurred. The reference to the *praetorium* in Philippians 1:13 and "Caesar's household" (4:22) point to the presence of imperial freedmen and soldiers in this city, the fourth largest in the empire.

Notice that in Philippians 1:12–26 Paul is uncertain how his case will be decided. Philemon 22, on the other hand, hints that Paul is about to be released. If 1 Corinthians 15:32 does refer to this imprisonment, then Philippians and Philemon must have been written before the Corinthian letters. When we come to 1 Thessalonians and Galatians, we do not even have these slender clues to help us. Galatians must have been written after the Jerusalem Council and Paul's departure from Antioch. However, was the church at Galatia founded after that separation or does it stem from an earlier period in Paul's mission? When compared with Romans, Paul's argument about the law is less nuanced. Paul defends his teaching about salvation through Christ against opponents who thought converts should also adopt Jewish practices. Galatians 2:10 mentions the collection for the poor, but unlike the Corinthian letters and Romans, Paul does not refer to provisions for gathering funds. Romans 15:26 speaks of churches in Macedonia and Achaia as contributors, but Galatia is not mentioned. Some scholars think that Galatians was written late in Paul's ministry. Others, more influenced by the theological contrasts with Romans, think that it belongs with the earlier letters, 1 Thessalonians and Philippians. Judaizing, that is, expecting Gentile converts to adopt circumcision, kosher food, and Jewish holidays, is also an issue in Philippians 3:2–21.

First Thessalonians mentions the apostle's travels. Paul then arrived in Thessalonica after suffering opposition in Philippi (2:2). Not only was he forced out of Thessalonica, the nascent community encountered persecution as well (1:6–8). Unable to return there from Athens, Paul sent Timothy to check on the church (3:2). First Thessalonians is his response to Timothy's glowing report. However, Paul does not refer to Athens in that context. Most scholars think that he was writing from Corinth during his first visit there. This letter does not voice concerns over the relationship between Paul's conversion of Gentiles and Judaism that appear in other letters. Nor does Paul mention the collection for poor believers in Jerusalem (Gal 2:10) to which the Macedonian churches contributed generously (2 Cor 8–9). Therefore, some scholars propose that 1 Thessalonians represents Paul's missionary effort prior to the Council in Jerusalem. In any case, 1 Thessalonians appears to be the first surviving letter from Paul to a church that he had founded. Our available evidence is so fragmentary or apparently contradictory that we must make a number of likely guesses in order to reach any results at all. Chart 8–1 gives you a rough outline of Paul's life.

CHRONOLOGY OF PAUL'S LIFE	[8–1]
ca. AD 10	Born (father a Roman citizen; leather worker). Raised in Tarsus (family may have had ties to Judea, e.g., Paul's insistence that he is a "Hebrew" [2 Cor 11:22] and from the "tribe of Benjamin" [Phil 3:5])
	Became a zealous member of the Pharisees
ca. AD 31/33	Is actively persecuting members of a new Jewish sect centered in Jerusalem that claimed Jesus as messiah (Gal 1:13; 1 Cor 15:9)
ca. AD 33/35	Called by God to preach to the Gentiles
ca. AD 35/38	Missionary activity in Arabia and Damascus (expelled under Aretas)
ca. AD 37/38	Two-week visit to Jerusalem; meets Peter and James but not the larger church (Gal 1:22)
after AD 37/38	Missionary activity in Cilicia; Syria; from the Antioch church; [also Greece?]
ca. AD 47/50	1 Thessalonians (?)
ca. AD 50/51	Gallio episode at Corinth
ca. AD 49/51	Jerusalem Council
ca. AD 52/57	Missionary activity in Asia Minor and Greece (Gal; Phil; Phlm; 1 and 2 Cor)
ca. AD 56/57	Writes Romans from Corinth
ca. AD 57/58	Arrives in Jerusalem with collection; arrested; two-year imprisonment at Caesarea
ca. AD 59/60	Sea journey to Rome
ca. AD 62	Executed after imprisonment at Rome

Reading a Pauline Letter

Students often find Paul's letters the most difficult part of the New Testament. Unlike the gospels, letters are not narratives. Yet each letter belongs to a bigger story about Paul and the individual churches. Usually Paul was addressing a crisis. What a given church did in response to Paul's letter is unknown. We can often tell what Paul was hoping they would do

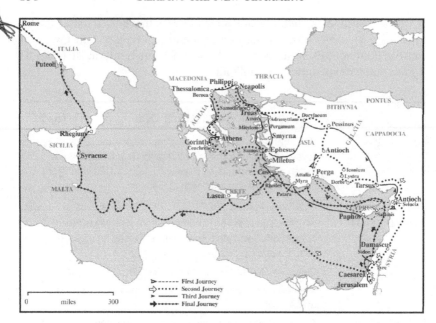

The travels of Paul

from the way in which he wrote. But we cannot be sure things actually happened that way. The Galatians, for example, may have resisted Paul's advice, though they did preserve the letter he sent them.

Paul is also difficult for us to understand because we are not trained to write or to make complex arguments in the style he used. The Greek language permitted very complex patterning of clauses within a single sentence. Chart 8-2 lists some of those patterns that you should watch out for in reading Paul.

Paul also drew upon material that his readers would recognize as "traditional," just as we hear phrases like "first amendment rights" or the "Ten Commandments." It is often possible to recognize traditional material by its vocabulary (words Paul does not use elsewhere), by a special introductory formula such as "we all know...," or "I handed on to you...," or by its form as a hymn, a list of virtues or vices, a set piece of ethical exhortation, a creedal formula, an acclamation in Aramaic like *marana tha*, "our Lord, come." Paul did not quote Jesus very often. Yet he must have taught his churches sayings and stories about Jesus. We find references to things the Lord taught in 1 Corinthians 7:10f (Mark 10:11 par.); 1 Corinthians 9:14 (cf. Luke 10:7); 1 Corinthians 11:23–24f (the words at the Last Supper); 1 Thessalonians 4:16f (cf. Mark 13). Allusions to other sayings of Jesus have been suggested for 1 Corinthians 14:37; Romans 12:14; 1 Corinthians 4:12 (Luke 6:28); 1 Tim 5:15; Romans 12:17 (Matt 5:39); Romans 13:7 (Matt 22:15–22); Romans 14:13 (Matt 7:1);

Romans 14:14 (Mark 7:18f); 1 Thessalonians 5:2 (Luke 12:39f); 1 Thessalonians 5:13 (Mark 9:50); 1 Corinthians 13:2 (Matt 17:20). Whenever Paul used traditional material like this, one has to figure out what function an appeal to tradition plays in the argument.

RHETORICAL FEATURES IN PAUL'S LETTERS   [8–2]

1. Use of parallel words and phrases or antitheses such as "life/death"; "flesh/spirit."

2. Chiasm: words and phrases developed in ab—b'a' patterns. Putting an element in the middle of a chiasmus so that the pattern becomes ab—c—b'a' emphasizes "c."

3. Use of paradoxes and expansion of metaphorical images.

4. Grouping of items for dramatic effect (pleonasm as in Gal 4:10, "You observe days, and months, and seasons, and years").

5. Diatribe style: Address a question, usually an objection to the line of argument that "someone" would raise (e.g., Rom 6:1, "What shall we say, then? Shall we remain in sin so that grace may abound?").

6. Use of a negative expression to convey a positive meaning (e.g., 1 Cor 1:25).

7. Formulaic summaries.

8. "Preaching" style, elaborate and solemn references to God (e.g., Rom 14:12, "So let each of us give account of himself to God....")

9. Autobiographical style: Paul makes use of autobiographical references in several different ways: (a) simple autobiography (e.g., Phil 1:12ff; 2 Cor 7:5); (b) apostolic autobiography, Paul's life as an example to be imitated (e.g., 1 Thess 2:1–12; 2 Cor 1:8–10); (c) apologetic: Paul is defending himself or his mission against charges made by others (e.g., 1 Cor 9; Gal 1:11–2:14; 2 Cor 12:1ff); (d) "pseudo-autobiography," as a way of generalizing (e.g., Rom 7:7ff).

Writing the Letter

In the age of electronic communication the formal types of letters are blurred. Many ancient letters fall into three groups: (a) relatively short, private letters whose purpose was to transact business between the parties, request a favor, recommend the bearer to the recipient, or convey some piece of news; (b) official public letters such as that of Claudius concerning Delphi in which Gallio is mentioned, which was written to the proconsul but was engraved on stone as a formal notice; (c) philosophical letters that philosophers wrote to friends or stuents and then later collected and published to explain their teachings.

Here is an example of a business letter. Notice that the whole family expects to work at making women's garments. They are planning to join other free workers who were textile manufacturers in Philadelphia:

> Greetings to Zenon from Apollophanes and Demetrius, brothers, makers of all sorts of woolen clothes for women. If you would like to and if you happen to have need, we are ready to supply what you want. We have heard of the glory of the city as well as of the goodness and justice with which you administer it. That is why we have decided to come to you, to Philadelphia, with our mother and wife so that we might be workers. Summon us if you would like us to work. We make, as you wish, cloaks, tunics, girdles, dresses, belts, ribbons, split tunics, trimming, everything to size. And we can teach our trade, if you wish. Tell Nicias to provide lodging for us. So that we won't seem strangers to you, we can provide references from people known to you, some from here whom you can trust, others from Moithymis. Farewell.

This letter gives you an idea of the kind of shop in which St. Paul worked.

A problem faced by people living in the Roman provinces was having labor, animals, and crops seized for use by the military (see Matt 5:41). Here is an official letter/decree from the emperor Domitian to the procurator in Syria forbidding that practice:

> From the orders of the Emperor Domitian Caesar Augustus, son of Vespasian Augustus, to the procurator Claudius Athenodoros: Among the special problems demanding great concern I am aware that the attention of my divine father Vespasian Caesar was directed to the cities; privileges, intent upon which he commanded that the provinces be oppressed neither by forced rentals of beasts of burden nor by importunate demands for lodgings. But purposely or not…that order has not been enforced…. Therefore I order you, too, to see to it that no one requisitions a beast of burden unless he has a permit from me; for it is most unjust that the influence or rank of any person should occasion requisitions which no one but me is permitted to authorize. Let nothing, then, be done which will nullify my order and thwart my purpose…to come to the aid of exhausted provinces, which with difficulty provide for their daily necessities; let no one in defiance of my wish oppress them and let no one requisition a guide unless

he has a permit from me; for if the farmers are snatched away, the lands will remain uncultivated. [The rest is lost.]

Ancient letters are very formal. Scribes and secretaries employed what we might call "boiler plate" language. Here is a letter to a husband and wife, who have just lost a child. Even the phrases of comfort are typical formalities:

> Mnesthianus to Apollonianus and Spartiate, be brave! The gods are witness that when I learned about my lord, your son, I was grieved and I lamented as I would my own child. He was a person to be cherished. I was starting to come to you, when Pinoution stopped me, saying that you, my lord Apollonianus, had sent him word that I should not come because you would be away in the Arsinoite nome [= a region in Egypt]. Well, bear it nobly, for this rests with the gods... [The sender goes on to discuss business details.] I too have had a loss, a houseborn slave worth two talents. I pray that you remain well, my lord, together with my lord [= Apollonianus's father], in the benevolence of all the gods.

You can see from the example that travel plans, especially when the sender does not come as expected, are often at issue in private letters. You can also see that many people had little else to say in the face of death beyond "keep your chin up" or "it's the gods' will." No wonder Paul's Thessalonian converts were concerned about the death of fellow Christians (cf. 1 Thess 4:13–18).

Teaching in Letter Form

One group of ancient philosophers, called Cynics (after the Greek word for "dog"), taught that people should give up all the false values, pleasures, and weaknesses created by society. They wandered about giving advice, possessing as little as possible, and challenging the false values of society. Here are selections from letters of the philosopher Crates to his wife, Hipparchia, also a Cynic philosopher:

> It is not because we are indifferent to everything that others have called our philosophy Cynic, but because we robustly endure those things which are unbearable to them because they are effeminate or subject to false opinion. It is for this reason that they have called us Cynics. Stand fast, therefore, and live the Cynic life with us, for you are not by nature inferior to us, for female dogs are not by nature inferior to male dogs, in order that you may be freed even from nature, since all people are slaves

either by law [the Greek word for "law" also carries the meaning of "customary behavior"] or through wickedness.

Crates objects to his wife following the social convention of weaving clothes for him rather than studying philosophy:

> Some people have come from you bringing a new tunic, which they say you made so that I could have it for the winter. Because you care for me, I approved of you, but because you are still unschooled and not practicing the philosophy I have taught you, I censure you. Therefore, give up doing this immediately, if you really care, and do not pride yourself in this kind of activity, but try to do those things for which you wanted to marry me. And leave the wool-spinning, which is of little benefit, to the other women, who have aspired to none of the things you do.

Crates wants his wife to bring up their new son as a little Cynic philosopher. These are his instructions:

> I hear that you have given birth—and quite easily, for you said nothing to me. Thanks be to god and to you. You believe, it seems, that toiling is the reason you did not have to labor [at giving birth]. For you would not have given birth so easily, if you had not continued to toil as athletes do while you were pregnant. Most women, however, when they are pregnant become enfeebled; and when they give birth, those who survive child-birth bring forth sickly babies. Take care of this little puppy of ours. And you will take care of him, if you go into childrearing with your usual concern. Therefore, let his bath water be cold, his clothes a cloak [= a philosopher's cloak], his food be milk, yet not to excess. Rock him in a tortoise shell cradle, for they say that this protects against childhood diseases. When he is able to speak and walk, do not dress him with a sword as Aethra did Theseus, but with a staff, cloak and wallet [= Cynic philosopher's attire], which can guard men better than swords, and send him to Athens. As for the rest, I shall take care to rear a stork for our old age instead of a dog.

The Cynic answer to the problem of death was to practice separation from all the concerns with the body. Here is a selection from a long letter of Diogenes to Monimus on that topic:

> ...practice how to die, that is, how to separate the soul from the body, while you are still alive....The practice is very easy.

Examine carefully what death means to you. (Don't we do the same thing when we ask what is according to nature and what is according to custom?) For in death alone is the soul separated from the body, while in other experiences it is not at all. When a person sees, hears, smells or tastes, the soul is joined to it. It so happens that if we do not practice for death a difficult end awaits us. For the soul bemoans its bad luck as if it were leaving behind some darling boys, and it is released with much pain....But whenever it meets the souls of philosophers [after death] they flee from it, since they know that it has erred in life by yielding direction of the whole person to the worst part of its nature....If you have practiced how to die, this exercise will accompany you whenever you have to migrate from here. First, life itself will be sweet, for you will live free, a master and not someone who is enslaved, and in a short time you will strip away all that belongs to the body. Now this leads to harmony, when one keeps silent, exercises dominion and considers what the gods have provided for those who are moderate and restrain themselves from life like wild animals. For the rest of humanity, robberies and mutual slaughter are committed, not for great and noble reasons, but for trivial and common ones, and not against men only but against animals as well. For when it is a question of possessing more, eating, drinking and indulging in one's lusts, they are all worthless and no different from animals.

For some people, the life of the wandering Christian missionaries, dependent upon support from others, or, in Paul's case, upon working as a craftsman, seemed to be like that of the Cynics.

Paul's letters do not exactly resemble any of these types of letter. Most include concerns typical of the private letter, arranging for lodging, explaining changes in travel plans, and recommending associates to the community. Another dimension of Paul's letters resembles official public correspondence. Unlike imperial proclamations, they are not engraved in stone, but they are read and circulated in the churches. Therefore, we find liturgical language used in them. Where a private letter might have followed the opening "x to y, greetings" with the wish for the health of the recipient (see the end of the condolence letter above), Paul's letters usually contain an elaborate thanksgiving for the faith of the recipients. These passages often introduce motifs taken up in the letter. The simple phrase opening "greeting" or "grace and peace" in a Jewish letter is often expanded with references to Paul's status as apostle, to one or more co-senders, and to Jesus Christ and God. The conclusion of the Pauline letter may have further benedictions and greetings. Thus, you can see a new form of Christian letter emerging in the Pauline collection.

The letter as a personal exchange between the apostle and a particular church at the same time creates a new form of "public" speech that employs the common language of worship and exhortation in that community.

Paul's letters are also related to philosophic letters. Each letter contains sections of *paraenesis* (the word for ethical exhortation). Sometimes, as in the case of the question about death in 1 Thessalonians 4:13–18, Paul is answering a specific question from the church. In other cases, as in the exhortation to holiness in 1 Thessalonians 4:1–12, Paul is reminding the churches of what he had taught them. Diogenes' letter on practicing for death is an example of that type of exhortation. Christians have preserved Paul's letters because his words are not limited just to the peculiar problems in first-century churches. They speak about the roots of Christian faith and life.

Philemon: Letters and Apostolic Authority

We will begin our study with the shortest and most specific letter, Philemon. Just a single chapter, it is a personal letter from Paul and his associate Timothy to Philemon, Apphia, Archippus, and the church that gathers in Philemon's house (vv. 1–2). It concludes with further greetings from Ephaphras, also in prison with Paul, and other fellow workers (v. 23). Thus even Philemon is not just a private affair, but speaks to the whole church.

The occasion for the letter is quite specific. Paul, who had converted Philemon, is returning the runaway slave, Onesimus, to his master. Perhaps the slave had once seen Paul in his master's house. Legally, Philemon could punish the slave severely. Paul's offer to repay in verse 19 suggests that Onesimus may have also stolen from his master when he ran away. The situation was not unusual. Nor was it peculiar for a friend to intercede with the master for a runaway slave. Here is an example from a plea by the Roman author Pliny on behalf of a young freedman (*Epist.* 9.21):

> The freedman of yours with whom you said you were angry has been with me, flung himself at my feet and clung to me as if I were you. He begged my help with many tears....I believe he has reformed, because he realizes he did wrong. You are angry, I know, and your anger was deserved, but mercy wins the most praise when there was just cause for anger. You loved the man once, and I hope you will love him again, but it is sufficient for the time being if you let yourself be appeased. You can always be angry again if he deserves it, and will have more excuse if you were once placated. Make some concession to his youth, his tears, and your own kind heart, and do not torment him or yourself any longer—anger can only be a torment to your gentle self.

OUTLINE OF PAUL'S LETTER TO PHILEMON   [8–3]

Greeting (vv. 1–3)

Thanksgiving for the love and faith Philemon has shown (vv. 4–7)

Body of the letter: Plea for Onesimus who is being returned as a beloved brother in Christ (vv. 8–16)

Body closing: Settling "accounts" between Philemon and Paul, which will settle Onesimus's account as well (vv. 17–22)

Final greetings (vv. 23–25)

When you read Philemon, you will notice a different tone. Paul is not arguing in terms of "worldly" standards of behavior between masters and slaves. He is not pleading the case on the grounds of mercy. Instead, the argument begins with a new set of relationships, those between Christians. We are not told why Onesimus ran away. Instead, we are told that Onesimus is now a beloved brother in Christ. As such, he represents the apostle himself. Paul expects that Philemon will treat Onesimus as he would treat him. In fact, Paul suggests that any future "fellowship" between himself and Philemon depends upon the way in which Onesimus is received. Since Paul ends with a request that Philemon prepare a guest room for Paul, we presume that Paul expects the situation with Onesimus to be settled as he directs.

We cannot tell concretely which of several actions Philemon might have taken. Clearly, to receive Onesimus back as a fellow Christian means that Philemon must cancel all "debts and punishments" that he might have claimed against Onesimus the runaway. Clearly, Paul does not make the "if he does it again" type of argument that we find in Pliny's letter. However, since Paul also says that he would have liked to keep Onesimus with him, that Onesimus is his "heart," and that he would like Philemon to "refresh his heart," some scholars think that Paul is hinting that Philemon should free Onesimus and allow him to work with Paul.

You may also have noticed that, unlike Pliny, Paul claims the authority to "command" Philemon to do what is right, but says he would rather exhort him to act out of love (v. 8). By opening the body of the letter in this way, Paul turns from command to persuasion. If Philemon is persuaded to treat Onesimus as a fellow Christian rather than a runaway slave, then Philemon will once again demonstrate the faithfulness and love for which he is well known (vv. 5–7).

If you trace the themes of faith and love in these verses, you will find an example of Paul's use of chiasm. Verse 5 introduces the pair: love (A)–faith (B). Then verse 6 picks up Philemon's acts of faith (B'), and verse 7 concludes with his love (A'). By having love at the beginning and end of the thanksgiving in this way, Paul puts special emphasis on "love" as the virtue he wishes to stress.

The letter shows how Paul exercised his authority. We are never in any doubt that as the one responsible for converting Philemon to Christianity, Paul has the authority to tell him how the gospel is to be lived in concrete circumstances. Since the letter is directed to the church that gathers at Philemon's house, the whole community is called to recognize that authority. However, Paul does not exercise authority through command but by persuasion. Philemon has to see that the very foundation of Christian fellowship is at stake in how he responds to Onesimus. Maybe you think that the words are all a fancy cover-up for a command. But look at the letter again. Philemon is left with a certain freedom in how he receives Onesimus. Though he is clearly not to extract all the penalties that the law allowed, he may still put the debt down to Paul's credit; he may simply forgive Onesimus, who will then remain the Christian slave of a Christian master, or he may send Onesimus back to Paul to aid him. Furthermore, the letter makes any such response a positive sign of Philemon's virtue, that he is a person who loves and cares for the community.

Philemon presents a picture of equality in an early Christian church that does not do away with all authority or hierarchy. Paul refers to his converts, like Onesimus, as his "children." He has begotten them and remains responsible for them. Nevertheless, they also share in Paul's mission. They can be examples of love and goodness for others. The whole community must come to see that it is right to treat Onesimus in a new way, as a fellow Christian. They must all shift away from the worldly categories that make him a runaway slave. On the other hand, Christianity did not yet challenge slavery as such. Paul tells the slaves at Corinth that their "worldly" status as slaves does not matter in the Lord. Christians must all recognize that their real master is God. Therefore, the slave can make use of whatever situation he or she is placed in (1 Cor 7:20–24). We can also see that the foundation for rejecting slavery is Paul's insistence that Christians treat the slave and free person as equally brothers and sisters in the Lord. Thus, even this short letter contains an important message about how Christians are to relate to one another.

Missionary to the Gentiles: 1 and 2 Thessalonians

Paul wrote that God called him to preach the gospel among the Gentiles (Gal 1:16). Thessalonica was the largest city in Macedonia (pop. 80,000). Many different religious cults flourished in the city, including that of Heracles, the Discouri, Apollo, Aphrodite, the Egyptian deities Isis and Osiris, as well as the cult honoring the Roman emperor. Paul arrived after suffering persecution for preaching in Philippi (2:3). When he was unable to visit Thessalonica again, Paul sent his associate Timothy, who returned with a glowing report (2:17—

3:6). Paul then wrote 1 Thessalonians to encourage them to continue in their faith and to answer questions caused by the death of some believers (4:13–18). Much of the letter is taken up with expressions of thanksgiving. Paul is thankful for the way in which they received him when he worked among them as well as for the way in which they have continued to set an example for other Christians through their faithfulness.

Second Thessalonians is more difficult to locate. The letter suggests that the Thessalonians were confused by false claims of inspiration, false prophecies, or even letters claiming to be from Paul himself (2:1–2). Some people claimed that the Day of the Lord (= judgment) had come. The way in which that theme is introduced, "concerning the coming of our Lord Jesus Christ and our assembling to meet him" (2:1), implies that the readers were familiar with 1 Thessalonians 4:17, "we…will be caught up in the air…to meet with the Lord in the air." Against those alleging that the Day of the Lord had arrived, 2 Thessalonians insisted upon a number of mysterious events and figures that must come before the judgment. Presently God was restraining the Man of Lawlessness (2:3–10).

Second Thessalonians 3:6–13 reflects the ethical advice of 1 Thessalonians 4:11–12. Christians are to gain respect from others by working at a trade and minding their own affairs. Second Thessalonians warns against Christians who are not following this advice but are living in a disorderly way, meddling in the affairs of others.

Scholars have often noticed that 2 Thessalonians is not written in Paul's usual style. It is much more impersonal. None of the apostle's relationships with the community or of his travel plans is mentioned. Where 1 Thessalonians 1:3 bases the thanksgiving on the triad, "faith, hope, and love," 2 Thessalonians 1:3 speaks only of faith and love. Has the coming Day of the Lord ceased to be a source of hope? Where 1 Thessalonians speaks of rejoicing when Christ comes in judgment (e.g., 1:10; 4:17–18), 2 Thessalonians highlights the punishment to come upon the wicked (1:6–9; 2:8–12). Therefore, many interpreters suggest that some associate wrote 2 Thessalonians. Second Thessalonians confirms Paul's teaching about the coming of Christ and the way in which Christians should live. However, since the letter has no references to Paul's activities, Silvanus or Timothy might have written it after Paul had been imprisoned. Learning about the confusion in Thessalonica, they sent a letter to clarify the apostle's true teaching.

Both letters to the Thessalonians deal with the basics of Christian life as set out in 1 Thessalonians 1:9b–10. Christianity means converting from "idols to serve a living and true God." Most of us do not have the experience of having worshiped some other gods, but we still understand that Christians "convert" when they change their values or way of life from the "idols" of the modern world to serve God. Salvation is described in these verses as a future event. It means being spared the judgment that is to come upon all evil persons.

OUTLINES OF 1 AND 2 THESSALONIANS   [8–4]

1 Thessalonians

Greeting (1:1–2)

Thanksgiving for the faith, hope, and love of the Thessalonians (1:3–10)

The example set by Paul's ministry (2:1–12)

Condemnation of those unbelievers who persecuted Christians and hinder the spread of the gospel (2:13–16) [Because of its bitter remarks about the Jews, some scholars think this passage was added to the letter after Paul's death and the destruction of Jerusalem]

Paul's desire to visit Thessalonica again has been thwarted (2:17–20)

Timothy's visit and glowing report about the Thessalonians (3:1–13)

Exhortation: Live a life of holiness (4:1–12)

Exhortation: Resurrection of dead Christians at the parousia so that all will be with the Lord (4:13–18)

Exhortation: Be watchful, since we do not know when the Lord will return (5:1–11)

Exhortation: Relationships within the church (5:12–24)

Final greeting (5:25–28)

2 Thessalonians

Greeting (1:1–2)

Thanksgiving for the faith and love that saves Christians at the parousia (1:3–12)

What must happen before the parousia (2:1–12)

God has chosen Christians for salvation (2:13–17)

Prayer for the apostle and the steadfastness of Christians (3:1–5)

Exhortation: Christians are to follow Paul's example by working, living quietly, and doing good to others (3:6–13)

Exhortation: How Christians should treat one who will not follow Paul's words (3:14–15)

Final greeting (3:16–18)

Christians expect that this divine judgment will occur at the parousia, a Greek word that was used for the visit of an important figure like the emperor. Christians use the word *parousia* for the second coming of Christ when Christ will come with the power of God to judge the world. Paul and his associates must explain what kind of life Christians are to lead now as they await the second coming.

One of the identifying characteristics of Christian life is the love that Christians show for each other and even for those outside their group (e.g., 1 Thess 4:9–10). This theme appears repeatedly in Paul's letters. Another common theme is that of sexual morality (1 Thess 4:3–8). Even though pagan philosophers warned against being slaves to passion and various laws punished adultery, permissive attitudes toward male sexual behavior were the norm. Frescoes in houses at Pompeii depicted sexual passion, comedy was full of sexual humor, and the gods of well-known myths were hardly examples of restraint. Grounded in their Jewish heritage, Christians insisted that the only appropriate place for sexual activity was in marriage. Paul told Christians at Corinth that buying sex from prostitutes violates the holiness of the body, a temple of God's Spirit (1 Cor 6:12–20). Christians also opposed the homosexual use of young boys as a perversion of God's natural order (e.g., Rom 1:26–27).

Perhaps you were surprised to see Paul insisting that Christians work and live quietly, minding their own affairs. The educated elite despised those who had to work for a living. The "gentleman" was able to live off the proceeds of his farms and could spend the whole day in public affairs, study, discussions, and athletic activities, in the company of friends. Others might live such a "leisured life" if they could find a rich patron to support them. When Paul insisted that the Christian should not be dependent upon others, he had patronage relationships in view. Christians who had decided that the events leading to the end of the world were already underway (2 Thess 2:2) might have made the situation even worse, if they were taking advantage of the charity of other Christians.

The early Christians generally expected the return of Christ within their own lifetime. False teachers in 2 Thessalonians saw the final events in which evil would show its powers happening in their time (2 Thess 2:3–12). Paul rejected that position. The final evil times were delayed because they were being "held back" (2 Thess 2:6–7). First Thessalonians 5:1–11 draws upon apocalyptic teaching that goes back to Jesus. No one knows when the "end" is coming by signs. However, since Christians live in holiness and not in darkness, they have no reason to worry about the judgment day. Whenever the Lord comes, Christians will rejoice because it is a time of salvation.

Questions about the deceased seem to reflect a worry that those who had died would miss out when the Lord came. Paul appeals to earlier traditions. Jesus will not just come with the angels of God. He will bring the risen Christians so that the whole community will be restored. Paul insists that Christians should not treat death like those who had no hope for anything afterward. All Christians will be reunited in the Lord. In these short letters, Paul has sketched out the plan of a Christian life from the time of conversion to the glorious future that awaits Christians with the Lord.

Paul's Missionary Associates: Philippians

First Thessalonians 2:2 reports that Paul had been persecuted for preaching the gospel at Philippi. Nevertheless, Paul was able to establish a strong church there. His close personal ties with that church are evident in the letter. We learn from Philippians 4:15–16 that the Philippians supported Paul's missionary work in Thessalonica by sending him gifts. These verses speak of the Philippians as the only church which "entered into partnership in giving and receiving" with Paul. Legally persons could enter into "partnerships" on the basis of a verbal agreement. No written documents were required. A partnership was an association of persons formed for some common goal. Usually these objectives were commercial. All parties had to agree about the goal of their partnership and all would share the profits. Paul and the Philippians had such a relationship. Believers at Philippi shared in Paul's missionary efforts both through gifts that supported the apostle and through the members of the Philippian church who were Paul's "fellow workers" in spreading the gospel. In Philippians 4:2–3, Paul asked an unnamed Christian to help reconcile two women from that group, Syntyche and Euodia. Paul did not mention what caused their falling out, but he did indicate that they had worked side by side with him for the gospel.

Obviously, the "profit" from such a partnership cannot be material reward as it would be in business. What the Philippians shared with Paul was the "rewards" of his suffering (Phil 4:14; 1:7) and the "riches" that God bestows on those who sacrifice to serve the gospel (4:19; cf. 2 Cor 9:6–13).

A partnership lasted only as long as the original parties agreed about their common purpose and as long as all the original parties were alive. When those conditions ceased to exist, the partnership was dissolved. Paul alludes to both possibilities. There is the possibility that some people will preach the gospel out of rivalry or motives that are not part of the original intent (1:15–18). There is also the possibility that Paul will not be released but will die in prison (Phil 1:19–26).

Paul speaks of the "unity of spirit" that Christians should share (1:27–30). A business partnership depends upon unity about a single project. Paul shows that Christian unity goes beyond that to the example of humility and concern for others that was given by Christ. He uses the early hymn praising Christ's humiliation and exaltation (2:6–11) to make this point. Whatever happens to Paul, the Philippians must hold on to the truth of their faith. Paul compares himself to an athlete running to win a medal (a wreath was used for victors in Paul's time). He will know that his "race" is successful only if the churches that he has founded remain faithful to the gospel (2:15–16; also 3:12–16).

The tone of the letter is suddenly broken in chapter 3. Instead of continuing with the plans to send Timothy to Philippi and the account of Epaphroditus's serious illness (2:19–30), Paul begins to condemn some persons he calls "the dogs" (an expression of scorn and contempt in Greek), "evil workers," and "those who mutilate the flesh." Clearly, such persons are rival preachers. Paul's opposition to them is much stronger than the warning about divisions within his own missionary association.

Those whom Paul condemns in Philippians 3 hold views similar to the Judaizers mentioned in Galatians. They appear to have been Christian missionaries who taught that in order to become Christians the Gentiles had to follow at least some Jewish customs. Men had to be circumcised, so Paul attacks them for "mutilating the flesh." These Christians also had to follow Jewish food restrictions, so Paul says they have made their god their belly (Phil 3:19). And from what Paul says elsewhere, they must have observed some of the Jewish religious feasts. Even today, there are small groups of Christians who hold similar views. In addition to believing in Jesus, they also follow Jewish food rules and keep the Sabbath and other Jewish holidays.

Paul is violently opposed to this view. He uses one of his favorite antitheses, spirit vs. flesh, to contrast the two positions. The Judaizers, he claims, put confidence in what is fleshly or material. Christians, on the other hand, know that the salvation they have received from God is spiritual. Paul introduces another important theme in Philippians 3:7–11, "righteousness through faith" rather than the law. He will develop this theme in Galatians and Romans. The only way to become acceptable to God is through faith in Jesus Christ. And that faith is based on Christ having suffered for us. It is not a faith that needs to be complemented by taking on a Jewish way of life. Paul reminds his readers that he had all the qualifications of a righteous Jew (Phil 3:6). But he has set all that aside now that he believes in Christ (3:20–21).

The end of Philippians mentions Epaphroditus again (4:18) but gives no hint of the serious illness that had prevented him from returning to Philippi once he had delivered their aid to the apostle. Neither chapter 3 nor chapter 4 mentions the danger to Paul's life referred to in chapter 1. Perhaps these peculiarities are clues that Philippians, as we have it, was adapted from three shorter letters that Paul wrote to the church: (a) a brief note thanking the Philippians for the aid they had sent him; (b) a warning against Judaizing preachers; (c) a letter brought by Timothy when Paul thought he might be in danger of death and wanted to assure the unity of purpose in his missionary partnership.

OUTLINE OF PHILIPPIANS   **[8–5]**

Sections from other letters that have been used in Phil:

Note thanking the Philippians for their gift, which Epaphroditus had just brought (4:10–20)

Letter warning the Philippians against the preaching of "Judaizing" missionaries (3:1—4:1)

Letter delivered by Timothy as Paul's case is about to be decided:

Greeting (1:1–2)

Thanksgiving for the "partnership in the gospel" with the Philippians (1:3–11)

Paul's situation: Whatever happens, it will advance the gospel (1:12–26)

Philippians' situation: Continue to be "of one mind" in following Christ (1:27—2:18)

Timothy and Epaphroditus are to come to Philippi (2:19–30)

[Against the Judaizers]

Exhortation: Euodia and Syntyche are to be reconciled (4:2–3)

Exhortation: Rejoice and be at peace (4:4–9)

[Thank-you for the gift]

Final greetings (4:21–23)

Summary

These short letters from Paul's mission in Asia Minor and northern Greece have shown us what it meant for people to become Christians. Becoming a Christian required a break with one's past. The gods and goddesses worshiped by the Gentiles in both private clubs and civic cults had to be abandoned for the God of Jesus. Converts also had to change their behavior. Sexuality could not be an "indifferent" pursuit of pleasure. It had to be controlled so that it reflected holiness and not lust. The old power and hierarchy could not be left unchallenged when it might destroy the relationships between fellow Christians. Even though Philemon had a legal right to punish his runaway slave, Paul made it clear that as a fellow Christian with that same slave, he could not use that right.

Early Christian communities were places of intense personal relationships between people. Paul was deeply concerned with the welfare of the churches he founded. But he was often prevented from returning to visit them, so he relied upon his close associates like Timothy and upon his letters. We can see that the churches kept those letters. They were read to the whole community. When there was confusion about Paul's teaching, an associate wrote 2 Thessalonians to clarify the apostle's teaching. Both letters were then preserved. The Philippians appear to have put three of Paul's letters together into the longer version we have. Even Paul's thank-you note to them was preserved. Paul's letter to Philemon about Onesimus might have seemed to be just a private matter. Its importance might have ended when Paul visited after his release from prison. Nevertheless, the Christians in that church clearly thought that the message of even that small letter was important and so they preserved it.

All of these letters mention the suffering that Christians faced. Paul was forced out of Philippi and then Thessalonica and would then be forced out of Corinth because of the opposition to his preaching. He wrote Philemon and Philippians from prison, probably in Ephesus. For a time, he even thought that he might be executed. Paul admits in Philippians 3:6 that he had even persecuted the Christian movement. We learn in 1 Thessalonians that major figures like Paul were not the only ones who might suffer. Other Christians in both Judea and Thessalonica found themselves under attack. However, in all of this suffering, especially in Philippians with his life in danger, Paul's attitude is one of rejoicing. He constantly reminds his converts of the great salvation that they have from God. As long as they remain faithful to the gospel, no one can take that from them.

STUDY QUESTIONS

Facts You Should Know

1. Name the sources scholars use in constructing a chronology for Paul's life and indicate the difficulties they face in doing so.
2. What are the three main types of letter found in the ancient world? Explain how Paul's letters are both similar to and different from each type.
3. Describe the reasons Paul has for writing each of the following letters: (a) Philemon; (b) 1 Thessalonians; (c) Philippians.
4. What was the reason for writing 2 Thessalonians? Why do some scholars think that 2 Thessalonians might have been written by one of Paul's associates?
5. What was the special relationship between Paul and the church at Philippi? How was this relationship threatened by Paul's imprisonment?

Things to Do

1. Read Paul's appeal for the runaway slave in Philemon. Compare it with the letter from Pliny about a similar situation. What do the two letters have in common? Where are they different? What difference does the fact that Onesimus is now a Christian make in Paul's argument?

2. Read Paul's words of consolation in 1 Thessalonians 4:13–18. Compare them with the approach to death reflected in the letters by Mnesthianus and Diogenes. How does the Christian approach differ from that of an average person (Mnesthianus) and that of a philosopher (Diogenes)?
3. Find as many examples of the rhetorical features of Pauline letter writing (Chart 8-1) in 1 Thessalonians as you can.

Things to Think About

1. What do you imagine Philemon's response to Paul's letter was? Do you feel that Paul was really forcing Philemon to give up his own authority over the runaway slave?
2. In reading these short letters, what elements in early Christian community life seem to you to be most appealing? What message do they have for people today?

Chapter 9

CHRISTIANS: JEW AND GENTILE

Jewish/Gentile Christianity: Its Variations

The letters of Paul are our earliest evidence for the missionary expansion of Christianity. There we find Paul calling non-Jews to believe in God and in Jesus, God's Son. They are promised that Jesus saves those who believe in him from divine judgment (1 Thess 1:9–10). A major shift has occurred, from Jesus and his disciples preaching that the prophetic promises are being fulfilled among the Jewish population of Syro-Palestine, to Christians converting those with little or no knowledge of Judaism. Acts 10–11 tells a story of Peter converting the centurion Cornelius, a Jewish sympathizer. Acts 8:4 suggests that some believers began preaching to Samaritans and Gentiles after the first martyr, a Greek-speaking Jew named Stephen, died in Jerusalem. Matthew 28:16–20 has the risen Lord send the disciples out to all the nations. Ephesians 3:1–11 combines the tradition that Paul received a divine call to preach to the Gentiles (v. 3) with the tradition that this commission was given to apostles and prophets as a group (v. 5).

Matthew 10:5–6 limits the disciples' mission to the lost sheep of Israel. Some Christians continued to think of their mission as converting fellow Jews to believing in Jesus as God's messiah. Paul's initial zeal in persecuting Christians (Phil 3:6; Gal 1:13–15; 1 Cor 15:9) points to a movement under the jurisdiction of local Jewish authorities. The speech that Luke attributes to Stephen in Acts 7:1–53 employs salvation history in a highly polemical way, as evidence of Israel's consistent disobedience and idolatry that culminated in the crucifixion of Jesus. Such apparent hostility toward the religious traditions of Israel may have been the catalyst in the early conflicts between Jesus' followers and Jewish authorities. Christians today recognize such rhetoric as the ancient equivalent to negative campaign advertising. It selects sound bites and images that will inflame an audience. It does not represent the rich history of devotion to God preserved in Israel's scripture.

The New Testament provides only snapshots of key moments in the emergence of a mission to non-Jews. In Paul's Letter to the Galatians, we learn of a heated dispute over the conditions under which Gentile converts might be included in the Christian community (Gal 2:1–14). Paul reports that he, Barnabas, and other Christians from a church in Antioch that had both Jewish and non-Jewish members, and the leaders of the Jerusalem church, Peter, James, and John, had all agreed that Gentiles did not have to become converts to Judaism to be saved by believing in Jesus. However, he also mentions others who continued to reject that view. Paul writes Galatians in response to a fresh crisis. An anonymous group of teachers has persuaded believers there that Paul's "gospel" is incomplete (perhaps de-

Fragment of the inscription on the gates leading from the court of Gentiles into the court of the Israelites: "No Gentile to enter the fence and barrier round the temple. Anyone caught is answerable to himself for the ensuing death."

signed to gain easy success, Gal 1:6–10; 5:7–12; 6:12–13). Christians should be circumcised and should follow at least some of the religious practices of Judaism (Gal 4:10, observance of the Jewish religious calendar?).

We have an example of a gradual conversion to Judaism in the Jewish historian Josephus about King Izates of Adiabene. A Jewish merchant had converted the king's wives to "worship God in the manner of the Jewish people." Through them, the king was also won over. The king's mother, Helena, was won over by another Jew. The conversion of the royal house was completed when a third Jew arrived preaching a stricter interpretation of the law. He also persuaded the king to be circumcised (*Antiquities* 20.17–54).

Father Raymond Brown detected four different types of Jewish/Gentile Christianity in the New Testament (R. Brown and J. Meier, *Antioch and Rome* [Paulist, 1983], 1–9):

(1) *Gentiles who became Jews.* Like King Izates, some converts to Christianity may have become Jewish proselytes. They would have received circumcision and taken on the full observance of the Jewish law, which Paul says is required of anyone who seeks to "come under the law" (Gal 5:3). Paul refers to persons who are preaching this view among Gentile converts as "false broth-

ers" and "spies" in Galatians 2:4. They may also be the "dogs" against which he warned his Philippian converts (Phil 3:2–21). Acts speaks of persons "of the circumcision" (Acts 11:2) and "Pharisees" (15:5) holding such views.

(2) *Gentiles living within Israel.* This approach, probably that held by James and Peter (Gal 2:9; Acts 15), does not require that Gentiles convert to Judaism. However, it does assume that they will follow some Jewish observances. The decree attributed to James and the Jerusalem community (Acts 15:28–29) suggests that these requirements are those stipulated in the law (Lev 17–18) for non-Jews living within Israel. They are to reject all meat sacrificed to idols, keep from *porneia* (sexual immorality), that is, sexual relations within forbidden degrees of kinship, and avoid eating blood and meat that comes from an animal with the blood inside, that is, non-kosher meat. (City officials in Sardis were required to provide "suitable food" for the Jewish community in the public market; cf. Josephus, *Antiquities* 14.259–61.) Such rules would make it possible for Gentile converts to associate with Jewish-Christian counterparts in one community. Some scholars think that the episode in which Jewish Christians from Jerusalem refused to associate with Gentile Christians (= share the Lord's Supper) mentioned in Galatians 2:11–14 was the occasion for the ruling in Acts 15:29.

(3) *Gentiles not under the law.* This is the view of Paul and other Christians with whom he worked. Salvation comes to all persons through Christ. It does not come through the law, which is broadly understood as the body of religious practices that governed the lives of Jews. Since even Jews must believe in Christ to be saved, there is no reason to require that Gentiles come under the law in any sense (e.g., Gal 3:10–13). Nor does Paul think that the fact that Gentiles are not "under the law" creates a barrier between Jewish and Gentile Christians sharing the Lord's Supper in a single community (a view shared by Peter until objections were raised by "people from James"—Gal 2:11–14). Notice what this view does not say. It does not say that Jews who have come to believe in Jesus abandon their heritage. Romans 9:4–5 suggests that Paul felt that it was possible for Jewish-Christians to find salvation through faith in Christ and maintain their Jewish heritage. Paul affirms his own place as a "Hebrew" (Phil 3:5; 2 Cor 11:22; Rom 11:1). However, he argues that God is making the Gentiles heirs to the promises to Abraham without requiring that they follow the law (Rom 10:1–4; 11:17–24). Acts 21:20–21 pictures the negative campaign ad by Paul's opponents: that he was leading Jews to abandon their traditions.

(4) *Jesus has replaced Judaism.* The radical critique of the Jewish temple cult represented in the preaching of the Hellenists in Acts 6:8–14 also appears elsewhere in the New Testament. In John, Jesus symbolically replaces the Jewish temple and the major Jewish feasts. The way to God lies only through Jesus, not Moses (e.g., John 1:14–18). The Letter to the Hebrews insists that Jesus' sacrifice as eternal, heavenly high priest has replaced all the imperfect images in the

earthly cult of the Jewish temple and priesthood (e.g., Heb 7:1—10:18). Mark
2:22 insists that the "new wine" cannot be put into old wineskins. For these
Christians, scripture testifies to Jesus and provides instructive examples for Christians, but the coming of Jesus as messiah has led to a sharp break with the past.

Righteousness, Faith, and the Law

Many Christians today identify the fourth option as their view of the
relationship between Christianity and Judaism without considering the long
history of Christian anti-Semitism built on the conviction that Christ ended
the story of God's love for the Jewish people. Small groups of "Christian
Jews" do advocate some form of the first alternative. But the disappearance
of mixed communities of Jewish and non-Jewish Christians quickly deprived
the middle two options of their social grounding. The accommodations of the
Petrine position were simply forgotten. Paul's arguments about "righteousness through faith in Jesus and not through the law" were transformed into
timeless theological principle, no longer anchored in the practical problem of
how God's salvation was opening up to embrace all humankind. For later theology, the question became one of how God is gracious to humans who always
stand condemned as "sinners," not one of how those who were "sinners"
because they lived outside the law and its holiness could be righteous.

Scholars continue to argue over what led Paul to make such a radical dis-
junction between faith in Christ and "the law." Paul insists that he was blameless in his observance of the law (Phil 3:6). We cannot conclude that he found
in Christ freedom from an obligation that he was unable to meet as a Jew.

Paul links "zeal" for the law with his opposition to the church. Some
scholars find the key to our problem in this experience. The one failing that
Paul repeatedly admits is persecuting the church, though his later sufferings
on behalf of the gospel certainly made up for that failure (1 Cor 15:9–10; Phil
3:10). These scholars have suggested that Paul's description of how the "good
law" can be "used" by sin to entrap humans in a "sin they do not even want
to do," in bondage and death (Rom 7:13–25), is based on Paul's experience.
When Paul was acting out of his own zeal for the law, he found himself
opposed to God. Zeal for the law led him to consider the "crucified Christ,"
the source of righteousness for all humanity, accursed, as he says in Galatians
3:13–14. Thus, Paul speaks of his own conversion as nothing less than a complete reversal of everything he had valued in the past (Phil 3:7–8). Paul could
not have freed himself from the impasse set by the law; only God acting in
Christ could do that (e.g., Phil 3:9–14; Rom 8:1–3).

Paul's reflection on the experience of "bondage to sin and death," even
by those who know the "good law," also has echoes of the story of Adam's disobedience. Romans 5:12–21 presents the figures of Adam and Christ as type

and antitype. Sin and death came to dominate humanity through Adam. Giving the law to Moses did not erase sin. It might be said to have increased it, since the law provided the norm against which sin is measured. However, if Adam's sin brought all that on humanity, Christ's death brought much more, the "free gift" of righteousness that leads to eternal life. Romans 7:7–13 reflects part of this story of how "sin" exploits the "commandment," which is good in itself, to bring about death.

Freedom for the Gentiles: Galatians

The location of the churches to which Galatians is written remains a puzzle, since Paul does not mention any specific cities. Had he been in the Roman province of Galatia, one would expect Paul to mention cities such as Pisidian Antioch, Iconium, Lystra, and Derbe, the scene of a missionary effort by Paul and Barnabas in Acts 13:13—14:20. Therefore, some scholars suggest that Paul is referring to an ethnic region, the "Galatian country" (Acts 16:6), which is located in the central highlands of Anatolia, where tribes of Celts had settled in Hellenistic times. Paul's *O Galatai* in Galatians 3:1 means "O Celts" or "O Gauls." Roman roads connected the three small cities in this area with such cities as Sardis, Nicomedia, and Paul's home city of Tarsus. Paul's mission in Galatia was the result of "weakness of the flesh" (4:13). He may have fallen ill while journeying through the region.

OUTLINE OF GALATIANS   **[9–1]**

Greeting (1:1–5)

Curse against those who preach another gospel (1:6–10)

Proof of Paul's gospel based on past events (1:11—2:14)

    (a) Paul's call as apostle to the Gentiles (1:11–24)
    (b) Jerusalem agreement about the Gentile mission (2:1–10)
    (c) Antioch episode (2:11–14)

Thesis: Salvation comes only through faith in Christ (2:15–21)

Proofs from Galatians' experience, scripture, and Christian tradition (3:1—4:31)

    (a) Galatians received the Spirit apart from the law (3:1–5)
    (b) Promise to Abraham is different from the law whose curse Christ removed (3:6–14)
    (c) The promise is fulfilled in Christ; the law is a later addition (3:15–20)
    (d) The law acts as "custodian" until all could become heirs of Abraham through Christ (3:21–29)

Continued

Continued

> (e) Gentiles were "under elemental spirits" until their adoption as heirs
>   in Christ (4:1–7)
> (f) Galatians' experience of conversion and relationship with Paul (4:8–
>   20)
> (g) Abraham's two sons (4:21–31)
>
> Conclusion: Maintain your freedom in Christ (5:1–12)
>
> Ethical applications: Freedom in the community (5:13–6:15, 17)
>
> (a) Freedom is walking in the Spirit/Love (5:13–26)
> (b) Maxims for relations between Christians (6:1–10)
> (c) Final warning against Judaizers (6:11–15, 17)
>
> Final Blessing and Greetings (6:16, 18)

Paul does not have any immediate plans to return (Gal 4:20). Nor does he indicate the source of his information about the crisis in the Galatian churches, only that people are preaching a "different gospel" from the one he had preached (1:7–9). They are insisting that believers be circumcised (5:2–12; 6:12) and that they observe certain Jewish holidays (4:10) and perhaps other provisions of the law, though Galatians 5:3 and 6:13 suggest that the Galatians were not becoming Jewish proselytes. Paul insists that for Gentile converts to seek to be "under the law" in any sense would be as bad as the slavery to the various spirits of the universe they had worshiped as pagans (4:8–9). Paul is so disturbed by the problems in Galatia that he omits the thanksgiving for the community's faith with which he usually begins a letter. Instead, he lashes out, cursing anyone who perverts the gospel message (1:6–10).

You can see from the outline that much of the argument against the Judaizing position refers to past events that Paul claims vindicate the truth of his teaching. Salvation comes through faith in Jesus. Attempting to "add the law" to that faith is really a rejection of that salvation (Gal 2:15–21; 3:1–5; 5:1).

During the argument, Paul sets up a number of antitheses. These paired opposites create negative associations with the opposition's proposed obedience to the law. Here are some of the most prominent:

faith in Jesus Christ	works of the law
live to God	died to the law
death of Christ	righteousness through the law
Spirit	flesh
blessing of Abraham (promise)	curse of the law
freedom	slavery (to law; to "elemental spirits")
faith working through love	freedom used as occasion for desires of the flesh

Surveying the various types of Jewish Christianity shows that Paul's treatment of the law would be controversial in Christian circles. Paul's opponents might even have used the example of Abraham's two sons to argue that the Galatians must adopt circumcision and some Jewish practices in order to be among the "free offspring" of Abraham, the descendants of Isaac. Even Abraham's older son, Ishmael, was circumcised as the symbol of God's covenant (Gen 17:9–23).

Paul rejects that interpretation of the story. Isaac is the child of promise just as Christians who are born "according to the Spirit" are (Gal 4:28–29). He finds in Genesis 21 an analogy with the present situation in which the "law-free" Christians are persecuted by those of the circumcision (Gal 4:29; cf. 5:11; 6:12).

Paul also invokes baptism to support his claim that "in Christ" differences between Jew and Gentile are abolished. Galatians 3:27–28 reflects a formula of the baptismal ritual. Other echoes of the formula are found in 1 Corinthians 12:13 and Colossians 3:11. It proclaims that baptism brings into being a "new human" in whom the fundamental divisions between humans—Jew/Gentile; slave/free; male/female—are eradicated. First-century Jewish interpretations of Genesis 1:26–27 thought of Adam as originally created "male/female." This androgynous Adam possessed the image of God as a "garment of light." After the fall, humans were divided into male and female, became mortal, and the garment of light was replaced by the "garment of skin." Colossians 3:10 speaks of the renewal of the image of the creator. Elsewhere Paul holds that our transformation into the image of the heavenly Christ occurs at the resurrection (1 Cor 15:42–49). But the baptismal rite symbolizes the truth of this new reality. Galatians 4:5–6 refers to another aspect of the baptismal ceremony. The Christian cries in the Spirit, "Abba, Father!" The Spirit by which the new Christians proclaim their adoption as children of God is the Spirit of God's Son. Therefore, Paul insists that the Galatians know from their own experience that they are heirs to the promises of salvation. They do not need any additional religious rites to assure their salvation.

The section of the letter devoted to ethical encouragement picks up themes from the body of the letter. Paul insists that the Christian, who is not under the law, will live a life that fulfills the positive teaching of the law because it is based on love (Gal 5:14). Some scholars suggest that the appeal of the Judaizers' preaching lay in its ethical seriousness. Galatians 6:1 explains how to deal with believers who have sinned. Paul expects Christians to handle this difficulty by mutual exhortation. He speaks of such actions as fulfilling the "law of Christ." Those who walk by the Spirit do not need to supplement their freedom in Christ with formal allegiance to the law. Paul speaks of constantly seeking to "do good" (6:9). Actions prompted by the Spirit are not ones that can be captured by laws (5:22–23). Yet they are the ones that the Christian who has "been crucified with Christ" will seek out because Christians no longer live as people dominated by what Paul calls the "passions of the flesh" (5:24). The examples that he gives are not limited to what we might think of as bodily desires. They include a variety of "social sins" like jealousy, anger, enmity, strife, selfishness, divisiveness, and envy (5:19–21, 26). Paul's vice list is open-ended. The vices listed are only examples of more general types of activity.

Righteousness and Salvation History: Romans

Scholars are uncertain about the relationship between the arguments in Romans and the actual situation of the Christian house churches in Rome. Paul did not found the church there. He hopes to come to Rome after delivering the collection for the poor in Jerusalem (Rom 1:10–13; 15:23–33). Paul plans to take his missionary work west to Roman Spain. He considers his work in Asia Minor and Greece to be completed. The greetings in chapter 16 include some twenty-five people. Prisca and Aquila (Rom 16:3) had been associated with Paul at Corinth (Acts 18:2–3) and then were living at Ephesus (1 Cor 16:19; Acts 18:11, 18–19, 24–26). Paul greets Epaenetus, the first convert in Asia (Rom 16:5), and writes a letter of recommendation for Phoebe, who is the patroness of the church in the eastern port of Corinth (Rom 16:1–2). Therefore, some scholars think that chapter 16 belongs to a copy of Romans that was sent to Christians at Ephesus as a farewell. (Acts 20:17–18 has Paul summon the leaders of the Ephesian community for a farewell.) According to this view, Romans is a summary of Paul's experience in Asia Minor and Greece. Its concern with the problem of righteousness through faith and the relationship between the Christian movement and Judaism in God's plan is dictated by Paul's impending visit to Jerusalem where he anticipates opposition from both Jewish and Jewish Christian leaders (Rom 15:30–31).

Other scholars think that Prisca and Aquila, who had left Rome when Claudius expelled Jews for rioting at the name of "Chrestus," had returned. The others whom Paul refers to as associates and heads of household churches (Rom 16:5, 11, 14, 15) have also migrated to Rome. A number of these people are Jewish converts to Christianity. The returnees may have found a Christian community quite different from the earlier churches that had emerged from Rome's extensive Jewish community in the 40s. Paul's words to the Gentiles warning against assuming superiority to "unbelieving Israel" (Rom 11:13–32) suggest a community that is largely Gentile. Paul insists that God has given faith to those who have heard the gospel message. God is also behind the "hardening of Israel" and yet may "undo" that hardening. The Gentiles have benefited from the "disobedience" of Israel. But Israel remains the people of God's promise.

The situation of the Roman church led Paul to reflect on the place of Israel in salvation history. He is much more positive about Israel in Romans 9–11 than he was in the allegory of Abraham's two sons in Galatians 4:21–31.

There he simply treated the present-day Jerusalem and her "children" as slave descendants of Abraham. Only Christians are the children of promise. In Romans, Paul is no less committed to the view that salvation comes to both Jew and Gentile through faith, but he leaves the story of Israel open to further saving acts of God. Paul's argument about the promise to Abraham in Romans 4 is also different from the version in Galations. First, he argues that scripture bases Abraham's righteousness on his faith. Abraham had that faith before he was circumcised. Paul even allows that circumcision served as a sign of Abraham's faith (Rom 4:11). In this way, Abraham is father of both circumcised and uncircumcised believers (4:12). The example of God's promise to Abraham's descendants drops the idea of two sons, slave and free. Paul only tells the story of Sarah and Abraham's trust in the promise God made (4:16–24).

Paul still wrestles with the problem of the law. He opens Romans with an extensive argument convicting all people, Jew and Gentile, of sin. Only faith can save humanity (Rom 1:16—3:31). Romans 3:24–26 uses a pre-Pauline formula to suggest how the death of Jesus "saves" a sinful humanity. God is the primary actor in the drama. Scholars have suggested that this formula refers to ideas connected with the death of the Maccabean martyrs. God responded to their faithfulness by forgiving the sins of the people and freeing the land from its oppressive rulers. This formula presents the death of Jesus as expiation for all the sins of humanity, which God had not punished as they deserved. Paul insists that the gift of righteousness to a sinful humanity does not destroy the law. By demonstrating God's righteousness, the gracious gift upholds the law (3:26–31). Romans 5:6–11 returns to the theme of Christ's death for a sinful humanity. Here it is presented as an act that reconciles those who are "enemies" to God.

You may notice from the outline of Romans that there is a structural parallel between the argument in chapters 5 to 8 and that in Galatians 5. Paul follows his arguments that Christ has freed Christians from the law with a reflection on what it means for the Christian to have "died with Christ" and to "live in the Spirit." Paul also makes use of references to shared convictions about baptism (Rom 6:3–5) and to the gift of the Spirit of God through which the "adopted children" call God "Abba" (Rom 8:14–17) as he had done in Galatians 3:26—4:6.

OUTLINE OF ROMANS [9–2]

Greeting (1:1–7)

Thanksgiving: Paul's desire to preach in Rome (1:8–15)

Thesis: God's salvation comes through faith for both Jew and Gentile (1:16–17)

Continued

Continued

Salvation through faith in Christ as God's response to the sinfulness of humanity (1:18–3:31)

Abraham as the ancestor of all believers (4:1–25)

As Adam's sin brought death to all, so Christ's sacrifice brings reconciliation with God and life for all (5:1–21)

The free gift of righteousness in Christ creates freedom, not increased sin (6:1–23)

(a) Baptism is sharing in Christ's death so that we will share life with God (6:1–11)

(b) "Dying" in baptism means dying to the passions that made us slaves to sin (6:12–23)

The law could not bring righteousness and life (7:1–25)

(a) Human example: The law only binds those who are alive, not the Christian who has died with Christ and now lives by the Spirit (7:1–6)

(b) Sin was able to pervert the law to awaken passions that led to death [Adam story implied] (7:1–12)

(c) The law itself is good but the "fleshly" nature of humans makes it possible for sin to enslave us even when we want what is good [Paul reflecting on his story] (7:13–25)

Christ has freed us from bondage by making life in the Spirit possible (8:1–39)

(a) Freedom is life in Christ/the Spirit and is opposed to the slavery of sin which works through the flesh (8:1–11)

(b) Baptism is our adoption as children of God/Abba in the Spirit (8:12–17)

(c) The Spirit helps us live in this world of creation waiting for its final redemption when we will have the image of Christ (8:18–30)

(d) Nothing can separate us from the love of God in Christ (8:31–39)

Though Israel is rejecting Christ now, God may still bring the people of the promises and covenants to salvation (9:1–11:36)

Ethical instructions on mutual love, service, and tolerance in the Christian community (12:1–15:13)

Paul's mission and plans to come to Rome (15:14–33)

Recommendation for Phoebe and greetings to fellow workers (16:1–16)

Final warning and greetings from Paul's associates (16:17–23)

[Doxology missing from many early manuscripts (16:25–27)]

Romans contains an extensive section of ethical exhortation (12:1—15:13). Many of the themes in this instruction, such as the necessity for Christians to love one another, the command to love and not retaliate against enemies, and the picture of the church as a body in which people exercise different ministries for the good of all (12:1–21), appear in Paul's earlier letters. But there are two new points, which may be linked to particular problems faced by Christians in Rome.

The first new instruction occurs in Romans 13:1–7. Christians are to be subject to the governing authorities. Paul echoes a common theme in writers of the time when he insists that political authority has a divine origin. Its purpose is to promote what is good and punish evil. Since the Christian seeks to do good, he or she has nothing to fear from governing authorities and should be respectful of the role God has given them. In this context, Paul explicitly instructs Christians to pay taxes and revenues to the appropriate persons (vv. 6–7). This concrete detail is missing from the other New Testament example of this teaching (1 Pet 2:13–17). Therefore, some interpreters think that Paul was concerned about the social rebelliousness against customs duties that the emperor Nero had imposed. The previous emperor Claudius had already expelled "Jews" from Rome for rioting at the name of Christ. Some of those expelled are greeted in Romans 16. Furthermore, many of the Christians in the city may have been artisans, merchants, and traders—exactly the persons most affected by the disputed levies. Paul makes obedience to the ruling authorities a matter of conscience (Rom 13:5).

The second new element emerges in chapter 14. Paul speaks of Christians who differ over religious customs: some obey dietary restrictions, others do not; some consider particular days holy, others do not (14:1–23). Though Paul himself does not think that the Jewish rules about clean and unclean foods need apply to Christians (14:14), he argues that Christians should tolerate their mutual differences in love. The only thing that counts is whether someone is serving the Lord (vv. 6–9). Since the conclusion of the whole section speaks of Jesus welcoming both Jews and Gentiles (15:7–12), the differences to which Paul refers may have been those separating different "house churches" in the city of Rome. Some of these assemblies would have been made up of the original converts from within the Jewish community. Others are Gentile converts or fellow Jews who had worked with Paul in the mission to the Gentiles in Asia Minor and Greece. The first group may have continued to follow Jewish customs about kosher food and observance of the Sabbath and other holidays. The second group would have considered itself free from such obligations. Paul is not trying to force all of the household churches in Rome into the same mold. Instead, he argues that as part of their service to the Lord, they should live together in harmony (15:5–6).

Summary

The problems of Jewish/Gentile Christianity that Paul faced in Galatians and Romans vanished as Christianity came to be a religion independent of its Jewish birthplace. Christians read the Jewish scriptures as their own by looking as Paul did for ways in which those scriptures pointed to Christ. They also found there general examples of how to live that were not tied to the specific practices of Judaism. Certainly the "freedom in Christ," which Paul worked so hard to defend, became a permanent possession of the Christian churches.

In the process, Paul also came to understand how sin could capture all people, even those who might consider themselves "righteous." He was able to see that our salvation comes to us only from God's love in Christ. We are not saved by our own efforts. At the same time, Paul knew that God's love is not an excuse for a freedom that says that anything goes. He insisted that the baptized Christian really has received a gift of the Spirit and can live by the Spirit. We have seen that Paul knows that Christians will not always live up to their ideals. He tells the Galatians that they will have to correct each other and bear with each other's failings. He tells the Christians in Rome that they are not to judge and condemn one another.

Along with Paul's insights about sin and righteousness, Romans has important lessons to teach Christians for their daily relationships. Christians are not radical revolutionaries. They support the authorities and laws that are necessary to have order and goodness in society. Christians should also avoid thinking that the Jews and others who may reject Christ are automatically God's enemies. God may yet find a way to bring about the change of heart necessary for them to be heirs to the promises in Christ. Finally, Paul's emphasis on the need for the different Christian house churches in Rome to accept each other should teach us how to relate to Christians who are of different churches. Their particular rules, customs, and beliefs may be different from ours, but what is important is that all Christian groups are seeking to serve the Lord.

STUDY QUESTIONS

Facts You Should Know

1. Describe the four different approaches to the conversion of Gentiles reflected in the New Testament.
2. What is the occasion for the writing of Galatians? How does the story of the conversion of King Izates help us understand the attraction of Judaizing among the Gentile converts of Galatia?

3. What is the relationship between Paul's teaching on "righteousness through faith in Christ" and the conflicts over the conditions under which Gentiles are to be included in the Christian communities?
4. What lessons does Paul expect the Galatians to draw from their experience of baptism and conversion?
5. Describe the situation in the Roman church as we see it reflected in Romans.

Things to Do

1. Read through Galatians, making a list of as many different antitheses as you can find. What are some of the other words that appear in the negative column along with *law*? How might a Jew or Jewish Christian who faithfully observes the law as God's revelation respond to this set of associations?
2. Read Romans 1–8 and Galatians 2:11—5:12. How is the treatment of Abraham different in the two letters? How does Paul argue for the universality of sin and the necessity of righteousness through faith in Romans? How does he argue the case for righteousness through faith in Galatians?
3. List all the allusions to baptism in Galatians and Romans. How does Paul picture the lives of persons being changed by becoming part of Christ?

Things to Think About

1. What are the implications of Paul's picture of the place of Israel in salvation history in Romans 9–11 for relationships between Christians and Jews today?
2. What do Christians today have to learn from Paul's insistence upon mutual tolerance in Romans 14–15 and on the unity of all in Christ in Galatians 3:16–18?

Chapter 10

DIVISIONS IN CORINTH

The Urban Environment of Corinth

Paul's Corinth was a city of "self-made men," descendants of the initial colonists who had turned Corinth into a thriving city in two generations. The city controlled two harbors, Cenchreae leading to Asia and Lechaeum to Italy, as well as the major land route from the Peloponnese. Merchants, envoys, pilgrims, and other travelers passed through the city. Travelers used to eastern cities in which the population overflowed the city walls were impressed by the open-spaces within the city walls of Corinth, which even included wooded hills at the base of the city's acropolis.

We hear of the city's temples and shops in Paul's letters to the Corinthians. Some Christians apparently continued to attend banquets thrown by their pagan friends in honor of the gods (1 Cor 10:18–21). Others worried about whether they could eat meat from sacrificed animals that was being sold in the meat markets (*marcellum*—Paul uses the Latin word in Greek dress in 1 Cor 10:25). Paul himself labored at leather working in the shops of the city (1 Cor 9:3–19). Excavations of the north market area show the shops to have been about 4 meters high and 4 meters deep and varying in width from 2.8 to 4 meters. Some had a door or window communicating with the next shop. The door was their only source of light. These shops would have been drafty and difficult to heat. Perhaps Paul's "big writing" (Gal 6:11) was caused by the effects of working long hours in cold, drafty conditions.

We will see that Paul constantly had to remind Corinthian Christians not to exalt themselves over others. Boasting and even expecting the apostles to demonstrate their authority in signs such as persuasive speech, revelations, and speaking in tongues turn out to be pervasive faults among the Corinthians. This tendency is consistent with the city itself. Its leading families could include descendants of slaves and other colonists who would not have obtained such distinctions in an older city with an established aristocracy. An inscription says that the limestone pavement east of the city's theater was given by "…Erastus in return for his aedileship, at his own expense." This pavement dates to before the mid-first century. Scholars wonder if this Erastus is the same one mentioned in Romans 16:23 as a "treasurer of the city." If the two are the same man, "treasurer" would have been an office held prior to becoming *aedile*. The *aediles*—two were elected each year—served under the two city magistrates. Their responsibilities included managing the public markets of the city.

Paul's readers might have had an image of the fourteen thousand-seat theater flash through their minds when he spoke of the apostle as a "spectacle" (*theatron*) to the world (1 Cor 4:9). When Paul used athletic imagery to describe himself (1 Cor 9:24–27), they could have imagined the great Isthmian games celebrated in honor of Poseidon. The games were held in the spring of AD 51. Paul himself could have repaired tents that housed those who traveled to the games. The officials in charge of these games had their offices in the upper agora of the city.

Finally, archaeology also tells us something about the tensions that arose when Corinthian Christians gathered for the Lord's Supper (1 Cor 11:17–34). When the Corinthians met to celebrate the Lord's Supper, which took place during a meal, some people were eating well and even becoming drunk. Others, the poor members of the community, were being left out and going hungry. At the time, a wealthy person might give a banquet at which his special friends were served the best food and wine, but lesser-status invitees would be served small portions of poor food and wine. Someone like Gaius (Rom 16:23) was wealthy enough to invite the whole church to meet at his house. Archaeologists have excavated such houses with dining rooms that opened off the atrium.

Even in the wealthiest houses, only forty or fifty people could assemble at one time. Couches for the host and friends to recline in a typical dining area could accommodate only nine or so guests. Others would be crowded sitting in the courtyard. Such customs reinforce social distinctions and they turn up when Corinthian believers gather for the Lord's Supper (1 Cor 11:33). Paul will insist that the Lord's Supper is not like a private dinner party. All Christians are equal in the Lord. Believers must see to it that their behavior treats all members of the church in this way. Otherwise, Paul says, they are really mistreating the "body of Christ."

Paul and the Corinthian Community

Paul came to Corinth from Athens, where he does not appear to have had much success (1 Thess 3:1). He spent about eighteen months in Corinth before he was forced to leave the city. By the time Paul wrote 1 Corinthians, there were groups of Christians meeting in different house churches in both the city itself and in its seaports. Since Romans 16:23 makes special mention of the fact that the "whole church" could meet in Gaius's house, the individual house church gatherings may have comprised no more than twenty people.

Paul maintained constant contact with the church in Corinth. A letter written prior to 1 Corinthians no longer survives (1 Cor 5:9). He had heard about divisions between Christians at Corinth from members of "Chloe's household," presumably her slaves or freedmen traveling on business (1 Cor 1:11). The Corinthians themselves wrote asking Paul to resolve some questions (1 Cor 7:1). In addition, Paul dispatched his associate Timothy to visit Corinth and reinforce his teaching (1 Cor 4:17; 16:10). The Corinthians also learned about Christianity from the preaching of another missionary, Apollos (1 Cor 3:5–4:7). Acts 18:24–28 identifies him as a Jew from Alexandria who had been converted at Ephesus by Priscilla and Aquila. Some of the Corinthians had formed parties around the names of famous apostles—Paul, Apollos, and Peter (Cephas, 1 Cor 1:11–13). We do not have any direct evidence that Peter had preached in Corinth as had Paul and Apollos, so the Peter party might have formed based on reports about that famous apostle. Paul also speaks sarcastically of an alleged "Christ" group.

Just as he did not approve of divisions at the Lord's Supper, so Paul does not approve of these divisions either, even though one group claims to be his supporters. He insists that it is not possible to divide Christ. Furthermore, only Christ is responsible for our salvation. The various apostles are just servants who will eventually be judged on the quality of their labor in preaching the gospel.

A painting of the celebration of the Lord's Supper from the catacomb of Priscilla in Rome, dating to the first half of the second century AD. The fresco depicts six men and a woman at a table. The sacrament of the Eucharist was performed over the altar tomb.

Episodes of division and misunderstanding continued throughout Paul's association with the Corinthians. Some people may have thought that Paul was responsible for the fact that Apollos had not returned to preach there. Paul claims that he had urged Apollos to go, but Apollos had decided it was not the right time (Cor 16:12). Some objected to Paul's working at a trade. The educated elite thought it was disgraceful to be compelled to work at a trade, especially one like leather working, which meant being confined in a small shop working "like a slave." Paul was not able to support himself entirely. The church at Philippi sent him assistance when he was preaching in Thessalonica and again when he was in prison. The Corinthians also knew that other apostles were supported by those to whom they preached. Well-off Christians may have even felt insulted that Paul continued to work at a slavish trade rather than accept their patronage. Paul devotes 1 Corinthians 9 to this topic. He admits that most of the other apostles like Peter receive support for themselves and their families. He also notes that both the Old Testament and Jesus teach that those who preach have the right to material support. However, Paul does not think that having a right means that he has to exercise it. He could never help preaching the gospel. God's call makes it impossible for him to do otherwise. Nevertheless, he can show that he is also preaching out of his own free will by giving up his right to demand support from the church and working at his trade instead. That way he can preach the gospel for free. Even though laboring adds to the hardships of his apostleship (cf. 1 Cor 4:12), Paul's willingness to take on this suffering means that he can boast about the freedom with which he preaches (9:15–18).

You can see that Paul's relationship with the Corinthians is very complicated. As the founder of the community, he is responsible for it just as a father is responsible for the behavior and well-being of his children (1 Cor 4:14–21). He has authority over the community, which he exercises through his letters and his associates. However, Paul is not in control of everything that happens in the different house churches. Nor is he the only source of missionary preaching, since Christians traveling though Corinth bring news of other apostles like Peter, and other missionaries, like Apollos, preach in the community.

When we turn from 1 Corinthians to 2 Corinthians, we find an even more complicated situation. First Corinthians may have solved some of the concrete problems about the Lord's Supper and spiritual gifts like tongues and prophecy and the questions about marriage. At least they are no longer mentioned. Nor are the "parties" attached to Paul, Apollos, and Peter in evidence. Nevertheless, new problems have arisen and some old suspicions remain. Accusations surround Paul's support. These might have been fueled by charges that the collection for the poor at Jerusalem (1 Cor 16:1–4) was really going to the apostle (2 Cor 11:7–11; 12:14–18). The collection had not yet been completed. Second Corinthians 8–9 makes an extended appeal for the Corinthians and churches in the province of Achaia to imitate the generosity of much poorer Christians in Macedonia. During a visit that Paul had paid to Corinth between the two letters, some incident insulted or humiliated the apostle. He fired off an anguished and tearful letter (2 Cor 2:1–4). Cancellation of another planned visit to Corinth led to accusations about his integrity (1:15–24). Second Corinthians 2:5–11 and 7:8–16 then indicate that reconciliation between Paul and the Corinthians had taken place. Paul's tearful letter and a subsequent visit by Titus had caused a change of heart. In addition, a member of the community, responsible for the affront to the apostle, had been disciplined. Paul wants the Corinthians to forgive the man.

However, this tone of reconciliation does not fit the bitter sarcasm of 2 Corinthians 10–13. There Paul rejects charges against himself and his mission made by outsiders whom he refers to as "false apostles," "super-apostles," who boast in their spiritual achievements (10:12; 11:4–6, 12–15; 12:11–12). Paul says that he is about to come to Corinth for the third time. If the Corinthians do not change their attitude, they will find Paul a stern father (12:14; 13:1–2, 10–11). Some scholars think that 2 Corinthians 10–13 was taken from the "letter of tears." The cancelled visit would be the one referred to in 12:14. Nevertheless, other scholars point out that these chapters reflect an impassioned defense of the apostle against the claims of outside "apostles" who are trying to discredit the divine authorization of Paul's ministry. They do not refer to the painful visit. According to this view, the reconciliation of the earlier chapters has again broken apart. Paul must face yet another challenge to his apostleship.

Many scholars think that 2 Corinthians 1–9 was not from a single letter either. It is easy to see that chapters 8 and 9 refer to the collection for the poor at Jerusalem. Second Corinthians 8:16–24 tells the community that Titus and those with him are authorized to complete the collection. The trustworthiness of these men guarantees that the money will be used for honorable purposes (2 Cor 8:20). You will notice that none of the defensiveness of chapters 10 to 13 occurs in this section. Since Paul refers to the example of the Macedonians twice (8:1–6; 9:1–5), and in the second instance speaks of "Achaia," the province of which Corinth was the capital, in slightly different terms than he speaks of the addressees in 8:6, the two chapters might even be separate appeals, one to churches in Corinth, another to the province as a whole. You may also notice some "breaks" in chapters 1 to 7. Paul takes up the theme of reconciliation in 2:1–13 only to break off into a lengthy description of true apostolic ministry in 2:14—7:1. With 7:2–16, the tone of rejoicing and reconciliation as well as the narrative of events leading to reconciliation returns. First Corinthians 6:11–13 takes the form of an appeal picked up again at 7:2. That appeal is interrupted by a dualistic exhortation that tells Christians to have nothing to do with unbelievers. These exhortations seem very unusual for Paul, who had told the Corinthians in 1 Corinthians 5:9–13 that he did not mean for them to avoid sinful non-Christians. Is 2 Corinthians 6:14—7:1 something from that earliest letter of Paul, which had led to the misunderstanding? Or is it from another type of Christianity altogether? Perhaps it is a piece of Jewish Christian preaching that encouraged Christians to isolate themselves from the pagan world and its evils just as God had told the Jewish people to do.

CORINTHIAN CORRESPONDENCE [10–1]

Letters between Paul and the Christians at Corinth

(1) **"Previous Letter" (cf. 1 Cor 5:9):** May have contained exhortation to "holiness" like that of the fragment in 2 Cor 6:14—7:1.

(2) **1 Corinthians.**

(3) **"Letter of Tears" (cf. 2 Cor 2:3–4; 7:5, 12):** May have contained 2 Cor 10–13.

(4) **On Paul's Apostleship (2 Cor 2:14—6:13; 7:2–4?):** May have been an exposition of true apostleship against the claims of false apostles such as those mentioned in 2 Cor 10–13, since Paul opposes those who bring (and demand) "letters of recommendation" (cf. 2 Cor 3:1–3).

(5) **Letter of Reconciliation (2 Cor 1:1—2:13; 7:5–16):** Many scholars think that this letter also included the piece on apostleship and an appeal to complete the collection.

(6) **Letter(s) of Appeal for the Collection (2 Cor 8–9):** The addressees are asked to complete the collection, which had been begun a year ago (9:1; cf. 1 Cor 16:1–2).

(7) **Against the "Super-Apostles" (2 Cor 10–13):** If these chapters are not from the "letter of tears," then they suggest accusations against Paul by traveling apostles [Paul's collection appeals could have refueled the debate about his finances and way of life—2 Cor 11:7–11; 12:13–18].

Paul writes Romans from Corinth before his departure for Jerusalem with the collection for the poor (Rom 15:25–28; 16:1–2, 23).

If all of the "pieces" that now make up 2 Corinthians came from different letters, we have quite an anthology of Paul's dealings with the community. In these days of web-based blogs as well as music and video clips, we can easily imagine churches creating mini-anthologies like 2 Corinthians and Philippians from Paul's correspondence. When all letters and books had to be hand-copied, loss of material from a letter collection is hardly surprising. Putting sections of Paul's letters together may have helped preserve them. However, it is difficult to determine whether all the disjointed sections of such letters are from separate documents or simply represent breaks in Paul's composition.

Church as Body of Christ: 1 Corinthians

First Corinthians deals with a variety of problems in the community. Ordinarily the thanksgiving section mentions virtues like faith, hope, and love. When we read 1 Corinthians 1:4–9, we find a different situation. Paul speaks of "speech," "knowledge," and "spiritual gifts." This thanksgiving assigns these gifts their proper place. God gives them for the purpose of sustaining and building the community so that it will be "guiltless" before God's judgment. First Corinthians 1:9 reminds believers that God called them into fellowship in Jesus Christ.

Many of the problems in Corinth stem from an individualistic use of "knowledge," "speech," and "spiritual gifts." The moral failures show that the community is far from the holiness to which God calls believers. Paul accuses them of "boasting" about a man who had married his stepmother. They should be sad and expel such a sinful person (5:1–6). Others think that whatever they do with their bodies doesn't matter. Paul rejects their claim that it is acceptable for a Christian whose body belongs to Christ to have sex with a prostitute (6:12–20). Others think that it is better for Christians not to have sex at all (7:1). They may even have been breaking up marriages and engagements to take on this new life. Paul insists that God gave humans marriage as the proper way to express their sexuality. It is not wrong for Christians to marry. But God also gives some people the special gift of remaining single in order to devote themselves to serving the gospel.

Paul also reminds the Corinthians that Jesus rejected divorce. However, Jesus' words do not cover every case. Christians should not seek a divorce to live an ascetic life. Nor should they seek a divorce out of fear that living with a non-Christian spouse would make them unholy. If anything, both the children of a Christian parent and, indirectly, the nonbelieving spouse are made holy. However, if a Christian is divorced by a non-Christian spouse, then Paul thinks that Jesus would certainly have said that the Christian is free to marry again (7:1–40).

As Paul works through the issues that come up, he keeps returning to the idea that Christians should always see themselves as part of a larger whole. We are not just isolated individuals who are free to do whatever we want. We have to think about how our actions affect other people. We have to be particularly concerned about actions that might cause them harm. Some actions that would be acceptable in one situation are not allowed by this principle in another. Remember the meat markets. Some Christians felt that they should not eat any meat from an animal that had been sacrificed to a pagan idol. Others argued that Christians know that those gods and goddesses are nothing. Paul agrees that the meat itself is just meat. Nevertheless, he also recognizes that for some converts it might be difficult to separate eating sacrificial meat from the feelings of worship they had once held for the pagan gods. They could be drawn back into paganism. Therefore, Paul tells the enlightened Christians that their knowledge isn't worth anything without love for others. They can buy any meat they want. However, in a situation where another person's faith might be destroyed if they eat such meat, their knowledge has to give way to love and they too have to refrain from consuming idol meat (1 Cor 8:1–13; 10:23—11:1).

Paul develops an important symbol for the church in 1 Corinthians: the church as the "body of Christ." Ancient philosophers described political communities as a body of which the citizens were members. The metaphor was employed to show that, despite diversity in origins, social status, and roles, members of a community or state were obliged to act together in a harmonious way. Paul expands that image using Christian belief that the Spirit links believers together as members of the body of Christ. The gifts that the Spirit gives to each person should be used to build up the community, not as opportunities for individuals to claim superiority to others. Paul emphasizes this point by reminding the Corinthians that the spiritual gift they should seek above all others is love (13:1).

The body of Christ imagery links a number of themes together. Christians should not abuse sexuality because their bodies are part of Christ's body. Because the bread and wine of the Lord's Supper represent the body of Christ, Christians should recognize that the same body is present in all who are at the Supper. They should not humiliate poor members of the community at the meal. They should also not try to mix up the Lord with feasts celebrated in pagan temples. Christians may accept invitations to a pagan friend's home (10:27), but a Christian cannot attend a banquet offered in a pagan temple (10:14–22).

In 1 Corinthians 15, Paul deals with another confusion about the body—the physical body. Some Corinthians were denying resurrection. Though they must have known that they could worship Jesus as Lord only if Jesus had been resurrected (15:3–8), the Corinthians apparently saw no connection between what happened to Jesus and what would happen to Christians. Paul insists that Christians would be raised as Jesus had been (15:12–28). He reminds those who think that it would be impossible to raise up the physical body that resurrection does not mean jumping back into the bodies we have now. It means being changed so that we have a new, spiritual body that carries the image of the heavenly Christ (15:35–58).

OUTLINE OF 1 CORINTHIANS   [10–2]

Greeting (1:1–3)

Thanksgiving: Spiritual gifts to keep the community blameless (1:4–9)

Against divisions in the church (1:10–31)

True wisdom found in the cross (2:1–16)

Imitate the apostles: God's fellow-workers (3:1—4:21)

Against immorality tolerated by the Corinthians (5:1—6:20)

- (a) Man married to stepmother to be expelled (5:1–13)
- (b) Christians should not have lawsuits against each other (6:1–11)
- (c) Do not unite the body, the temple of the Spirit, with a prostitute (6:12–20)

Questions raised by the Corinthians (7:1—11:1)

- (a) Some are called to marriage and others to remain single for the sake of the kingdom (7:1–40)
- (b) Christians will not seek divorce (7:10–16)
- (c) Christians follow God's will in any way of life (7:17–24)
- (d) On meat offered to idols (8:1–13)
- (e) Paul's example: Give up rights for the sake of others (9:1–27)
- (f) Do not participate in cults at pagan temples (10:1–22)
- (g) Use your freedom for the good of others (10:23—11:1)

Questions related to worship (11:2—14:40)

- (a) Suitable dress for male and female prophets in the assembly (11:2–16)
- (b) Show unity with all at the Lord's Supper (11:17–34)
- (c) God gives different spiritual gifts to create unity in the body of Christ (12:1–31)
- (d) Love is the highest gift Christians can pursue (13:1–13)
- (e) Rules for prophecy and speaking in tongues (14:1–40)

Christians believe they will be raised like Jesus (15:1–58)

Gather the collection for Jerusalem (16:1–4)

Paul's future travel plans (16:5–12)

Respect those who serve among you (16:13–18)

Final greetings from Paul and his associates (16:19–24)

Division and Reconciliation: 2 Corinthians

We have already discussed various sections of 2 Corinthians. We have seen that Paul faced serious challenges to his position as an apostle. As a result of these challenges, 2 Corinthians contains two sections on the true nature of apostleship. Second Corinthians 10–13 is a passionate self-defense in the heat of the struggle. Second Corinthians 2:14—7:4 presents Paul as the apostle of a new covenant that God writes in the Spirit on the hearts of those who believe. A letter of reconciliation in which Paul instructs the Corinthians to forgive the man who had offended him provides the framework in which an early editor set these two pieces along with the appeal letter for the collection at Jerusalem.

It is difficult to draw a clear picture of Paul's opponents in 2 Corinthians, since we are not always certain when Paul is representing actual accusations and when he is mocking the opposition. We know from 2 Corinthians 1:17–19 that Paul's cancelled travel plans led to accusations that he was insincere, vacillating, and perhaps even deceitful. Paul insists that neither he nor his associates have ever acted that way. God is the source of both Paul's apostolic authority and the Corinthians' faith. They should know that such accusations are false. Though Paul cancelled his visit, his "letter of tears" had brought the Corinthians around so that Paul is later able to speak of a joyous reconciliation that will even include forgiveness for the person who had offended the apostle during his second visit (2:1–11).

Outside apostles carried with them letters of recommendation. They may have suggested that Paul's apostleship was deficient because he did not have such letters. Paul argues that the Corinthians themselves are his recommendation. Because their faith is a "letter" that all people can "read," Paul does not need written documents (3:1–3). (You may remember that Paul praised the Thessalonians for the way in which their faith had become known to others [1 Thess 1:7–9].) Paul accuses these "super-apostles" of a false competitiveness, comparing themselves to one another in claims of spiritual power and making comparisons unfavorable to Paul (2 Cor 10:12; 11:5–6, 18–20). Paul answers by speaking of a "heavenly revelation" in an ironic manner. It doesn't matter what visions he has seen or what angelic languages he has heard. The true sign of Paul's apostleship is his consistent suffering and weakness for the sake of the gospel. This suffering is a "sign" that even God would not take away (12:1–10). Some even attacked Paul's letters, alleging that the letters were a way of "lording it over" the Corinthians from a distance. But when Paul was actually present, he showed himself to be weak and not strong (10:8–10).

OUTLINE OF 2 CORINTHIANS   [10–3]

Greeting (1:1–2)

Blessing God for comforting the apostle in his sufferings (1:3–11)

Reconciliation between Paul and the Corinthians (1:12–2:13; 7:5–16)

Paul's ministry: Ambassador for a new covenant (2:14–6:13; 7:2–4)

  (a) The apostle relies on God, who writes with the Spirit in the hearts of
      believers (2:14–3:3)
  (b) The new covenant in the Spirit is not like the Mosaic covenant: it
      reveals God's glory (3:4–18)
  (c) The truth is only hidden from those who do not hear the call to
      believe (4:1–6)
  (d) The weakness of the suffering apostle demonstrates the glory of
      God that we will share in the resurrection (4:7–5:10)
  (e) Everything the apostle does is to call people to be reconciled with
      God in Christ (5:11–21)
  (f) The apostle is even willing to suffer to bring people to Christ (6:1–
      13; 7:2–4)

[Fragment on holiness as separation from the world (6:14–7:1), possibly non-
Pauline]

Appeals for the Jerusalem collection (chapters 8–9)

Against the "super-apostles" (chapters 10–13:10)

  (a) Paul rejects their standard of boasting in human accomplishments
      (10:1–18)
  (b) Do not be led astray by their flattery (11:1–6)
  (c) Against suspicions raised by Paul's working and the collection
      (11:7–15)
  (d) True sign of an apostle is God's power manifested in suffering and
      weakness (11:16–12:13)
  (e) Paul's love for the Corinthians (12:14–21)
  (f) Paul's plans for a third visit to Corinth (13:1–10)

Final greetings (13:11–14)

Paul does not deny that in correcting the Corinthians he exercises authority over their faith. Paul claims that God has given him the Corinthian community as part of the "assigned territory" for his mission (2 Cor 10:13–16). Unlike the outsiders, Paul sticks to his territory and does not try to boast of work that someone else has done. Paul also uses parental images to describe the special relationship between himself and the church. He is like a father who is responsible for seeing that his daughter is a "pure virgin" for her husband (11:2). He is like a parent working hard to save up money for his children (12:14–15). His heart goes out to these "children," and he hopes that they will find a place for him in their hearts in return (6:11–13).

All of these images of the apostle as a loving parent who is willing to work and suffer for his children are grounded in an understanding of what it means to be an "apostle of reconciliation." Paul describes the new covenant in Christ as one in which the glory of God is made manifest. Every believer who sees that glory will also be changed into the "glory of Christ, who is the image of God" (3:7—4:4). However, the apostle who is the minister of this new covenant should never think that the light and knowledge that he brings to others somehow "rubs off" on its messenger. Quite the opposite, the apostle shares in the "death of Jesus" through weakness and suffering (4:7–18). Like all Christians, Paul is confident that he will share in a glorious future, but that future is in heaven with Christ (5:1–10). He reminds the Corinthians that we cannot judge Christ "from a human point of view" or we would not see that in Christ's death God reconciles the world to himself (5:16–21). Similarly, anyone who looked at Paul from a "human point of view" without understanding the gospel would only see the weakness, suffering, poverty, punishment, and "bad reputation" of the apostle. One would never suspect that the apostle is God's "co-worker" (6:1–10).

Summary

The Corinthian letters provide us with our most extensive look at Paul's ministry in a single community. We often wish we knew more about the Christians to whom these letters were addressed as we catch glimpses of their struggles and divisions. The Corinthians appear to reflect the city from which they come, a "new city" without many of the established ways of old cities; a thriving, mobile seaport; a city of diverse people who are often "on the move." Some of the problems that surface in Corinth seem quite dated. Most of us are not likely to be invited to celebrate a banquet in honor of a pagan god or to require rules for how men and women prophets should dress or for speaking in tongues. We no longer assemble for worship in the house of a wealthy patron or celebrate the Lord's Supper in the context of a meal. We are not likely to encounter Christian preachers who advocate breaking up a marriage so that the man can follow the "noble" practice of "not touching a woman" (1 Cor 7:1).

Even in these cases, we see Paul looking for ways in which love and unity can be made the primary experiences of the community. We do still have lawsuits with one another, though we are not likely to call upon the churches to find people to mediate disputes in order to keep Christians out of the civil courts (1 Cor 6:1–8). We are certainly as confused as the Corinthians were about the body, sexuality, and marriage. Most of us have experienced divorce in our families or among our friends. Most of us know the pressure generated by the idea that the body can be used for anything, so that "date rape," incest, and sexual abuse of young children are increasing problems in our society. To all these, not to mention our various forms of drug and alcohol abuse, the same advice Paul gave the Corinthians applies: the body is "for the Lord" and is to be treated like the "temple of the Spirit," which it is.

Paul has also given us a number of images for the church. The most significant is that of the "body of Christ." We have to remember that symbol when we are torn apart by conflicts and even competing "spiritual gifts." Paul gives concrete examples from his own life and suffering as an apostle of what it means to put love and the building up of others first. But the most important example stands behind Paul's own apostleship, the example of Christ. Paul never lets us forget that the cross is a "paradox," not an example of human wisdom or power. As a result, the life of those who are Christ's servants must also image the glory hidden in weakness that we find in Christ.

STUDY QUESTIONS

Facts You Should Know

1. Describe the controversy over eating "meat sacrificed to idols" and participating in meals in the pagan temples in 1 Corinthians. What were the different views held by the Corinthians? How did Paul seek to resolve the conflict?
2. Describe the tensions that arose over the celebration of the Lord's Supper. How did those divisions reflect the social customs of the time? What is Paul's answer in his instruction to the Corinthians?
3. How does Paul use the metaphors of the "body as temple of the Holy Spirit" and the community as the "body of Christ" to deal with the following problems in Corinth: (a) sexual morality; (b) relationships between Christians at the Lord's Supper; (c) differences in "gifts" within the community; (d) the destiny of Christians after death?
4. What accusations were raised against Paul's apostleship in 1 and 2 Corinthians? How does Paul use the imagery of the crucified Christ to respond to such charges?

Things to Do

1. Find as many references to "body" in 1 Corinthians as you can. List those that refer to the physical body, those that speak of the community as a "body," and those that speak of "body" in connection with Christ.

2. Find as many references to the "weakness of the apostle" in 1 and 2 Corinthians as you can. How is "weakness" understood to be a sign of true apostolic ministry in Paul?

3. Find as many exhortations to "love" as the principle of relationships between Christians in 1 and 2 Corinthians as you can. What problems does Paul invoke the principle of love to resolve?

Things to Think About

1. Are we more like Paul or the Corinthians in our evaluations of persons, status, power, and success?

2. Is our attitude toward the "body" shaped by any Christian symbols or expectations, for example, the "body" as the seed of the "body" we are to have in the resurrection? Or do we tend to agree with those Paul opposes at Corinth that the body is an indifferent "tool" for humans to use as they will?

Chapter 11

UNIVERSALIZING PAUL'S MESSAGE

Pauline Christianity in Colossians and Ephesians

Colossae was famed for wool working and cloth dying, especially for a dark red wool known as *colossinum*. Ephesus, 110 miles to the west, was a major port city in Asia Minor. According to Acts 18:19–21, Paul sailed here from Corinth with Prisca and Aquila. Paul returned to Ephesus on subsequent missionary journeys. He was there when he wrote 1 Corinthians (1 Cor 16:8) and was probably imprisoned there when he wrote Philippians and Philemon. Paul's "fellow prisoner," Epaphras (Phlm 23), may have served as Paul's representative to Colossae and the neighboring cities of Laodicea (see Col 2:1; 4:13–16) and Hieropolis. The thanksgiving in Colossians attributes the recipients' faith to Epaphras (Col 1:7–8).

According to Colossians 1:24 and 4:3–10, the apostle is once more in prison. If you compare Colossians with Philemon and Philippians, letters from Paul's earlier imprisonment, you will notice that this situation is different. In the earlier letters, Paul expected to be released and that he would resume his work among those to whom he wrote. Colossians never speaks of release, though Paul's imprisonment is an "open door" for the word (Col 4:3), nor does it speak of future visits by the apostle. Colossians 2:1–2 mentions those who have never seen the apostle. Colossians takes great pains to emphasize the growth in faith that its recipients experience through the ministry of persons who are Paul's associates (Col 1:7–8; 4:7–17) and encourages sharing Paul's letters with other churches in the region (4:16). Archippus, another person known to us from Philemon 2, is being charged to undertake a permanent ministry in the area (Col 4:17). You have probably already figured out one possible reason for this new tone: Paul's imprisonment in Rome. A severe earthquake occurred in the region of Colossae in AD 60 or 61. Colossae was already declining in contrast to nearby cities of Laodicea and Hieropolis before the earthquake.

Afterward it became an insignificant town. Since Colossians shows no awareness of these events, many scholars think that it was written before AD 60/61.

Although Colossians follows the outline of a Pauline letter (see Outline of Colossians, Chart 11-1), many of the expressions and images do not quite sound like the letters written during Paul's missionary work in Asia Minor and Greece. Look for some of these differences in your reading. There is only one reference to the Spirit (Col 1:8). Instead of speaking about the perfection that Christians should have when Christ comes at the judgment (see Phil 3:20–21), Colossians speaks of Christians participating in a life oriented toward the Christ who is now in heaven (Col 1:5, 12–14; 3:1–4). Notice that Colossians 3:1 speaks of Christians as having been raised with Christ already and Colossians 3:4 of Christians appearing with Christ in glory. Paul's earlier letters speak of Christians who had died coming with the Lord (1 Thess 4:16–17) and those who are alive being transformed (1 Cor 15:51–52). Look for the word *church* in Colossians. Paul's earlier letters used *church* to refer to Christians gathered in local communities just as in the expression *church* that meets in Nympha's house (Col 4:15). However, elsewhere in Colossians *church* takes on a new, universal sense. It is pictured as a cosmic "body" with the heavenly Christ as its head (Col 1:18).

OUTLINE OF COLOSSIANS   **[11–1]**

Greeting (1:1–2)

Thanksgiving: faith, hope, and love of the community (1:3–8)

Prayer for the well-being of the community (1:9–14)

The exalted Christ as source of our heavenly salvation (1:15–2:23)

    (a) Hymn to Christ as image of God and Savior (1:15–20)
    (b) Apostle's ministry reveals God's salvation (1:21–2:7)
    (c) Against those who preach a false salvation based on "angelic worship" (2:8–23)

Living the Christian life (3:1–4:6)

    (a) Holiness manifests the "new creation" that Christians have become in baptism (3:1–17)
    (b) "Household code": behavior of wives and husbands, children and fathers, slaves and masters (3:18–4:1)
    (c) Continue in prayer and wise conduct toward outsiders (4:2–6)

Concluding greetings (4:7–18)

    (a) Tychicus and Onesimus will report on what has happened to Paul (4:7–9)
    (b) Greetings from associates of Paul (4:10–14)
    (c) Greetings to those at Laodicea and instructions for an exchange of letters between churches (4:15–18)

Christ's death is mentioned only in the hymnic passage of Colossians 1:20 and very indirectly in Colossians 2:14. Such an elliptical way of speaking is very different from Paul's earlier emphasis on his preaching as "portraying Christ crucified" (Gal 3:1). It is also a very peculiar contrast to the Paul who gloried in his sufferings as ways of participating in the death of Christ (see 1 Cor 4:6–13; 2 Cor 11:21–29; Gal 6:14–17; Phil 3:10). Instead of looking to Christ crucified for the meaning of his suffering, Colossians 1:24–29 makes the sufferings of the apostle an addition to those of Christ for the sake of the cosmic body of Christ, the church. These verses also picture Paul as a triumphant figure, charged with revealing the "mysteries" that God had kept hidden for ages (v. 26). Elsewhere Paul speaks of "mysteries" either as the paradox of Christ's crucifixion (1 Cor 2:6–13) or as the "end-time" events of salvation (1 Cor 15:51–52; Rom 11:25–27). Highlighting the apostle's role in making these mysteries known establishes his significance as founder of these churches. The Jewish sect of new Covenanters spoke in a similar fashion about its Teacher of Righteousness, "to whom God made known all the mysteries of His servants the prophets" (1 QpHab 7.4–5).

Although Colossians 1:27, 2:11–15, and 3:11 speak of the salvation of the Gentiles in Christ, a central theme of Paul's mission, the other pole, "the Jews" or "Israel," has disappeared. So have the links that Paul forged between his insights about "righteousness through faith" and the Old Testament. While Paul's theological imagery and his way of speaking about Christ, the church, and his own mission may have changed during his long imprisonment, two years in Caesarea followed by Rome, many scholars doubt that so many little details would be different. They think that Colossians was composed by one of the associates mentioned, perhaps Timothy or Epaphras. Since they had worked with Paul for such a long time, they knew his general way of writing. The danger of false teachers (Col 2:4, 8) and the impending death of the apostle made it imperative that the churches left behind in Asia Minor be instructed and encouraged by apostolic letters. If Paul was still alive, he may have been able to add the final greeting (4:18).

Ephesians: A Circular Letter?

When we turn to Ephesians the questions of authorship become even more complex. Colossians instructed churches in the region to exchange letters. The apostle's letters were not just for one church and its problems. They were instruction for all churches. Ephesians may have originally been a circular letter. Our oldest manuscripts do not name a particular church in the opening greetings. Nor does the conclusion refer to any particular people. The only one mentioned is Tychicus, in verses (Eph 6:21–22) that appear to have been copied from the conclusion to Colossians (Col 4:7–8). Compare the opening of Ephesians (1:1–2) with Colossians (1:1–2). They are almost identical except that Ephesians does not mention Timothy and employs a more "Pauline" expression by adding the reference to "our Lord Jesus Christ" at the end of verse 2.

You can see from these examples something that a more detailed comparison of the two letters also shows. Whoever penned Ephesians was very familiar with Paul's language but also reworked parts of Colossians for this letter. Chart 11-2 gives the main parallels between the two letters.

PARALLELS BETWEEN EPHESIANS AND COLOSSIANS [11–2]

Ephesians	Colossians
1:1-2	1:1-2
1:15-17	1:3-4, 9-10
2:5-6	2:12-13
3:1-13	1:24—2:5
4:17-32	3:5-14
5:19-20	3:16-17
5:22—6:9	3:18—4:1
6:18-20	4:2-4
6:21-22	4:7-8

In some cases, Ephesians has taken the framework of a Colossians passage and expanded it considerably. Ephesians emphasizes the theme of the church as the body of Christ. For example, Colossians 1:19 and 2:9–10 describe Christ as the one in whom the "fullness" (*pleroma*) of God dwells. Ephesians understands that "fullness" to be embodied in the church as the body of Christ (1:23; 3:19–21; 4:10–13). Compare the two examples of the "household code" (Col 3:18—4:1 and Eph 5:22—6:9). You will notice that Colossians thinks that the instructions address situations in which only one member of a pair is Christian. Ephesians, on the other hand, has given a Christian cast to the whole section. Marriage is compared to Christ and the church. Children are reminded of the Ten Commandments. Slaves are to view their masters as "the Lord," and masters are to remember that they too have a "Lord."

In reading through Ephesians, you may also notice that the image of Paul as the heroic martyr is emphasized even more strongly than it was in Colossians. The Gentile audience of this letter (Eph 1:11–14; 2:1–3, 11–22; 3:1; 4:17–19; 5:8) is reminded that Paul's suffering is on their behalf (3:1, 13). They are to be inspired by the example of Paul's suffering (4:1). Following Paul's own example, Colossians refers to the apostle's prayer for the churches (Col 1:9; 2:1). Ephesians gives actual examples of Paul's prayer in addition to the normal thanksgiving with which Paul began his letters. Look at Chart 11-3. You will see that the first half of the letter, which is usually the theological part of one of Paul's letters, is mostly composed of prayer formulas.

You may have noticed that the content of Ephesians is very general. It is not possible to point out a particular problem that the author must resolve. Instead, the author presents us with a cosmic vision of the church as the source of salvation. Since Ephesians used Colossians and since most of the particular names and references that we find in Colossians are missing in Ephesians, Ephesians was not written by the same person as Colossians. The emphasis upon Paul's heroic imprisonment on behalf of the Gentiles suggests that Paul may have already been martyred at the time this letter was penned. Ephesians is a way of providing a general summary of his teaching for the churches in Asia Minor.

OUTLINE OF EPHESIANS   [11–3]

Greeting (1:1–2)

Thanksgiving for redemption and knowledge of heavenly mysteries in Christ (1:3–14)

Through the apostle God has made the Gentiles alive in Christ (1:15–3:21)

  (a) Prayer for the faith, love, and hope of those whom God has made part of the body of the heavenly Christ (1:15–23)
  (b) Contrast between their old "death" in sin and life in Christ (2:1–10)
  (c) Reconciliation of the Gentiles to God in the one body of Christ (2:11–22)
  (d) Paul's suffering and ministry to bring the Gentiles into the body of Christ (3:1–13)
  (e) Prayer for faith and love among Paul's converts (3:14–21)

Christian life in the world (4:1–6:20)

  (a) Unity in the body of Christ that is built up by different ministries (4:1–16)
  (b) Old life in "darkness" contrasted with new life as "children of light" (4:17–5:21)
  (c) Household code: Marriage in Christ; children and parents; slaves and masters (5:22–6:9)
  (d) Battle against evil (6:10–20)

Christ as Lord of the Cosmos: Colossians

Both Colossians and Ephesians have shifted from the earlier letters in which the glory of Christ is associated with the end of the world to picturing the heavenly glory of Christ as the reality of Christian salvation. Both use the apocalyptic contrast of light and darkness to speak of the transformation that Christians have experienced in baptism. They have been taken from the world of darkness, a life lived in opposition to God, and been made part of the heavenly world of light (e.g., Col 1:12–13).

Colossians 1:15–20 appears to quote an early Christian hymn. The first section describes Christ as the "image" of God through whom the universe was created. The second section speaks of the risen Lord as the fullness of God and head of the "body," the church:

> who [= the Son, from v. 12] is the image of God,
> the first-born of all creation;
> in him all things were created,
> in the heavens and on the earth,
> visible things and invisible ones;
> whether thrones or dominions;
> whether principalities or powers—
> all things were created through him and in him;
> he is before all things,
> and all things hold together in him;
> he is the head of the body, the church; (vv. 15–18ᵃ)

> who is [the] beginning, first born from the dead
> so that he might be pre-eminent in all things;
> in him the whole fullness was pleased to dwell,
> and through him all things were reconciled to him [= God]
> making peace through the blood of his cross [through him]
> whether things on earth or those in the heavens. (vv. 18ᵇ–20)

The images of this hymn make an important point. The special role that Christ has in salvation is not something that was added to his earthly life when he was exalted into heaven after his death. Rather, it is part of the role that Christ, as the "image" of God, played in creation. The fullness of God's creative power in Christ is the same fullness that brings salvation in Christ.

At first, you might think that Colossians has quoted this hymn simply to back up the exhortation in 1:21–23. Christ's death has made us part of this reconciliation, but we must continue to show that we belong to the "body" in lives of holiness. However, when we come to Colossians 2:8–23, we find out that this picture of Christ is being challenged by another form of religious teaching described as "philosophy and empty deceit." The accusation of being "human tradition" often occurred in debates between philosophical schools. It implies that the opposition had simply made up their teaching and did not base it on authentic sources. The contrast between "according to the elements of the universe" and "not according to Christ" (2:8) is more difficult to interpret. "Elements of the universe" could refer to demonic beings or astrological powers—usually opposed to the ascent of the human spirit into the heavenly regions. If so, the contrast would be between the inspiration of the false teaching and Christian truth. But the expression usually referred to the fundamental physical elements out of which the universe was made. If that is what the author means, then the contrast is between human speculations about the makeup of the universe—which usually associated the dark, heavy elements of earth and water with the realm of change and death, and the light elements of air and fire with the immortal stars—and the Christian picture of Christ as the one in whom all is created. The "fullness of deity" mentioned in verse 9 would refer to the "fullness" mentioned in 1:19.

Colossians 2:9–15 emphasizes the role of Christ in the salvation of the Gentiles, who had been caught in sin and did not know God. Several themes from Paul's earlier conflicts over the salvation of the Gentiles appear in a slightly different form here. In Christ, the uncircumcised are the same as the "circumcised," though not in a physical sense. Paul uses this pairing in Romans 2:29; cf. also Philippians 3:3. The image of baptism as dying and rising with Christ (Col 2:12) recalls Romans 6:4. Paul had described the conflict between the crucified Christ and the law as Christ becoming "sin" (2 Cor 5:21) or "cursed" (Gal 3:13). Colossians 2:14 pictures Christ setting aside the claims of the law against humanity by nailing its "bond" to the cross. This verse is connected with verse 16. Christians should not accept new obligations or judgments being passed by others. We found a similar train of thought in Galatians 4:8–11. Paul had told his Galatian converts that if they took on observances of the Jewish calendar, they might as well be going back to paganism.

Paul made the argument against Judaizing practices by appealing to Christian freedom (e.g., Gal 5:1). Colossians uses the imagery of the cosmic role of Christ to make its point by pointing to the victory of Christ over all the powers in the universe (Col 2:10, 15).

It is difficult to reconstruct the religious practices that Colossians is opposing. Clearly regulations involved food, possibly some other cultic objects, and subjection of the body through ascetic practices such as fasting and sexual renunciation. The opponents also promoted a peculiar religious calendar. The puzzling references to "elements of the cosmos" and "self-abasement and worship of angels" suggest that these practices were linked with some form of "heavenly ascent" or vision. Perhaps the "elements" were thought to keep the soul down in the earthly realm. Only through the practices of asceticism and worship of angelic guardians could the soul ascend to the divine realm.

Colossians assures its readers that Christ embraces the whole cosmos. Through baptism, they have become one with the heavenly risen Christ. They should not think of salvation as some dangerous trip that the soul still has to make. Instead, Colossians 3:1–4 tells them how Christians should seek the "things above." The nature of that quest is spelled out in the ethical life by which Christians "put to death" the desires and passions that cut people off from God and "put on" the virtues of those who belong to the body of Christ (3:5–17). Colossians also speaks of the cultic practices of Christians that are the basis of salvation. Baptism has united all believers in Christ (3:10–11). Christians continue to worship God through mutual teaching, encouragement, psalms, hymns, and other "spiritual songs." They are not involved in worshiping angels or even claiming visions of the angels praising God in heaven. Christians are giving thanks to God through Christ (3:16–17).

All United in Christ: Ephesians

You can see from Chart 11-3 that Ephesians emphasizes the contrast between life in Christ and that in the world. Ephesians also stresses the unity that binds the whole church together as the body of Christ. Where Colossians presents us with the image of the cosmic Christ as the source of salvation, Ephesians describes the embodiment of salvation in the "body of Christ," the church. Colossians speaks of "fullness" belonging to Christ and communicated to Christians (Col 1:19; 2:9, 10). Ephesians 1:23 identifies the "fullness" with the church as Christ's body. The different ministries in the church have the task of bringing Christians to full maturity (Eph 4:11–16).

The image of Christ's cosmic victory over the powers (Col 2:5) has been expanded in Ephesians 4:8–10. Ephesians cites Psalm 68:19. Christ has filled the universe by descending to the earthly regions and ascending to the highest heavens. The "captives" of the psalm are presumably the "powers and authorities" mentioned in Colossians. Ephesians 4:11 picks up the second theme in the psalm text to explain: "He gave gifts to men." Those gifts are the spiritual gifts that enable the church to grow in love. Ephesians 3:10 pictures the church/body of Christ as the cosmic manifestation of God's wisdom. What was originally a cosmological description of Christ as the "wisdom of God" (divine image in Col 1:15; in whom "treasures of wisdom are hidden" in Col 2:3) has been transferred to the church in Ephesians.

Even though the symbolic language of Ephesians can be difficult to follow, this letter presents a very important insight about the nature of the church. "Body of Christ" is not just a nice metaphor for a particular collection of people. "Body of Christ" says that the church really does have some of the same attributes that belong to Christ, her head. She is the manifestation of God's wisdom. She is holy. She is different from other social groups in the world. You can see how deeply this idea is worked into Ephesians when you compare what Ephesians 5:22–33 says about the relationship between Christian husbands and wives with Colossians 3:18–19. Colossians merely adopts the standard social conventions about a well-ordered household. Husbands are told not to be harsh with their wives and are reminded to love them. Ephesians has taken over this simple pattern of ethical teaching and "explained it" by describing the relationship as like that between Christ and the church. This development describes the wife's relationship to her husband as like that of the church and Christ.

The major new development concerns the role of the husband. It becomes the source of a reflection on love and self-sacrifice. This reflection is important on a number of levels. Some people think that because the New Testament tells wives to "be subject" to their husbands, women have to "put up with it" when husbands abuse them or their children. You can see from this description of love that abusive behavior of any sort does not belong in a Christian marriage. On another level, you can also see that the holiness of the church is not something that its human members create on their own. The holiness of the church comes from the sacrifice and love of Christ. Finally, we live in a time when people always seem to be criticizing the church. For some the church is too conservative; for others, too liberal. For some the church is not involved enough in social causes; for others, it seems to have lost its religious focus to become a social reform movement. Ephesians challenges us to forget all the squabbling and to imagine the church as the object of Christ's love. Those who love someone treat his or her "faults" differently than they do the failures of others. We may criticize people we love, but we also are willing to accept their struggles, peculiarities, and even weaknesses.

Just as holiness is a gift, so salvation comes to Christians as God's "grace." Ephesians 2:1–10 reminds readers that without God's grace they would have remained lost in sinfulness. Throughout the letter, Christians face a world of darkness and sin. The "new creation" that Christians become in baptism is not some static form of divine salvation. It appears in the "good works" that are part of the new life of Christians (2:10). Ephesians speaks of Christians being strengthened by the Spirit and growing to maturity in love and knowledge (3:16–19; 4:11–16). Promoting growth and unity is the primary function of the various "gifts" that God has given people in the church (4:11–13). Thus, Ephesians reminds us that Christian life is not merely static or defensive, holding on to salvation like a possession. Rather Christian life involves constant growth. Christians cannot be naive about the task that faces them. Ephesians reminds us that "putting away" the old life of sin that shows itself in speaking deceitfully to others and in anger as well as in more obvious crimes like theft means working against a tough enemy, the "devil" (4:25–32; 6:10–18).

Summary

We have seen that Colossians and Ephesians reflect the situation of Pauline Christianity after the apostle himself was removed from the scene by imprisonment and death. Ephesians is particularly conscious of how much the Gentile churches that Paul founded owe to his efforts and suffering on their behalf. Ephesians 3:3–4 also mentions the important role of Paul's letters in conveying his teaching to those who had not known him personally.

Christians could read and exchange these letters. Believers had no official Christian scriptures to go with the Old Testament at this time. Even the collection of Pauline writings that we have been studying was not in circulation. We have seen that these letters preserve Paul's teaching by developing images from Paul's earlier letters in new ways. They emphasize the cosmic significance of Christ and the universality of the church as the body of Christ. They speak of others who must carry on the work of "building up" the body of Christ that the apostle left behind. They remind Christians of the holiness that comes from being in Christ.

STUDY QUESTIONS

Facts You Should Know

1. How is Paul's imprisonment in Colossians and Ephesians different from the imprisonment in Philippians and Philemon?
2. How does Colossians picture the cosmic role of Christ? List some of the elements of the religious movement that this letter opposes. How does the "cosmic Christ" make those religious practices unnecessary for Christians?
3. Explain how Ephesians has taken over and expanded the following metaphors found in Colossians: (a) the cosmic victory of Christ over the "powers of the universe"; (b) Christ as "head" of the church; (c) the relationship between husband and wife in Christian marriage.
4. According to Ephesians, what is the basis for the Christian claim that the church is holy?

Things to Do

1. The thanksgiving in Colossians praises the addressees for "faith in Christ Jesus," "love for all the saints [= Christians]," and "hope laid up for you in heaven" (Col 1:4–5). Read the rest of the letter and find as many examples as you can of each of these virtues.
2. Compare the "household code" of Ephesians 5:22—6:9 with that in Colossians 3:18—4:1. How has Ephesians "Christianized" the moral teaching of the household code in each of the three cases?

Things to Think About

1. Do Christians today really believe that Christ is victorious over the "powers" that hold the cosmos in bondage to evil and sin? How do they demonstrate that they have such a faith?

2. Ephesians emphasizes the need for Christians to grow into Christ by putting aside the vices of their past, which the "rulers of this world" still encourage, and taking up the armor of Christ. What "vices" would go into a modern-day catalogue of things that the Christian must struggle to put aside?

Chapter 12

MARK:
JESUS, SUFFERING MESSIAH

The Composition of Mark

Paul's letters presumed that the readers knew some sayings of Jesus, that Jesus was a Jewish teacher who had followers including a special group referred to as "the Twelve," and that Jesus had been crucified at the time of the Jewish Passover and had been raised from the dead. Paul also mentioned the origins of the Lord's Supper as the final meal that Jesus shared with his disciples. Clearly stories about Jesus played a role in the earliest Christian preaching and worship. But for Paul the "story of Jesus" as such was not yet written down for his readers to consult. Paul uses the word *gospel* to mean the message of salvation that he preaches (e.g., Gal 1:11; Rom 1:1; 2 Cor 4:3). The noun *euangelion* has its roots in the verbal form, "to bring or announce news," which is used in Isaiah 40:9; 41:27; 52:7; and 61:1 for the announcement of the "good news" that God is going to bring captive Israel out of exile. A Roman inscription describes the birthday of the emperor Augustus as "good news" for the whole world.

Mark begins with the words, "The beginning of the gospel of Jesus Christ, Son of God" (1:1). *Gospel* does not mean "book" here either. Mark 1:14–15 uses *gospel* for Jesus' preaching that the reign of God is at hand. That usage reminds us of the Old Testament use of *gospel* for the announcement that God is coming to free the people. (Luke 4:18–19 has Jesus begin his ministry with the words of Isaiah 61:1–2.) The sayings about suffering for "Jesus' sake and for the sake of the gospel" (Mark 8:35; 10:29) link Jesus and the preaching about him (also 13:10; 14:9). Mark's opening, then, would not have led its readers to expect a reporter's biography about Jesus. They would expect preaching about Jesus as Son of God.

Look at Mark 14:9. It suggests something more by *gospel* than just repeating stories and sayings. By promising that a particular woman's action will be remembered wherever the gospel is preached, it treats the story of Jesus as a larger whole into which the sayings and stories fit. Some of the individual stories may have belonged to small collections, such as the parables in Mark 4:1–34. The doubling of several miracle stories (calming the storm: Mark 4:35–41; 6:45–52; feeding the multitude: 6:34–44; 8:1–9; healing the blind: 8:22–26; 10:46–52) suggests that there may have been separate collections that had different versions of the same story. The story of Jesus' passion that we find in Mark 14–15 might have been based on an earlier written account.

As far as we know, Mark was the first person to bring the diverse stories about Jesus together in a single narrative. Mark writes in Greek for an audience that does not understand the Aramaic words that occur in some of the stories (5:41; 7:34; 15:34). They are also unfamiliar with Jewish customs (7:3–4). Mark 13:2 suggests that the fall of Jerusalem to the Roman army either has occurred or will soon. The warnings against false messiahs and the command to flee (13:5–7, 14–16, 21–22) could be directed against expectations about the return of Jesus that had been awakened by those events. Mark has strung together these prophetic sayings with an address to the situation of readers in 13:9–13. They must expect to suffer for Jesus' sake at the hands of various political authorities: synagogue officials, Roman governors, and even kings. This suffering is linked with the preaching of the gospel throughout the world. Mark 14:9 also referred to the gospel being preached "in the whole cosmos."

Church tradition identified the author of this gospel with the Mark said to have been with Peter in Rome (1 Pet 5:13). We also find a Mark associated with Paul's imprisonment there (2 Tim 4:11; Col 4:10). If the gospel was composed for believers in Rome, the references to suffering could be associated with Nero's persecution. Another old tradition held that Mark had founded the church in Alexandria. Citations from a gospel claiming to be a "secret version" of Mark preserved in Alexandria appear in a letter that is said to be by the third-century teacher Clement of Alexandria. Some modern scholars favor an alternate geographical location, the region of Syro-Palestine. Concern with the impending destruction of the Jerusalem temple and the theme of Jesus' kingship fit the time of the Jewish rebellion of AD 66 to 70. Christians would have suffered at the hands of both Jews and non-Jews in the conflict. To Jewish nationalists, they are traitors. To Roman officials and the Gentile inhabitants of the region, they are "Jewish sympathizers." Perhaps the promise that the disciples would see the risen Lord in Galilee (Mark 14:28; 16:7) addressed the community's flight from hostilities in Judea.

Whatever the circumstances, the gospel leaves little doubt that the truth of Jesus is found in the cross. The center of the plot comes with Peter's confession that Jesus is messiah, Jesus' passion prediction, and the rebuke of

Peter (Mark 8:27–33). Christians are told that they too must be prepared to suffer (8:34–38).

As you read Mark, you will notice that the story is broken up into small units that begin and end abruptly. You will find other passages that provide a generalized summary to fill in between two episodes (see 1:21–22, which fills in between the call of the disciples and the first exorcism that attracts attention to Jesus). One of Mark's favorite methods of composition is to fit two stories together by putting one in the middle of the other. In Mark 2:1–12 and 3:1–6, healing stories have sayings about Jesus' authority to forgive and the appropriateness of healing on the Sabbath inserted in them. The story of the withered fig tree forms the outside framework for Jesus' cleansing of the temple in Mark 11:12–25. The healing of Jarius's daughter is interrupted by the healing of a woman who has been hemorrhaging for twelve years (Mark 5:21–43). Both of these stories emphasize the faith of those who ask Jesus for healing. The mission of the twelve disciples frames the story of John the Baptist's death (6:6–30).

The biggest puzzles in Mark center on what is called the "messianic secret." Even though Jesus is Son of God and a powerful teacher and healer, he sometimes commands people to remain silent. This theme leads to a story of a leper in 1:40–45 immediately disobeying Jesus by telling everyone. The disciples are also commanded to keep silent about the transfiguration (Mark 9:9). Even Jesus' teaching sometimes seems to be a riddle, which his disciples have a hard time understanding (4:10–13). The key to this puzzle lies in the middle of the gospel. Peter recognizes that Jesus is God's messiah and is immediately told not to tell anyone (8:27–30). The reason for the silence must be connected with what follows. Jesus tries to explain to his disciples that his role as messiah is one of suffering and death (8:31–33). The "messianic secret" points to the paradox of who Jesus is: the powerful Son of God who is destined to die on the cross.

OUTLINE OF MARK   **[12–1]**

Jesus comes preaching the kingdom (1:1–3:6)

    (a) Introduction to Jesus' ministry: John the Baptist (1:1–15)
    (b) Calling of the disciples and Jesus' powerful deeds (1:16–45)
    (c) Controversies with religious authorities (2:1–3:6)

Teaching and healing around the Sea of Galilee (3:7–6:6a)

    (a) Reactions to Jesus: Who are the true relatives? (3:7–35)
    (b) Disciples hear the parables (4:1–34)
    (c) Miracles of Jesus (4:35–5:43)
    (d) Rejection at Nazareth (6:1–6a)

Continued

Second cycle of teaching and powerful deeds (6:6b–8:21)

    (a) Sending out of the disciples / death of the Baptist (6:6b–30)
    (b) Feeding, walking on water, healing (6:31–56)
    (c) Controversies over keeping the traditions (7:1–23)
    (d) Healings, feeding (7:24–8:10)
    (e) Demand for a sign; the "leaven" of the Pharisees (8:11–21)

Discipleship: following the Son of Man who is destined to suffer (8:22–10:52)

    (a) Healing the blind (8:22–26)
    (b) Jesus is "messiah"; first passion prediction; discipleship means suffering (8:27–9:1)
    (c) Transfiguration; disciples fail to heal; second passion prediction (9:2–37)
    (d) Dispute over greatness / beware of temptation (9:38–50)
    (e) True discipleship: marriage, children, wealth (10:1–31)
    (f) Third passion prediction / dispute over greatness (10:32–45)
    (g) Healing the blind (10:46–52)

Jesus comes to Jerusalem as messianic king (11:1–13:37)

    (a) Entry to Jerusalem / cursing of the fig tree / cleansing the temple (11:1–25)
    (b) Controversies with religious authorities / Parable of the Wicked Tenants (11:26–12:44)
    (c) How disciples are to react to the coming destruction of Jerusalem / no one knows the hour of the parousia (13:1–37)

Jesus' passion and death (14:1–16:8a)

    (a) Woman's anointing / Judas's betrayal (14:1–11)
    (b) Last Supper (14:12–31)
    (c) Gethsemane: Jesus' prayer / arrest (14:32–52)
    (d) Trials of Jesus (14:53–15:20)
    (e) Crucifixion / "Truly this was the Son of God" (15:21–41)
    (f) Burial of Jesus / empty tomb: 'He has been raised' (15:42–16:8a)

Jesus as Powerful Savior

Take a look at the outline of Mark's gospel. You will notice that the first half of the gospel can be described as a combination of Jesus' miracles that show powers of healing and control over nature, and his teaching. Jesus' teaching takes two forms. The parables about the kingdom of God in Mark 4 are directed toward sympathetic followers of Jesus. Perhaps you noticed that the seed parables of Jesus collected in Mark 4 all emphasize the "great harvest" that comes out of hidden, insignificant, or difficult beginnings. The saying about the lamp in Mark 4:21–22 reminds the disciples that they are not to hide the light they have received.

The second form of teaching occurs in controversies between Jesus and religious teachers like the Pharisees. Mark 1:22 leads the reader to expect Jesus to teach with *exousia*, "power" or "authority," not like the scribes. The same word, *exousia*, reappears in the crowd response after an exorcism (Mark 1:27). There *exousia* is used for the power to cast out the demons. Jesus' teaching and exorcisms are linked again in the summary of his mission in 1:39. Mark has prepared the reader to expect a form of teaching that is like the healings and exorcisms described in 1:23–27, 30–31, 40–44. Jesus will speak with authority. He will "command" and vanquish his opponents.

The debate over *exousia*, "authority," appears in the healing that opens the first cycle of controversy stories (Mark 2:1—3:6). Jesus has the authority to forgive sins. His opponents charge that he has blasphemed by taking on a power that belongs only to God (2:5–10). In this episode, the physical healing of the paralytic takes second place to the issue of whether or not Jesus can speak God's word of forgiveness to the sinner. The reaction of Jesus' opponents and of the crowd shows what is "new" in Jesus' teaching. This theme is repeated throughout the section. We see Jesus summoning a tax collector as disciple and are told that the scribes of the Pharisee party object to the tax collectors and sinners who have become followers of Jesus (2:13–17). Jesus answers their objections by insisting that the sick need healing, not the healthy people.

Controversy stories also have Jesus challenge some of the practices by which righteous people showed devotion to God: fasting and refraining from any kind of work on the Sabbath. Jesus never denies that these practices have their place. However, they cannot be used to obstruct the new presence of salvation that has appeared with Jesus' ministry. It is not right to fast when the savior is present. Jesus' ministry is "new wine," which cannot be forced into old skins (2:18–22). Jesus insists that even the law itself recognizes that human need has priority over the obligation to refrain from work on the Sabbath (2:23–28; 3:1–5). Although Jesus wins the arguments, his strategy creates enemies. Mark 3:6 pictures the Pharisees and Herodians leaving to plot a way of destroying Jesus.

The narrative in the first part of Mark moves on two levels. On the human level, Jesus' powerful miracles and teaching attract crowds of followers, but they also lead to strong opposition from both religious (scribes, Pharisees) and political (Herodians) authorities. On the cosmic level, Jesus' ministry is pictured as a conflict with Satan. His healings and exorcisms are breaking up the hold that Satan has on human beings. Destruction of the power of evil is one of the signs of the coming of God's messiah (see Mark 3:22–27). Some of the demons even complain that Jesus is "destroying them" (1:24; 5:7). Jesus is also portrayed with power over nature. He can provide

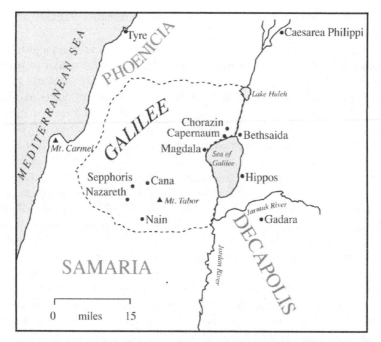

Some towns and cities in Galilee at the time of Jesus' ministry

food for the crowd from a small amount of bread and fish (6:30–42; 8:1–10) and rescue his terrified disciples from a storm at sea (6:45–52; 4:35–41).

You might think that anyone who has such divine powers would silence all opposition: human and demonic. That is where we run into the paradox. No matter what Jesus does, misunderstanding and hostility seem to grow. People in Jesus' hometown do not believe (6:1–6). We hear of the death suffered by John the Baptist and of Herod's fears that Jesus might be another John the Baptist (6:14–29). We even see that Jesus' own disciples have trouble understanding and believing in him (4:13, 40; 6:52; 7:18; 8:21). The first half of Mark, then, presents Jesus as a powerful divine savior who is consistently misunderstood and rejected.

Jesus, Suffering Son of Man

The first part of the gospel builds up to the revelation of Jesus as the messiah who must suffer in Mark 8:27–33. Now you can also see why that revelation is so important. Jesus' mission does not depend upon using divine power to get the crowds to follow him and to destroy his enemies. Jesus' mission is one of suffering and death. The rejection that he faced in Galilee is only a prelude to the final events of his life: his crucifixion by the religious and political authorities in Jerusalem.

Perhaps you noticed that in the outline of Mark there are only three healings in the second half of the gospel. The exorcism of the boy after the transfiguration repeats the lesson that faith is crucial to receiving salvation from Jesus. It shows that Jesus' disciples do not yet have such faith (9:14–29). Two others are healings of blind persons. Then there is one nature miracle, the cursing of the fig tree, which is associated with Jesus' condemnation of corruption in the Jerusalem temple and his prediction that the temple will be destroyed (11:12–21; 13:1–2). Mark often creates a "frame" for important parts of his gospel. Healing the blind men provides the frame for the revelation of Jesus as God's suffering messiah. There are three predictions of the passion in this section. Each one is more detailed. Each time the disciples become more and more frightened and perplexed (8:31–33; 9:30–32; 10:32–34). By framing this section with the healings, Mark points up the "blindness" of the disciples that will be healed.

Since Jesus' destiny is rejection and death, the final revelations about Jesus occur during the events of his passion. Jesus comes to Jerusalem "in the name of the Lord" (11:9), the royal messiah who is to restore the Davidic kingdom. His prophetic condemnation of corruption in the temple evokes the same official plotting to destroy him that his teaching had in Galilee (11:18; 3:6). A final sequence of controversy stories is introduced by a challenge to Jesus' *exousia*, "authority" (11:27–33). Jesus does not answer the question about the source of his authority directly. Instead, he exposes the falseness of the "chief priests, scribes, and elders" who posed the challenge. They cannot answer because they did not recognize divine authority behind the Baptist's preaching. However, they do not dare reject the Baptist's claim to speak God's word because they are afraid of the populace who revere John. Jesus' Parable of the Wicked Tenants serves as a thinly veiled condemnation of the religious and political leaders (12:1–11). It evokes further hostility (12:12).

Each additional controversy story begins with a challenge from either political or religious leadership. Jesus' responses often do not speak to the question posed directly. Instead, they show that these individuals have no understanding of what really belongs to God. Jesus even condemns the scribes for exploiting the poor and contrasts the seemingly pious, wealthy people with a poor widow's offering (12:35–44). There is one exception to this universal condemnation: the scribe in 12:28–34. He is not sent to challenge or trap Jesus like the others. Mark pictures him as hearing the debates and asking Jesus about the "greatest commandment." They agree that worship of God and love of God and neighbor are the greatest commandments in the law. Jesus praises the scribe for his insight. At the same time, the wisdom of this one scribe makes the perversity of Jesus' opponents all the worse. It is not impossible to recognize that Jesus speaks with God's authority if a person truly understands what God has revealed in the law.

The events of the passion show that Jesus dies as the messianic king of Israel. The woman who anoints Jesus in Mark 14:3–9 pours her costly ointment over his head as though anointing a new king. The charge that Jesus is "king of the Jews" runs through the trial before Pilate (15:1–32). Jesus is even mocked by the two men who are crucified with him for this claim. The onlookers insist that Jesus could not be "king" since he has no power to save himself or others. These accusations reflect the final irony of the gospel. As he dies, the Roman centurion will be the only one to see the truth: "Truly, this man was the Son of God" (15:39). God does "rescue" Jesus, not by giving him great earthly power, but by freeing him from death. Though his opponents may have appeared to have been victorious when they crucified Jesus, they were not successful. Jesus did not remain dead in the tomb (16:1–8).

Discipleship in Mark

Discipleship is one of the central issues in Mark. The gospel was written for Christians suffering persecution. They may have wondered why the powerful Jesus, now exalted with God in heaven, did not step in to rescue them. They could have been tempted to follow false messiahs who made promises about Jesus' return from heaven as Son of Man. Mark 13:32–37 warns about speculation like that. It insists that not even the Son knew when God would bring the judgment. If Jesus did not know, then no human being can claim to know either. The proper response for disciples is to always be ready for the coming of the Lord.

But discipleship will not be easy. Mark 13:9–13 prophesies suffering for those who preach the gospel. At the same time, they are to be confident that God is with them in suffering and that they will be saved. The same message about discipleship is delivered in the section framed by the healings of the blind. Disciples have to expect to suffer the same fate as their master (8:34–38). They are warned against thinking in terms of human greatness and power, when the example set by Jesus as the suffering Son of Man is one of humility, service, and suffering (9:33–37; 10:35–45). The story of the rich man whom Jesus loved but who could not bring himself to give up that wealth to become Jesus' disciple points out that disciples may even have to make material sacrifices to follow Jesus (10:17–31).

Even at the very end of the story, the women who have heard the angel announce the good news that Jesus has been raised run away from the tomb in fear (16:7–8). But for all the fears, hesitation, misunderstanding, opposition, and even flight that we see in Jesus' disciples, we also know that they finally did follow Jesus. We are reminded of this knowledge twice. Though reprimanding the sons of Zebedee for seeking positions of honor in the kingdom, Jesus does prophesy that they will suffer martyrdom (10:39–40). The prediction of Peter's denial elicits a vehement protest of willingness to "die with Jesus" (14:29–31). Mark's readers cannot have failed to think of Peter's martyrdom in Rome just a few years before the gospel was written. Though Peter failed to follow Jesus to the death in Jerusalem, he did so at the end of his life.

When we take the readers' familiarity with the story into account, we can see that the way in which Mark portrays the fears, weakness, and lack of understanding by Jesus' first disciples is part of the encouragement he offers Christians. Their weaknesses, just as much as the hostility of Jesus' enemies, were part of the divine plan for suffering and service. The divine forgiveness and love that is extended to all in Jesus' death was not less because of human failure. At the same time, the readers are also encouraged to follow Jesus faithfully, since they know that he is the source of divine salvation.

Summary

Mark's gospel paints a powerful picture of Jesus as the suffering Son of Man. We see the divine authority of Jesus in both miraculous deeds and teaching. We see a full range of human reactions to Jesus, from the great love of the woman who anoints him before his passion to the fears of his disciples and the mocking hostility of religious and political authorities. Since Jesus has power to break up Satan's empire and to control natural phenomena, we cannot agree with the crowd that he failed to save himself from the cross because he was unable to do so. Instead, we are forced to accept the death of Jesus as part of God's plan for the salvation of humanity.

That insight about the cross is so central to Mark that it shapes the whole gospel. It also shapes Mark's vision of discipleship. For Mark, the concrete issues of Christian life are very few. They are summarized in love of God and neighbor and in the willingness to follow Jesus' example of self-sacrificing service. No persons are excluded from God's love and forgiveness. No one can claim that being a disciple of the suffering Son of Man gives him or her a position of superiority over others. No one should be so naive as to think that the life of discipleship will be without failures and setbacks. But whatever the difficulties and confusion, whatever the cost in personal or material terms, Mark insists that Jesus is there "ahead of his disciples," always reaching out to save them.

STUDY QUESTIONS

Facts You Should Know

1. What did the word *gospel* (*euangelion*) originally mean? How did it come to be associated with a narrative account of Jesus' life?
2. What hints does Mark give us about the situation of the Christians for whom the gospel was written?
3. How does the composition of Mark emphasize the paradox of the suffering Son of God?
4. How does Mark emphasize the "authority" (*exousia*) of Jesus? Why is this emphasis important for the gospel's portrayal of the suffering of Jesus and his disciples?

Things to Do

1. Find the passages in which "Son of God" is used for Jesus in Mark. Who knows Jesus' identity in each case? How does the final example illustrate Mark's theme of the "crucified savior"?
2. Trace the reactions of the disciples of Jesus to his deeds and words through the gospel. Where do misunderstanding and fear cause the disciples to fail Jesus?

Things to Think About

1. What is the cost of discipleship for Christians today? Are we just as repelled by the message of suffering and lowliness as the disciples in Mark?
2. What happens to faith that is based upon Jesus "the powerful miracle worker" in Mark's gospel? How do people today base their faith on demonstrations of divine power by religious figures?

Chapter 13

MATTHEW: JESUS, TEACHER OF ISRAEL

The Composition of Matthew

Though Matthew incorporates much of the material in Mark, comparison of the two gospels shows that Matthew also reshapes it. He does so to include additional material from other sources, to improve the order in which material is presented, or to correct details. Or Matthew may revise his sources to bring out the message in a particular episode. You can see Matthew at work by comparing the presentation of John the Baptist and Jesus in the two gospels. Mark 1:2–15 contains four narrative episodes:

(a) Presentation of John the Baptist as the messenger in the wilderness (vv. 2–8)

(b) Jesus' baptism by John (vv. 9–11)

(c) Jesus' testing in the wilderness (vv. 12–13)

(d) Jesus comes preaching the kingdom (vv. 14–15)

Each episode has its counterpart in Matthew.

Matthew 3:1–12 has reworked the appearance of the Baptist. The first rearrangement is one that a writing teacher might tell you to make in a story. Matthew moves the reference to John the Baptist from after the quotation to the opening of the story, which creates a smoother introduction to the episode. Next, compare the two quotations. You may need help from the footnotes in your Bible to figure this one out. Matthew omits the part about the messenger in Mark 1:2. This change is an example of a correction. The prophecy being fulfilled is identified as that of Isaiah. However, Mark included the words of Malachi 3:1 before he gets to Isaiah 40:3. You can see that the reference to a messenger preparing a way would make it natural to link the two together. But Matthew, who highlights prophetic passages that point to Jesus, corrects the citation so that only the words of Isaiah are used. Now look at the content of the Baptist's preaching. Matthew has sayings about judgment (vv. 7–10, 12) not found in Mark. In addition, Matthew has taken the reference to fire from the judgment sayings and added it to the prediction of Jesus' coming to baptize with the Spirit from Mark 1:7–8 (see Matt 11). Luke's version of this episode (Luke 3:1–20) shows that these sayings were also known to Luke in this context. Therefore, we can conclude that Matthew was using material about the Baptist from Q in addition to Mark.

Besides concern for prophetic tradition, the Matthean version of this episode has other themes that will be repeated in the gospel. Compare Matthew 3:7 with Luke 3:7. In Luke, you will notice that John speaks his words of condemnation to the crowd. In Matthew, he has a particular target, the Pharisees and Sadducees. As you read through Matthew, you will find the Pharisees condemned for hypocritical behavior and for making detailed commandments more important than mercy. This preoccupation with the Pharisees could be motivated by the circumstances of Matthew's time. After the destruction of Jerusalem and its temple (AD 70), the idea that the whole nation might become holy, not simply the temple and its priests, gained influence. Pharisaic interpretation of the law may even have influenced Jewish Christians in Matthew's community. Matthew does not think that Christians need to create their own copy of Pharisaism. Jesus has shown them a way to a greater righteousness (Matt 5:20). Right from the beginning, then, Matthew makes readers suspicious of the Pharisees. Another theme that Matthew will emphasize is judgment. A different problem in Matthew's church may lie behind this emphasis: Christians who do not follow Jesus' ethical teaching. Matthew 7:15–23 warns against persons who are "false prophets," who do not bear good fruit, and against some who think that they are saved because they have worked miracles in Jesus' name. Matthew reminds readers that they will be judged by their faithfulness to Jesus' teaching.

Now compare Matthew's version of the baptism of Jesus with Mark's version (Matt 3:13–17; Mark 1:9–11). This episode shows Matthew providing a new perspective on the tradition. There are two major changes. Matthew adds a dialogue between Jesus and the Baptist in verses 14–15. This dialogue makes it clear that Jesus was not baptized because he needed to repent of sin. Rather, Jesus is being baptized as an act of righteousness, to fulfill God's plan. You will also notice another difference. Where Mark 1:11 has the divine voice speak to Jesus alone (the Greek indicates a second person singular), Matthew 3:17 has a public declaration that Jesus is "beloved Son."

The episode of Jesus' testing in the wilderness is much more extensive than in Mark (Matt 4:1–11). Matthew's version supplies what Mark 1:12–13 lacks: the content of the "test" that Jesus faced. Once again, Luke has a version similar to Matthew's; though the "tests" occur in a different order, it is likely that Matthew used Q material for the entire episode.

Finally, look at the final scene in the series, Matthew 4:12–17. By now, you should be familiar with the types of change that Matthew has made. First, you can see that Matthew has given this episode a longer introduction describing Jesus' geographical movements and even suggesting that Capernaum rather than Nazareth became Jesus' home (v. 13). With his interest in fulfillment of prophecy, Matthew provides another citation from Isaiah in verses 15–16. This citation may be the reason that Matthew added the explanation of Jesus' movements. Also notice that Matthew has shortened the words used by Jesus in verse 17 (compare Mark 1:15). He does not have to mention fulfillment, since he has already shown that Jesus fulfills the prophecy, so he drops Mark's phrase "the time is fulfilled." Then Matthew takes the call to repent to introduce Jesus' words. However, Matthew recognizes that to have Jesus speak like a Christian missionary and call people to "believe in the gospel" (Mark 1:15c) is out of place, so he drops that expression as well.

So far, we have seen Matthew use traditions from Mark, from Q, and from the Old Testament. However, there is also material in Matthew found only in this gospel. A quick comparison of Matthew's chapter of parables (chapter 13) with Mark 4 provides an example of this type of tradition (see Chart 13–1). Matthew has included a number of parables that are not found in Mark (or Luke). Yet variants of them do turn up in the second-century-AD *Gospel of Thomas*. Therefore, Matthew probably derived these parables from another source or tradition. The extra interpretations provided for them and the Matthean theme of judgment both appear to be the work of the evangelist.

You will also notice that Matthew has taken the hints about Jesus' mode of teaching in Mark and expanded them. He gives prophetic support for the suggestion that the teaching of the parables was in some sense "hidden" from those who heard it. However, he also wants the reader to be sure that Jesus' disciples were not ignorant of Jesus' true meaning. Therefore, Matthew has reshaped the whole discourse so that such confusion could not arise.

MATTHEW'S REDACTION OF MARK 4   [13–1]

(a) Introduction: Teaching from a boat (Mark 4:1; Matt 13:1–2)

(b) Parable of the Sower (Mark 4:2–9; Matt 13:3–9)

(c) Explanation of why Jesus speaks in parables (Mark 4:10–12; Matt 13:10–11, 13 [Matt 13:12 = Mark 4:25] [Matt 13:14–15, quotation from Isaiah being fulfilled] [Matt 13:16–17, Blessing on Jesus' disciples (from Q see Luke 10:23–24)])

(d) Explanation of the Parable of the Sower (Mark 4:13–20; Matt 13:18–23)

(e) Sayings of Jesus as warnings to disciples about how they hear (Mark 4:21–25: v. 21 see Matt 5:15; v. 22 see Matt 10:26; v. 23 see Matt 13:43 and 11:15; v. 24 see Matt 7:2; v. 25 = Matt 13:12)

Continued

Continued

(f) Parable of the Seed Growing Secretly: in Mark 4:26–29 this is an image of seed growing up "of itself" until harvest, but in Matt 13:24–30 we have a story of a man whose enemy has planted weeds in with his wheat [a version of this parable occurs in *Gos. Thom.* 57].

(g) Parable of the Mustard Seed (Mark 4:30–32; Matt 13:31–32) [Matt 13:33, Parable of Leaven (also *Gos. Thom.* 96)]

(h) Jesus speaks to crowds in parables, but explains to disciples in private (Mark 4:33–34; Matt 13:34 = Mark 4:33) [Matt 13:35, Fulfillment quotation] [Matt 13:36–43, Jesus explains the Parable of Wheat and Tares to his disciples in private] [Matt 13:44, Parable of the Hidden Treasure (*Gos. Thom.* 109, has a related story)] [Matt 13:45–46, Parable of the Pearl of Great Price (*Gos. Thom.* 76)] [Matt 13:47–48, Parable of the Hidden Fishnet (*Gos. Thom.* 8)] [Matt 13:49–50, Explanation of the fishnet] [Matt 13:51, Jesus' disciples have understood his teaching (see Mark 4:34)] [Matt 13:52, Saying about the scribe trained for the kingdom of heaven]

Matthew's emphasis on Jesus' role as the true interpreter of the will of God is evident in the structure of this gospel. At the beginning of Mark we saw references to Jesus' teaching as manifesting the same power as his miracles (Mark 1:27). Matthew puts the teaching before the miracles of Jesus. He picks up Mark's reference to Jesus' activity in Galilee (Mark 1:35–39) and reformulates it to provide a general summary of Jesus' activity (Matt 4:23–25). You will notice that the geographical range of Jesus' activities has been increased in Matthew's version. Look at a map of Palestine in Jesus' time. You can see that all the major regions are covered by the crowds that come to hear Jesus. In addition, Matthew 4:24 asserts that Jesus' reputation has spread even into Syria. With the exception of the reference to the Roman governor in Luke 2:2, this is the only mention of Syria in the gospels. Matthew's gospel has often been linked with Christianity in the region of Antioch in Syria. This brief reference may be another "footprint" that points toward Matthew's audience.

Now look at the outline of Matthew's gospel. You will see two major changes in the presentation of Jesus' story. The first change involves expanding the beginning and end of the narrative. Mark began with John the Baptist. Matthew has brought together early traditions about Jesus' Davidic heritage in a genealogy (Matt 1:1–17), Jesus' birth as the one who is to save Israel (1:18– 25), and the persecution by the evil king Herod that drives the family to repeat the journey of the people of Israel by going down into Egypt and then being brought back by God (2:1–23). As you read through, you will notice that Matthew has inserted quotations from the prophets to show that Jesus is fulfilling God's plan. Mark originally ended his gospel with the women fleeing the empty tomb because they were afraid. We know from the angel's words in Mark 16:7 that Jesus will meet the disciples again in Galilee, but Mark's original version ended before that part of the story. We also know from Paul that Jesus did appear to groups of disciples and to Paul himself (1 Cor 15:3–10). Matthew's gospel ends the story as Christians would expect. The women do not simply run away. Jesus appears to them and repeats the angel's message. At the very end of the gospel, the risen Lord appears to the eleven disciples in Galilee. They are told of Jesus' divine authority and of his continued presence with the church, and they are given a mission to spread Jesus' teaching to all the nations (Matt 28:16–20).

The Sermons: Jesus Instructs the Community

The second major structural change you could predict. Jesus is presented throughout the gospel as a teacher. Matthew has Jesus deliver five sermons. Each one begins with the people or disciples gathering around Jesus. Each one ends with a reference to the fact that Jesus had finished speaking. We have already seen that Matthew is concerned about the theme of judgment. Each one of the five sermons concludes with that theme. Matthew often uses parables about judgment to make his point:

(a) Sermon on the Mount: Two types of foundation (7:24–27)
(b) Kingdom parables: Interpretation of weeds and wheat (13:36–43)
(c) Community relationships: The unforgiving servant (18:21–35)
(d) On judgment: Wise and foolish servant girls (25:1–13); talents (25:14–30); sheep and goats, the judgment of the nations (25:31–46)

OUTLINE OF MATTHEW   **[13–2]**

Infancy narrative (1:1–2:23)

Beginning of Jesus' ministry (3:1–4:25)

Sermon: Sermon on the Mount (5:1–7:29)

Healings and gathering of followers (8:1–9:34)

Sermon: Disciples on mission to Israel (9:35–11:1)

Jesus' teaching in Galilee (11:1–12:50)

Sermon: Parables of the kingdom (13:1–52)

Continued

Continued

Ministry in Galilee and surrounding areas (13:53–16:12)

Jesus as messiah who will suffer (16:13–17:23)

Instructions for the community (17:24–18:35)

  (a) On paying the temple tax (17:24–27)
  (b) Sermon: Relationships within the community (18:1–35)

Jesus teaches disciples on journey to Jerusalem (19:1–20:34)

Jesus in Jerusalem (21:1–25:46)

  (a) Entry into Jerusalem and cleansing of the temple (21:1–22)
  (b) Controversies with religious authorities (21:23–22:46)
  (c) Denunciation of scribes and Pharisees (23:1–39)
  (d) Sermon: The end of the world and judgment (24:1–26:1)
    (i) Prediction: Temple will be destroyed (24:1–2)
    (ii) Coming of the end: Always be watchful (24:3–51)
    (iii) Parables of judgment (25:1–46)

Passion of Jesus (26:1–27:66)

Resurrection of Jesus (28:1–20)

  (a) Empty tomb (28:1–8, 11–15)
  (b) Jesus appears to the women near the tomb (28:9–10)
  (c) Jesus appears to disciples in Galilee: Go preach to the nations (28:16–20)

Each one of these parables concludes with a warning to the audience to be ready for the judgment.

The missionary discourse in Matthew 10 concludes with a different kind of reference to judgment: the reward for those who treat the disciples well even if they do not actually become Christians (Matt 10:40–42). In a world of wandering preachers who are completely dependent upon others, such help would be crucial to survival. Whatever such hospitable outsiders have done for Jesus' disciples will be treated as though it were done for God. Perhaps you are already familiar with the Parable of the Sheep and the Goats (Matt 25:31–46). There you will find a similar teaching about judgment. Jesus comes to judge all the nations of the world. But the grounds on which judgment is made turn out to be the way in which individuals have treated the poor, oppressed, and suffering "little ones" with whom Jesus identifies himself.

Matthew does not want readers to think that, just because God will reward or punish based on the justice and mercy shown to others, there is no real point to being a Christian. Remember that at the end of the gospel the risen Jesus instructed his disciples to go and teach all the nations what he had taught. Christians have the advantage of Jesus' teaching and of Jesus' help in following it. But Matthew is also realistic, warning believers who are not concerned with producing good fruit that they will face judgment. Matthew also recognizes the Christian churches as a minority group living in a much larger world, much like the situation of the Jewish communities from which the Jesus movement emerged. Matthew knows that sympathetic outsiders have often helped Christians. He knows that nonbelievers can be just and merciful. God will never forget the good that people have done for the poor and suffering humanity with which Jesus identifies.

Jesus as Fulfillment of the Law

In Matthew 3:15, Jesus says that he is to be baptized by John because "it is fitting for us to fulfill all righteousness." The verb *fulfill* usually appears in Matthew in the introduction to a quotation from the prophets (e.g., Matt 1:22; 2:15, 17; 4:14; 8:17; 12:17). However, in Matthew 5:17, we find the affirmation: "Do not think that I have come to destroy the law and the prophets; I have not come to destroy but to fulfill." Matthew 5:17–20 affirms the abiding validity of the Mosaic law and asserts that entering the kingdom requires a righteousness "greater than the scribes and Pharisees." Thus, the teaching of Jesus that follows is set in the context of "fulfilling" the law and prophets and presenting a "higher righteousness" than that of this particular group of interpreters. Disagreements over how to interpret the law were as much a part of Jewish life in the first century as they are today. The Pharisaic movement claimed to base its application of the law on oral traditions that had as much validity as the written text (Matt 23:2). Many of their particular concerns are reflected in the New Testament: purity (Matt 23:25–26); tithing (Luke 11:42); fasting (Mark 2:18); Sabbath observance (Mark 2:23–28); proper religious deportment in public (Matt 23:5–7, 27–33). As the controversies with Jesus indicate, Pharisees were active in promoting their understanding of holiness among the populace at large (Matt 22:16). The overlap between scribes and Pharisees points to the emphasis on grounding this teaching in scripture. Understood within this first-century Jewish setting, Matthew's Jesus is staking his claim to be the superior to the Pharisees in interpreting the law. He is not rejecting Judaism as a religious way of life.

Matthew's preoccupation with the Pharisaic teachers of the law is evident throughout the gospel. Matthew 23:2–3 suggests that believers might even "obey" the teaching of the Pharisees but not their conduct. If you compare the controversy stories about the greatest commandment and who the "Son of David" is in Matthew 22:34–40, 41–46 with their Marcan source (Mark 12:28–34, 35–37a), you will notice that Matthew has changed the focus of the story. A Pharisee (not a scribe as in Mark) questions Jesus. Matthew omits the exchange of praise (Mark 12:31–34a) that culminates in Jesus saying that the scribe is "not far from the kingdom." Now the story presents Jesus' declaration about the double love command as fulfillment of the law in opposition to the Pharisees. The next episode, the question about the "Son of David," has also been shifted from a general statement made before a crowd to a question that Jesus puts directly to an assembly of Pharisees. Their inability to answer (v. 46a) demonstrates Jesus' authority as the true interpreter of God's will. The condemnation of the teaching and practice of the scribes and Pharisees in Matthew 23 draws together sayings from Q as well as tradition special to Matthew.

Compare Matthew 23:23–24 with Luke 11:42. Matthew has added "scribes" and the epithet "hypocrites" to the "Pharisees" in the saying. He has also shifted the expression of what is neglected from Luke's "justice and the love of God" to "the weightier matters of the law, justice and mercy and faith," and then attached an additional condemnation of these teachers as "blind guides, straining out a gnat and swallowing a camel." The Sermon on the Mount draws a sharp contrast between the way in which Christians are to give alms, pray, and fast and the ostentatious, public display of the "hypocrites" (Matt 6:1–6, 16–18).

But Matthew's concerns are not simply directed against the influence of Pharisaic teaching. His references to "their synagogue" (4:23; 9:35; 10:17; 12:9; 13:54) and "your synagogue" (23:34) suggest that Matthew's church has its own assemblies separate from those of its Jewish neighbors. Compare Matthew 23:34–36 with the Q version of the woe oracle reflected in Luke 11:49–51. In Q, God's Wisdom pronounces judgment against the people for killing and persecuting the prophets and messengers sent by God. Matthew is attacking the scribes and Pharisees (v. 29) for hypocritical behavior. They consider themselves better than their ancestors, who had persecuted the prophets. But their deeds prove otherwise. Identifying Jesus with Wisdom, Matthew omits the reference to Wisdom as speaker. Jesus becomes the "I" who sends "prophets, wise people, and scribes" who are killed, crucified, and scourged in "your synagogues" and persecuted from town to town. The separation between Jewish and Christian groups is not a polite agreement to go separate ways. It has resulted from the hostility that Christian preachers experienced (also see 5:10–12, 44; 10:23). Remember Paul himself once persecuted the church out of zeal for ancestral traditions (Gal 1:13–14).

Matthew 23:8–12 warns Christians against copying the behavior attributed to scribes and Pharisees. They are not to seek titles and positions of honor. Some of the sharp polemic against them as "hypocrites" may just as well be aimed at Matthew's own community. Matthew warned against other Christians who are not the "prophets" sent by Jesus but "false prophets" (7:15). Matthew 24:9b–13 expands the warning about persecution from Mark 13:13 to include evils within the community: (a) betrayal and hatred; (b) false prophets leading people astray; (c) love growing cold and an increase in lawlessness.

Yet Matthew does not seek to establish a Christian Pharisaism. His gospel concludes with an affirmation that Jesus' teaching is to be spread to "all the nations." The word *ethne*, "nations," is often used to mean "Gentiles." Matthew has even based his gospel on Mark, a work that originated among Gentile Christians. He acknowledges that Christians are engaged in converting Gentiles (10:17–18) even in the missionary discourse that limits the activity of the disciples to the lost sheep of Israel (10:5–6).

James, the leader of Jewish Christianity in Paul's time, had been martyred circa AD 62, and the Christian community at Jerusalem had been scattered during the Jewish revolt against Rome in AD 66 to 70. Matthew's portrayal of hostility toward Jesus and his followers suggests that by the time he writes there is not much of a continued mission to Israel. His gospel concludes with Jesus authorizing a mission to the Gentiles. But such a shift could have seemed to mean rejecting the Jewish Christian heritage of the community. Matthew's presentation of Jesus and the law responds to suspicions that Jesus believers are not heirs of God's promised salvation but lawless apostates.

Jesus is presented as the "fulfillment" of the law whose teaching emphasizes the fundamental elements of the law: love of God and neighbor, justice, mercy. Now look at the way in which Matthew 15:1–14 handles the controversy with the Pharisees over the custom of ritual washing before meals from Mark 7:1–15. Naturally, he has no need to explain Jewish purification rituals (Mark 7:3–4). He then relocates the argument that Pharisaic "traditions" are contrary to the commandments of God from its Marcan position after the Isaiah prophecy to before the quotation. The reader sees that the "traditions" that the Pharisees seek to enforce are the human doctrines and false worship about which Isaiah speaks. Matthew adds a brief exchange between Jesus and the disciples about Pharisaic objections to Jesus' teaching (vv. 12–14). They are "blind guides" whose teaching does not come from God and who will be destroyed. In the explanation that follows (Matt 15:15–20//Mark 7:17–23), Matthew omits Mark's generalizing of the episode to imply that Jesus had also suspended kosher rules (Mark 7:19b). Perhaps Jewish Christians in his community still observed them.

Jesus' teaching presents the true commandment of God. Traditions that are ways of sidestepping the will of God expressed in the commandment should be rejected. In this episode, Jesus points to the example of declaring some part of one's property "Corban," dedicated to God, and thus avoiding the obligation to support one's parents. The controversy over divorce in Matthew 19:3–9 (Mark 10:1–12) presents another example of such a distinction. This time a provision of the Mosaic law, granting the divorced woman a certificate of divorce (Deut 24:1), is rejected as an accommodation to human "hardness of heart" but not part of God's will exemplified in creation.

You can see that Matthew has been careful to make it clear that Jesus' teaching expresses the will of God, which is the norm for all obedience to the law. The way in which Matthew links the double love command with the affirmation that Jesus is Son of David in 22:34–46 reminds us that Jesus is more than just another sectarian interpreter of the law. Speaking as the messianic Son of David, who fulfills the prophets, Jesus' word about the will of God is more than a human interpretation. It expresses God's own intention in giving the law. Indeed, by going beyond the law as the possession of Israel and its custodians, the scribes and Pharisees, Matthew sees that Jesus' teaching will be preached as God's word to all the nations (28:19).

Discipleship in Matthew

The commission in Matthew 28:19 calls upon Jesus' followers to "make disciples" from all the nations. The verb *matheteuein,* to "make a disciple of someone" or to "be a disciple," occurs in Matthew 13:52 and 27:57. In the latter, it designates Joseph of Arimathea as Jesus' disciple. Matthew 13:52 speaks of "every scribe who has been made a disciple for the kingdom." Such a person is able to bring out of his treasure both old things and new things. Perhaps this verse is the evangelist's description of himself. We have seen hints that Matthew's community needs both "new things" and "old ones" to meet the situation in which it finds itself. Externally disciples must face persecution, opposition from both Jews and Gentiles. Internally the community appears sharply divided. There are conflicting voices among the teachers and prophets. There is confusion about how the community should proceed in the future and about how it should relate to its Jewish Christian heritage.

We find hints that relationships between Christians are also deteriorating. This problem emerges most clearly in Matthew 18 in the discourse on relationships within the community. As in the other discourses, Matthew has gathered together material from Mark, Q, and his own tradition and reshaped it. The chapter opens with an affirmation that only one who is willing to be humble, of no importance, like a child, is great in the kingdom. Notice how Matthew 18:3–4 has reformulated the tradition of Mark 10:15. The issue is no longer "receiving" the kingdom like a child or, as in verse 5, receiving a child in Jesus' name (cf. Mark 9:37). Rather the disciple must become like a child. Remember that in the first century being a child did not have warm, positive feelings associated with it. Being a child was like being a slave, someone of no significance or importance. Matthew 18:4 emphasizes that point by speaking of one who "humbles" himself or herself.

Matthew 18:6–9 shifts abruptly to a severe warning against those who cause others to stumble. Matthew adds verse 7 to material he has taken over from Mark 9:42–48. Even if it is necessary, one of the evils at the end of the age that stumbling blocks will come, the person responsible is condemned. From this general warning against leading others to sin, Matthew turns to leaders of the community. He uses the Parable of the Lost Sheep from Q (Matt 18:12–

13//Luke 15:4–6) to remind them that they must always seek out one of the "little ones" who has gone astray. God wants them to be saved, not to perish.

Several sayings about relationships between Christians follow in verses 15–21. A simpler Q saying exhorting Christians to forgive one another (cf. Luke 17:3–4) has been expanded to form a set of rules for handling disputes between believers. Whatever decisions the community reaches in resolving such conflicts are viewed as binding in heaven (v. 18). Finally, this teaching on forgiveness is concluded with the Parable of the Unforgiving Servant (vv. 23–35). Christians are warned that if they do not forgive, they are liable to judgment. This emphasis upon mutual forgiveness appears to be Matthew's response to the betrayal, hatred, and "love growing cold" that afflict the community. We have seen that Matthew constantly warns readers that Christians must always be prepared for God's judgment. Otherwise they could find themselves excluded like the wedding guest without the proper attire (Matt 22:11–14).

Matthew also has a message of comfort for a troubled church. They can trust in Jesus' eternal presence (Matt 28:20). Matthew reworks a sequence of three Marcan stories of Jesus and the disciples in a boat to show how Jesus strengthens the "little faith" of the disciples. The first is the storm at sea (Matt 8:18, 23–27//Mark 4:35–41). Where Mark has Jesus rebuke the disciples for having no faith after he has calmed the storm (Mark 4:40), Matthew has Jesus ask why they are afraid, like persons of little faith, and then he calms the storm. Those changes present Jesus' gesture as one of reassurance. Trust and reassurance for a battered community become the focus of Matthew's presentation of the walking on water miracle (Matt 14:22–23//Mark 6:45–52). In Mark the episode concludes with a severe chiding of the disciples for being persons whose hearts are hardened. Matthew's version, on the other hand, demonstrates Jesus' ability to save. Not only are the disciples rescued, but even Peter could have walked on water if his faith had not failed him. At the end of the story, the disciples acknowledge that Jesus is the Son of God.

The final example shifts from the realm of miracles to that of teaching. The warning about the leaven of the Pharisees (Mark 8:14–21//Matt 16:5–12) again finds the Marcan disciples chided for their lack of understanding and hardness of heart. In Matthew Jesus refers to the "little faith" of the disciples. He then explains to the disciples that the "leaven" means the teaching of the Pharisees and Sadducees. Thus Matthew suggests that it is not just the presence of Jesus helping the community, but also Jesus' teaching that can sustain them during this time of "little faith." Matthew states that the disciples understood that teaching in 13:51 and 17:13. He omits the elements of fear and misunderstanding from their response to the passion predictions (Matt 20:17–19; contrast Mark 10:32–34).

The Sermon on the Mount provides the basic description of what it means to be a disciple of Jesus at the opening of Jesus' public ministry. The

Beatitudes describe the blessings on Jesus' "little ones" who are persecuted for the sake of the kingdom (5:3–12). The sayings about salt and light admonish the disciples never to surrender their mission of witnessing before humanity (5:13–16). Then the "higher righteousness" that Jesus has made possible is described first in a series of antitheses that culminate in love of enemy (5:21–48). Teaching about true almsgiving, fasting, and worship again emphasizes the need for forgiveness (6:1–18; see 6:14–15). Disciples must be devoted to the kingdom. Neither desires for earthly possessions nor anxieties about how they are to survive are to deter them (6:19–34). Matthew 7 turns to teaching and warning directed at some of the tensions within the community. Once again, readers are reminded not to judge others (7:1–5). Only "hypocrites" try to take a grain of dirt out of someone else's eye while they have a log in their own. Whatever happens, disciples are not to abandon their confidence in God as the source of "good things" when they turn to ask (7:7–11). But as in the earlier teaching about prayer, the disciple's prayer is complemented by love of others. Here the golden rule summarizes the positive ethical teaching of the Sermon (7:12). These instructions on discipleship conclude with warnings about judgment (7:13–27).

Summary

We have seen that Matthew is more than a collection of traditions about Jesus gathered together in the framework of the ministry and passion of Jesus. The evangelist has shaped the traditions about Jesus to address the situation of Christians who must find their way outside the original confines of Judaism. Matthew assures them that Jesus and his teaching bring that tradition to its fulfillment. They can go out to the nations with a treasure that embraces both old things and new ones. In the teaching that Jesus gave the disciples, Christians have a guide to the true expression of God's will for humanity.

For those who are troubled by the ongoing hardships of discipleship and even the internal turmoil that divides the community, Matthew shows the disciples how to overcome their "little faith" by trusting in Jesus' power to save them. As long as it exists in this age, the church will be a mixed community of good and bad. God's judgment will be the time of separation. In the present, Christians must remember that discipleship asks them to be always ready for the Lord's return. Their relationships with one another are not to be marked by legalism, judgment, or exclusion. They are to be characterized by justice, mercy, forgiveness, and a repeated willingness to go out to the "lost." Matthew ends with a ringing affirmation of the Lord's presence to the community of "little ones" (28:20b). This presence fulfills the promise given in the naming of Jesus "Emmanuel," "God-with-us," at the beginning of the gospel (1:22–23).

STUDY QUESTIONS

Facts You Should Know

1. List five ways in which Matthew has revised material taken over from Mark and give an example of each one.
2. Give three examples of Matthew's emphasis on judgment. To whom is the warning about judgment directed in each example?
3. Give three examples of Jesus as "true interpreter of the law" from Matthew. How is Jesus contrasted with other teachers in the context from which you have taken your examples?
4. Give an example of how Matthew has shifted Mark's picture of Jesus' disciples away from "misunderstanding" and "fear" toward one of little or immature faith. What characteristics has Matthew given the disciples in his portrayal?
5. How does Matthew use the warnings against the "hypocrites" (Pharisees) to address dangers within the Christian community?

Things to Do

1. Using a concordance, find the passages in which Matthew uses the verb *to fulfill*. What do these passages tell the reader of the gospel about Jesus?
2. Using a gospel parallel, study the five sermons in Matthew's gospel. How has Matthew brought together traditional material in each case? How do the concluding warnings about judgment fit in with the teaching given in each sermon?

Things to Think About

1. Matthew addresses a warning about judgment to the Christian community of his day. What failures in Christian discipleship today call for such warnings?
2. Both the sermon on relationships within the community (Matt 18) and the condemnation of the Pharisees (Matt 23) carry lessons about leadership for Christians. How could those lessons be applied today?

Chapter 14

LUKE: JESUS, THE LORD

The Composition of Luke

Luke opens with a prologue (1:1–4), which in one elegant sentence presents the evangelist's relationship to other accounts of what has happened among the Christians. The prologue is comparable to those of other ancient literary works with two puzzling exceptions: its brevity and lack of the author's name. The Jewish historian Josephus wrote an apologetic work, *Against Apion*, that is addressed to a distinguished figure and that picks up the account in a second volume (*Against Apion* 1.1.1–3; 2.1.1) as Luke will do in Acts. Josephus points to his own earlier history, *Antiquities of the Jews*, and assures his distinguished reader that his book is written to "convict our detractors of opprobrium and deliberate falsehood, to correct the ignorance of others, and to instruct whoever desires to know the truth about the antiquity of our race."

Luke's preface is similar. The purpose indicated in verse 4b is [that you] "may know what assurance (*asphaleia*) you have for the matters about which you have been instructed." This phrase suggests that the evangelist has apologetic concerns comparable to those reflected in Josephus. Luke is defending Christianity against false accusations before a sympathetic audience. A similar expression, "to know the *asphales*," "certainty/truth," occurs in Acts 21:34. There the uproar of the crowd shouting contradictory opinions makes it impossible for the tribune to tell what Paul is being accused of. Paul is taken inside and speaks in his own defense. This pattern is repeated in Paul's speech before the council in Acts 22:30. When Paul is brought before King Agrippa in Acts 25:26, the Roman procurator says that he has nothing *asphales* to charge Paul with. In the realm of law and politics, the word *asphaleia* refers to the reliability of information whether from a source or a written document or report. In verse 2, Luke mentions both eyewitnesses and written material. These examples suggest that *asphaleia* means knowing the truth about the Christian message.

Anyone who knows this truth will reject accusations brought against those who preach the gospel. Theophilus is not an outsider like the officials in the trial stories. He has already received reports about or perhaps even been instructed in Christian matters. Therefore, scholars have suggested that Luke has more in mind than apologetics. He wishes to assure the reader that what the church is preaching goes back to the *kerygma* (preaching) of Jesus and the earliest disciples.

Luke's preface indicates the evangelist's literary goal: to present material from earlier written traditions in a more appropriate order. Like Matthew, Luke takes over much of Mark and adds material from the sayings collection Q along with that found only in Luke ("L"). Two sections of Mark do not show up at all in Luke: Mark 6:45—8:26; 9:41—10:12. One of the most striking departures from Mark's narrative order is the block of material between Luke 9:51 and 18:14. This new section follows the transfiguration, healing of the possessed boy, passion prediction, and dispute about greatness (Luke 9:28–50) adapted from the Marcan teaching on discipleship (Mark 9:2–41). Luke returns to this section of Mark at 18:15–43.

Luke 9:51 is phrased in formal language, similar to the Greek Old Testament. Jesus turns toward Jerusalem to fulfill a divine plan by which he will be "taken up" (to heaven) from Jerusalem. Luke turns that journey into a lengthy period of instruction. Over half of the "L" material in the gospel is found here. It includes famous parables of Jesus: Good Samaritan (10:29–37); Persistent Friend (11:5–8); Rich Fool (12:16–21); Fig Tree (13:1–9); Lost Coin (15:8–10); Prodigal Son (15:11–32); Dishonest Steward (16:1–8a); Rich Man and Lazarus (16:19–31); Unjust Judge (18:1–8); Pharisee and Tax Collector (18:9–14).

By creating this new section, Luke narrates the ministry of Jesus in three parts: (a) Galilean ministry (4:14—9:50); (b) journey to Jerusalem (9:51—19:27); (c) ministry in Jerusalem (19:28—21:38). Luke introduces the gospel with an account of the births of John the Baptist and Jesus in fulfillment of God's plan of salvation (1:5—2:52) and the career of the Baptist as preparation for the opening of Jesus' ministry (3:1—4:13). The gospel ends with the passion (22:1—23:56a) and resurrection (23:56b—24:53) of Jesus. However, Luke makes it clear that the end of the gospel is not the end of his story. The disciples are told to wait in Jerusalem for the coming of the Spirit; then they will be witnesses of all that has happened to the nations (24:47–49). This instruction anticipates the opening of his second volume, the Acts of the Apostles.

Luke also shifts the order of episodes taken from Mark to provide better narrative continuity. He finishes with the Baptist before Jesus' public ministry begins by mentioning John's imprisonment (3:19–20). Jesus' rejection at Nazareth (from Mark 6:1–16) is incorporated into a synagogue scene that inaugurates Jesus' ministry in Luke 4:16–30. There we learn that the Spirit rests on Jesus in fulfillment of the messianic prophecies. But we also see that

Jesus will have a double fate. Some will receive the news with joy. Others will reject God's salvation. Luke has also built the same contrast into the infancy narratives. Read Luke 2:24–38. When Jesus is brought to the temple the prophetic figures Simeon and Anna, who represent the pious of Israel, receive him with joy. Anna becomes a "witness," telling others who are looking for the promised redemption about him. Simeon proclaims that God's salvation has come for all people. However, his blessing on Mary warns of opposition to her son. Luke relocates the episode about Jesus' real relatives (Mark 3:31–35) after the interpretation of the Parable of the Sower (8:19–21). In its new position, the story becomes an example of hearing and following the word of God.

Further evidence of the care with which the evangelist has planned this gospel is evident in the parallel episodes found in each of the three sections. These episodes are another way of contrasting those who welcome Jesus with those who reject him.

We also find another block of special Lucan material in the passion and resurrection accounts of the gospel. The passion includes an appearance before Herod (23:6–12) and explicit declarations of Jesus' innocence by Pilate (23:4, 14–15, 22). Luke's narrative suggests that Pilate turned Jesus over to the hostile crowd for execution (23:25–26). This emphasis may be apologetic. Luke wishes to demonstrate that Jesus was not guilty of the charges of rebellion and insurrection that were the alleged reason for his death. Even those involved in his execution knew that he was innocent.

DIVISIONS IN JESUS' MINISTRY			[14–1]
	Galilee	**Journey**	**Jerusalem**
rejection:	Nazareth (4:22–29)	Samaria (9:52–56)	Jerusalem (19:42–48)
sends disciples:	"the 12" (9:1–6)	"the 70" (10:1–20)	"the 12" (22:35–38)
relatives/women:	true relatives (8:19–21)	mother blessed (11:27–28)	women of Jerusalem (23:26)
true greatness:	receive child (9:46–48)	Jesus' "baptism" (12:50)	one who serves (22:24–27)
Herod:	his opinion (9:7–9)	Jesus warned about (13:31–35)	Jesus appears before (23:6–16)

OUTLINE OF LUKE   [14–2]

Prologue (1:1–4)

Infancy narratives: John the Baptist and Jesus (1:5—2:52)

Preparation for Jesus' ministry (3:1—4:13)

    (a) The Baptist's preaching and imprisonment (3:1–20)
    (b) Jesus: Baptism, genealogy, and temptation (3:21—4:13)

Jesus' ministry in Galilee (4:14—9:50)

    (a) Proclamation and rejection at Nazareth (4:14–30)
    (b) Healings and calling of Peter (4:31—5:16)
    (c) Controversies with Jewish authorities (5:17—6:11)
    (d) Teaching: Sermon on the Plain (6:12–49)
    (e) Healings: Testimony to Jesus (7:1–50)
    (f) Galilean women disciples (8:1–3)
    (g) Parables: Hearing and doing the word (8:4–21)
    (h) Miracles: Jesus' power (8:22—9:6)
    (i) Jesus' identity, passion prediction, and transfiguration (9:7–36)
    (j) Exorcism, passion prediction, and instruction of disciples (9:49-50)

Journey to Jerusalem (9:51—19:27)

    (a) Departure: Rejection in Samaria (9:51–56)
    (b) Disciples and their mission (9:57—10:24)
    (c) Parables and sayings of Jesus (10:25—13:21)
    (d) Rejection of Jesus: Warning about Herod, departure from Galilee, and lament for Jerusalem (13:22–35)
    (e) Sayings and parables of Jesus (14:1—18:14)
    (f) Conditions of discipleship, passion prediction (18:15—19:27)

Jesus' ministry in Jerusalem (19:28—21:38)

    (a) Entry, lament over Jerusalem, and cleansing of the temple (19:28-46)
    (b) Reaction to Jesus: Hostility and acceptance (19:47–48)
    (c) Teaching: Controversies with authorities (20:1—21:4)
    (d) Teaching: Fate of Jerusalem, persecutions, end-time (21:5–38)

Passion of Jesus (22:1—23:56a)

Resurrection of Jesus (23:56b—24:53)

    (a) The empty tomb (23:56b—24:12)
    (b) Appearance on the road to Emmaus (24:13–35)
    (c) Appearance commissioning the disciples (24:36–49)
    (d) Jesus is taken up into heaven (24:50–53)

You will also notice that the crucifixion scene is quite different in Luke. Instead of praying Psalm 22:2 (see Mark 14:34) Jesus speaks like a heroic martyr. He forgives his enemies and prays Psalm 31:6, entrusting his spirit to God (23:24, 46). Even the two criminals crucified with Jesus are divided. One shares the mockery of the crowd, challenging Jesus' claim to be savior (23:39); the other acknowledges his own sinfulness and Jesus' innocence. The repentant criminal is promised eternal life with Jesus (23:40–43). This exchange shows readers the value of repentance and faith in Jesus.

Luke's resurrection traditions include appearances of the Lord near Jerusalem and the disciples' vision of Jesus being taken up into heaven (promised in 9:51). These stories include the famous encounter on the road to Emmaus (24:13–35) as well as an appearance to the disciples at a meal (24:36–43). That meal story includes Jesus commissioning the disciples to mission (24:44–49), a tradition that Matthew 28:16–20 located in the context of a Galilee appearance. We saw that in Matthew the final scene reflected key concerns of the gospel. Luke's commissioning scene plays a similar role. The message that the disciples carry involves repentance and forgiveness of sin. They are the witnesses upon whom the faith of the later community depends. Luke has a pattern of salvation history in which Jesus fulfills God's promises in his suffering, death, and resurrection that will be proclaimed to all the

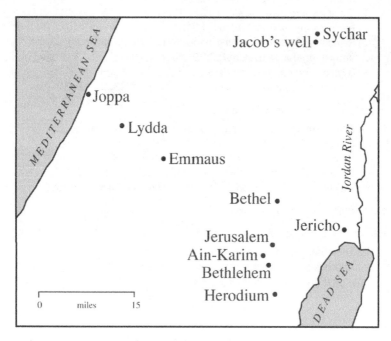

Some towns and cities in Judea at the time of Jesus' ministry

nations. The last episode in that story will be the theme of Luke's second volume, Acts.

You may have noticed that in Luke blocks of teaching are not organized into identifiable sermons as they are in Matthew. Look up Luke's version (6:17—7:1) of material that is more famous in Matthew's Sermon on the Mount. The section has a formal ending (7:1) but its beginning has Jesus teaching and healing crowds, not teaching disciples as in Matthew 5:1–2. The opening Beatitudes address those who have come for healing. Luke links material together around particular themes to create some of the smaller units in the gospel. Read chapter 15. Verses 1 to 2 create a setting for the three parables that make up the chapter: the accusation that Jesus welcomes tax collectors and sinners and eats with them. Readers have already met this objection in the story of the calling of Levi (Luke 5:27–32). There Jesus answered the objection by quoting a familiar proverb about the sick needing a doctor and asserting that his mission is to call sinners to repentance.

Here Jesus tells three stories focused on the finding or return of what has been lost. The first, the lost sheep, was used in Matthew to instruct community leaders (Matt 18:10–14). Luke's version suggests that a repentant sinner brings more joy in heaven than many righteous people (v. 7). Luke pairs the story of the lost sheep with that of a woman searching for a lost coin. We frequently find such pairs in Luke. Again, the emphasis is on the joy in heaven that comes from a repentant sinner (v. 10). In both parables, the person who finds what is lost also calls together neighbors to rejoice. The Parable of the Prodigal Son picks up this theme in an even more dramatic way. The father gives a great banquet for his lost son. He also answers the objections of the dutiful older son. Rejoicing at the return of one who is lost does not mean that the older son is excluded from his father's love. Of course, Luke's introduction leads the reader to think of the older son as representative of the complaining Pharisees in verses 1 to 2. If they continue to refuse to rejoice in the return of the lost being brought about by Jesus' ministry, then they will be shut out of the feast.

You can see how these stories provide readers with an explanation for the eventual rejection of Jesus. The charges against Jesus at his trial were recognized as false. No one should claim that because Jesus was executed by crucifixion he was a criminal. Rather, the rejection of Jesus is grounded in the attitudes exhibited by certain religious leaders. Jesus' ministry to sinners and his table fellowship signifying their place in God's kingdom led to that hostility. Like the older brother in the parable such people were unable to see that God's will makes it "right" to call what is lost to repentance and to celebrate their return as the sign of salvation.

The Time of Salvation

Jesus' sermon in Luke 4:16–30 proclaims that the promised time of salvation is being fulfilled in Jesus. The celebrations of joy in response to Jesus' preaching are further signs that a new age of salvation is beginning. People break out in words praising and glorifying God. Both Elizabeth's blessing upon Mary and Mary's Magnificat speak of the joy of faithful people now that God's promises are being fulfilled (Luke 1:42–45, 46–55). Zechariah blesses God (1:64, 68–79). So do the angels in heaven (2:13–14). The people respond to miracles by praising God (5:26; 7:16; 9:43 [are astonished at the majesty of God]; 13:17; 17:15 [proper response to healing]; 18:43). Luke's version of the entry to Jerusalem adds praises by a crowd of disciples for the great works they had seen Jesus perform (19:37). In Mark, the centurion at the cross recognized the true secret of Jesus' identity, that he was Son of God (Mark 15:39). In Luke, that episode becomes recognition of Jesus' innocence and praise of God (23:47). And at the very end of the gospel we see the disciples returning to Jerusalem in joy and praising God in the temple (24:52–53).

These examples show that the faithful of Israel received Jesus as the fulfillment of God's promises. Luke thus presents readers of the gospel with a pattern of "salvation history." First God's promises to Israel formed those pious ones who are waiting for salvation from the Lord like Simeon and Anna. John the Baptist is the culmination of that part of salvation history. This period is followed by the salvation experienced in Jesus' ministry (16:16). The Spirit had been at work guiding Israel and shaping its faithful people during the first period of salvation history (1:15, 35, 41, 67; 2:25–26). It has come to rest on Jesus and guides his ministry (3:22; 4:1, 18).

Salvation history does not move from the ministry of Jesus directly to the second coming. Luke uses Jesus' Parable of the Master Entrusting Servants with Money [Parable of the Talents] (19:11–24), to caution those who think that the kingdom is to appear immediately. He also formulates Jesus' predictions about the fate of Jerusalem so that the destruction of Jerusalem is not a prelude to the end-time as it is in Mark 13 (21:20–24; cf. Mark 13:14–20). Instead, the destruction of Jerusalem is the prelude to the "times of the Gentiles" (v. 24), which must be fulfilled before the end-time. This shift, along with the commissioning of the disciples (24:44–49) and the continuation of the story into Acts, points toward a third epoch, the period of the church's mission. Luke 24:49 looks toward another outpouring of God's Spirit to inaugurate that time of salvation. It comes upon Jesus' Jewish disciples at Pentecost (Acts 2:4) and then upon the first Gentile converts (Acts 10:44–48).

Luke has also set the scene for this time of salvation at several points in the infancy narratives. We have seen that Simeon's prophecy spoke of a salvation for all the peoples (2:31–32). The evangelist also makes the birth of Jesus an event that belongs to "world history" in 2:1–2. Instead of dating

Jesus' birth using the kingship of Herod as in Luke 1:5 for John the Baptist, Jesus' birth is linked to events in the Roman history of Judea. The angelic announcement in Luke 2:10–14 also has similar overtones. The "peace" announced by angels would have reminded readers of the "peace" that the Roman emperor Augustus claimed to have brought to the civilized world. Three times the doors of the temple of Janus, open in wartime, were closed and the great altar to the Augustan peace was constructed in the Campus Martius. Inscriptions hailed Augustus as "savior of the whole world" and said of his birthday, "[the birthday] of the god has marked the beginning of the good news through him for the world." These themes were repeated on coins and inscriptions throughout the empire. Luke's readers would easily get the message of the angelic announcement: Jesus, not the emperor, is the source of peace and salvation. Luke 19:38 has this theme picked up by the crowds as Jesus enters Jerusalem. From the point of view of salvation history, the story is still incomplete. The "good news" must be brought from the faithful of Israel to the Gentiles. Geographically Luke will depict the progress of the gospel outward from Jerusalem (24:47).

Jesus as Universal Savior

Luke's narrative uses the dynamic movement of history unfolding according to God's plan to explain the place of non-Jews in a salvation rooted in Israel. Graeco-Roman society was grounded in tradition. Roman piety respected the ancestral religions of conquered peoples. As a form of Judaism, Christianity might have claimed a legitimate place in the world. But what of a religious movement that is converting non-Jews away from their ancestral traditions? Is this movement really a form of piety or a malicious superstition that threatens the good order of families and society? The Roman historian Tacitus reports the trial of a Roman noble woman, Pomponia Graecina, on the charge of practicing a "foreign religion" (*Annals* 13.32.3–5). Scholars have suggested that she had been attracted to Judaism or perhaps even to a Jewish Christian group. In his account of Nero's persecution, Tacitus describes Christianity as a pernicious superstition:

> Nero…inflicted most extreme punishments on those, hateful by reason of their abominations, who were commonly called Christians. Christus, the originator of that name, had been executed by the procurator Pontius Pilate. The pernicious superstition, checked for the moment, was bursting out again not only throughout Judea, the birthplace of the plague, but also throughout the city into which all that is horrible and shameful streams from every quarter and is constantly practiced. Therefore first

those who confessed were arrested, then on their information a
huge throng was convicted not so much on a charge of arson as
because of their hatred of the human race. (*Annals* 15.44.2–8)

The apologetic function of Luke–Acts provides a way of answering such
charges. For Paul the problem had been to defend the inclusion of Gentiles
in salvation based on their faith in Christ against objections from the Jewish
side of the movement. Luke's situation is different. He must ground a Gentile
movement in its Jewish heritage. By doing so, Luke shows that Christianity is
not a pernicious superstition but a religion with an ancient tradition founded
on divine revelation. However, Luke must explain that what begins with
Israel is appropriately expanded to others. Acts will tell the story of how that
came about in the earliest period, the "rebirth" after the crucifixion to which
Tacitus refers.

Luke's gospel incorporates another form of universalism, which is
sometimes reflected in the opponents who present Christians as social mis-
fits. Luke depicts Jesus dealing with women and men from all levels of society. Tax collectors, often wealthy men, are frequently mentioned (5:27,
29–30; 7:29, 34; 15:1; 18:10– 13; 19:2–10). They exemplify the larger class of
"sinners" who hear Jesus' message, repent, and find salvation (7:36–50, sinful
woman; 15:11–32, prodigal son as an example story). Women are numbered
among Jesus' disciples. Some like the Galilean women (8:1–3) and Martha
and Mary (10:38–42) have houses or other financial resources under their
own control. But we also meet the poor in the persons of widows (7:11–17;
18:1–8; 21:1–4) and the Parable of Lazarus and the Rich Man (16:20). The
poor are singled out in Jesus' announcement of salvation (4:18; 6:20).

"Seeking and saving what is lost" (19:10) is the mission of Jesus. The
sweep of Luke's vision recognizes that everyone is to be included. This perspective is expressed in Acts 4:12: "Salvation comes through no one else, for
there is no other name under the heavens given to human beings by which
we must be saved." Luke suggests that true peace and unity among peoples
is not created by the order of the Roman Empire but by a common hope for
salvation that is open to all.

Where Paul often speaks of salvation as the future destiny of Christians
(Phil 2:12; 3:20), Luke presents it as already achieved. Jesus is "savior" (2:11;
Acts 5:31; 13:23). Luke frequently mentions salvation (1:69, 71; 19:9; 2:30;
3:6; Acts 4:12; 7:25; 13:26, 47; 16:17; 27:34). Christ's role as savior is to forgive
sins, an expression that appears in the other Synoptics only at Mark 1:4 and
Matthew 26:28. Forgiveness is the focal point of the disciples' mission to the
world (24:47). This mission is fulfilled in Acts (2:38; 5:31; 10:43; 13:38;
26:18). Lucan use of expressions like "peace," "joy," and "life" underlines the
presence of salvation. Luke even speaks of the resurrection as the way in

which Jesus became "the leader of life" (Acts 3:15). Thus, the coming of Jesus has opened up new possibilities of life for humanity.

Discipleship in Luke

These new possibilities have to be embodied in a life of discipleship. Repentance and conversion mark a person's entry into that new life. Luke takes pains to emphasize the diversity of persons who are called to discipleship. We meet women and men from all social categories. The calling of Peter in Luke 5:1–11 exemplifies the response required of a disciple. Peter's first response is to confess his sinfulness (v. 8). He, James, and John accept the Lord's call and "leave everything and follow him" (v. 11). Levi the tax collector also responds by "leaving everything" to follow Jesus (5:28). The women disciples in Galilee are providing for Jesus and the disciples (8:1–3). In the story of Mary and Martha, Mary is commended for her single-minded devotion to the word that Jesus teaches (10:38–42). True discipleship is "hearing and keeping the word of God" (8:19–21). Throughout the gospel, Jesus' mother Mary is pictured as the first disciple for her hearing of the word.

Luke's emphasis on "leaving everything" to follow Jesus draws attention to an important theme: the danger of wealth and position to the life of discipleship. Luke's version of the Beatitudes blesses the poor and condemns the wealthy who have achieved satisfaction of their desires in this life (Luke 6:20–26). Jesus speaks to the poor directly, promising them the kingdom (6:20). Several parables from Luke's special material deal with the traps posed by wealth: the Rich Fool (12:13–21), the Unjust Steward (16:1–8a), and the Rich Man and Lazarus (16:19–31). The conversion of the rich tax collector Zacchaeus exemplifies the kind of response such a person should make to the message of salvation (19:1–10).

Compare Luke's story of the rich ruler (18:18–30) with the Marcan version (Mark 10:17–31). Luke shifts Mark's "go sell what you have and give to the poor" to emphasize the radical nature of the "selling" to "sell *all* that you have" (Luke 18:22). In Mark the rich man goes away sad and the dialogue about wealth takes place between Jesus and his disciples. Luke omits the reference to the man leaving so that he remains among the audience for Jesus' words about the difficulty rich persons have in entering the kingdom.

Luke's interpretation of the Parable of the Sower emphasizes the danger that the concerns of daily life will rob people of their enthusiasm for the gospel. Some may fall away because of "testing," perhaps when their faith is challenged by persecution. Others never gain any mature faith because "cares, riches, and pleasures of life" choke it off (8:11–15). Luke recognizes that true discipleship requires not only hearing the message but also holding on to it. It means a whole lifetime of "bearing fruit," which comes from the "good heart" of the faithful disciple.

Luke's model of the "first disciple" is Mary. He uses the episode of Jesus' mother and brothers to show that the true disciple "hears the word of God and does it" (8:19–21). This is the example that Mary set in the infancy narratives at the beginning of the gospel. Representing all of the faithful, pious ones of Israel, she heard and accepted the word of the Lord so that the promises of salvation could become realized through her. The same devotion is held up to all disciples in the gospel.

Summary

Luke makes readers aware that the gospel stands at the center of a larger story of salvation. Its roots go back into the Old Testament. God's promises to the holy people of Israel are being fulfilled in Jesus. Its branches reach into the spread of the gospel throughout the known world by the disciples whom Jesus has selected as his witnesses. Luke will tell that story in his second volume, Acts. From the beginning, Luke reminds the reader that the coming of Jesus is not just an event in Jewish history. It is an event in the history of all humanity. He is careful to link the events of Jesus' birth with the Roman Empire. Jesus, not the emperor Augustus, is the real savior of humanity. Jesus is the real source of God's peace.

Luke has also told the story of Jesus in such a way as to answer some of the charges and suspicions that people had about Christians. He emphasizes the fact that there is no evidence for the charges against Jesus. Jesus dies as an innocent person. His last words are a message of forgiveness and salvation. Christianity is not some new, dangerous superstition. It is rooted in the piety of Israel. The founder whom Christians revere is not subversive. He teaches people the way to peace. Christians are the ones who are following along the way that Jesus set out for them.

STUDY QUESTIONS

Facts You Should Know

1. How do the following themes fit into the picture of Luke as a "defense" of Christianity: (a) the piety of Jesus' family in the infancy narratives; (b) the declarations of innocence at the trial of Jesus?
2. Give examples of the Lucan theme of repentance and joy. How do these examples show that salvation is open to all?

3. What are the three major divisions in Luke? How does Luke tie the three sections together?
4. How does Luke show the reader that the events he is narrating belong to "world history" and not just the story of the Jewish people?
5. Give three examples in which Luke deals with the theme of wealth and discipleship. What message does he have for the Christian about possessions?

Things to Do

1. Luke often uses pairs of stories in which one has a man and the other has a woman as its central character. Find examples of such pairs in the gospel.
2. Luke 7:36–50 contains a variant of the tradition of Jesus' anointing (cf. Mark 14:3–9). Compare Luke's story and Mark's version. Which themes in the Lucan version are special emphases of the gospel?
3. Using a gospel parallel, compare Luke's account of Jesus in Gethsemane (Luke 22:39–46) with Mark's (Mark 14:32–42). How is Luke's picture of the relationship between Jesus and the disciples different?
4. Using a concordance, find all of the times that Luke mentions prayer. What role does prayer play in the life of Jesus according to Luke?

Things to Think About

1. How can we preach a "time of salvation" for today's world?
2. What is the role that prayer plays in our lives?

Chapter 15

JOHN:
JESUS, THE DIVINE SON

The Composition of John

The Fourth Gospel presents a picture of Jesus strikingly different from that in the Synoptics. Read John 1:1–18. Notice the allusions to the opening chapter of Genesis: "in the beginning," references to God's word as a creative power, the creation of light in the darkness, and all things, including humans, coming to life through the word. Where Genesis 2:1–3 ended with God "resting" and making the Sabbath holy, John 1:17 contrasts the law of Moses, which included the Sabbath, with the "grace and truth" in Jesus. John's prologue uses poetic language to cast the story of Jesus as the divine Word coming to dwell with humanity. The Word is rejected by those who should receive it (1:11) but is the source of salvation and rebirth as children of God for those who believe (vv. 12–13). There is no other way to "know" God except through the Word in Jesus (vv. 14, 18).

References to the story of Jesus have been incorporated into the prologue. John the Baptist is sent to give testimony to the light (vv. 6–8, 15). The presentation of the Baptist in John 1:19–37 mixes traditions familiar from the Synoptics with elements found only in the Johannine material. "Testimony" or "witness" (Gk. *marturia*) governs the whole story. The familiar citation from Isaiah 40:3 describes the mission of the Baptist (v. 23; cf. Mark 1:3; Matt 3:1; Luke 3:4). The Synoptics have the narrator introduce the quotation. In John's gospel, the Isaiah passage forms the Baptist's response to questions about his identity. John 1:23 collapses the second two phrases of the passage into one. Instead of "preparing the way" and "making straight his footsteps," we have "making straight the way."

The saying about the relationship between John and Jesus reappears in John: "One stronger than I is coming after me, the strap of whose sandals I am not worthy to undo" (Mark 1:7; Luke 1:16; Matt 3:11 shifts the final phrase to "carry his sandals"). John 1:27 comes closest to the synoptic version of the saying where it is attached to John's testimony that the true prophet-messiah is present but unknown to those challenging John's authority: "the one who comes after me, of whom I am not worthy to undo the strap of his sandal." The evangelist has created "cross-references" to this saying. John 1:15 makes the content of the Baptist's testimony: "the one who comes after me ranks before me because he was before me." John 1:30 repeats the variant in 1:15.

You can see that the evangelist is assuming that readers already know a story about Jesus. The reader knows that John is engaged in baptizing (v. 25). The "Christological titles" about which the Baptist is questioned by the Jewish authorities are being used as they were traditionally used among Christians. Curiously, the Baptist denies being "Elijah." The Synoptics know a tradition in which the Baptist was "Elijah," the forerunner of the messiah (e.g., Mark 9:11–13). While the Q tradition presented the Baptist preaching a message of judgment and repentance (Luke 3:7–9; Matt 3:7–10), in the Fourth Gospel his message is about Jesus from the beginning. The evangelist has shaped two parallel episodes using different groups from Jerusalem to make the point. Each ends with one of the traditional sayings (vv. 19–23, 24–28). The culmination of the Baptist's testimony comes on the next two days. First, the traditional story about Jesus' baptism in which the Spirit descends on Jesus and the divine voice announces that Jesus is God's Son (Mark 1:9–11; Matt 3:13–17; Luke 3:21–22) is no longer addressed to Jesus. Instead, the Baptist has the vision of the Spirit descending on Jesus as a dove and testifies that Jesus is "Son of God." Second, John's witness leads two of his own disciples to become disciples of Jesus (vv. 35–37).

You can see from the examples that the Fourth Gospel differs from the Synoptics in its presentation of individual episodes, in the wording and use of traditional sayings, and even in matters of chronology. You will hardly be surprised to discover that in the Johannine stories about the calling of disciples (1:35–51) those who follow Jesus do so because they recognize his messianic identity. From the outset we are presented with the story of God's Word come from heaven confronting a world in which there will be two reactions, unbelief (remaining in darkness) and belief (achieving salvation as God's children).

The narrator steps into the story to address the reader and to point out corresponding events. Sometimes the evangelist appears to be summarizing the message about Jesus but has not marked the shift. Look at John 3:31–36, for example. John 3:30 has the Baptist testify to the relationship between himself and Jesus. Verses 31–36 summarize the significance of Jesus' mission in terms that recall the prologue of the gospel. Jesus has come from above to speak the words of God. His appearance divides humanity into two groups: believers who receive eternal life and unbelievers. Summary passages like this one give the reader insight into the gospel's understanding of Jesus.

John 4:1–3 returns to the theme of Jesus and the Baptist. The transition

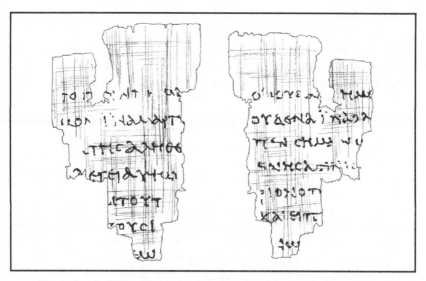

The Rylands Library Papyrus 52 showing John 18:31-33 (front), 37-38 (back). This is the earliest surviving manuscript of the New Testament. It is dated from around AD 125.

is very awkward. Verse 1 reads "when the Lord [or "Jesus" in some manuscripts] knew that the Pharisees had heard that Jesus...." This transition is an example of a number of puzzles in the gospel. Sometimes carefully crafted discourses are patched together with rough transitions or even illogical sequences of events or places. Unlike the Synoptics in which Jesus' ministry moves from Galilee to Jerusalem and the crucifixion, the Fourth Gospel has Jesus alternating between Galilee and Jerusalem. Sometimes the alternations separate material that seems to belong together. For example, chapter 4 has Jesus leaving Judea for Galilee (v. 3). He meets a Samaritan woman on the way (vv. 4–42) and then arrives in Galilee where the healing of the official's son is set in Cana. But John 5:1 shifts back to Jerusalem where a Sabbath healing leads to controversy and a lengthy discourse by Jesus. John 6:1 does not mention Jesus' return to Galilee, but seems to presume that Jesus is journeying around Galilee. John 7:1a seems to contain the transition to Jesus going about in Galilee because of danger in Judea that would fit the gap at 6:1.

Many scholars think that the gospel passed through more than one edition. Similarly Jesus' Supper discourses appear to be over at John 14:31, but we now have more discourses in chapters 15 to 17. In addition, passages like John 16:5 pick up a theme of the earlier discourse about "Where is Jesus going?" but contradict the development of the theme there (13:36 where Peter does ask where Jesus is going). The gospel concludes in 20:30–31 after resurrection appearances in Jerusalem. Suddenly, John 21 provides a new story of Jesus' appearance in Galilee in which the disciples seem to have no knowledge of what happened before. One suggestion is that the version of the gospel that we possess was edited after the death of the original evangelist in order to preserve traditions circulating in the Johannine communities.

John and Synoptic Tradition

The Johannine Jesus speaks in long discourses about himself and his mission. The short parables and sayings about the kingdom of God found in the other gospels are missing here. This shift makes the Johnnine Jesus sound quite different. Yet there are sayings and even blocks of tradition that are similar to material found in the Synoptics. One of the most striking appears in the story of the feeding of the multitude in John 6. Chart 15-1 lists the parallels between this section of John and material in Mark.

JOHN 6 AND MARCAN TRADITION		[15–1]
Episode	**John**	**Mark**
Feeding Crowd	6:1–15	6:30–40 (8:1–10)
Walking on Water	6:16–21	6:45–54
Request for a Sign	6:22–34	8:11–13
Jesus' Parentage	6:41–44	6:1–6
Misunderstanding	6:60–65	8:16–20
Peter's Confession	6:66–69	8:27–30
Passion Prediction	6:70–71	8:31–33

Other links can be drawn between sayings in John and the traditions of Jesus' sayings in the Synoptics. Compare John 12:25 and Matthew 10:40; John 5:9 and Mark 2:11; John 12:24 and Mark 3:24. The evangelist reformulated a tradition of "Son of Man" sayings. Chart 15-2 illustrates parallels between Johannine traditions and the three types of sayings found in Mark: (a) the coming of the Son of Man in glory; (b) the present authority of the Son of Man; (c) the suffering Son of Man. In each case the transformations reflect important themes in the Fourth Gospel. John 1:51 picks up the pattern of ascent/descent that is a structural feature in the gospel. The disciple is promised a vision of Jesus' true glory. John 5:27 appears in a discourse that has gone beyond the forgiveness of sins linked to a healing miracle (cf. 5:14) to insist on Jesus' identity with God. The Son can exercise the functions of the Father—judgment and the giving of life. The final example is a passion prediction. But for John the passion is Jesus' return to the Father. It is the hour of Jesus' being "lifted up" or glorified (cf. 3:13–14; 8:28).

JOHANNINE SON OF MAN SAYINGS AND MARCAN TRADITION   [15-2]

(a) coming in glory:

John 1:51

Truly, truly I say to you,
you will see the heaven
opened, and the angels of
God ascending and descending
upon the Son of Man.

Mark 14:62

You will see the Son of Man
seated at the right hand of
Power and coming with the
clouds of heaven.

(b) authority of the Son of Man:

John 5:27

and has given him authority
to execute judgment because
he is the Son of Man.

Mark 2:10

that you may know that the Son
of Man has authority on earth to
forgive sins.

(c) Son of Man must suffer:

John 12:34

We have heard from the law
that the messiah remains
forever; how can you say
that the Son of Man
must be lifted up?

Mark 8:31

And he began to teach them that

the Son of Man
must suffer many things...

Even though John does not appear to employ the Synoptics as written sources in the way that Matthew and Luke recast texts from Mark or Q, the evangelist may have known of one or more of them. Others feel that the Jesus material circulating in the Johannine community developed from a variant line of tradition that was related to that in the Synoptics. John also has its own special material as each synoptic writer did. The discourses in the gospel may have been formed in the preaching of the Johannine community. Their distinctive style and symbolism go back to the "Beloved Disciple" who founded the Johannine group.

OUTLINE OF JOHN   [15-3]

Book of Signs: Jesus reveals the Father (chapters 1-12)

Prologue (1:1-18)

Gathering disciples (1:19—4:54)

    (a) Jesus as messiah, Son of God, Son of Man (1:19-51)
    (b) Miracle at Cana: Jesus' glory (2:1-12)

Continued

(c) First Passover: Cleansing of the temple (2:13-25)
(d) Nicodemus: Rebirth from heaven (3:1-21)
(e) Judea: Jesus and John the Baptist (3:22—4:3)
(f) Samaritan woman: Water of life (4:4-42)
(g) Healing official's son: Second Cana sign (4:43-54)

Disputes: Jesus' True Identity (5:1—12:50)

(a) Healing cripple: Son is like the Father (5:1-47)
(b) Feeding five thousand: Son is bread of life (6:1-70)
(c) Tabernacles discourse: Light of the world (7:1-52)
(d) Divine I AM: Jesus greater than Abraham (8:12-59)
(e) Healing blind man: Walk in the true light (9:1-41)
(f) Jesus' sheep: True shepherd (10:1-42)
(g) Raising Lazarus: Jesus gives life to the world (11:1-44)
(h) Officials decide to kill Jesus (11:45-54)
(i) Mary anoints Jesus (12:1-11)
(j) Jesus' final public appearances in Jerusalem (12:12-50)

Book of Glory: Jesus returns to the Father (Chapters 13-21)

At the Last Supper (13:1—17:26)

(a) Foot washing: Example of service (13:1-30)
(b) First discourse: Jesus' presence with disciples (13:31—14:31)
(c) Second discourse: Remain on the true vine (15:1—16:4a)
(d) Third discourse: Paraclete to console disciples (16:4b-33)
(e) Fourth discourse: Jesus' prayer of unity (17:1-26)

Passion of Jesus (18:1—19:42)

Resurrection of Jesus (20:1—21:25)

(a) Empty tomb (20:1-10)
(b) Appears to Mary Magdalene (20:11-18)
(c) Appears to disciples at meals (20:19-29)
(d) First ending to the gospel (20:30-31)
(e) Appears by the sea in Galilee (21:1-23)
(f) Second ending to the gospel (21:24-25)

The gospel falls into two major sections. The first presents Jesus' public ministry up to the final rejection of his message in Jerusalem. It is punctuated by a series of miracles that climax in the raising of Lazarus, which demonstrates that Jesus is the source of eternal life. The second section presents the culmination of Jesus' mission as the Son returns to his Father. The two divisions fit a pattern that dominates the whole gospel. Jesus is the one who has come from heaven to reveal God to those who believe. Jesus is the one who returns to heaven from the cross. There he lives in the glory of God, which he has since the beginning.

Jesus, the Jews, and the World

The sharp division between Jesus, who comes from heaven, and those who belong to this world is reinforced by dualistic symbols. We have already met some of the most important: belief/unbelief; light/darkness; life/death. Jesus' final prayer expresses the division between believers and the world (John 17:13–19). Jesus is not "of the world." His disciples are being left "in the world" as witnesses. Like Jesus, they now have a mission to the world, but are also to be made holy, which requires being kept safe from a world that John pictures as ruled by "the evil one." Like Jesus they must expect hostility from a world that remains unwilling to hear the word of God (15:18–26).

The positive side of this separation is an intense unity of love with Jesus, the Father, and fellow believers. The gospel even speaks of believers as having passed into eternal life already (5:24; 6:51; 8:52). Of course, everyone knows that believers will die at the end of this life. The gospel includes the traditional Christian view that Jesus will raise the faithful to new life on the last day. But the gospel presents the life-giving power of Jesus as already effective. The story of the raising of Lazarus in John 11:1–44 makes this point very dramatically. Martha already believes that her brother will be raised on the last day (11:21–24). Jesus tells her that because he is the "resurrection and the life" she will see something even greater than that: "Whoever lives and believes in me shall never die" (v. 26).

As you read chapters 5 to 12 you will notice that dualism in the gospel takes a very sharp form in disputes between Jesus and Jewish opponents. "The Jews" in these chapters represent the forces of unbelief. They are like villains in an adventure movie always plotting to kill Jesus. Jesus lashes back that his opponents fail to worship God, or to understand what Moses taught. He even describes them as "children of Satan" rather than children of Abraham (8:39–47). When engaged in debate, the Johannine Jesus always answers an objection with an even more extraordinary statement. Each episode moves from its initial tension toward greater hostility. In John 8:12–59, for example, Jesus finally claims for himself the name of God "I Am." The original Jewish charge that Jesus is not from God because he bears witness about himself becomes an angry debate over Jesus' claim to an identity with God that makes him even greater than Abraham.

Arguments like this would not be much good in persuading skeptical Jews to accept Jesus as the messiah. The hostility toward "the Jews" here goes well beyond anything we find in the other gospels. What could be responsible for this picture? The gospel gives a hint when it speaks about Jews forcing Christians out of the synagogue community and even putting some to death. Read the story of the healing and conversion of the blind man in John 9:1–41. A group of Pharisees investigated him. His parents tried to avoid becoming involved. The evangelist tells us that they did this "because they feared the Jews, for the Jews had already agreed that if any one should confess him to be the messiah [Christ], he was to be put out of the synagogue" (v. 22). When the man would not give up his belief that Jesus was "from God," he was called a sinner and thrown out (v. 34).

John 12:42–43 returns to the theme of fear: "Many, even among the authorities, believed in him, but for fear of the Pharisees they did not confess it lest they should be put out of the synagogue." John 16:1–4a warns Jesus' disciples not to "fall away" when such persecution comes. They will be put out of the synagogues and may even be killed. You can see from these examples that these Christians had lived through a period of severe persecution that not only led to suffering but had also divided families and the community. The evangelist recognizes that there were other Jews who did not share the hostility of the leaders of the persecution. He even gives us a portrait of such a sympathetic, "hidden believer" in the figure of Nicodemus. Nicodemus comes to question Jesus, but he does so "at night" (3:1–15). Later he attempts to defend Jesus when the Pharisees are plotting to kill him (7:45–52). Finally, he reappears to help Joseph bury Jesus (19:38–42).

The accusations against Jesus in the Fourth Gospel may well represent those faced by Johannine Christians. John 7:47 refers to persons being "led astray," a formal charge against those who were held to be false prophets. You may have noticed in both this chapter and chapter 9 that the "Pharisees and authorities" are pictured as pitting themselves against the crowds who are uncertain about whether to believe in Jesus. But the charge, which runs throughout the whole gospel, is that Jesus is a "blasphemer" because as a human being he is claiming equality with God. John 5:9b–18 explains to the reader that the accusations of "Sabbath-breaking" are not the real reason for hostility toward Jesus. The real reason is the special relationship between Jesus as "Son" and God as "Father" that makes Jesus equal with God.

Jesus, Revelation of the Father

The equality with God, which fuels dispute in the gospel, is linked with another important theme: Jesus is the one who reveals the Father. The prologue ends with the assertion that Jesus alone makes God known to humanity. In the last discourses, Jesus tells his disciples that having known him they have "known" or "seen" God (14:8–11). The vision of God in Jesus appears in a number of other places in the gospel. The messianic titles collected in chapter 1 end with a promise that like Jacob the disciples will see a vision of Jesus linking heaven and earth (1:51; for Jacob's vision at Bethel see Gen 28:12). Even the patriarch Abraham is said to have "seen" Jesus and rejoiced (8:48–59). You can see from the debate over Jesus' relationship to Abraham that "seeing God" in Jesus is part of the definition of salvation in John. The person who "sees" and believes in Jesus has eternal life.

Another way in which the gospel describes the relationship between Jesus and God is in the use of symbols. These symbols are collected in the "I Am" sayings of the gospel. Jesus is identified with major religious symbols: flowing water (4:14, interpreted as the gift of the Spirit in 7:39); bread of life (6:35, 41, 48, 51); life (8:12; 9:5); sheep gate (10:7, 9); good shepherd (10:11, 14); resurrection and life (11:25); light (8:12; 12:46); way, truth, and life (14:6); the vine (15:1, 5). One could say that there is no image or hope for salvation that is not fulfilled in Jesus.

As the Abraham episode in 8:48–59 makes clear, Jesus represents the goal of all human hopes for salvation because he is one with God. This unity is expressed in the most striking of the "I Am" sayings, those that do not have some symbol after the verb but simply use "I Am." Any Jewish reader would recognize the divine name of God, which was revealed to Moses at the burning bush (Exod 3:14; 20:4; Isa 45:5–6, 18, 22). The Greek translation of Isaiah 43:10–11 contains a number of parallels to the language used in the gospel:

> You are my witness and I am a witness says the LORD God and the servant whom I have chosen, that you may know and believe and understand that I AM. Before me there was no other God, and after me there will be none. I AM God and no one saves except me.

Notice the importance of "witness" language in John 8:13–30. John 8:28 affirms that when Jesus is "lifted up," his divine "I Am" will be made known. Belief in the crucified and exalted Jesus is the only source of salvation (cf. John 3:14–15). Throughout the gospel Jesus defends his equality with the Father by insisting that he does what the Father has sent him to do. The words he speaks are God's words and are recognized as such by those who are truly "children of God." Many people reacted to such claims about Jesus with outrage. The evangelist offers some possible reasons for that response. Some might prefer to remain "in darkness" because of their evil deeds (3:16–21). Some are afraid of the human consequences of believing in Jesus (12:42–43). But the evangelist also points out the mystery involved in coming to faith. God draws people to Jesus (10:26–30; 17:6). Thus faith is not simply an individual, personal achievement. It is the response to a call that comes from God.

Discipleship in John

The kind of teaching about the kingdom of God and discipleship found in the Synoptics is missing from John. The gospel repeatedly issues a call to faith in Jesus' identity: "I and the Father are one" (John 10:30). Humanity is divided by its response. John even speaks of those who fail to believe in Jesus as already judged (3:16–21; 5:19–29). But belief had concrete consequences. Johannine Christians had been persecuted and thrown out of the synagogues. Thus we know that discipleship means a willingness to "bear witness" to one's faith in Jesus in a hostile world.

This impression is strengthened by the farewell discourses and the resurrection stories in the second half of the gospel. Jesus turns to instruct his disciples at the Last Supper. John's story of Jesus' final meal is different from the other gospels. The formula that designates bread and wine as the body and blood of Christ had already been introduced during Jesus' ministry as the culmination of a discourse that identified Jesus as the heavenly "bread of life" (John 6:51–59). At the Last Supper, Jesus makes a striking gesture of humility by performing the slave-like act of washing the feet of his disciples (13:1–20). The evangelist reminds readers that this gesture is a sign of how much Jesus loves "his own" (13:1; see 10:17). It might be easy to let the emphasis on Jesus' divinity in the gospel overshadow the goal of Jesus' mission: to save humanity by offering his life out of love. The evangelist never forgets the importance of love. When Jesus raises Lazarus, we see how much Jesus loved his friend (11:3, 36). They repay Jesus' love with their own when Mary anoints Jesus before his death (12:1–8).

In the Last Supper discourses, Jesus draws his disciples into the relationship of love that exists between himself and the Father. They are promised a share in that love if they fulfill Jesus' command to love one another (14:21–24; 16:27). Jesus prays that there will be the same unity among his followers as exists between himself and the Father (17:21–24). The earlier parts of the gospel already hinted at one of the threats to such unity: external persecution.

Matthew and Luke understand the resurrection appearances as Jesus' commission to his followers. These scenes point forward to what the disciples must do now that Jesus is glorified in heaven. The Fourth Gospel follows a similar pattern. Jesus' first appearance, to Mary Magdalene, warns against clinging to the earthly Jesus. Jesus must return to glory with God, who is Father both to him and to his disciples (John 20:11–18). When Jesus appears to the disciples at a meal (20:19–23), he commissions them and gives them the Spirit. They are now "sent" just as Jesus had been sent by God. However, John has something unique, a second meal appearance to Thomas (20:24–29). The evangelist is conscious that those who read his gospel no longer belong to the first generation of Christians. Even the disciples who were witnesses to Jesus have died (21:20–23). Jesus prayed for these believers in John 17:20–21. Now Thomas is made to represent them. They might feel as though their faith is somehow inferior to that of the first generation of believers. Thomas shows that even among that group there was disbelief. The episode concludes with a blessing on those who have believed "without see-ing" (20:29).

The issue of faith lies at the heart of discipleship in John. Many charac-ters in the gospel find it impossible to believe that Jesus really is one with God. But the Fourth Gospel insists that without believing in God's Son we cannot enter into any relationship with God. Those who do believe have a special relationship of love with God. That relationship is expressed in the life of love and service among those who follow Jesus (John 13:31–36). It is also manifest in willingness to testify to one's belief in Jesus despite hostility from outsiders. Disciples do not simply believe for their own benefit. They also have a mission to be a witness to the world just as Jesus had been.

Summary

Everything that happens in the Fourth Gospel is a consequence of Jesus' mission from the Father. Jesus is the Word of God sent into the world to summon people to faith and salvation. Jesus' death expresses God's love for the world in sending the Son. But even though Jesus represents God the mys-tery of human freedom remains. Instead of welcoming the Word some per-sons turn away from it. Some even react with hostility and seek to kill both Jesus and those who follow him.

John 20:30–31 says that the point of the gospel is to bring its reader to faith in Jesus as messiah, Son of God. We have seen that the gospel presumes that we already know something about Jesus. This is not a beginner's gospel. It is addressed to those whose faith may be weak like Thomas's or who may be unsure of how to respond to charges that for Christians to honor Jesus as "one with" God is blasphemy. Only God, the evangelist insists, can do the signs that Jesus does. Only God can offer those who believe eternal life. Those who are unable to believe are blind to the presence of God in Jesus.

STUDY QUESTIONS

Facts You Should Know

1. Explain how John differs from the Synoptic Gospels (Matthew, Mark, and Luke) in each of the following areas: (a) use of messianic titles for Jesus; (b) teachings that Jesus gives; (c) reason given for Jewish hostility against Jesus.
2. Give examples of Johannine variants of synoptic-like stories that support the view that the Johannine church must have known traditions about Jesus like those in the Synoptic Gospels.

3. What is the symbolic role played by "the Jews" as characters in the Johannine narrative?
4. How is Jesus' equality with God demonstrated in the gospel? What arguments does John give in response to Jewish claims that it is blasphemy for a human being to claim such a relationship to God?
5. What are the obligations of discipleship as they are presented in the Fourth Gospel?

Things to Do

1. Using a concordance, trace the images of "life" and "light" from the prologue through the rest of the gospel. What do they show us about Jesus each time they occur?
2. Find all of the "I Am" sayings in the gospel. What symbols does Jesus identify himself with? How is the relationship between Christians and Jesus as the source of salvation represented in those symbols?
3. Read John 9. Trace the stages by which the "blind man" develops faith in who Jesus is. How does the story of the blind man reflect experiences of Christians in the Johannine community?

Things to Think About

1. John claims that the disciples are now "sent" to the world as Jesus was. How do we participate in that mission today?
2. How does Jesus reveal God to us?

Chapter 16

ACTS:
THE GOSPEL
TO THE NATIONS

The Composition of Acts

Acts picks up the story that is left unfinished in Luke's gospel. Like other multipart writings of its time, the prologue to Acts reminds the reader of the earlier work (1:1–5). Unlike other multivolume works, Acts never appears after the gospel in ancient manuscripts. If Luke intended to compose a two-part narrative from the outset, then there is an additional question of what its title would have been. Therefore some scholars doubt that Luke originally planned to follow his gospel with a sequel. You may have detected another puzzle in these verses. Luke 24:50–51 pictures Jesus blessing the disciples and being carried up into heaven on Easter Day. Acts 1:3–4 paints a different picture. It suggests Jesus appearing to the disciples and teaching them during a forty-day period before his ascension.

If you look closely at other references to Jesus' resurrection, you will notice that the time span of Jesus' appearances was not fixed. First Corinthians 15:3–9 suggests a lengthy period of appearances culminating in the conversion of Paul, nearly two years after Jesus' death. Mark hints at an appearance in Galilee, sometime after Easter Day (Mark 14:28; 16:7). Luke knows that "forty" is a symbolic number. Israel wandered in the wilderness forty years. Jesus was in the wilderness forty days after his baptism. The forty days of resurrection appearances establishes the disciples as witnesses (by Philip in Acts 8:12; by Paul in Acts 14:22; 19:8; 20:25; 28:23, 31). Acts 1:6 has Jesus correct a misunderstanding about the "kingdom of God." One is not to expect the second coming immediately. This correction recalls the "time of the Gentiles" in Luke 21:24. Acts 1:4–5 refers back to the gospel. Jesus told the disciples to wait in Jerusalem "for the promise of the Father" in Luke

24:49. Here he indicates what that promise of "power from on high" will be: the "baptism with the Holy Spirit" predicted by the Baptist (Luke 3:16).

These passages illustrate an important feature in Luke's composition. When Luke repeats an episode, he creates a different version. Usually that version contains new information appropriate to the particular point in the narrative. You can see this process at work in the three accounts of Paul's conversion (Acts 9:1–19; 22:4–16, 17–21; 26:12–18). The introductions are very close in all three, though the final version expands the description of the light, suggests that Paul's companions also fell to the ground, specifies the language as Hebrew, and expands the reprimand (26:13–14). Acts 9:11–19 focuses on the story of Paul's blindness and the "miraculous healing" by Ananias that accompanies Paul's formal conversion: reception of the Spirit and baptism. The healing element is shortened in Acts 22:10–13a, which suggests that the blindness was the result of the intensity of the light. Acts 22:16 seems to reflect Christian baptismal practice, since the "washing away of sins" and "calling on Jesus' name" are part of the process.

Acts 26 reports what was hidden from the reader in the earlier versions: the words of the commission given to Paul on the road to Damascus (26:16–18):

> I have appeared to you for this reason: to appoint you for service and witness to the things in which you have seen me and in which I will appear to you, rescuing you from the people and from the Gentiles among whom I am sending you, to open their eyes, that they may turn from darkness to light, and from the power of Satan to God, and may receive forgiveness of sins and inheritance among the saints through faith in me.

Hints of Paul's commission are contained in God's words to Ananias (9:15–16):

> ...he [Paul] is my chosen instrument to carry my name before the Gentiles and kings and children of Israel. I will show him how much he must suffer on account of my name.

Notice that this commission is similar to that of the disciples at the opening of Acts (Acts 1:8):

> You shall be my witnesses in Jerusalem and in all Judea and Samaria and to the end of the earth.

Ananias refers to God's commission in Acts 22:14–15:

> The God of our fathers appointed you to know his will, to see the Just One, and to hear sounds from his mouth; for you will be a witness for him to all people, of what you have seen and heard.

Acts 22:21 makes Paul's departure from Jerusalem for the Gentile mission a response to the hatred generated by his earlier activity as persecutor of Christians. Luke assumes that Paul must have been present at the martyrdom of Stephen (8:1; 22:20) though neither Paul himself nor Luke's own tradition gives Paul an active role in that episode. By the time we come to the final version of Paul's conversion we know that the apostle has fulfilled the commission to witness to the Gentiles, before kings and before the children of Israel. Paul is about to be sent as a prisoner to Rome where he will eventually die as a martyr. You can see from the outline that Acts follows a geographical pattern that moves from Jerusalem to Rome:

OUTLINE OF ACTS   [16–1]

Prologue (1:1–5)

Commission and ascension (1:6–11)

Earliest days of the community in Jerusalem (1:12–8:1)

  (a) Successor to Judas chosen (1:12–26)
  (b) Pentecost and Peter's sermon (2:1–13, 14–41)
  (c) Life in fellowship (2:42–47)
  (d) Healing and Peter's sermon (3:1–10, 11–26)
  (e) Witness before the council (4:1–22)
  (f) Prayer and life in fellowship (4:23–5:16)
  (g) Miraculous escape and witness before the council (5:17–42)
  (h) Appointment of Hellenist leaders as deacons (6:1–7)
  (i) Martyrdom of the deacon Stephen (6:8–8:1)

Christianity spreads in Judea and Samaria (8:2–12:25)

  (a) Philip: Into Samaria and the Ethiopian eunuch (8:4–40)
  (b) Paul's conversion (9:1–31)
  (c) Healings by Peter (9:32–43)
  (d) Conversion of Cornelius: Spirit to Gentiles (10:1–48)
  (e) Peter defends conversion of Gentiles in Jerusalem (11:1–18)
  (f) Church at Antioch (11:19–30)
  (g) James martyred and Peter delivered from prison (12:1–19)
  (h) Death of Herod (12:20–23)

Barnabas and Paul (Saul) sent out by Antioch (13:1–15:40)

  (a) Cyprus, Pisidian Antioch, Iconium, Lystra (13:1–14:28)
  (b) Jerusalem Council: Conditions for Gentile Christians (15:1–35)
  (c) Barnabas and Paul separate (15:36–41)

Paul's missionary journeys in Asia Minor and Greece (16:1–20:38)

  (a) Journey to Macedonia (16:1–15)
  (b) Philippian imprisonment and danger in Thessalonica (16:16–17:15)

Continued

One might expect Acts to end with the story of Paul's martyrdom. Instead, we last see him "…preaching the kingdom of God and teaching about the Lord Jesus Christ with all boldness, unhindered" (28:23–31). "Unhindered," the final word, points to the larger purpose of this story, describing the spread of the gospel from Jerusalem to the ends of the earth. Peter and the disciples carry the story in the first half of Acts. Their last contribution to the outward spread of the gospel appears when James and the others set the terms under which Gentiles are to be admitted to the new movement (15:1–35). After that, the story belongs entirely to Paul as God's "instrument." At this turning point in the narrative, Luke introduces sections that sound like a travelogue. They are told in the first-person plural "we" instead of the third person (16:10–17; 20:5–15; 21:1–18; 27:1—28:16).

Some scholars think that one of Paul's companions based the shift to the first-person plural on some form of travel diary. Others point out that there are examples of shifts into first-person narrative in both fiction and history writing that do not indicate firsthand knowledge by the author or a source. Scholars also debate the extent to which information in Acts provides sufficiently accurate details to complement what can be gleaned from Paul's own letters. Only in Acts do we learn such facts about Paul as: being from Tarsus (e.g., 11:25); held Roman citizenship (e.g., 16:37); was a tent-maker or leather-worker (e.g., 18:3); expelled from Corinth under Gallio (18:12). The historical accuracy of its depiction comes into question where Acts seems much different from the Paul of the letters. One can hardly imagine the Paul who insisted that he kept the Jerusalem Council from imposing any restrictions on Gentile Christians (Gal 2:1–10) obediently carrying a decree from James that says they must avoid marriages forbidden by Jewish law and nonkosher food (Acts 15:28–31; 16:4). How could the apostle maligned for weakness by the "super-apostles" (2 Cor 12:7–13) emerge as the powerful miracle-worker of Acts

(13:4–12; 14:8–10; 16:16–18; 19;11–20; 20:7–12; 28:3–6, 7–10), or the individual charged as a weak, unimpressive speaker in 2 Corinthians 10:9–10 (also 11:6) be the powerful orator of Acts (14:12; 17:16–34)?

None of Paul's favorite theological themes appears in the sermons attributed to him in Acts (e.g., 13:16–41; 17:22–31; 22:2–21). Scholars have divided the various speeches given in Acts into two categories. Some are "kerygmatic," that is, they set forth the basic message of salvation (e.g., 13:16–41, by Paul and speeches by Peter in 2:14–39; 3:11–26; 4:18–22; 5:29–32; 10:34–43). Others are "apologetic," that is, the apostle is making a defense of Christianity in a "law court" setting (7:2–53, by Stephen, and Paul's speeches in 20:18–35; 22:3–21; 24:10–21; 26:1–23; 28:17–20, 25–29). The speech Paul makes in Athens is like an apology, since it is set in the Areopagus, a famous court in ancient Athens, even though Paul is not using judicial rhetoric. He is making a plea for belief to the pagan philosophers of Athens (17:22–31).

Ancient historians used to formulate speeches for their characters that reflected what the person ought to have said in a given situation. Acts contains a greater percentage of speech-making and direct discourse (over 50 percent) than other ancient writers typically employ. The kerygmatic speeches in Acts provide glimpses of what Luke thought early missionary preaching was like. Perhaps they were based on models used in his own community. These speeches follow a typical outline. Read the most famous, Peter's Pentecost sermon in Acts 2:14–39:

(1) Introduction locates the speech in the narrative (vv. 14–21).
(2) Outline of the message about Jesus using proofs for Jesus' messiah-ship from the Old Testament (vv. 22–36).
(3) Call for repentance and conversion (vv. 37–39).

Notice that repentance includes forgiveness of sins, baptism, and the gift of the Holy Spirit to new believers (v. 38). Even though the official mission to the Gentiles has not begun by this point, Pentecost points toward the spread of the gospel throughout the earth. Everyone heard the apostles speak in his or her own language (2:5–11; notice how many countries Luke includes). Peter points out that the promise of salvation through Jesus is to all, even those who are far off (v. 39). Luke also insists that all these different believers gathered in the community life of the church for teaching, fellowship, breaking bread, and prayer (v. 42).

The Church in Salvation History

Luke's emphasis on the geographical spread of Christianity underscores the important role of the church in salvation. In the picture of Pentecost with which Acts begins, pilgrims from nations, east and west, hear the good news. They join together in a single fellowship that hears the teaching of the apostles, shares meals, and prays together. Acts 2:43–47 repeats this picture with two additional elements: (1) signs of God's power in the miracles done by the apostles; (2) community members sharing all things in common. Each person is provided with whatever he or she needs through the sacrifice of those who had sold property to provide for the poor.

At the same time, Acts also preserves stories about the early Jerusalem community that are less than idyllic. Acts 4:32–37 repeats the tradition that Christians sold property to provide for the poor. But the next episode, 5:1–16, tells the story of a couple who lie about the amount received for their property. The result of such an attempt to deceive the Holy Spirit is immediate death. Other examples of divine "punishment" in Acts are the death of Herod (12:20–23), the blinding of the magician Elymas (13:8–11), and the attack of an evil spirit on the sons of Sceva (19:11–16). In short, Christians are not spared divine punishment. Some interpreters think that the temporary blinding of Paul is meant to be read as punishment for his persecution of Christians.

Acts 6:1–7 links the appointment of Stephen and others as deacons with a quarrel between Aramaic- and Greek-speaking Christians. The latter claim that their widows are being neglected. Although the role of the deacon seems to be distribution of food among the poor, the most famous member of the group, Stephen, is martyred for preaching the gospel. Luke concludes that the persecution that followed led to the spread of Christianity outside Jerusalem (8:1–3). Thus, the persecution has a providential side enabling the realization of God's plan to spread the gospel to the "ends of the earth."

The Holy Spirit frequently intervenes in the story in Acts. Often divine action is required at a critical juncture in the mission. Dreams and visions are the medium of communication. Ananias is instructed to find Paul in a vision (9:10–16). Visions are involved in the conversion of the first Gentile, Cornelius (10:1–16). Paul takes the critical step of expanding his ministry into Greece (Macedonia) when summoned by a vision (16:6–10). He is told by the Lord not to fear the opposition aroused by his preaching in Corinth (18:9–10). The Holy Spirit warns him of the coming imprisonment in Jerusalem (20:23). In other cases, the words of community prophets serve as guides to future events. Agabus, a prophet from Antioch, is said to have foretold a famine under Claudius (11:28). Community prophets direct the church at Antioch to send Barnabas and Paul on a missionary journey (13:1–3). Agabus prophesies that Paul will be "bound" by the Jews and handed over to the Gentiles (21:11). Many other smaller acts are also attributed to the Holy Spirit.

Modern readers may find persistent references to divine guidance either unreal or triumphalistic, as though whatever happens in the history of the church is automatically God's doing. Luke's audience would have recognized these parts of the story as supporting the claim that this history is God's doing. Luke has taken great pains to emphasize connections between the

Christian story and the larger world of Roman rule. References to the Roman governors in different provinces, to the death of Herod Agrippa, and to the famine under Claudius are part of this pattern. Roman historians saw their own history as divinely guided, concluding that they were destined to rule the civilized world. Luke presents the Christian reader with a "counter-history." The Roman world is the framework within which God's providence is working to spread salvation to all peoples. It is not a "divine event" in itself.

Although Luke emphasizes divine deliverance, joy, and harmony among the first Christians, we are never far from persecution, incarceration, or courtroom defense. Almost a third of the narrative involves apostles in prison (4:3–31; 5:17–41; 6:12—7:60; 12:1–17; 16:22–40; 17:6–9, 19–33; 18:12–17; 21:30—28:31). Initially "Jews," who resist the preaching about Jesus, stir up hostility. Once the story moves out of Jerusalem, they enlist local magistrates and Roman officials. But sometimes the enemies are persons whose financial interests in pagan religious practices are challenged by the gospel (e.g., owners of the possessed girl, 16:14–24; silversmiths at Ephesus, 19:24–41). Luke expresses the view that Jewish refusal to accept the gospel caused the apostles to turn away from the synagogue to the Gentiles (e.g., 13:44–47; 18:5–11; 28:23–28). Since this paradigmatic shift occurs in each of the three geographic areas of the Pauline mission, Asia Minor, Greece, and Rome, it appears that Luke no longer considers the conversion of Israel part of the missionary effort. On the other hand, he mentions devout Jews who became believers (e.g., Crispus, 18:8; unnamed Jews in Thessalonica and Borea, 17:4, 11–12). Perhaps Luke views this group of believing Jews as the "renewed Israel."

Just as Luke's evaluation of the "Jews" is a mixture of negative and positive, so the evangelist's presentation of magistrates and Roman officials has good and bad elements. Authorities often rescue the apostles from mob actions. Roman officials move Paul into custody outside Jerusalem in order to foil a plot against him (23:12–35). They sometimes provide a sympathetic hearing for apologetic speeches (e.g., 22:30; 24:22–24; 25:13–22). But we also find magistrates beating Paul, though he is a Roman citizen (16:37–39; 22:24–29), and holding him in prison without proven charges in hopes of being paid a bribe for his release (24:26). Some scholars think that the benign acts of Roman officials are intended to lessen the hostility toward such authorities felt by Christians who themselves have suffered beatings and imprisonment. Others treat imprisonment stories as opportunities to answer the charges that outsiders routinely directed against Christianity: that it was a "superstition" that turned people away from the ancestral gods and caused civic disruption. Paul is charged with "being a Jew" and advocating customs "unlawful for Romans" (16:20–21). Jews accuse him of leading people to worship in a way contrary to their law (18:13–15; 21:21, 28). Paul attacks the pagan gods and goddesses who were protectors of their cities (19:25–26).

Though readers know that those hostile to the gospel fabricate these charges, they persist throughout the narrative. Luke presents the charges against Paul in Jerusalem as an "inner Jewish" squabble (23:6–10; also in the episode before Gallio, 18:13–15). On occasion, the apostles are freed from jail by divine intervention (e.g., 5:17– 26; 12:6–11; 16:19–40). They are not let off through their own efforts. The reader knows that Stephen and James have been martyred. The Lord tells Paul that he will have to "bear witness" not only in Jerusalem but also in Rome (23:11). Thus, the defense that Acts gives is not in terms of human legal judgments. The suffering of the apostles is ultimately seen in light of the divine plan for the spread of the gospel.

The Apostle Heroes: Peter and Paul

Acts focuses on Peter and Paul as the "heroes" of its story. Peter dominates the first half of the book, which deals with the spread of Christianity from Jerusalem to the surrounding areas. The second half is the story of Paul's missionary activity in Asia Minor and Greece. Then the scene returns to Jerusalem for one last time to describe Paul's arrest and testimony there. As a prisoner, Paul makes the trip that brings him to Rome. Luke has shaped both the gospel and Acts so that Jerusalem provides a focal point for the dramatic action. Jerusalem is the city of destiny in the story. But with Paul's imprisonment and appeal to Rome for trial, Jerusalem has lost its place. Christianity is now to unfold within the larger world of the Roman Empire.

Both Peter and Paul play a central role in the shift from being a Jewish messianic movement to a Christianity that presents salvation in Jesus' name to all peoples. Paul is God's chosen instrument for the spread of the movement into the Greek-speaking cities of Asia Minor and Greece. Peter follows God's directions in baptizing Cornelius and his household, the first Gentile converts. Although their various imprisonments indicate that Peter and Paul will suffer for the gospel, Luke never tells the story of how they died. Yet we have already seen allusions to the fate of Paul in Ephesians (Eph 3:1; 4:1; 6:20) and to Peter's martyrdom in John 21:18–19, so Luke can hardly be ignorant of the fact that they were martyred.

Luke shapes the stories of the two heroes so that they run along parallel lines as you can see from Chart 16–2. The extensive parallels between the two sections of Acts make it clear that both apostles are following the plan that has been laid out for them by God.

Luke also shows the divine plan guiding the Christian mission in another way. He introduces parallels between the account of Jesus' life and the story in Acts; for example, the miracles that the apostles do to awaken faith in the crowds are like miracles that Jesus performs. Luke also patterns

Paul's journey to Jerusalem after Jesus' journey there in the gospel. Chart 16–3 shows some of the parallels between Jesus' story and Acts.

PETER AND PAUL: PARALLEL STORIES	[16–2]	
	Acts 1–12 [Peter]	Acts 13–28 [Paul]
STRUCTURE OF APOSTLE'S MISSION		
Witness to risen Christ	1:21–22	23:11; 26:16
Spirit initiates	2:1–40	13:1–40
Heals lame and speech	3:12–26	14:8–17
Persecution (stoning) leads to wider mission	[6:8–8:4, Stephen]	14:19–23
Defends Gentile mission in Jerusalem	ch. 11	ch. 21
Imprisoned at Jewish feast	12:4–7	21:16–28
Conclusion: Success of word of God	12:24	28:30–31
DEEDS OF THE APOSTLE		
Encounters a magician	8:9–24	13:6–12
Gentiles try to worship him	10:25–26	14:13–15
Raises the dead	9:36–43	20:9–12
Delivered from prison	12:6–11	16:24–26
Laying on hands gives Spirit	8:14–17	19:1–6
Appoints leaders with prayer/laying on hands	6:1–6	14:23
Defended by Pharisees in Sanhedrin	5:34–39	23:9
Accused of acting vs. Moses	[6:13–14, Stephen]	21:20–21; 25:8

JESUS' STORY AND ACTS	[16–3]	
	Luke	Acts
OPENING SEQUENCE OF EVENTS		
Spirit descends in physical form	3:21–22	1:14, 24; 2:1–13
Opening sermon: Scripture fulfilled and Jesus rejected	4:16–30	2:14–40
Preaching/healing prove fulfillment of promises; conflict and rejection	4:31–8:56	2:14–12:17

Continued

Continued

	Luke	Acts
lame healed	5:17–26	3:1–10
vs. leaders	5:29—6:11	4:1—8:3
pious centurion	7:1–10	ch. 10
widow/dead raised	7:11–17	9:36–43
Pharisees criticize	7:36–50	11:1–8
JOURNEY TO JERUSALEM		
Divine necessity	19:51	19:21
Dangers in Jerusalem	13:33	21:12
Resolved to go	19:11, 28	21:15, 17
Enthusiastic welcome	19:37	21:17–20a
Enters temple	19:45–48	21:26
Sadducees do not believe in resurrection; support from scribe(s)	20:27–39	23:6–9
Bless/break bread	22:19a	[27:35]
Seized by mob	22:54	21:30

Discipleship in Acts

In the gospels, teaching about discipleship is expressed in sayings of Jesus. Paul's epistles speak directly to particular churches and situations. Acts is different from both the gospels and the epistles. Its sermons repeat the basic themes of salvation history. God's promises have been fulfilled in Jesus. All people are called to believe in Jesus, to repent, to receive forgiveness for sin, and to join the new fellowship of believers. Luke is conscious of the fact that the Christian movement is something new. He uses a distinctive name for the group, "the way" (9:2; 19:9, 23; 22:4; 24:14, 22). This name appears to be a pre-Lucan term taken from Palestinian traditions. The Essenes spoke of persons who joined their community as "choosing the way." Their community rules were "regulations of the way of the master." Luke may have found this term appropriate since it picks up on one aspect of discipleship for Luke, the journey motif. A disciple follows Jesus along his journey. The parallels between the story of Jesus and the lives of the apostles make this point.

Acts looks back to the stories of the earliest community as examples for discipleship. Three themes are particularly strong in those stories. One is the theme of hospitality and sharing with the poor. Luke emphasizes the unity of the first Jerusalem Christians. He insists that they shared things in common. Wealthy Christians sold possessions to provide for the poor. In Acts 16:11–15, Lydia, who apparently was engaged in the business of selling dyed cloth, becomes a benefactor of Paul's mission. (This passage is a parallel to the women who provided for Jesus' mission in Luke 8:1–3.) Luke contrasts this "moderate" sharing of possessions to the radical attitude of renunciation of all possessions, a tradition he also preserves. The apostles are without money (Acts 3:6). Members of the Jerusalem community are said to have sold all their possessions (2:44–45; 4:35–37). Such examples serve as memory of a past ideal. The present application of Jesus' teaching appears to be generosity and community concern for the poor. Such efforts may call for rich Christians to make resources available by selling some property, as in the ill-fated case of Ananias and Sapphira (Acts 5:2–11), but does not suggest that Christians in Luke's day are adopting a radical poverty.

Another key theme in Acts is piety. The gospel emphasized Jesus' own roots among the faithful, pious persons of Israel. This motif is emphasized in the portrayal of the earliest Jerusalem community. Its members gather daily in the temple area for prayer. They also offer prayers in house-church gatherings. Acts 4:24–30 includes a lengthy prayer in which the community rehearses "salvation history" and asks for boldness in its witness to Jesus despite persecution. Prayer accompanies all-important acts of the community. It is part of the appointment of leaders (6:6; 13:2–3). The apostles are also shown praying to the Lord individually (9:11; 10:9). It accompanies healings (9:40). It is clear that both communal and personal prayer is a central feature of the Christian life.

There is another element in the treatment of piety in Acts: rejection of pagan religious practices. Throughout Acts, the apostles maintain contact with the piety of Judaism in both the temple at Jerusalem and the synagogues of various cities. Paul even takes pious vows (18:18; 21:23–26). The apostles also confront a spectrum of religious beliefs representative of the pagan world. Magicians, soothsayers, and other demon-possessed prophets are decisively defeated (e.g., 8:9–24; 13:8–12; 16:17–19; 19:13–20). Christianity is thus shown to be opposed to demonic and magical practices. In other cases, pagans think that the divine powers shown by the apostles mean that they are "divine" and must be prevented from worshiping them (10:25–26; 14:12–18; 28:3–6). Once again, Christianity is established as a form of "piety" and not gross superstition. However, educated pagans might still be suspicious of the new movement. It does turn people away from worshiping the traditional gods of a city. The riot by the silversmiths at Ephesus (19:23–41) makes this point: that the only persons "hurt" by such conversion are dubious types who are making a profit from the famous shrine. Finally Luke speaks to the most "enlightened" form of pagan piety, that schooled by philosophy. Paul's famous speech in Athens insists that those who already know that the divine is a cosmic, beneficent force, and not resident in magic rites or human temples, should now turn to accept Christianity (17:16–31). Thus, Luke answers the objections that Christianity is a base form of mass superstition by showing it to embody only the noblest forms of piety.

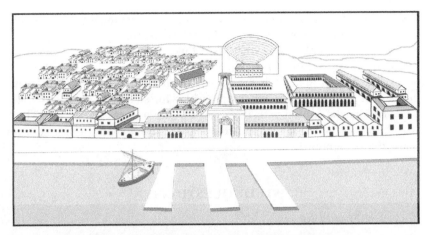

Reconstruction of the ancient city of Ephesus

A third theme is persecution. It dogs the steps of the apostles throughout the whole book. We are shown the first disciples praying for boldness in proclaiming the gospel despite persecution. Episodes of persecution have different results. But in every case, the apostle never hesitates to make a stirring defense of the gospel. Because he is acting out of divine necessity, the apostle will never be moved by human orders to cease preaching. Luke insists that only persons who have some motive such as envy, jealousy, or greed create trouble for Christians. All others should recognize that neither they nor their preaching are harmful. Whatever happens, the disciples accept persecution without anger. They rejoice in the salvation that God is bringing to many people through their testimony.

Summary

Acts shows readers how God guided the process that brought salvation out from Jerusalem to the whole world. Acts is not "church history" in the way we think of history: a collection of events that happened to Christians in the past. Rather it is the story of how God's providence worked through such famous apostles as Peter and Paul to bring into being the church and traditions that Luke and his readers have inherited.

Acts also establishes an important pattern for later generations of Christians by teaching us to look back to the story of the earliest community for a vision of what it means to be followers of Jesus. Paul's farewell speech to the elders of the Ephesian church (Acts 20:17–38) makes the difference between the time of the apostles and that of Luke's readers very clear. Now that the apostles are gone, those who have charge of the churches are responsible for teaching and admonishing others so that the community does not fall victim to divisions and predatory teaching. The departing apostle holds up his own life as an example. Notice that when Luke looks back on Paul's practice of working to support himself, he does not think of it as a sign of Paul's weakness. Rather he presents it as the way in which Paul not only met his own needs (and showed that he was not preaching for money) but also was able to share what he earned with the weak and unfortunate (20:17–38). This speech directs the message of Acts to all Christians who live in the generations after the apostles.

STUDY QUESTIONS

Facts You Should Know

1. How does the outline of Acts reflect Luke's understanding of salvation history?
2. What are the two kinds of speeches in Acts? Give an example of each type of speech.
3. How does the picture of the early Jerusalem community given in Acts serve as a model for Christian discipleship?
4. How are Roman authorities pictured in Acts? Give an example for each of the points you make. What purpose might this picture of the Roman authorities have served in Luke's "apology" for Christianity?
5. Describe Luke's treatment of each of the following themes: (a) wealth; (b) piety; (c) persecution.

Things to Do

1. Compare Paul's picture of pagan religiousness in Romans 1:18—3:31 with the speech Paul gives in Acts 17:22–31. What common themes are there? How do the two speeches differ?
2. Using a concordance, find the references to the "spirit of the Lord" or the "Holy Spirit" in Acts. What role does the Spirit play in the early community?
3. Read the stories of persecution in Acts. How does Luke show the reader that the apostles are innocent of the charges being brought against them in each story?

Things to Think About

1. How might the picture of the early community serve as a model for Christians today?
2. What role does the guidance of the Holy Spirit play in the life of Christians today?

Chapter 17

HEBREWS:
THE HEAVENLY
HIGH PRIEST

The Thought World of Hebrews

Although Hebrews found its way into the New Testament as an epistle of Paul, early Christian writers recognized that Hebrews is quite different from the Pauline letters. The third-century exegete Origen noted that its elegant Greek is quite different from the awkward style of the apostle. He finally concluded that the thought of Hebrews is worthy of apostolic teaching, but that it must have been written by someone else (in Eusebius, *Ecclesiastical History* 6.25). He reports suggestions that Luke had been the author or perhaps the Roman bishop Clement who appears to be citing Hebrews in a letter to the Corinthian church written in AD 96 (cf. *1 Clem* 36.2–5//Heb 1:3–12; *1 Clem* 17.7//Heb 11:37; *1 Clem* 17.5//Heb 3:5). Our oldest manuscript of Hebrews (ca. AD 200) places it after Paul's Letter to the Romans. Several comments in the work suggest an author looking back to the earlier days of the community. He and his readers depend upon the witness of a previous generation (Heb 2:3). They revere "leaders" whose lives have already ended (13:7) and look back on a time in which they suffered persecution. That suffering has ended but they are in danger of letting their first enthusiasm cool (10:32–36).

Although Hebrews is traditionally called a "letter," it lacks the formal structure of a letter. Only the concluding verses (13:19–25) have been shaped to sound like the conclusion of a Pauline letter with a final exhortation, prayers, mention of travel plans, and greetings from the sender to the recipients. Mention of Timothy's release (13:23) enabled later identification of the author with Paul. Timothy is co-sender with Paul in Philemon 1, when Paul was in prison. The personal reference in Hebrews 13:19 could be seen as similar to Philemon 22. Some exegetes find in these details hints that

Hebrews was written to the church at Rome by a second-generation Christian. The Italians mentioned in 13:24 would be immigrants from Italy. Roman Christians would have been concerned about Timothy's fate since he had been there when Paul (2 Tim 4:9, 11, 21) and Peter (1 Pet 5:13) were martyred. However, as Origen recognized, only God knows for sure. Hebrews does not provide enough information to identify either the author or the recipients of this discourse.

OUTLINE OF HEBREWS [17–1]

Prologue: God has spoken through the Son (1:1-4)

The Son's superiority to the angels (1:5-14)

Exhortation: Do not drift away from such a salvation (2:1-4)

By suffering, the Son brings many to salvation (2:5-18)

Jesus is greater than Moses (3:1-6)

Exhortation: Do not fall away like Israel in the wilderness (3:7—4:13)

Jesus is the sympathetic high priest (4:14—5:10)

Exhortation: Do not be immature in faith (5:11—6:12)

God's promises are confirmed by an oath (6:13-20)

Jesus **is** the high priest in the order of Melchizedek (7:1—10:18)

  (a) Melchizedek symbolizes an eternal priesthood higher than the levitical priesthood of the old covenant (7:1-28)
  (b) Christ ministers in the true, heavenly sanctuary that fulfills the promise of a new covenant (8:1-13)
  (c) Christ as mediator of the new covenant makes the sacrifices of the old covenant unnecessary (9:1-22)
  (d) Christ's sacrifice for sin takes place once for all in the heavenly sanctuary (9:23—10:18)

Exhortation: Hold fast to your faith and good works; there is no sacrifice for the sin of turning away from Christ (10:19-39)

Heroes of faith grasp the reality of heavenly things (11:1-40)

Exhortation: Persevere, remembering Christ's example and those who went before you (12:1—13:19)

Letter-like closing (13:20-25)

Hebrews 13:22 describes the writing as a "word of exhortation." Acts 13:15 uses this term of a sermon. Hebrews employs classical rhetorical patterns and mentions speaking to its audience rather than writing (2:5; 5:11; 6:9; 8:1; 9:5). Sections of Old Testament proofs about Christ in Hebrews are followed by exhortation to the community. Hebrews presents Christ as the heavenly high priest who has made sacrifice for sin "once for all" in the heavenly sanctuary. Christians must never waver in their own hope of attaining salvation.

New Testament writers often encouraged steadfastness and hope by invoking the coming judgment. Paul strives for the prize that lies ahead, the transformation when the Lord returns (Phil 3:12–21). He reminds readers that "salvation is nearer now than when we first believed" (Rom 13:11–14). Hebrews retains the language of judgment. Scripture has revealed that the Lord will judge apostates (Heb 10:30–31). The final judgment will be more traumatic than the worst earthquake, since even the heavens will be shaken (12:25–29). But future judgment is not a dominant image in Hebrews.

Hebrews employs a contrast taken from philosophical thought and applied to interpreting the Bible by Jewish exegetes like the first-century writer Philo. From this perspective, everything connected with the material world is imperfect and changing. Platonism held that this imperfect, changing material world was just a pale reflection of an unchanging, divine, heavenly world. Human beings could access the divine world through the mind or reason. A philosopher whose mind was constantly trained on that heavenly realm attained perfection. Philo of Alexandria applied this understanding of reality to the Jewish scriptures. God is the unchanging source of all that exists. The journeys of heroes like Abraham and Moses represent what takes place within the soul as it sought to know God. For such great figures, knowledge of God meant a union with the divine brought about through the working of God's word or wisdom within the soul.

Hebrews uses this contrast throughout the letter. Christ is our access to the heavenly world. Hebrews even uses the motif to interpret the judgment (12:25–29) by observing that the "cosmic destruction" associated with the time of judgment is really a purging away of all that is imperfect and earthly. What is true reality, the heavenly realm, cannot be shaken. It remains after the judgment. The kingdom that Christians have received belongs to that eternal dimension of reality (vv. 27–28). Other basic Christian categories are given a new interpretation by means of this philosophic understanding of the world. Philo had argued, for example, that the "Sabbath rest" in the Bible points to the unchanging nature of God. Moses was able to "soar above to hold fast to God." Thus Moses shared in that rest. Hebrews encourages Christians to seek the rest through their pilgrimage to a heavenly homeland. The famous definition of faith in Hebrews 11:1–3 speaks of it as our way of knowing the invisible, heavenly realities that lie behind everything that is created.

Another concept typical of this philosophic tradition is the idea of an education of the soul. Elementary teachings are for the immature, who must learn to lead a life of virtue through discipline. As the soul progresses it no longer needs the milk of elementary teaching but can receive true teaching. The soul in which God's wisdom dwells no longer experiences virtue as discipline because it has become good. The education theme is part of the exhortation in Hebrews. Hebrews 5:11—6:12 encourages readers not to remain "sluggish." They should not still be going over elementary school lessons but should be among the mature. Hebrews 6:1–3 lists the beginning doctrines of Christianity: repentance; faith in God; baptism [washings]; laying on of hands; resurrection and eternal judgment. Hebrews 6:4–8 points toward a difficulty in the community: persons who had once been Christians are falling away. Hebrews warns that apostates cannot be restored to the community. It also invokes the education motif when it tells the readers to accept any of the hardships they experience as God's discipline. Like parental discipline of a child, divine discipline is part of the training necessary to become a mature Christian.

Another unusual element in Hebrews, its emphasis upon the cultic liturgy of Judaism, can be seen as part of the tradition of Alexandrian biblical interpretation. Philo's writings discuss the priestly functions of Moses in the heavenly sanctuary. They contain elaborate allegories for the vestments worn by the high priest. Hebrews is unique in the New Testament for its treatment of Christ as the heavenly high priest. For Philo, the patterning of the earthly cult after the heavenly one meant that persons gained access to heavenly realities when practicing the earthly cult. Hebrews takes a more polemical turn. The earthly cult of Judaism is an inferior copy, which is to be rejected now that Christ has provided the believer with access to the heavenly sanctuary. Jewish visitors, hearing passages from Hebrews read in Christian churches, often feel insulted. It is important to remember two facts. First, everything Hebrews says about "Jewish worship" is constructed from the author's reading of Exodus. Second, by the time Hebrews was written the Jerusalem temple was in ruins, so none of the earthly sacrifices treated as inferior images could be carried out.

Christ as Heavenly High Priest

Hebrews develops two key images of Christ: Christ is the divine Son who is the eternal image of God; Christ is the heavenly high priest who belongs to an eternal order of priesthood that was prefigured by the mysterious figure of Melchizedek in Genesis 14. The tradition of Christ as image of God emerges in early Christological hymns. The prologue to Hebrews, like the prologue to John, opens with a poetic depiction of the Son's mission:

> ...whom [= the Son] he appointed heir of all things, through whom
> he created the world. He reflects the glory of God and bears the
> stamp of his nature, upholding the universe by his word of power,

> who, having made purification for sins, sat down at the right hand
> of the majesty on high, having become as much superior to the
> angels as the name he has obtained is superior to theirs. (1:2–4)

This fragment follows a pattern common in other hymnic passages. Christ preexists as the creative power of God, creating and upholding the universe. The role of Christ in salvation is then described in terms of earthly activity, frequently an effect of his death, and subsequent ascent to glory at the right hand of God. Philippians 2:6–11 described the final exaltation in terms of a "superior name" and subjection of the powers. There the name was "Lord." Hebrews 1:5–6 makes it clear that the name that marks Christ's superiority to the angelic powers is "Son."

The liturgical traditions establish Christ's unique place in the heavenly realm. The description of Christ's death as "making purification for sins" points toward description of Christ as high priest, whose self-offering is the perfect sacrifice for sin that will occupy much of the letter. Before turning to that topic, the author draws out the imagery of "subjection" and exaltation as it applies to Christ. Hebrews 2:7–9 admits that the subjection of all things to the "Son" is not something that we actually see now. Traditionally that subjection is evident only at the judgment (cf. 1 Cor 15:22–28). But Christians do see that the Son who had suffered death is exalted with God. Using the education tradition that suffering is a way of perfecting the soul along with the liturgical tradition of purification, Hebrews argues that the Son's suffering was the source of perfection for many brothers and sisters (Heb 2:10–13). Christ can be the source of salvation only if he shares their human nature, flesh and blood, suffering, and death. His heavenly place above the angels does not mean that Christ is a non-human, divine figure. He is a real descendant of Abraham (2:14–16). Christ's humanity and education through suffering are part of his service as a faithful and merciful high priest (2:18–19; 4:14–5:10).

Emphasis on the suffering humanity of the Son modifies one of the presuppositions of the philosophical language Hebrews adopted. In the philosophical tradition, rest, standing, and unchangeableness are all attributes of the divine that the soul seeks to attain. Suffering and the passions imply imperfection. Hebrews insists that the perfection of Christ is not lessened by suffering with humanity or by knowing the temptations to which humans are subject. These experiences are part of the obedience that the Son learned. Christ's obedience is the basis for the sinlessness that made the self-offering in death a perfect, unrepeatable sacrifice. Hebrews 10:5–10 uses the prophetic critique of insincere cultic worship to show that God did not desire cultic activity. What God sought was perfect obedience. Only one who has come into a body in this world can offer such obedience.

Hebrews 7:1—10:18 uses the language of cult and sacrifice in a series of arguments that the new order, which has come into being with Christ, surpasses the old Mosaic covenant and Levitical priesthood. For example, Hebrews 9:1–14 contrasts the effects of the old sacrifices and that of Christ. The Levitical cult established rules for worship in an earthly sanctuary. But such rules could only affect the body. They did not perfect the conscience. The earthly tent symbolizes the present age. Christ's sacrifice does not take place in the earthly tent. It implies entry into the heavenly world. The "blood," superior to all the blood of slaughtered sheep and goats, is the whole self-offering of Christ (9:14, 23–25; 10:4, 19–20). The superiority of this offering lies in its ability to cleanse what is inner: conscience. Thus unlike the older cult, Christ's offering takes away sin (9:13–14; 10:4, 22).

Comparison with exegetical tradition in Philo makes this emphasis on cleansing the conscience clearer. Philo says of the earthly cult, which images the heavenly, "It is not possible to express our gratitude by means of buildings, oblations and sacrifices, for even the whole world was not a temple adequate for Him" (*Plant*. 126). True worship of God must take place in the purity of the soul. Hymns, prayer, and virtue are ways in which the rational part of the human person serves God, who is incorporeal. Only those with "pure souls" can approach the heavenly altar. Conscience can be described as the divine Word sent into the soul that brings to light its transgressions (*Spec. Leg*. 1.272). Hebrews argues that by making forgiveness possible once and for all, Christ cleanses the conscience of believers.

Discipleship in Hebrews

The primary danger faced by Hebrews' audience is apostasy. Some have turned away from the faith that they once possessed. Even those being addressed must be encouraged to hold fast and endure (3:6, 14; 10:36–39). Instead of progressing to maturity and perfection, some have a faith that has not gone beyond the beginner's stages (5:11—6:2). The author reminds them to encourage one another in good works. Some are reprimanded for neglecting to meet together (10:23–25). Yet this same community can look back to a past in which its members were willing to endure much suffering. They knew that loss of perishable earthly possessions was nothing compared with the permanent salvation that awaited them (10:32–36).

Throughout the work, Hebrews emphasizes the certainty and permanence of God's promises (e.g., 10:36–39; 6:13–20). The audience is warned that just as the heavenly salvation received through Christ is much superior to the old covenant, so the penalties for failure to remain faithful are greater (10:28–31). Hebrews 12:18–29 draws a dramatic comparison between Israel coming to Mount Sinai in the wilderness and the people of the new covenant who belong to the "city of the living God, the heavenly Jerusalem." The terrifying appearance of God on Sinai meant death for any living creature that touched the mountain. But the terrifying appearance associated with the new covenant will be the judgment that will consume all transitory earthly things. Christians must take care to remain part of the "kingdom which is unshaken."

The philosophic tradition insisted that virtue, cleansing of the soul, was the appropriate worship of God. Christian sacrifice, that appropriate to those who belong to the heavenly city and not the earthly realm, takes the form of praising God, doing good, and sharing what one has (13:14–16). Hebrews 13:1–5 lists some of the obligations of love among Christians: hospitality; care for prisoners and those who are ill treated; respect for marriage and avoidance of adultery; freedom from greed and contentment with what one has. This list follows common patterns of ethical exhortation. The emphasis upon remembering the lives of leaders of the community and avoiding false teaching (13:7–8) reflects the concerns of Christians in the generation after the death of the apostles.

However, the warning against false teaching is followed by polemic against eating sacrifices from the "earthly altar" (13:9–10). Combined with the constant reminders that the Jewish cult has been superseded in Christ, this passage may indicate that there are Christians who expected an earthly replacement for the cult of the Jerusalem temple. We have already seen that Acts presented its readers with a picture of the Jerusalem community gathering in the temple for prayer as well as making private vows and sacrifices there. The emperors Vespasian and Titus presented their destruction of the great Jerusalem temple as a triumphant moment on coins and monuments. An audience in Rome need not have been of Jewish origin to be interested in the temple's fate. Impressive temples with processions and sacrifices to the god or goddess formed part of the civic life of every major city. Christians could not adopt pagan rites without becoming idolaters, but they might have been attracted by the cultic elements in Christianity's Jewish heritage.

If Hebrews was directed to such Christians at Rome, then we can see that its negative portrayal of the Levitical cult did not win the day. *First Clement*, a letter from that church (ca. AD 96) that alludes to Hebrews, speaks of the temple cult as a divinely established order in which each group (high priest, priests, Levites, laity) has an appropriate place (40.1–5; 41.42). This order is replicated in the Christian sphere where Christ is high priest followed by apostles, bishops, and deacons (ch. 42). *First Clement* 44.4 insists that one of the main functions of the bishop is to offer sacrifices. Rather than reject the Levitical priesthood as transitory and imperfect in contrast to the heavenly sanctuary of Christ's sacrifice, *1 Clement* shows us that Roman Christianity had combined it with the tradition of Christ as high priest. That combination would provide the beginning point for extensive development of a cultic understanding of priesthood within Christianity.

Another point at which the tradition did not follow the lead of Hebrews concerns forgiveness of sin after baptism. In its warnings against apostasy,

Hebrews insists that there can be no forgiveness for sin committed after baptism (6:4–6; 10:26–27). The second-century visionary work from the Roman community *Shepherd of Hermas* offers limited forgiveness for those willing to repent with their whole hearts (*Vision* 2.2–4; *Similitude* 9.26). However, its hearers must hurry to repent of blaspheming or denying the Lord before the period of repentance is past. Popes took an even more liberal approach to the problem of forgiveness of post-baptismal sin in the early third century. Despite its use in *1 Clement*, Hebrews does not appear to have been treated as canonical in the early third century. Only thirteen Pauline letters appear in the Muratorian canon list (ca. AD 200). By the time Hebrews is clearly accepted as canonical in the West, forgiveness for sin committed after baptism even if that sin was apostasy had become an established part of penitential discipline in the church.

For Hebrews, disciples are on an exodus journey toward the promised land, their share in God's rest in the unshakable, heavenly kingdom. Faith is the access we have to those realities that we cannot see. Hebrews 11 catalogues all the great heroes of faith from the Old Testament. Their faith, the author concludes, was particularly exemplary because they did not receive what was promised. They had to wait until the fulfillment of all God's promises in Christ (11:39–40). Christians who have experienced the promised salvation in Christ and have such witnesses as their heritage should be even more eager to lay aside sin and to perfect their faith (12:1–2).

Summary

The unknown author of Hebrews has fashioned a discourse that points to future developments in Christian imagery and thought just as much of the work also draws on well-established themes from the past. Its picture of the Christian people as journeying toward the heavenly city set in contrast to the earthly city became an important way of understanding how Christians are to orient themselves in the world with St. Augustine's *City of God*. Adaptation of Platonic philosophy to understanding the biblical message of salvation and the soul's progress toward God became an essential part of Christian spirituality. The definition of faith in Hebrews 11:1 became a classic definition in the Christian tradition.

Even in those areas where subsequent tradition differed from the position expressed in Hebrews, evaluation of Jewish cultic imagery and post-baptismal sin, the discourse voices important insights. Hebrews recognizes that the washing of baptism can never be repeated. Hebrews is also right to be horrified that someone who has experienced all the richness of the Christian life would throw all that away. Finding in Christ's sacrifice a forgiveness that could extend even to such people if they repented did not mean that

Christians had become casual about apostasy. Even though the Old Testament would shape the language of Christian priesthood, Christians did not reestablish multiple sacrifices. The only sacrifice offered by the Christian priest is the eternal sacrifice of Christ.

Though Jesus was not of a priestly family, Hebrews recognizes his death as the supreme priestly act. Hebrews finds in the mysterious figure of Melchizedek indication of an eternal order of priesthood that is different from the earthly priesthood based on descent. Consequently, it is in Hebrews that we find the clear affirmation that Christ is the supreme priest. Hebrews also gives us moving images of the divine humanity of Christ as Son. Jesus genuinely shares the suffering and temptations of human beings even though he is without sin. This education of the divine Son should make Christians willing to turn to Christ the high priest for mercy and understanding.

STUDY QUESTIONS

Facts You Should Know

1. What type of writing is Hebrews? How did it come to be included in the New Testament?
2. What is the philosophical picture of reality used by Hebrews? How does the letter reinterpret the traditional teaching about judgment?
3. What images does Hebrews use for Christ? How is Christ the high priest different from all other high priests?
4. What is the importance of the suffering of Christ according to Hebrews?
5. What dangers does Hebrews see facing its audience? How do the words of exhortation in Hebrews address those dangers?

Things to Do

1. Trace the theme of journey to the promised "rest" in Hebrews. How does the author use this theme in his exhortation to remain faithful?
2. List the arguments that Hebrews gives for the superiority of Christ's sacrifice. Why could there never be another sacrifice like that of Christ?

Things to Think About

1. How do we fall into the danger of letting our initial enthusiasm for Christianity lapse?
2. Do we make an effort to attain a mature understanding of our faith, or do we remain content simply to repeat its elementary doctrines?

Chapter 18

THE PASTORAL EPISTLES: A PAULINE TRADITION

The Image of Paul in the Pastorals

We have seen in Acts and Hebrews that by the end of the first century Christians looked back on the apostles as heroes from the past. Christians no longer assumed that the second coming was in the immediate future. The church must go on preaching and living in this world for an indefinite period of time. How will Christians preserve the heritage of apostolic teaching against fragmentation? In Acts, the apostles formally appoint leaders in local communities. Paul gives his farewell instructions to such a group, elders from the church at Ephesus (Acts 20:17–35). Hebrews instructs readers to remember the example of past leaders and to obey those who now guide the community (Heb 13:7–9, 17).

First and Second Timothy and Titus make these developments even clearer. In the thirteenth century, St. Thomas Aquinas called 1 Timothy "a pastoral rule." Eighteenth-century commentators began referring to the group as Pastoral Epistles. They are cast as letters from Paul to his two closest associates, Timothy and Titus, about how elders or bishops of local churches should conduct their ministry. Unlike the earlier group of letters that remain close to Paul's language and theology (e.g., Col, Eph, 2 Thess), the pastorals do not attempt to recapture Paul's own language even though an associate may have composed the letter in his name. During Paul's lifetime Timothy and Titus were traveling missionaries who often filled in for the apostle when he could not visit a community (1 Thess 3:2; 1 Cor 4:17; 2 Cor 8:23). In the pastorals, these seasoned associates have become inexperienced resident leaders of local communities who need instructions.

OUTLINE OF 1 TIMOTHY   [18-1]

Greeting (1:1-2)

Timothy's task: Maintain apostolic faith against heretics (1:3-20)

   (a) False teaching and immorality (1:3-11)
   (b) Thanksgiving for Paul's conversion (1:12-17)
   (c) False teachers condemned by the apostle (1:18-20)

Specific instructions on community order (2:1—6:19)

   (a) Prayer for all and proper conduct of men and women (2:1-15)
   (b) Qualifications for bishops and deacons (3:1-13)
   (c) Maintain proper behavior in the "household of God" (3:14-16)
   (d) Reject false teaching: ascetic denial of creation (4:1-4)
   (e) Timothy's good example against false teaching (4:6-16)
   (f) Respect for persons of different ages (5:1-2)
   (g) Rules for enrolling widows (5:3-16)
   (h) Rules for treatment of elders (5:17-22)
   (i) Rules and sayings (5:23-25)
   (j) Behavior of Christian slaves (6:1-2)
   (k) Against disputes about teaching (6:3-5)
   (l) Against greed: be contented with what you have (6:6-10)
   (m) Persevere in the "good fight of faith" (6:11-16)
   (n) To the rich: Trust in God and do good deeds (6:17-19)

Conclusion: Guard what has been entrusted to you (6:20-21)

OUTLINE OF 2 TIMOTHY   [18-2]

Greeting (1:1-2)

Thanksgiving for Timothy's faith (1:3-7)

Remember Paul's faithful testimony to the gospel (1:8—2:13)

Reject heretical teachers: some claim resurrection is past (2:14-26)

People will fall into evil in the last days (3:1-9)

Remember Paul's conduct and your own heritage of faith (3:10-17)

Fulfill your ministry by preaching even to those unwilling to hear (4:1-5)

Paul's life is ending (4:6-18)

   (a) He has faithfully fulfilled his calling (4:6-8)
   (b) Faithful and unfaithful associates (4:9-16)
   (c) The Lord will uphold the apostle (4:17-18)

Final greetings (4:19-22)

OUTLINE OF TITUS   [18–3]

Greeting (1:1–3)

Titus's work: order the churches in Crete (1:5–16)

(a) Qualifications for elder-bishop (1:5–9)
(b) To counter false teachers: Judaizing mythologies (1:10–16)

Titus's work: teaching sound doctrine (2:1–3:11)

(a) Proper behavior for men, women, and slaves (2:2–10)
(b) Renounce passions and await the appearing of the savior by leading "godly lives" (2:11–15)
(c) Rules for obedience, honest work, and gentle speech toward all (3:1–2)
(d) Salvation as regeneration and hope for eternal life (3:3–8)
(e) Insist on the truth and avoid useless controversies (3:8b–11)

Travel plans for Paul's associates (3:12–14)

Final greetings (3:15)

You can see from the outlines that 1 Timothy and Titus might easily serve as a handbook for church leaders. They give qualifications for those appointed elders or bishops in the churches. They incorporate rules about proper conduct for Christians. Preservation of sound teaching is one of the primary responsibilities of local bishops or elders.

The distinctive themes of Paul's theology are absent from these letters. The apostle is being presented as the authoritative source for general rules of community life. These rules have some ties to the earlier Pauline tradition. In his earliest letter, 1 Thessalonians, Paul exhorted Christians to live in holiness, not dominated by passions, quietly minding their own affairs, working with their hands so as to be dependent on no one, and commanding the respect of outsiders (1 Thess 4:3–11). Paul had established rules for the proper dress of men and women who were prophesying in the assembly (1 Cor 11:2–26), and had given advice to widows (1 Cor 7:7, 8–9, 39–40) and to slaves (1 Cor 7:17–24). Colossians and Ephesians included advice about relationships between husbands and wives, parents and children, masters and slaves in the form of a "household code" (Col 3:18—4:1; Eph 5:22—6:9). The pastorals view the Christian community as the "household of God." The rules set forth are intended to maintain proper behavior among members of that household (1 Tim 3:14–16).

Second Timothy shares with the other two letters warnings against heretical teaching and instructions for ministry. However, its focus is on Paul as an example. The letter takes the form of a farewell discourse from the apostle to Timothy. In the farewell discourse, the dying patriarch gathers his children, admonishes them to live virtuously drawing upon his own past life as an example, and predicts their future. The speech to the Ephesian elders in Acts 20:28–35 is such a discourse. Second Timothy provides us with a fascinating glimpse of how Paul was remembered in churches at the end of the century.

Second Timothy pictures Paul's suffering on behalf of the gospel (e.g., 2 Tim 1:8; 3:10–11; 4:6–8). He provides a model to follow when Christians have to bear witness to the gospel entrusted to them. Acts concluded with a benign picture of Paul as imprisoned witness to the gospel in Rome (Acts 28:17–31). Second Timothy tells a very different story. It picks up an element of Paul's biography missing from Acts: Paul faced enemies within the Christian movement itself. Notice the references to persons who have deserted the apostle (2 Tim 1:15; 4:9, 14–16). The apostle is almost completely abandoned in jail (4:6–18). Second Timothy 1:16–18 praises Onesiphorus and his household for not being ashamed of Paul's imprisonment but seeking diligently to find him. Has Luke omitted embarrassing facts about the end of Paul's life? Or is the abandonment of the apostle in 2 Timothy another way of connecting the sufferings of the apostle and those of Christ? We do know that before his ill-fated trip to Jerusalem, Paul wrote Romans, seeking to gain support in the Roman community. He fears that the church in Jerusalem might not accept his collection (Rom 15:31). If the polemic against the Jewish cult in Hebrews addresses sentiments among Christians in Rome, then there may have been believers in Rome who were less than enthusiastic about helping the controversial apostle.

True Doctrine in the Pastorals

One of the major motifs in the pastorals is concern to preserve apostolic teaching. The letters warn against those who like to dispute and to devise clever myths. Paul predicts that deceitful and divisive teaching that has been adapted to what people want to hear will become common in the last days (e.g., 2 Tim 3:1–9; 4:1–5). The pastorals employ rhetorical moves common in disputes between rival schools of philosophy. The opposition is always pictured as divided into numerous factions while true teaching is unanimously held by its followers. Those who teach such "false doctrines" are presented as morally corrupt, out to satisfy their own passions or greed. False teachers are often accused of gaining by appealing to women who lack the education or rational self-mastery required to resist such appeals (e.g., 2 Tim 3:6–7).

The polemical rhetoric makes it difficult to figure out the actual content of false teaching. However, three areas seem to be disputed:

(a) an asceticism that rejected marriage (1 Tim 2:15; 4:3; 5:14) and required abstaining from some foods (1 Tim 4:3; 5:23; Tit 1:15)

(b) individuals who taught that the resurrection had "occurred already" (2 Tim 2:18)

(c) some form of speculation characterized as Jewish myths and genealogies (1 Tim 4–7; Tit 3:9)

Paul himself dealt with questions about asceticism from Corinthian believers who thought they should dissolve their marriages in order to avoid sexuality (1 Cor 7). Romans 14:1–3 mentions disputes about food. Although we cannot tell what those who claimed the resurrection had already occurred meant, there was a tradition in Pauline churches of speaking of the Christian as "raised with Christ" (e.g., Col 3:1; Eph 2:5–6). That tradition could have led to the conclusion that resurrection referred to an experience of spiritual illumination, not to a future transformation of persons. We do not know what form the speculations about Jewish myths and genealogies took. In the second century, various movements of a general type called *gnostic* claimed secret knowledge about the origins of the heavenly world and the fall of a heavenly being whose offspring is the "evil creator" of this material world. Gnostic mythologies included genealogies of the various heavenly and demonic powers and incorporated the Old Testament creation stories.

Since there are no arguments against the heretical views, we cannot reconstruct those positions. What is the "true doctrine" that the successors to the apostles are to teach? There is no sustained development of theological themes in the pastorals. We find out clues to the tradition of faith in the short formulaic expressions that the author uses. The unusual expression *pistos ho logos*, "the word is trustworthy," appears five times (1 Tim 1:15; 3:1; 4:9; 2 Tim 2:11; Tit 3:8). First Timothy 4:9 adds a parallel expression: "It is worthy of all recognition." This formula marks some of the passages in which such traditional material is being quoted. First Timothy 1:15 refers to the conviction that Jesus came "to save sinners." First Timothy 4:9 may anticipate the affirmation that Christ is "savior of all people, especially believers," in 4:10. This affirmation is directed against heretical teaching that overemphasized "bodily discipline." The previous verse stated that while bodily discipline has some value, the real source of salvation is "piety." The reference of 1 Timothy 3:1 is equally ambiguous.

Second Timothy 2:11 introduces a formula contrasting the faithful Christian who will live and reign with the Lord and the unfaithful who will be rejected (vv. 12–13). Titus 3:8 refers to what has come before in verses 4 to 7. These verses summarize the "story of salvation" found in the formulas. Humanity is separated from God through sinfulness. Thanks to the mercy of God, the savior appeared so that humans could be reborn in baptism and the Spirit. Consequently, believers now have the hope of eternal life. In this passage, the title "savior" applies both to God and to Jesus Christ. First Timothy 2:3–6 describes God as savior and Jesus as ransom for us. Titus 1:2–3 speaks of God's promise of external life manifested in Jesus. Second Timothy 1:10 reminds the reader that the "appearing" of Christ abolished death.

There are also a few cryptic allusions to a story of Jesus' coming, though you will notice that the characteristic Pauline pattern of cross and resurrection is not present. First Timothy 3:16 comments that the "mystery" of "our piety" is:

> who [= Jesus] was manifested in the flesh; vindicated in the Spirit; preached among the nations; believed in the world; taken up in glory.

First Timothy 6:13 refers to Jesus making "good confession" in his testimony before Pilate. God, for the pastorals, is the invisible creator, king of kings (e.g., 1 Tim 3:15–16), who stands behind the salvation Christians have received.

Church Organization in the Pastorals

The New Testament mentions many different roles within Christian communities: apostles, prophets, teachers, elders, deacons, overseers ("bishops"), and the like. Matthew's community may even have had persons described as Christian "scribes." As long as the communities were small groups that could seek advice from their apostle-founder or his associates, the differing patterns of leadership and community service "inspired by the Spirit" (e.g., 1 Cor 12:28–31; Rom 12:6–8) posed no problem. However, in Acts in response to a concern to establish more permanent forms of church office, individuals were formally installed as leaders and missionary representatives of the community. Prayer and laying on of hands are part of the ceremony. Second Timothy 1:6 links Timothy's appointment in this manner with a gift of the Spirit to help him fulfill his duties.

The terms *overseer* (*episkopos*), which is usually translated "bishop," and *elder* (*presbyteros*) seem to have been used in different communities for the person in charge of the community. The term *deacon* was apparently used for those who played a role in assisting them. Thus, Paul addressed Philippians to "all the saints in Christ Jesus at Philippi together with their overseers and deacons" (Phil 1:1). In addition to these leaders, other people served as missionaries in the Philippian community, including the two women, Euodia and Syntyche (Phil 4:2). The rules of both "elder" and "overseer/bishop" are rooted in Jewish practice. *Elder*, as the term suggests, indicates older men who oversaw the affairs of the local community. They might also serve as "judges" when disputes arose between individuals. *Overseer* is paralleled by the Hebrew term *mebaqar*, which referred to the head of a community in the new Covenanters' sect. He was in charge of admitting members and other affairs of the sect, though in some cases another official may have assisted him. The community also had a ruling council of older members, which some scholars have compared to the way in which the group of "the Twelve" functioned in the earliest church at Jerusalem.

In Titus 1:5–9, the terms *bishop* and *elder* are used interchangeably for the person in charge of the local community. A man appointed to that office, as well as his wife and children, must be above any reproach morally. He must have a firm grasp on sound teaching so that he can convey it to others and refute those who are propagating false opinions. First Timothy mentions the qualifications for bishops and deacons in one place (3:1–13), and for elders, who are apparently subordinate to the bishop, in another (5:17–22). The bishop might have been an "elder" who had risen to preeminence because of his aptitude for teaching. In any event, we have the basic elements of the threefold order of pastoral ministry and supervision that would become established practice: bishops, elders, and deacons. As Christianity assumed the cultic language of the Old Testament, the *elders* would be referred to as "priests." According to the pastorals, the "bishops/elders" are the successors of the apostles, since it is their responsibility to preserve and to continue apostolic teaching and witness in the Christian communities.

As you can see from the list of qualifications in 1 Timothy 3:1–13, those appointed to these offices had to be well-established Christians. They also had to be well-thought-of in the larger community, since it would be part of their responsibility to represent the Christian groups in the larger community. Since the Christian church thought of itself as a "household," the bishop had to be a person who was able to manage his own household well. That ability was part of someone's standing in the local community. You can see that the situation of the bishop or elder is different from that of a traveling apostle like Paul. This person has to be able to guide a single, local community over a long period. In the ancient world, only a man who was the head of his own household would enjoy sufficient respect to accomplish that task. Even though women did manage households independently, like Lydia in Acts 16:14–15, they would not have been the respected leaders of a local community. The same considerations would have also excluded a younger man who was not in charge of his own household but still under the power of his father.

It is not clear that the role of deacon was entirely restricted to men at this period. First Timothy 3:11 inserts a reference to women into the qualifications for that office: "The women likewise must be serious, not slanderers, but temperate and faithful in all things." The roles that women played in the early household churches of the Pauline mission may have been understood as diaconal. But as the threefold structure developed further and deacons often went on to become priests and bishops, women were no longer designated deacons. Later this verse came to be understood simply as a reference to the qualities that the wife of a deacon had to have.

Christian Women in the Pastorals

The model of the church in the pastorals was that of a "patriarchal household." The church was like the "households" of the surrounding society in which everyone—younger men, women, children, and slaves—had a role subordinate to that of the older male who was head of the family. The bishop had to fill this role for the Christian family. In the ancient world, women or young men would head households only in extraordinary circumstances. The rules for the Christian household did not reflect such unusual cases. They sought to make the Christian household an example of what was considered appropriate and correct behavior in society at large.

The social model adopted for church order always considered women inferior to men. Indeed, they often had much less education, were much younger than their husbands, and could not assume important roles of public leadership. We have seen that in the earlier period women did prophesy in community worship (1 Cor 11:2–16; also the daughters of Philip in Acts 21:9). However, as leadership in the community was shaped by the patriarchal model women could not be designated as leaders of the community. Just as they did not teach or exercise authority over men in the larger society, so they were not permitted to do so in the church (1 Tim 2:12; cf. also 1 Cor 14:33b–36).

First Timothy 2:9–15 expects Christian women to dress and behave as any well-bred matron would. Such behavior would show her superiority to the weaknesses that people commonly attributed to women as a group. Because of her piety, the Christian woman accomplished even more. What Eve had to suffer as a punishment for her transgression, that is, childbearing, would become for the Christian woman a means of salvation (vv. 14–15).

The most extensive discussion of women's affairs occurs in 1 Timothy 5:3–15 on widows. The likelihood of death in childbirth meant that women as a group lived shorter lives than men. But because most were married in their early teens to older males, women who did not die young could expect to be widowed. Some might have sufficient resources either of their own or inherited from their husbands to continue to live in their own households. Or an adult son might become the head of the household. Others would be dependent upon their natal families if they did not or could not remarry. Paul had said in 1 Corinthians 7:39–40 that a Christian widow could remarry if she wished, though she should be married to a fellow Christian. However, he thought that she, like others who had the calling to it, might be happier to remain unmarried. First Timothy 5:11–15 limits this possibility to women who are quite old by ancient standards (over sixty—v. 9). Perhaps drawing upon some unfortunate cases or reflecting common social sentiments about unattached women, the author thinks that younger women without a family to care for and a household to manage may become idle or even fall into sinful behavior.

First Timothy 5:4, 8, 16 also insists that Christians should assist widowed relatives so that they do not become a burden on the resources of the community. When these two groups of persons are excluded, those women who have led exemplary lives as Christian women are given a special role in the church, which will also provide for their support. Squabbles over inequitable distributions to different groups of widows had broken out in the Jerusalem community (Acts 6:1). First Timothy deals with several different abuses of the church's tradition of supporting pious widows. Second Timothy 1:5 speaks of Timothy as the third generation in a family that included a pious Christian mother, Eunice, and grandmother, Lois. The rules in 1 Timothy presume that these widows have Christian families. Their relatives, children, and grandchildren have an obligation to assist them. First Timothy suggests that a number of women sought to be enrolled as widows. Though we cannot be sure of the basis for their claim, they may have appealed to 1 Corinthians 7:39–40 in doing so. Some have later broken the "promise" they made when enrolled to remain "wife of one husband," that is, a widow for life. Others, those accused of becoming busybodies, might have been targets for the spread of divisive teaching in the community. Their decision to remain unmarried would certainly provide a receptive audience for the ascetic teaching against marriage that is rejected in 1 Timothy 4:3.

In the coming centuries, devout Christian women would form households, often in the homes of wealthy widows, in which women might choose to follow a calling to remain unmarried and devote themselves to lives of prayer and good works. Such communities would provide alternatives to the rules about Christian widows made in the pastorals. They would also provide a place for women who would never include marriage and family as part of their Christian life.

Summary

The Pastoral Epistles met the problem of creating a community structure that could maintain itself and its tradition after the apostle founders had passed from the scene. Though many of the specific rules would be dropped or modified, the basic models of installing persons in offices that claim to stand in apostolic tradition and of the church as a hierarchically ordered household community with the bishop as the father figure responsible for teaching and overseeing all that goes on in the community have continued to this day. Our concerns about divergent teaching in the church are also shaped by the polemical rhetoric of the pastorals. We may be very quick to consider those whose teaching challenges common views of the faith to be personally immoral. Some Christians feel that any differences in teaching and preaching among the faithful must be stamped out before they can lead to quarrelsome divisions and idle speculation.

We face a serious difficulty in interpreting many of the statements in the pastorals. These letters do not provide many clues about the particular situations in the churches that led the author to formulate the tradition in given rules. Yet the rules are clearly directed at real concerns. There is no effort to give a systematic or complete set of rules for ordering Christian communities. Although there are references to prayer and citations of what are clearly liturgical phrases, we are not told anything about celebrations of the Lord's Supper or gatherings for worship, for example. Though we know qualifications for bishops and deacons, we do not know anything about how communities went about selecting them. Consequently, even though the pastorals have had a profound influence on our understanding of church and faith as a deposit of apostolic tradition, they have not provided a complete blueprint for how the church must be ordered in order to remain in faithful continuity with the apostles.

STUDY QUESTIONS

Facts You Should Know

1. What are the qualifications for a person to fill each of the following roles in the churches of the Pastoral Epistles: (a) bishop (*episcopos*); (b) deacon; (c) "enrolled" widow? How do these qualifications relate to the behavior, duties, and obligations expected in the Graeco-Roman "household"?

2. Give three examples of advice or community rules in the Pastoral Epistles that expand or develop themes already found in Paul's letters.

3. How do the pastorals describe the "false teachers" whom the bishop is to oppose? How are some of the actual issues raised by the disputes over teaching related to problems that Paul had faced during his ministry?

4. How is the term *elder* used in Titus? How is it used in 1 Timothy? What do the pastorals show us about the development of the threefold pattern of church offices: bishop, elder (later "priest"), and deacon?

5. What are the social patterns behind the behavior expected of Christian women in the pastorals?

Things to Do

1. Read the pastorals, picking out the sections in which we are given glimpses of "Pauline biography." Create a biographical sketch of the apostle based upon these passages.

2. Read the pastorals and pick out the passages in which Paul gives advice about conduct directly to Timothy or Titus. What are the characteristics of the "ideal" leader that emerge in these passages?

Things to Think About

1. If you had to make a list of qualifications for candidates to be "bishop" or "deacon" today, what would be on your list? How many of those characteristics overlap those in the pastorals? Are there any "new" ones that are derived from the special circumstances of the church today?
2. What virtues might be included in a contemporary version of "appropriate conduct" for Christian women and men such as we find in the pastorals?

Chapter 19

THE CATHOLIC EPISTLES: AN APOSTOLIC HERITAGE

1 Peter, the "Holy People of God"

First Peter is one of a group of seven letters known as the Catholic Epistles: 1 and 2 Peter, James, Jude, and 1, 2, and 3 John. They are called "catholic," or "general," letters because they are not addressed to a specific church. Some like 2 and 3 John are short, private letters. Others like 1 John and James are really short treatises. In this chapter we will study 1 and 2 Peter, James, and Jude. The Johannine epistles will be treated separately in the next chapter.

First Peter follows the basic skeleton of a letter comparable to those in the Pauline collection: expanded opening (1:1–2); a blessing [thanksgiving] (1:3–9); body opening (1:10—2:10); body middle (2:11—4:11); body closing [eschatological] (4:12–19); final exhortation (5:1–12); concluding greeting (5:12–14). However, there are none of the personal elements typical of Paul's letters. The letter is a circular to churches scattered in northern Asia Minor (1:1). One of Paul's associates, Silvanus (1 Thess 1:1), is referred to as drafting the letter under the author's direction (1 Pet 5:12). "Babylon" in 5:13 is a traditional "code name" for Rome in Jewish and Christian apocalypses (2 Esdr 3:1–2; Rev 18:2). By using the name "Babylon," the author highlights the status of suffering aliens and exiles that Roman Christians share with believers in Asia Minor. Perhaps the designation "fellow elder" in 5:1 (contrast the "apostle" used in 1:1) indicates that the author was an "elder" in the Roman church.

The northern half of Asia Minor encompassed Pauline mission territory. There are significant thematic parallels between 1 Peter and Romans. Compare the teaching on relationship to civil government in Romans 13:1–7 and 1 Peter 2:13–17 or the treatment of brotherly love in 1 Peter 3:8–12 and Romans 12:10–17a. Numerous other parallels can be found that are grounded in the liturgical language of early Christian communities (e.g., the "stone" images from Isaiah in 1 Pet 2:6–8 and Rom 9:33; descriptions of

Jesus' resurrection, 1 Pet 1:21//Rom 4:25; 1 Pet 3:21–22//Rom 8:34). These parallels to Pauline language suggest that 1 Peter draws upon sources of Christian tradition that were widely shared.

OUTLINE OF 1 PETER   [19–1]

Greeting (1:1–2)

Thanksgiving: Future hope for Christians being tested by suffering now (1:3–9)

Live in purity and holiness as God's chosen people (1:10–2:10)

(a) The prophets predicted salvation for the Gentiles; the sufferings and glory of Christ (1:10–12)

(b) Having been reborn and ransomed from your sinful past, live in holiness (1:13–2:3)

(c) You are the "royal priesthood" offering spiritual sacrifices to God (2:4–10)

Obligations of Christian life (2:11–3:22)

(a) Maintain good conduct so that "Gentiles" [= non-Christians] who accuse you of wrongdoing will be proven wrong at the judgment (2:11–12)

(b) Silence your opponents by living in free obedience to all human institutions (2:13–17)

(c) Slaves follow Christ by accepting even the unjust treatment of harsh masters (2:18–25)

(d) Wives should be obedient and of exemplary modesty so they need not fear nonbelieving husbands, and husbands should be considerate of their wives (3:1–7)

(e) Remain free from evil; love those who abuse and revile you while being ready to give a gentle defense of your faith (3:8–22)

Suffering as the imitation of Christ (4:1–19)

(a) Suffering shows you have ceased from the sinful ways of your past even to those who abuse you because you no longer join them (4:1–6)

(b) Remember your gifts of Christian service to one another (4:7–11)

(c) This ordeal of suffering is a share in Christ's suffering if you suffer because you are a Christian (4:12–19)

Stand fast in humility and you will share Christ's eternal glory (5:1–12)

(a) Humility in elders caring for the flock and in "younger persons" toward them (5:1–5)

(b) Resist the devil who would use this suffering to destroy your faith (5:6–12)

Final greetings (5:12–14)

First Peter is concerned with shaping Christian life in the face of ongoing experiences of persecution. Listing Christian duties takes up a significant portion of the work. Even the treatment of conventional duties such as the household code section on the behavior of slaves, wives, and husbands in 1 Peter 2:18—3:7 is shaped by the ever-present reality of persecution. Christian slaves may be subject to abusive masters. Christian women may be married to suspicious, non-Christian husbands. In each instance, exemplary behavior is a strategy for alleviating the tension in these situations.

The Christians addressed are called "resident aliens" and "visiting strangers" (2:11). These terms are not merely a metaphorical way of saying that the Christian's true home is heavenly, with Christ. They were political terms for persons who were not citizens of the cities in which they lived. The resident alien at least had some status as a registered member of the city. The visiting stranger was merely a transient visitor who could be expelled at any time.

Not only are these believers coping with a social and legal status that is precarious; they also have awakened the suspicion of their neighbors by converting to Christianity. Much of the random abuse and persecution they face is the result of their changed behavior (4:1–5). Conversion has meant breaking off past ties and associations (1:3–5, 10–12, 18, 21; 2:4–10) to enter the new familial community of mutual love that is God's holy people (1:17; 2:5,10; 5:9). Though interpreters have tried to link the suffering in 1 Peter to a specific period, the letter speaks of persecution in a number of forms. Some people harass believers out of ignorance (2:15) or a twisted curiosity to see what these persons will do (3:15). Others suspect them of wrongdoing (2:12; 4:14–16). Still others are openly hostile to Christianity as such (3:13–16; 4:4). First Peter takes pains to emphasize the civic loyalty of Christians (2:13–17).

Whatever its source, suffering will not destroy the faith of the community. Christians can look to the example of Jesus and to that of Peter (5:1) as models of suffering. From the same examples, they can be sure that their suffering will be rewarded with glory. By writing a general letter to these churches, the elder from the Roman church also reminds them that they are part of a worldwide fellowship of brothers and sisters.

OUTLINE OF JAMES   [19-2]

Greeting (1:1)

Perfection through faith and single-hearted steadfastness (1:2-8)

Wealth and those who trust in it fade away (1:9-11)

Temptation is not from God but the enticement of desire (1:12-18)

Doing the word that one hears (1:19-27)

Continued

Continued

Against partiality toward the rich in the Christian assembly (2:1–13)

Faith without works is dead (2:14–26)

Control the tongue (3:1–12)

Wisdom from above is evident in a life of goodness (3:13–18)

Passions are the root of war (4:1–10)

Do not judge or speak evil of one another (4:11–12)

Human boasts and plans vanish like mist (4:13–17)

Woe against the rich who have lived by injustice (5:1–6)

Christians remain patient (5:7–11)

Against oaths (5:12)

Christian prayer: anointing the sick; confession and forgiveness (5:13–18)

Winning back a sinner brings forgiveness (5:19–20)

OUTLINE OF JUDE   [19–3]

Greeting (vv. 1–2)

Struggle for the faith against those who pervert it (vv. 3–4)

Judgment will come upon the ungodly (vv. 5–16)

   (a) Proven by Old Testament examples: wilderness generation, fallen angels, Sodom and Gomorrah (vv. 5–8)
   (b) Michael contending with the devil for Moses' body (v. 9)
   (c) So irrational they are like Cain, Balaam, Korah (vv. 10–11)
   (d) They pollute your "love feast" and are driven like waterless clouds, dead fruitless trees, wild waves, wandering stars (vv. 12–13)
   (e) Enoch prophesied their judgment (vv. 14–16)

Apostles predicted such people would come in the last days (vv. 17–19)

Build up your faith and try to win some back (vv. 20–23)

Final benediction (vv. 24–25)

James and Jude, the Legacy of Jewish Christianity

The list of Jesus' relatives in Mark 6:3 (Matt 13:55) includes a James, later the leader of the Jerusalem community, and a Jude who does not appear elsewhere. Both the writings that came into the canon under their names reflect Jewish Christian traditions. However, James is written in an elegant Greek style, which suggests its origins lie in a Greek-speaking Jewish community. Jude, on the other hand, is a short piece of apocalyptic tradition directed against unspecified false teachers. James has only a brief epistolary introduction. It then continues as a work of exhortation. Jude takes the form of a very brief letter. Neither of the two letters provides concrete details about its author. Yet both James (5:19–20) and Jude (vv. 22–23) end with a very concrete instruction to members of the church: they are to seek to bring back fellow Christians who have strayed. The content of Jude implies that straying would mean following the perverted teachers. We cannot tell what the content of that teaching might have been, since Jude follows the conventional rhetorical pattern of describing the opposition as completely immoral. In James, straying could apply to any failure to live up to the teaching about a life of holiness.

James contains passages that come close to sayings of Jesus in the Sermon on the Mount (e.g., 4:11//Matt 7:1–5; 5:12//Matt 5:34–37), yet Jesus is mentioned by name only in 2:1. He is not invoked as the authority for the instructions about moral conduct that make up the body of the work. Its teaching is presented as general wisdom by which people should recognize what is pleasing to God.

In addition to general moral advice, James lashes out against those who claim "faith saves" (2:14–26). The author even takes one of Paul's favorite passages for the priority of faith (Gen 15:6; see Rom 4:3) and argues that it proves the necessity of works. Abraham's faith was expressed in works when he believed God and went to offer Isaac as a sacrifice. It is impossible to tell whether James had Pauline arguments or slogans in mind. Of course, the works that Christians must perform—providing charity for the poor brother or sister—are not the "works" of Gentiles adopting Jewish religious observances against which Paul was arguing. Some interpreters think that James is dealing with slogans about faith that originated in popular reports of Pauline teaching.

Another concrete problem with which James deals is that of partiality in the Christian assembly (2:1–13). On the one hand, the warnings about trusting in wealth and the concluding woes against the rich (4:13—5:6) suggest that James and its readers view the wealthy from the position of outsiders. On the other, there seem to have been sufficient differences of wealth and poverty within the community itself that led to preferential treatment of rich members of the assembly. James 2:7 mentions in passing that the rich drag Christians into court simply for being Christians. By honoring a rich person and dishonoring a poor one in their own group Christians become like the unjust judges whom they face in other settings.

At the conclusion to the letter, we get another glimpse into the concrete life of the community. They have institutionalized healing in a ritual of anointing and prayer for the sick by the elders of the church (5:13–15). They have also developed some form of mutual confession and prayer for forgiveness. James argues against skeptics that the miracle of Elijah and the rain proves that the prayer of a righteous person is powerful. The unstated conclusion to the argument is that if the prayer of an Elijah can control the weather, then that of the community can effect forgiveness for sin.

James 2:8–13 shows that, even with its insistence that faith is not living unless manifested in works, the vision of true religion in James cannot be described as legalistic. The royal law of James 2:8 (also 1:25, "perfect law, law of liberty") is summed up in the love command. Throughout the work, James emphasizes not only the good works of caring for the poor, which are traditionally associated with that command (e.g., 1:27), but also the socially divisive effects of other sins. Several passages warn against anger and other sins of speech (e.g., 3:1–12; 4:11–12). Wealth also divides Christians, not only in the danger that the church will adopt the attitudes of a larger society in showing preference to the wealthy, but also in the false confidence it engenders in its possessors. People can even come to the point of not seeing the obligations of charity and justice (e.g., 2:15–16; 5:3–6). James draws upon a wisdom tradition that sees perfection as a single-hearted and humble devotion to God. In the writings of Greek-speaking Jews (e.g., *Testaments of XII Patriarchs*) this Jewish tradition is often linked with a stoic concern for the necessity of a victory over the disruptive effects of passions in the soul. Consequently, the inner passions that tear at the soul are the ones that ultimately destroy the outer fabric of society in wars (4:1–6). The tradition of ethical preaching found in James makes extensive use of nature images to describe the shifting character and deceitfulness of false human reasoning. The images for the steadfast purpose of the morally perfect person are linked with the heavenly perfection of God, who sends the humble wisdom from above (1:5, 17; 3:17).

While James reflects a Greek-speaking Jewish Christianity that drew on the ethical traditions of Hellenistic Judaism, Jude incorporates some apocryphal material from Jewish apocalyptic. The short, single chapter does not provide any concrete information about the false teachers it opposes. Its exhortation to remember that the apostles foretold the emergence of divisions, evildoers, and deceivers in the last days (v. 17) indicates that the writing belongs to the post-apostolic period. The apocalyptic material provides the author with further evidence that heretics will be condemned. The examples in verses 5, 7, and 11 are taken from the Old Testament. Stories of the fallen angels tethered in celestial prisons until the judgment (v. 6) are part of the Enoch tradition. The seer in 1 Enoch sees their locations. Jude verse 14 refers to Enoch as the prophet of divine judgment. Apocalyptic traditions also elaborated on the judgment of Sodom and Gomorrah (v. 7; cf. *Testament of Naphthali* 3, 4–5). Finally, the legend of Michael and Satan contending over the body of Moses (v. 9) appears in such apocryphal writings as the *Assumption of Moses*.

2 Peter, Christian Eschatology

The collection of apocalyptic warnings in Jude had little impact on early Christianity with the exception of 2 Peter, which faced a crisis of belief in divine judgment. False teachers rejected the traditional teaching about the second coming (3:3–4). They may also have appealed to those philosophers who insisted that the world was eternal to back up their views. In addition, 2 Peter accuses them of supporting their views with false interpretations of Paul's letters (3:15–16). Second Peter is cast as a defense of traditional Christian eschatology. It is put in the mouth of the dying apostle as a farewell discourse to the community.

The material from Jude is incorporated into the argument that the false teachers will be judged in 2 Peter 2. However, careful comparison of the two writings shows that 2 Peter has not simply taken over arguments from Jude. Second Peter has reordered the argument to follow what is found in the canonical Old Testament traditions. Apocryphal traditions that have no basis in scripture, like the contest between Michael and Satan for the body of Moses, have been dropped. This reordering fits with a theological principle that is stated at 2 Peter 1:19–20: we have prophecy, God's own word, to prove the truth of our belief in judgment. People did not invent this teaching. Rather it came through "prophets," that is, human beings moved by the Holy Spirit. The arguments set out in 2 Peter are to be understood as proof that the tradition of a divine judgment is grounded in the prophetic word of scripture.

Second Peter has a more developed sense of the authority of a canon of scripture than we find expressed in the other New Testament writings. Second Peter 1:14 makes the written testimony of the apostle the medium through which the community is to remember his teaching once he has died. Second Peter 3:1 refers back to the existence of a previous letter of Peter as the community's heritage of true teaching. The explicit use of the transfiguration as an apostolic witness to the truth of a coming parousia (1:17–18) suggests that at least one of the Synoptic Gospels enjoyed authoritative status as "apostolic testimony." The reference to disputes about the meaning of Paul's letters (2 Pet 3:15–16) suggests that there was a collection of the Pauline epistles with authoritative status as well.

Second Peter represents another important development in meeting the problem of continuity of apostolic tradition: emergence of a Christian canon of authoritative scripture. Second Peter does not claim that everything in scripture is directly inspired. Rather, human beings who have been moved by the Spirit speak the prophetic words of scripture. Second Peter recognizes that there are difficult passages in scripture that will be the subject of debate. However, the solution that this writing explores will become a central element in the theological use of scripture. Second Peter finds a consistent witness in prophecy, sayings of Jesus, and apostolic testimony to the central

Christian belief that the world is to be judged. Given that witness, the arguments advanced by the opponents cannot be accepted as legitimate interpretations of Paul's meaning. But 2 Peter does not simply condemn the opposition with the conventional rhetoric taken from Jude. Second Peter also provides counter-arguments to the claims that they make about the "irrationality" of the traditional belief.

OUTLINE OF 2 PETER   [19-4]

Greeting (1:1-2)

Remember the apostle's teaching: faith, knowledge, and virtue will gain entry to an eternal kingdom with Christ (1:3-15)

First proof: prophetic word made more certain by the transfiguration (1:16-21)

Condemnation of false teachers: divine judgment is certain (2:1-22)

(a) They bring on their own destruction (2:1-3)
(b) Examples of God's judgment against the evil and rescue of the righteous: fallen angels, Noah's generation, Sodom and Gomorrah (2:4-10)
(c) Their irrationality and immorality lead them to follow Balaam (2:11-16)
(d) Once freed from defilement through knowledge of the savior Jesus, they are now caught in even worse corruption (2:17-22)

Further arguments that the world will be judged (3:1-10)

(a) Remember predictions of the prophets and commandments of the Lord that you received through the apostles, which spoke of "scoffers" in the last days (3:1-3)
(b) Against arguments from the eternal sameness of the world: God's word created the earth out of water, reduced it to water in the flood, and now upholds the world until the judgment by fire (3:4-7)
(c) Against arguments from the "delay of the parousia":
(i)   time is not the same with God as in human reckoning (3:8-9a)
(ii) the "delay" is God's patience giving people time for repentance (3:9bc)
(iii) the day will come suddenly and the heavens and earth be destroyed (3:10)

Since we believe God's promise of a "new heaven and earth" we live in holiness (3:11-15a)

Paul's letters agree with this teaching, though false teachers twist the meaning of difficult passages to lead people to destruction (3:15b-17)

Final benediction (3:18)

Summary

The four writings we have studied show us different aspects of the preservation of tradition in communities that were not directly part of the Pauline group of churches. Both of the letters attributed to Peter have links with Pauline material. In 1 Peter these ties take the form of common traditions and even some link to members of the Pauline circle, Silvanus and Mark. By the time 2 Peter was written, both 1 Peter and a collection of Paul's letters had authoritative status in the churches. It is also possible that the treatment of faith and works in James was directed against the distortions of slogans from Paul's letters. Thus, some scholars have argued that the influence of the Pauline churches extended beyond their own circles. Paul's use of the letter as a way in which the apostle could be present to the churches became a way of preserving ties with apostolic tradition in churches that traced their roots to other apostles.

The influence of the apostolic letter appears in Johannine churches as well. Even the Book of Revelation, a Christian apocalypse, includes letters to major churches in Asia Minor. However, its letters are the word of the exalted Lord to the angelic supervisors of the churches. Thus, the letter form is part of a larger pattern of prophetic revelation. Second Peter witnesses the beginning of another way of preserving apostolic tradition: creation of an authoritative collection of writings in which God's word is found. Second Peter recognizes that the tradition will be handed down to later generations of Christians in writings that have come down from the first century.

STUDY QUESTIONS

Facts You Should Know

1. What are the ties between 1 Peter and Christianity in Rome?
2. What is the situation of the Christians to whom 1 Peter is written? How does 1 Peter advise Christians to react to the hostility?
3. What kinds of Jewish Christian tradition do we find in James and Jude?
4. What is the ethical teaching contained in James on the following topics: (a) rich and poor Christians; (b) the necessity of "good works"; (c) forgiveness of sin within the Christian community?
5. What views are being opposed in 2 Peter?
6. What does 2 Peter show us about the influence that Paul's letters were having in early Christianity?

Things to Do

1. Read 1 Peter and pick out the passages in which the author contrasts the "past life" of Christians with the new life they have received in Christ. How has their change led to hostility against Christians?
2. Read James. How does the "love command" play a role in the ethical teaching of the letter? Find the passages that echo the teaching of Jesus.

Things to Think About

1. Conversion and baptism changed the lives of Christians according to 1 Peter. What differences does "being Christian" make to people's lives today?
2. James insists that faith without works is dead. What "works" show others a living faith today?

Chapter 20

THE JOHANNINE EPISTLES: A CHURCH DIVIDED

The Story of Johannine Christianity

The three writings that we speak of as "Johannine epistles" do not claim to have been written by the author of the Fourth Gospel but by an unknown person who calls himself "the elder" (2 John 1; 3 John 1). He may have belonged to a school of teachers in the Johannine churches who were disciples of the beloved disciple. The author suggests the existence of this group in referring to a "we" whose testimony about Jesus the hearers accept (1 John 1:1–4). First John frequently calls upon traditions that the audience learned when they became Christians (e.g., 1:5—2:17). First John is not a letter but a tract or homily on true Johannine tradition. The introduction to 1 John (1:1–4) resembles the prologue to the Fourth Gospel (John 1:1–18). But although it employs a theological language similar to that in the gospel, 1 John never cites the gospel directly. It lacks the distinctive Christology, identifying the Son with the Father as God, for example. Therefore some scholars suggest that the elder did not know the Fourth Gospel in its canonical form.

Second and Third John, on the other hand, are short letters from the elder. Second John directs a church in the Johannine circle to exclude persons who have separated themselves from the community and are enticing others away with false teaching about Jesus (2 John 7–11). These are the same persons whose teaching is attacked in 1 John. Some scholars think that 2 John might have been accompanied by a copy of 1 John. Third John deals with a different crisis. It is a private letter to a certain Gaius. The elder wants Gaius to provide hospitality for missionaries, since another Christian in the region, Diotrephes, has refused to receive persons who come from the elder (3 John 5–10).

Many of the later writings in the New Testament are concerned with the divisive effects of false teaching. But it is only in the Johannine epistles that we have clear evidence that conflicts over teaching had led to the creation of a completely independent group that also claimed to be the heirs to the Johannine tradition. The Fourth Gospel indicated that the Johannine church had been divided before when believers were expelled from the Jewish community. Some had preferred to remain in the synagogue, denying belief in Jesus as God's Son and messiah (John 9:22–23). The Johannine picture of the "ideal community" as it is drawn in chapters 13 to 17 emphasized the unity in love of believers with one another and with the Father and Son.

Salvation depends upon being part of this unity. John 15:1–17 reminds Christians that they must remain attached to Jesus, the true vine. Their unity with Jesus is evident by the love that they have for one another. Johannine Christians are aware that they would not be part of this community if they had not "been chosen" by the Lord. The love command plays a central role in the catechesis of the Johannine community as 1 John shows (e.g., 1 John 2:7–11).

With these strong images of love and unity as a backdrop, the shock caused by the new division within the Johannine churches becomes evident. First John 2:18–26 speaks of the "going out" of a dissident group. How could people leave the community in which the Father and Son are present? The author answers first by invoking a view that frequently shows up in discussions of false teachers: at the end-time, false teachers will come to lead the faithful astray (Mark 13:22; 1 Thess 2:9–12). This image has its roots in apocalyptic traditions. First John is responsible for coining a new way to refer to the enemy of the end-time, the "antichrist" (1 John 2:18; 4:3; 2 John 7). The author's second explanation is that such schismatics could not really have been "of us," that is, chosen by Jesus, or they would have remained in the community (1 John 2:19).

The sharp language of 1 and 2 John strikes many people. Love applies only to those who have remained within the community. The dissidents are agents of the antichrist and are treated accordingly. Some interpreters think that this sharp tone indicates that the dissidents have been very successful in winning over Johannine Christians. First John 4:5–6 uses a contrast familiar from the gospel: those who are "of the world" opposed to those who are "of God." Because the opponents are "of the world," they gain a hearing that those faithful to the tradition taught by the elder cannot match. Believers should not to be taken in by the apparent success of the opponents.

Since a key element in the dissident preaching was denial of the significance of Jesus' humanity (e.g., 2 John 7), many scholars think that the Johannine splinter groups eventually formed sects that believed that Jesus embodied a heavenly divine revealer from a world outside this evil creation, such as one finds in second-century Gnostic heresies. The Fourth Gospel placed such emphasis on Jesus' divinity and on the pattern of descent from heaven and return that it could easily be read as the myth of a divine savior in a way that ignored the humanity of Jesus. First John insists that the authentic Johannine tradition is committed to Jesus' "coming in the flesh."

Some scholars have suggested that the gospel as we have it was edited to make these connections between the divinity and humanity of Jesus clearer. Discourses like chapter 15 with its emphasis on remaining attached to the vine might reflect the crisis of the epistles period. The gospel presents a striking division among Jesus' disciples in John 6:51–59, where some leave Jesus when he insists that the bread of the Eucharist really is his flesh. Reference to Jesus' death as an offering for sin is strengthened by the insistence on blood and water, flowing from the side of Jesus at his death on the cross (John 19:34–35). This element in the crucifixion scene might well fit with the insistence on the testimony of blood, water, and the Spirit in 1 John 5:6–8.

If the dissidents became gnostic sectarians, what happened to the Johannine churches that preserved the traditions of the elder? Some scholars find a clue in John 21. This chapter was added onto the gospel after it had already concluded. The story focuses upon Peter even though the beloved disciple is present. Peter draws in the net with many fish. He is also commissioned by Jesus to shepherd the flock (21:15–19). Peter asks about the fate of the beloved disciple (21:20–23). We learn from verse 23 that the beloved disciple had died by the time this chapter was written. If this chapter was added to the gospel during the final editing, it may contain a clue to the destiny of Johannine Christians. We saw in the Pastoral Epistles that an important way of preserving the community against dissident teaching was establishing a succession of apostolic leaders charged with true teaching. The Johannine letters do not contain any hints of such emergent organization. Some scholars think that this emphasis on Peter provided a way in which Christians who belonged to the tradition of the beloved disciple could join communities that had an apostolic succession based on Petrine tradition. When they did so, they took the unique emphasis on the divinity of Jesus with them. This emphasis when combined with the infancy stories of Jesus' birth provided the basis for what would become the orthodox doctrine of the incarnation of Jesus.

1 and 2 John, Christian Fellowship, and the Crisis of Division

There is no doubt that the crisis to which the elder is responding was a severe one. The elder argues that the dissidents have violated the fundamental commandment of the Johannine tradition: love one another (2:3–11; 3:10–11; 4:20–21). Second John 7 describes the false teaching of the opponents as false teaching about Jesus: "Do not confess the coming of Jesus Christ in the flesh." But 1 John is preoccupied with another topic as well: freedom from sin. First John 1:6—2:2 takes up a series of sayings about sin. Those who argue that they are free from sin are liars. The author insists that the

Christian can claim to be free from sin only because Christ's death has atoned for sin (1:7). Christians who do sin can turn to Jesus as their heavenly advocate (2:1–2). You may have recognized that this picture of Jesus' death as atonement for the sin of the world and of the exalted Jesus as the one to whom Christians are to turn is much like the tradition of Jesus as high priest in Hebrews 4:14–16. First John uses this tradition of the atoning death of Jesus as part of the argument against those who deny the significance of Jesus' coming in the flesh. Without Jesus' death on the cross there would have been no atonement and our sins would not have been forgiven.

OUTLINE OF 1 JOHN   [20–1]

Prologue (1:1–4)

Walking in light (1:5–2:17)

(a) God is light (1:5)
(b) Freedom from sin (1:6–2:2)
(c) Keeping the commandments (2:3–11)
(d) Address to three groups (2:12–14)
(e) Reject the world (2:15–17)

Reject the antichrists (2:18–29)

(a) Divisions are a sign of the last hour (2:18–19)
(b) Anointing preserves the true faith in the hearers (2:20–27)
(c) Confidence at the judgment (2:28–29)

Love as the mark of God's children (3:1–24)

(a) God has made us children now (3:1–10)
(b) We must love one another like Christ, not like Cain (3:11–18)
(c) Our confidence before God, who is greater than our hearts (3:19–24)

Reject the antichrists (4:1–6)

(a) They do not confess Jesus (4:1–3)
(b) They have not overcome the world (4:4–6)

God is love (4:7–21)

(a) Christ has shown God's love (4:7–12)
(b) We know God's love through the Spirit (4:13–16a)
(c) Our confidence: abiding in God's love (4:16b–21)

Belief in the Son (5:1–12)

(a) Faith overcomes the world (5:1–5)
(b) Testimony: Son came in water and blood (5:6–12)

Conclusion (5:13)

Continued

Epilogue: sayings and rules (5:14–21)

  (a) Confidence in prayer: God hears our prayer; prayer for sinners (5:14–17)
  (b) Confidence sayings: one born of God does not sin; we know the true God and have eternal life (5:18–20)
  (c) Keep from idols (5:21)

OUTLINE OF 2 JOHN   [20–2]

Greeting (vv. 1–3)

Thanksgiving: your children are walking in truth (v. 4)

Body: no fellowship with the dissidents (vv. 5–11)

  (a) Johannine tradition is to love one another (vv. 5–6)
  (b) Deceivers deny Jesus is come in the flesh (v. 7)
  (c) Warning: not abiding in the teaching about Christ could cost your fellowship with God (vv. 8–9)
  (d) Anyone who aids or even greets a dissident shares that person's wickedness (vv. 10–11)

Plans for a visit (v. 12)

Final greeting (v. 13)

The picture becomes somewhat muddied when we turn to 1 John 3:4–10. There we have the clear assertion that those "born of God," that is, Christians (cf. John 1:12–13), do not sin (vv. 6, 9). How does this view of perfection differ from the view rejected earlier? One answer is to insist that the dissidents cannot claim to be "children of God" since they have destroyed the community. They are not living in the sinless unity with God that they claim. The second answer is based on the picture of Christ as the heavenly intercessor in 1 John 2:1–2. The sayings on prayer that are appended to 1 John suggest that the community had a formal way of dealing with sin, since they speak of prayer for the sinful Christian. Only one sin is excluded, that called "the sin unto death." Although the author does not explain what this sin is, parallels with Jewish legislation would suggest a sin that required that a person be expelled from the community. Comparison with Hebrews 10:26 suggests that that sin would be apostasy, denial of one's faith in Christ. These rules may have first been formed to deal with those who denied their faith in the face of external persecution. First John has appended them because the author wants the dissidents excluded from all fellowship with Johannine Christians.

First John constantly reassures Christians that if they are faithful to its teaching they do not have to worry about the judgment (2:28; 3:2–3, 19–21;

4:17–18). First John 3:14 affirms that the mutual love among Christians is evidence that they have "passed from death to life." The conclusion to 1 John emphasizes the fact that the faithful have eternal life. This constant emphasis on the certainty of salvation suggests that the opponents preached a form of perfectionism that made Johannine Christians unsure of their own salvation. First John insists that the "child of God" is sinless, has eternal life, and through faith has overcome Satan.

3 John, Broken Hospitality

You can see from the outline of 3 John that there is no reference to the crisis addressed by 1 and 2 John.

OUTLINE OF 3 JOHN   [20–3]

Greeting (v. 1)

Health wish (v. 2)

Thanksgiving: You are following the truth (vv. 3–4)

Body: Rendering hospitality to missionaries is "of God" (vv. 5–11)

   (a) You do a good thing in aiding traveling missionaries (vv. 5–8)
   (b) Diotrephes' refusal to allow anyone to aid missionaries from the
       elder (vv. 9–10)
   (c) Exhortation: continue to imitate what is good (v. 11)

Recommendation for Demetrius (v. 12)

Future visit (v. 13)

Final greeting (v. 14)

The elder is writing a private letter to Gaius, a Christian known for showing hospitality to traveling missionaries. His letter follows an episode in which a certain Diotrephes turned away some missionaries who bore the recommendation of the elder. The elder does not accuse Diotrephes of siding with the dissidents but of being arrogant, speaking evil of the elder, and rejecting his authority. The immediate practical purpose of 3 John is to secure hospitality for traveling missionaries. The Demetrius who is recommended at the end of the letter was probably its bearer and a "test case" of Gaius's willingness to undertake these new obligations of hospitality.

Some scholars have tried to connect 3 John with the crisis of 1 and 2 John by presuming that Diotrephes' actions were motivated by the dissident crisis. After all, his treatment of the elder's emissaries is exactly what the elder called for in 2 John 10–11. However, there is nothing in the brief letter itself that makes this connection. Third John 10 suggests that the author still expects to talk the matter out with Diotrephes, something that is clearly beyond possibility in the case of the dissidents. Therefore, we may assume that this brief note was preserved because it came from the author of 1 and 2 John, but that it originally referred to a different situation.

Summary

The Johannine epistles present us with the severest crisis to confront the early small Christian communities: schism. The elder makes a strong plea to his readers to remain in communion with the authentic Johannine tradition that they have "heard from the beginning." He also takes drastic action to prevent dissident teaching from gaining any further hearing in Johannine churches. Many people today feel uncomfortable at branding one's opponents agents of Satan and expelling them from any contact with the community. But we can view the elder's actions only as a reflection of how severe the crisis had become. It seems evident that there was no longer any possibility of winning the dissidents back. There are no hints of a hoped-for reconciliation such as we find in the Diotrephes case. If the dissidents were indeed gaining ground among Johannine Christians, then the elder and other teachers in his circle may have seen the very survival of Johannine Christianity at stake. In such a crisis there seems little room for compromise.

STUDY QUESTIONS

Facts You Should Know

1. Describe the crisis in the Johannine churches that is reflected in 1 and 2 John. Why was division in the community such a shocking event for Johannine Christians?
2. How does 1 John emphasize the importance of the humanity of Jesus?
3. How does the author of 1 John understand sin and forgiveness in the Christian community?
4. Describe the situation being addressed in 3 John.

Things to Do

1. Pick out all of the passages in 1 John that refer to the love command. How is this command to be practiced in the Johannine churches?

2. Pick out all of the passages in 1 John that refer to the confidence Christians have in the judgment. What is the basis for this confidence?

Things to Think About

1. What situations do we face today in which church communities have become divided even though they share a common tradition? What lessons could we learn from the Johannine churches to help avoid the sharp break into two hostile groups that we find there?
2. First John 4 contains the famous definition: "God is love." How is the love of God shown in Christian communities today?

Chapter 21

REVELATION: CHRISTIANITY AND THE EMPIRE

The Composition of Revelation

The final book in the New Testament continues to be the most puzzling in the entire collection. It belongs to a literary type called an "apocalypse" (from the Greek word for "revelation"). Because Revelation presents visions of divine judgment, many people interpret Revelation as a detailed, event-by-event allegory of the end of the world. Such interpretations neglect the imagery familiar to the first-century audience of Revelation. You can get some feeling for this tradition by turning to your Old Testament and reading the visionary material in Daniel 7–12; Ezekiel 1–9, 26–27, 39–44; and Zechariah 9–14.

We can find a number of images and familiar story patterns being reused by the seer of Revelation. Here are some examples:

(1) The inaugural vision (1:12–20) combines features of the visions in Daniel and Ezra.
(2) Revelation 5 depicts the heavenly assembly of the gods, an ancient mythological motif that the prophets used for the divine council of Yahweh.
(3) Another ancient mythic motif that the Old Testament frequently used for Yahweh was that of a holy war in which the god defeats the forces of chaos. That theme appears in the defeat of the Satanic forces in Revelation 19:11—22:5.
(4) The idea that judgment is based on what has been recorded in a book (20:11–15) is another common theme.
(5) Apocalypses have a sharp contrast between the heavenly realm and the earthly one. Here they are exemplified in two cities, Babylon and the heavenly Jerusalem (14:8–21; chapters 17–18 and 21).

287

(6) Another mythological theme with parallels in both the ancient Near East and Greek mythology is that of a battle against the chaos monster to save the divine child (12:1—14:5; 19:11–20).

(7) Revelation 6:1—7:17 reuses traditional material about world cataclysms.

(8) The plagues of the Exodus story are evoked and intensified in Revelation 8:1—11:4; 15:5—19:10.

(9) The motif of the winepress of God (Rev 14:9–20; 19:13) has been taken from the prophets (Isa 63:3; Joel 4:13).

Revelation incorporates three scenes in which the prophet has a commissioning vision (1:12–20; chapters 4–5; 10:1–11). Other visions in Revelation show the heavenly liturgy. The work is punctuated with antiphonal hymns (4:9–11; 5:9–12; 7:10–12; 11:15b–18; 16:5b–6, 7b; 19:1b–3, 4b, 5b–6b, 8a). Unlike the Old Testament prophet who might have a vision of the divine council, heavenly altar, and throne and then carry out his commission on earth (as in Isa 6), the seer remains in heaven, and watches the scenes unfolding on earth from that perspective.

The Seven Letters

Revelation shows the influence of the apostolic letter in early Christianity. The seer's vision opens with letters to the angels of seven churches in Asia Minor. These letters were composed as a group, since they follow a standard format (see Chart 21–1). The rewards promised the faithful are picked up at the end of Revelation (e.g., 2:7 and 22:2, 14, tree of life; 2:11 and 21:18, second death; 2:17 and 19:12, new name; 3:12 and 21:2, heavenly Jerusalem). We meet some familiar themes in these letters. Christians must not be surprised by the persecution they suffer. Others are less endangered by persecution than by loss of their initial enthusiasm. Some are complacent in prosperity. Still other churches are divided by false teaching. Thus the letters easily serve as a general admonition to all churches, as the author of the Muratorian canon observed: "John also in the Revelation writes indeed to seven churches, yet speaks to all."

THE SEVEN LETTERS IN REVELATION 2–3   [21–1]

1. Address and command to write:
   (a) To the angel of the church in [i. Ephesus, ii. Smyrna, iii. Pergamum, iv. Thyatira, v. Sardis, vi. Philadelphia, vii. Laodicea]
   (b) write
2. Prophetic messenger formula + description of Jesus:
   (a) the words of...
   (b) *description:*

Continued

Continued

      i. holds the seven stars in his right hand; walks among the seven golden lampstands

      ii. first and the last; died and came to life

      iii. has the sharp two-edged sword

      iv. Son of God; eyes like a flame of fire; feet like burnished bronze

      v. has the seven spirits of God; seven stars

      vi. holy one, true one; has the key of David; opens and no one shall shut; shuts and no one shall open

      vii. the Amen; faithful and true witness; beginning of God's creation

3. I know...

  (a) *the situation:*

      i. works, toil, endurance, cannot bear evil persons but tested those called apostles but are not; enduring patiently for my name's sake, not grown weary

      ii. tribulation, poverty (though you are rich), slander from those who say they are Jews but are synagogue of Satan

      iii. dwell where Satan's throne is; did not deny my faith even in days of faithful martyr Antipas

      iv. works, love, faith, service, endurance, latter works greater than the first

      v. works

      vi. works

      vii. works, neither cold nor hot

  (b) *but I have it against you:*

      i. abandoned the love you had at first

      ii. some hold teaching of Balaam: eat food sacrificed to idols and practice immorality; some hold teaching of Nicolaitans

      iii. tolerate false prophetess Jezebel: practice immorality and eat food sacrificed to idols

      iv. have name of being alive and are dead

      v. would that you were hot or cold; say: rich, prosperous, need nothing but are wretched, pitiable, poor, blind, naked

  (c) *admonition to repent:*

      i. remember from what you have fallen; do the works you did at first

      ii. repent

      iii. gave her time, she refuses to repent

      iv. remember, keep what you have received and heard

      v. buy from me gold refined by fire (rich); white garments (clothing and cover shame of nakedness); salve (heal eyes); those whom I love I reprove

  (d) *"behold": prophetic revelatory saying:*

      i. do not fear what about to suffer; devil about to imprison some of you; be tested for "ten days"

      ii. will throw her and those who commit adultery with her on sick bed, tribulation; strike her children (disciples) dead; all will know I search

Continued

Continued

    mind and heart and give each as they deserve; but those do not fol-
    low this teaching and have not learned "deep things of Satan," no
    other burden
   iii. make those of synagogue of Satan, claim be Jews but are not, come
    and bow at your feet; learn that I have loved you; because you have
    kept my word of endurance I will keep you from trial coming on the
    whole world to test those who dwell on earth
   iv. I stand at the door and knock
  (e) *promise the Lord is coming:*
   i. if do not repent, will come and remove lampstand
   iii. will come and war against them with the sword of my mouth
   v. will come like a thief, you know not what hour
   vi. am coming soon
   vii. one who hears and opens, I will come and eat together
  (f) *exhortation to endure:*
   i. this you have, you hate the Nicolaitans
   ii. be faithful unto death and I will give you crown of life
   iv. to the rest who have not "learned the deep things of Satan," no fur-
    ther burden
   vi. still a few not soiled their garments, worthy to walk with me in white
   vi. hold to what you have so that no one may seize your crown
 4. Eschatological promise to the victors
  (a) *description of victor:*
   i–iii. one who conquers
   iv. one who conquers and keeps my works until the end
   v–vii. one who conquers
  (b) *the reward:*
   i. eat of the tree of life, in paradise
   ii. not hurt by the second death
   iii. hidden manna, white stone with new name known only to the recip-
    ient
   iv. power to rule over the nations (as I given power from God); the
    morning star
   v. white garments; not blot name out of book of life; I will acknowledge
    before God and angels
   vi. a pillar in the temple of my God, never go out of it; inscribed: name
    of my God, name of God's city, the new Jerusalem, my own new
    name
   vii. sit with me on my throne (as I on Father's throne)
 5. "Let him who has ears to hear, hear what the Spirit says..." (2:7, 11, 17,
  29; 3:6, 13, 22)

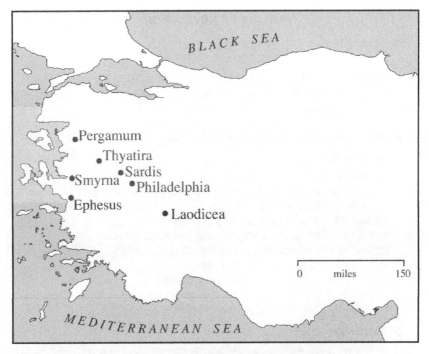

BLACK SEA

•Pergamum
•Thyatira
•Sardis
•Smyrna •Philadelphia
•Ephesus
• Laodicea

0   miles   150

MEDITERRANEAN SEA

The seven churches of Asia mentioned in Revelation 2–3

The Vision Cycles

Most of Revelation is taken up with visions that the prophet is shown in heaven. These visions can be divided into cycles of seven, punctuated by the contrasting visions of the two great cities: the earthly Babylon and the heavenly Jerusalem. Some visions form numbered sets. For others, we have divided the sequence to exhibit the numerical pattern of seven. There is considerable interlocking between cycles of visions. This technique suggests that the visions do not represent a linear, temporal sequence but that they are repetitions of the same pattern raised to another level of intensity. The cycles have also been linked together by internal references to three woes. The final woe is the cycle of seven plagues. The epilogue returns to the opening of the book. Both pronounce blessings on those who heed the words of the prophecy it contains (1:3; 22:7b). Both emphasize that these are things that God's plan has destined to happen soon (1:1; 22:6, 12a). Both remind the reader that Jesus, the faithful martyr, is the beginning and end of all things (1:8, 17). The beatitudes in the epilogue recall the promises made to the victorious in the letters. The final blessing in 22:21 may also call to mind the conclusion of the Christian letter form.

OUTLINE OF REVELATION   [21–2]

Prologue (1:1–8)

    (a) Preface (1:1–3)
    (b) Greeting to churches in Asia (1:4–6)
    (c) Prophetic sayings (1:7–8)

Call vision (1:9–20)

Letters to the seven churches in Asia (2:1–3:22)

Seven seals (4:1–8:5)

    (a) Vision of God's throne (4:1–11)
    (b) Vision of the enthroned Lamb with the scroll (5:1–14)
    (c) Seals #1–4: Four horsemen (6:1–8)
    (d) Seal #5: Martyrs crying out for judgment (6:9–11)
    (e) Seal #6: Earthquake, proleptic judgment (6:12–17)
    (f) Sealing of servants from the twelve tribes (7:1–17)
    (g) Seal #7: Silence in heaven (8:1–5)
        (i) Silence—preparation of the trumpets (8:1–2)
        (ii) From the altar: heavenward, the incense of prayers to God; toward
            earth, burning coals, thunder, earthquake (8:3–5)

Seven trumpets (8:2, 6—11:19)

    (a) Trumpets #1–4: Plagues fall from the heavens (8:6–13)
    (b) Trumpet #5: Falling star opens abyss, locust plague led by angel of the
        abyss (9:1–11) [End of first woe, two more to come, v. 12]
    (c) Trumpet #6: Deadly cavalry from Euphrates released (9:13–21)
    (d) Seer eats the little scroll from the hand of angel: commissioning to
        prophesy again (10:1–11)
    (e) Seer measures the temple and the altar (11:1–3)
    (f) Testimony of the two witnesses in Jerusalem; martyred by the beast;
        taken to heaven; deadly earthquake in the city (11:4–13) [End of sec-
        ond woe, third to come, v. 14]
    (g) Trumpet #7: Heavenly acclamation of Christ who rules for ever; vision
        of the ark with lightning, voices, thunder, earthquake, hail (11:15–19)

Unnumbered visions: Followers of Lamb vs. the beast (12:1—15:4)

    (a) Woman and her offspring vs. the dragon (12:1–17)
    (b) Beast from the sea (13:1–10)
    (c) Beast from the earth (13:11–18)
    (d) On Mount Zion: song of the 144,000 (14:1–7; cf. 7:1–17)
    (e) Angelic heralds: warning and promise to the saints (14:8–13)
    (f) Son of Man and angels harvest the earth (14:14–20)
    (g) Sea of glass: those who have conquered the beast (15:2–4)

Seven bowls of wrath (15:1, 5—16:21)

    (a) Introduction: bowls are end of wrath of God (15:1)

(b) Angels given the seven bowls by throne creature (15:5-8)

(c) Bowl #1: poured on earth: sores on those who worship the beast (16:1-2)

(d) Bowl #2: in sea: becomes like blood, everything in it dies (16:3)

(e) Bowl #3: rivers and fountains: become blood, just judgment for blood of martyrs acclaimed (16:4-7)

(f) Bowl #4: on sun: it scorches humans, who blaspheme God and do not repent (16:8-9)

(g) Bowl #5: on throne beast: kingdom darkened; humans curse God for sores, do not repent (16:10-11)

(h) Bowl #6: on Euphrates: demonic spirits from mouths of dragon, beast and false prophet assemble armies at Armageddon (16:12-16; cf. 9:13-21)

(i) Bowl #7: in air: voice sounds from temple, thunder, quakes, cities split, islands and mountains vanish, hail (16:17-21)

Babylon and her destruction (17:1—19:10)

(a) "Babylon the Great," harlot to the kings of the earth, drunk with the blood of the saints (17:1-6)

(b) Angelic interpretation of the vision: Rome, her rulers, client kings, and wars (17:7-18)

(c) Heavenly announcement: the hour of judgment on Babylon has come (18:1-8)

(d) Laments for the fate of Babylon by kings of the earth, merchants, captains, and sailors (18:9-20)

(e) Angelic announcement: Babylon and all who dwell in her to be thrown down (18:21-24)

(f) Heavenly praise to God for judgment against Babylon (19:1-4)

(g) Praise to Lamb: Celebration of divine marriage feast (19:5-10)

Unnumbered visions: Judgment of the earth (19:11—21:8)

(a) Rider on the white horse (19:11-16)

(b) Victory feast on bodies of the slain (19:17-21)

(c) Angel binds Satan for a thousand years (20:1-3)

(d) Victorious martyrs reign with Christ a thousand years (20:4-6)

(e) Fire from heaven consumes the Satanic hosts (20:7-10)

(f) Judgment of all humanity: Book of life (20:11-15)

(g) New heaven and earth: Righteous to dwell with God (21:1-8)

Bride of the Lamb: The heavenly Jerusalem (21:9—22:5)

(a) Jewels that adorn the bride (21:2, 9-21)

(b) God's presence in the heavenly city (21:22-27)

(c) River of water, tree of life, and God as its light (22:1-5)

Epilogue: Transmission of the prophecy and beatitudes (22:6-21)

The Apocalyptic Imagination

Revelation draws on a rich tradition of mythic and Old Testament imagery. The prophet also reminds readers of Christian traditions such as the earlier predictions of judgment and exhortations to watchfulness (e.g., Mark 13; Matt 24); the death and resurrection/exaltation of Jesus to God's throne, where Jesus is now "king" over the nations; titles and epithets of Jesus such as Son of Man, Son of God, Son of David, and Lamb of God.

Two Jewish apocalypses written at about the same time as Revelation, *4 Ezra* and *2 Baruch*, speak of the suffering and disorientation felt by Jews after the Romans had destroyed Jerusalem in AD 70. Like Revelation, these Jewish apocalypses are concerned with the question of why God does not send the messianic age soon and destroy the forces of evil, especially the Satanic Roman Empire. They both reassure the faithful that the end of the evil age is coming and that faithfulness to God will not be lost or forgotten.

Apocalyptic writings often speak for people who are oppressed, especially by a larger political power that they cannot control. Revelation emphasizes the imagery of the faithful martyr. Jesus is the prime example of the martyr. There is a special thousand-year reign on earth for those Christians who have been martyred. The prophet John is suffering exile to the island of Patmos for his preaching (Rev 1:9). The letter to the church at Pergamum mentions another famous martyr, Antipas, who had died in that city. As you can see from the outline, there is a major turning point in the book at chapter 12. From chapter 12 on, we are shown the conflict between the children of the heavenly Jerusalem and those who worship the beast. Just before that turning point, we are shown a vision of two martyrs in Jerusalem. Their fate is like that of the Lord for whom they died. After three days, God sweeps them up to heaven (Rev 11:4–13). This manifestation of divine power includes an earthquake, a frequent sign of divine presence. Earthquakes, thunder, and signs in the heavens were also a common part of the scenery of the end of the world. Matthew 27:51–54 has the apocalyptic signs of earthquake and raising of the dead in Jerusalem associated with the crucifixion. Matthew 28:2 introduces another great earthquake and descent of an angel with the opening of Jesus' tomb.

Revelation centers its confidence on Christ. By transporting the hearer into the heavenly court where the victory of the Lamb is proclaimed, the prophet shows that Christ is Lord over the kings of the earth. Suffering Christians are swept up into that glorious victory. Throughout Revelation we are reminded that Jesus has triumphed over death (e.g., 1:7, 8; 2:8; 5:5–6). We are also shown images of the faithful, the holy people ransomed by the Lamb's blood (1:5–6); the 144,000 from the tribes of Israel (7:1–8; 14:1–7); the martyrs clothed in white (6:10–11; 7:13–17); and multitudes from all the nations (7:9–10). These visions of the community of the redeemed provide powerful symbols with which readers can identify.

Most apocalypses are presented as pseudonymous works from an ancient figure that was hidden until the "end of the age." Revelation is quite different. The concluding sayings against tampering with the revelation (22:18–19) also insist that it is not to be sealed up (22:10). Its author does not speak as a voice from the distant past but as a fellow Christian. He gives his name, John (1:1), and suggests that he belonged to a group of Christian prophets active in the churches of Asia Minor (22:9). Thus, the first readers of Revelation were receiving a divine message mediated through one of their own prophets. Since the author is in exile because of his preaching, he may have been very well known in the region.

The Political Message of Revelation

The symbolism of Revelation provides a powerful description of the true divine kingship and its heavenly manifestations. The Christian reader is drawn into identifying with the holy ones who follow and sing praises to the Lamb. At the same time Revelation stands in a tradition that used apocalyptic symbolism to condemn the powerful empires of the ancient world. Daniel 7–12 had already established the pattern of using a succession of beasts to describe successive empires. Daniel 7 also uses the figure of a Son of Man exalted to God's throne as judge over those empires and as vindication of the suffering martyrs of Israel. Apocalypses use the code name "Babylon" for the Roman Empire. No first-century reader would have any difficulty figuring out that the number of the beast in Revelation 13:18 was the spelling of "Nero Caesar" in a Semitic alphabet. Nor would they have had any difficulty recognizing in the laments of the merchants and sea captains a frequent criticism of Rome in the "underground" oracles and apocalypses from the eastern part of the empire. Rome is routinely pictured as raping the provinces of Asia for their wealth. Here are some examples of that perspective taken from the Jewish *Sibylline Oracles*:

> However much wealth Rome received from tribute-bearing Asia, Asia will receive three times that much again from Rome and will repay her deadly arrogance to her. Whatever number from Asia served the house of the Italians [i.e., as slaves], twenty times that number of Italians will be serfs in Asia; in poverty they will be liable to pay ten-thousandfold. (3.350–55)

> Great wealth will come out of Asia, which Rome itself once plundered and deposited in her house of many possessions. She will

then pay back twice as much and more to Asia, and then there
will be a surfeit of war. (4.145–48)

...the famous, lawless kingdom of the Italians...will show many
evils to all men and will expend the toils of the men of all the
earth...the beginning of evils will be the desire for deceitful gold
and silver...If the huge earth did not have its throne far from the
starry heaven, men would not have equal light, but it would be
marketed for gold and would belong to the rich, and God would
have prepared another world for beggars...Having abundant gold,
[Hadrian] will also gather more silver from his enemies and strip
and undo them...[Marcus Aurelius] will control dominions far and
wide, a most piteous king, who will shut up and guard all the wealth
of the world in his home, so that when the blazing matricidal exile
[Nero] returns from the ends of the earth, he will give these things
to all and award great wealth to Asia...Woe to you, Italian land,
great savage nation. You did not perceive whence you came, naked
and unworthy to the light of the sun, so that you might go again
naked to the same place and later come to judgment because you
judge unjustly. (8.9–11, 17–18, 33–36, 68–72, 95–99)

These examples show that descriptions of the corruption and fall of Rome
similar to that in Revelation 17–18 would have been familiar in the provinces
of Asia Minor. For the *Sibylline Oracles* Roman power is to be smashed in a
military victory, led by the emperor Nero leading armies out of Asia.
Revelation does not share this political hope. The only armies to come from
the east are the demonic forces from the Euphrates region. The legend of
Nero redivivus is mentioned in Revelation 13:3 as the head with a "mortal
wound" that heals and then seduces the earth. Revelation 17:15–18 pictures
the client kings of Rome (also represented by the beast from the earth in
13:11–17) finally revolting and waging a war against her. But the saints in
Revelation do not participate in any such military actions. Their opposition to
the beast consists in refusing to grant the beast worship and in continuing as
faithful witnesses even at the cost of their own lives.

Honoring the Emperor?

What is implied in these warnings against worshiping the beast (e.g.,
13:4, 8, 15)? It is difficult for modern readers to understand what was
involved in cultic and civic honors paid to the emperor. Everyone knew that
the emperors were not divine in the same sense that the gods and goddesses
of pagan mythology and cults were. But from the time of Julius Caesar on,
Roman art depicted the deceased emperor being carried up to heaven to join

the company of the gods. Temples were erected and sacrifices offered to the "divine Caesar." Under his successor, Augustus, such honors could be paid to the living emperor. Honors included temples dedicated to the "genius of the emperor," sacrifices and festal games in his honor, or ceremonial inscriptions describing the emperor as the great benefactor and savior of humanity. Often such honors were voted by a city in hopes that the emperor would respond by bestowing some benefit such as relief from a particular form of taxation. In some cities of Asia Minor wealthy freedmen could aspire to the honor of holding a priesthood in the local imperial cult.

The emperor did not have to compel people to worship him as a god in the manner of a twentieth-century dictator. Imperial honors might come from cities as a matter of civic pride or as a shrewd political calculation. Perhaps you noticed that Revelation 13:12–15 speaks of those who received their power from the beast creating a miraculous statue of the mortally wounded head and causing people to worship it. In a well-known incident the emperor Caligula (ca. AD 40) had ordered his governor in Syria to get his statue erected in the Jerusalem temple even if he had to use armed force to do so (see Josephus, *War* 2.185–87; *Antiquities* 18.261–309; Philo, *Embassy to Gaius* 188–348; Tacitus, *Histories* 5.9). Our sources have varying accounts of the episode, though all agree that the Jewish people were willing to risk death in war rather than violate the law by setting up such a statue. Philo's account, written after he had been part of an embassy of Alexandrian Jews to the emperor Gaius Caligula, emphasizes the emperor's manic desire for divine honors. While Josephus and Tacitus claim that erection of the statue

Reconstruction of the Antonine altar at Ephesus

was prevented only by the emperor's death in AD 41, Philo reports that he had relented (after extensive lobbying by the Roman governor and the Herodian king Agrippa II, who lived in Rome at the time). However, at the same time, Caligula ordered the governor to encourage the dedication of temples and statues in other cities. Imperial images were forced on Jewish synagogues in Alexandria. Failure to pay honors to the emperor could easily be construed as evidence of subversion and civic disloyalty.

Several of the cities to which the letters in Revelation are addressed were involved in promoting the imperial cult. Ephesus and Smyrna competed with each other in paying honors at festivals. Pergamum was the regional center of the cult. It had received permission in 29 BC to build a temple to "the divine Augustus and the goddess Roma." This famous temple might be the "throne of Satan" referred to in Revelation 3:13. People in Thyatira worshiped the emperor as Apollo incarnate and son of Zeus. In AD 26, Sardis was one of ten cities competing for the right to build a temple honoring the emperor but lost out to Smyrna. Since Laodicea was the wealthiest city in Phrygia and especially prosperous under the Flavian emperors (Revelation was most likely written under Domitian, d. AD 96), we would certainly expect some form of emperor cult to be present in that city as well.

Such dedications and honors were not only the responsibilities of civic officials alone. Individual trade groups might offer such honors on a smaller scale. Revelation 18 singles out merchants and sea captains as persons who lament the fall of Rome. Some mercantile associations might make offerings in the name of the emperor or erect statues in his honor. Some of these honors were not strictly "worship," that is, they were not sacrifices that solicited benefits in return for piety as one might expect from a god. However, the distinction between cultic activity directed toward the gods and sacrifices offered for the well-being of the emperor was not always carefully maintained. When the distinctions became blurred, then common activities using the emperor's name or image would appear idolatrous to Jews and Christians. Images of the emperor on coins, for example, pictured the emperor as though he were one of the gods. Local mints put out such coins. Consequently, Revelation 13:17 remarks that no one could buy or sell unless he had the mark of the beast. The "mark" in question could refer to the images of the emperor on coins. In addition the name of the emperor, with appropriate god-like epithets (the "blasphemous name" of 13:1), was used on public occasions. Contracts and oaths in court might refer to the emperor, as would the ceremonial libations poured out at public banquets.

As the Caligula episode shows, the Jewish community had limits that it would not transgress. As long as the temple was standing in Jerusalem, the priests there did offer daily sacrifices to God for the emperor's welfare. But the Jews would not violate the first commandment by putting up statues or images of the emperor. Jesus sided with those who treated the images on imperial coins as unimportant (Mark 12:13–17), though coins without such iconography were used within the temple itself. Both the Pauline (Rom 13:1–10) and the Petrine (1 Pet 2:13–17) tradition instructed Christians to honor the emperor. These traditions were shaped by contexts in which the "honor" due the emperor did not exceed the boundaries of appropriate respect for one who stood at the top of the social and political order of a great empire. However, Revelation insists that such accommodation is no longer possible. Christians must resist Satanic divinization of Roman power in all of its forms.

Discipleship in Revelation

With its praise of martyrdom and its uncompromising refusal to venerate the emperor, Revelation calls Christians to a costly form of discipleship. Revelation considers the "mark of the beast" (Rev 13:16–17) a parody of the mark that the Christian receives (7:1–8). Anyone who has the "mark of the beast" is destined for eternal punishment (14:9–11; 16:2). This rigorous position would clearly have economic consequences for Christians like those in Laodicea who were condemned for wealth and prosperity that apparently derived from the city's extensive textile industry (3:15–18).

The Jewish community retained its policy of nonparticipation in veneration of the emperor by appealing to its ancestral religion and special privileges granted to the Jewish community by Roman emperors. The letters in Revelation refer to tension between Christians and "those who claim to be Jews but are not" in the cities of Smyrna (2:9–10) and Philadelphia (3:9). The message to Smyrna links the "synagogue of Satan" with the persecution of Christians. Perhaps members of the local Jewish community had accused Christians before the local magistrates. In the second century, the city's bishop, Polycarp, was martyred as the result of such opposition (ca. AD 156). The hostile references to Judaism in these passages of Revelation reflect clear separation of the two communities. Christians claim to be the true heirs to the tradition of Israel. They may have thought that they ought to have the same rights as "resident aliens" permitted to settle their own affairs as the local Jewish community did.

Another struggle in the churches of Asia Minor was internal. The author attacks a group known as the Nicolaitans and the followers of other Christian teachers treated as examples of Old Testament false prophets and idolaters, Balaam and Jezebel (2:14–15; 2:20–23). By the second century, the Nicolaitans was the name of a gnostic sect. John claims that the prophetess Jezebel had been given an opportunity to repent (2:21). He may have delivered a prophetic oracle against her teaching at some earlier time. The accusations directed against "Balaam" and "Jezebel" involve "eating food sacrificed to idols and prostitution." The decree of the Jerusalem Council reported in Acts 15:28–29 forbids eating food used in idol sacrifices, food slaughtered in violation of kosher laws, and sexual immorality. Clearly, Revelation expects this ruling binding on Christians. We have already met two different positions in the New Testament. Some Christians at Corinth held that whatever Christians did was indifferent. Their views could be represented as idolatry and sexual immorality. Some visited prostitutes and others accepted meat sacrificed to an idol as indifferent since the idol was no god. Paul rejected their views. He held that Christians had to avoid prostitutes (6:12–20). However, he permitted eating idol meat in situations where it was clear that no worship of the gods was implied, at home or the house of a friend but not in a ritual meal at a pagan temple (e.g., 1 Cor 8:8–10; 10:25–29). This middle-ground position kept open the possibility of social and business contacts with non-Christian associates and relatives. The "false prophets" attacked by Revelation may even have been advocating more extreme forms of accommodation like those advocated by the "strong" at Corinth. It is impossible to tell.

You can see that the Christianity advocated by Revelation would have to form its own trade associations, burial societies, and the like, since it would be difficult for Christians to participate in groups that included non-Christians. Christians could not engage in any of the associations, clubs, or even occupations that would require any form of gesture, word, or ritual that might be construed as "worshiping the beast." The martyrs are praised for virginity (14:4). The author himself may have been an ascetic prophet who had gone from city to city until he was exiled. Though Revelation does not suggest that all Christians must refrain from marriage, its ideal of Christianity does seem to require sectarian withdrawal from the everyday world of association with non-Christians.

Worship with Angels—Revelation as Liturgy

Its visions of heavenly hosts praising God, myriads of the faithful joined with them, and the woman clothed with the sun who is mother of the messiah and his followers make Revelation an important part of Catholic worship. A version of the "holy, holy, holy" sung ceaselessly before God's throne (4:8) is sung or said during every Mass. Other hymns from Revelation (e.g., 4:11; 5:9–10, 12, 13) are recited as canticles in the Liturgy of the Hours. Several passages from Revelation may be selected to console the faithful in celebrating a Catholic funeral (14:13; 20:11—21:1; 2:1–5a, 6b–7; 7:9–10, 15–17; 21:1a, 3–5a). The woman clothed with the sun celebrates the Blessed Virgin Mary. It is the first reading at Mass celebrating the Assumption of the Blessed Virgin on August 15 (11:19a; 12:1–6a, 10ab). Though bits of the judgment oracles or descriptions of faithful martyrs are occasionally read at Mass, the Catholic liturgy focuses on the triumphant celebrations and hymns in heaven.

The words of consolation heard during the funeral liturgy, "and God himself will be with them; he will wipe every tear from their eyes. Death will be no more..." (21:3b–4a, NRSV), sets the leitmotif for the resolution of Revelation. As such, it also forms an appropriate culmination to the entire Christian scripture in which God's plan of salvation that began in Genesis with creation achieves its goal. In the final chapter of Revelation angels who had once been agents of plagues on earth conduct the seer around the glorious new Jerusalem in which God and the Lamb dwell (21:9—22:5). These visions transpose elements from the great prophetic images of the new Jerusalem from Isaiah and Ezekiel into the eternal heavenly city. Eucharistic Prayer II of the third edition of the Roman Missal uses awkward English in remembering the deceased: "...and all who have died in your mercy welcome them *into the light of your face.*" But it captures a tiny bit of the vision in Revelation 22:3–5: "But the throne of God and of the Lamb will be in it, and his servants will worship him; and *they will see his face*, ...they need no light of lamp or sun, for *the Lord God will be their light*" (NRSV).

At one point John, the prophet, makes a curious mistake, prostrating himself in worship before his angelic guide (22:8–9). He is immediately reprimanded. Angels are as much God's creatures as human beings are. There is one activity that draws angels, saints, and faithful believers together in a great chorus, worshiping God.

Summary

Anyone who takes the time to study Revelation carefully can see that this visionary prophet has a clear and consistent message for the churches of his region. He sees the danger that Christians in Asia Minor will be led to accommodate with the surrounding culture in ways that constitute denying their faith. Some may have been trying to avoid persecution or the general forms of harassment mentioned in 1 Peter. Others could have had more secular goals: adaption to the demands of business associates or social relationships. The sharp polemic against other Christian teachers indicates that not all Christians saw the situation in Asia Minor in the same dark tones as Revelation does.

The dramatic imagery of the beast warring against the offspring of the heavenly woman clothed with the sun (Israel, the church; Rev 12:13–17) makes it clear that there is no "middle ground" in this situation. Christians are engaged in the cosmic struggle between evil and the power of God. For humanity at large, the prophet predicts that no matter how dramatic or severe the divine signs are, people will blaspheme God rather than repent (e.g., 16:8–11). These visions are not expected to scare non-Christians into conversion, as some of Jehovah's Witnesses who ring the doorbell on Saturday morning seem to think. John's message is directed toward his fellow Christians. They can repent and recover their former enthusiasm. They can be encouraged to stand fast when confronted by times of suffering. They can be inspired by its visions of heavenly victory with the Lamb, heavenly worship, and celebration that believers will one day share.

STUDY QUESTIONS

Facts You Should Know

1. Give examples of old "mythic themes" that are used by the author of Revelation.
2. What are the basic elements in the letters to the seven churches? How are the letters linked to the rest of the book?
3. How is the vision section of Revelation constructed? Which cities represent the earthly and heavenly worlds?
4. According to Revelation what is the role of suffering and martyrdom in the life of Christian disciples? Why do Christians find themselves faced with martyrdom?
5. How does the criticism of the Roman Empire in Revelation compare with other non-Christian writings from this period?
6. Describe what actions were considered "worshiping the emperor" in the first century. How had Jews come into conflict with Roman authorities over "emperor worship"?

Things to Do

1. Read the seven letters, making a list of those who are praised and those who are condemned in each letter. What ideal of Christian discipleship emerges from your lists?
2. Read Revelation and pick out each time Jesus is shown as a "faithful martyr" or the Lamb who has triumphed over death. Also, pick out each time we are shown the fate of Christian martyrs. How do these images encourage the audience of Revelation to remain faithful disciples?

Things to Think About

1. Revelation warns Christians against making easy compromises with the culture that surrounds them by showing that some parts of the culture are "Satanic." What warnings would Revelation address to Christians today?
2. The visions of plagues show that even with the most terrible devastation of the earth, the nations do not repent. What is the cause of this blindness? How is it evident in our world?

BIBLIOGRAPHY FOR
FURTHER STUDY

Chapter 1: Why Study the Bible?

Some basic tools for studying the Bible might include:

A Concordance: Lists all occurrences of a word in the Bible. For example, J. R. Kohlenberger, *NRSV Concordance. Unabridged.* Grand Rapids: Zondervan, 1991.

A Gospel Parallel: Sets out the parallel passages in the gospels side by side, so that it is easier to compare different versions of the same stories or sayings across the four gospels. For example, K. Aland, ed. *Synopsis of the Four Gospels in English.* United Bible Societies, 1972.

A Bible Dictionary: Provides definitions of terms; identification of persons and places; information on the individual books of the Bible along with theological and other topics that the student of the Bible encounters. For example, D. N. Freedman, ed. *Eerdmans Dictionary of the Bible.* Grand Rapids: Eerdmans, 2000; K. D. Sakenfeld, ed. *The New Interpreter's Dictionary of the Bible.* 5 vols. Nashville: Abingdon, 2006–9. More focused on literary and rhetorical features of the New Testament, David E. Aune, *The Westminster Dictionary of New Testament and Early Christian Literature and Rhetoric.* Louisville: Westminster John Knox, 2003. Dictionaries on more specialized topics related to the Jewish context of New Testament writings include J. J. Collins and D. C. Harlow, eds. *The Eerdmans Dictionary of Early Judaism.* Grand Rapids: Eerdmans, 2010; T. Lim and J. J. Collins, eds. *The Oxford Handbook of the Dead Sea Scrolls.* Oxford: Oxford University, 2010.

Commentary Series: The quality of individual volumes varies across any given series. The following series are written by scholars with general readers in mind: Dianne Bergant and Robert J. Karris, eds. *Collegeville Bible Commentary.* Liturgical Press; *Interpretation* series. Louisville: Westminster John Knox, 1989; *Abingdon New Testament Commentary* series. Nashville; Abingdon. A twelve-volume set that covers the entire

Bible for general readers, seminary students, and pastors, Leander E. Keck, ed. *The New Interpreter's Bible*. Nashville: Abingdon, 1995–2002 [NT in vols. VIII–XII]. A more academic, one-volume commentary by Roman Catholic scholars: R. E. Brown, J. A. Fitzmyer, and R. E. Murphy, eds. *New Jerome Biblical Commentary*. Englewood Cliffs, NJ: Prentice Hall, 1990.

A Bible Atlas: H. G. May, ed. *Oxford Bible Atlas*. New York: Oxford University, 2009.

Greek Language: F. Danker, *The Concise Greek-English Lexicon of the Greek New Testament*. Chicago: University of Chicago, 2009; J. J. Clabeaux, *New Testament Greek: A Systems Approach*. Scranton, PA: University of Scranton, 2009; G. L. Stevens, *New Testament Greek Intermediate. From Morphology to Translation*. Eugene, OR: Cascade, 2008.

New Testament Apocrypha: Occasionally you will find references to apocryphal gospels, such as the *Gospel of Thomas*, and other early Christian writings that are not part of the scriptures. A comprehensive one-volume collection of these writings is J. K. Elliott, *The Apocryphal New Testament*. Oxford: Clarendon, 1993.

Methods of Analyzing the New Testament: D. J. Harrington, *Interpreting the New Testament. A Practical Guide*. Collegeville: Liturgical Press, 1990; idem, *How Do Catholics Read the Bible?* Lanham, MD: Rowman and Littlefield, 2005; idem, *How to Read the Gospels*. Hyde Park, NY: New York City Press, 1996; J. A. Fitzmyer, *The Interpretation of Scripture. In Defense of the Historical-Critical Method*. Mahwah: Paulist Press, 2008.

Chapter 2: The World of Jesus

History and archaeology

Bond, H. K. *Caiaphas. Friend of Rome and Judge of Jesus?* Louisville: Westminster, 2004.

Goodman, M. *Rome and Jerusalem. The Clash of Ancient Civilizations*. New York: Knopf, 2007.

Levine, L. I. *Jerusalem. Portrait of the City in the Second Temple Period (538 B.C.E.–70 C.E.)*. New York: Jewish Publication Society, 2002.

Reed, J. L. *The HarperCollins Visual Guide to the New Testament. What Archaeology Reveals about the First Century*. San Francisco: HarperCollins, 2007.

———. *Archaeology of the Galilean Jesus*. Harrisburg, PA: Trinity Press International, 2000.

Richardson, P. *Building Jewish in the Roman East*. Waco, TX: Baylor University, 2004.

Sociological studies

D'Ambra, E. *Roman Women*. Cambridge: Cambridge University, 2007.

Neyrey, J. H., and Stewart, E. C., eds. *The Social World of the New Testament. Insights and Models*. Peabody, MA: Hendrickson, 2008.

Osiek, C., and MacDonald, M. Y. *A Woman's Place. House Churches in Earliest Christianity*. Minneapolis: Fortress, 2006.

Stegmann, E. W., and Stegemann, W. *The Jesus Movement. A Social History of Its First Century*. Minneapolis: Fortress, 1999.

Jewish literature

Charlesworth, J. H., ed. *The Old Testament Pseudepigrapha*. 2 vols. New York: Doubleday, 1983/1984.

Collins, J. J. *The Scepter and the Star. The Messiahs of the Dead Sea Scrolls and Other Ancient Literature*. Revised edition. Grand Rapids: Eerdmans, 2011.

Lim, T. H., ed. *The Dead Sea Scrolls in Their Historical Context*. Edinburgh: T. & T. Clark, 2000.

Solomon, N., ed. *The Talmud. A Selection*. New York: Penguin, 2009.

Sparks, H. F. D. *The Apocryphal Old Testament*. Oxford: Oxford University, 1984.

VanderKam, J. C. *An Introduction to Early Judaism*. Grand Rapids: Eerdmans, 2001.

Vermes, G. *The Complete Dead Sea Scrolls in English*. New York: Penguin, 1997.

Chapter 3: The Life of Jesus

Reconstructing the life of Jesus

Evans, C. A. *Encyclopedia of the Historical Jesus*. New York: Routledge, 2007.

Levine, A. J., Allison, D. C., Jr., and Crossan, J. D., eds. *The Historical Jesus in Context*. Princeton: Princeton University, 2006.

Meier, J. P. *A Marginal Jew. Rethinking the Historical Jesus. Vol. 1: The Roots of the Problem and the Person*. New York: Doubleday, 1991; *Vol. 2: Mentor, Message and Miracles*. New York: Doubleday, 1994; *Vol. 3: Companions and Competitors*. New Haven: Yale Univeristy, 2001; *Vol. 4: Law and Love*, New Haven: Yale University, 2009.

Special topics

Brown, R. E. *The Birth of the Messiah*. 2nd edition. New York: Doubleday, 1993.
———. *The Death of the Messiah*. New York: Doubleday, 1994.

As others see Jesus

Kaltner, J. *Ishmael Instructs Isaac. An Introduction to the Qur'an for Bible Readers.* Collegeville: Liturgical Press, 1999.
Khalidi, T. *The Muslim Jesus. Sayings and Stories in Islamic Literature.* Cambridge, MA: Harvard University, 2001.
Levine, A. J. *The Misunderstood Jew. The Church and the Scandal of the Jewish Jesus.* New York: HarperCollins, 2006.
Levine, A. J., and Brettler, M. Z., eds. *The Jewish Annotated New Testament: NRSV.* New York: Oxford University, 2011. An annotated edition of the New Testament with the introductions, notes, and essays by Jewish scholars.

Chapter 4: The Preaching of Jesus

Perkins, P. *Jesus as Teacher.* Cambridge: Cambridge University, 1990.

Parables

Beavis, M. A., ed. *The Lost Coin. Parables of Women, Work and Wisdom.* London: Sheffield, 2002.
Hultgren, A. J. *The Parables of Jesus.* Grand Rapids: Eerdmans, 2000.
Scott, B. B. *Hear Then the Parable.* Minneapolis: Fortress, 1989.
Snodgrass, K. *Stories with Intent. A Comprehensive Guide to the Parables of Jesus.* Grand Rapids: Eerdmans, 2008.

Sermon on the Mount

Allison, D. C. *The Sermon on the Mount. Inspiring the Moral Imagination.* New York: Crossroad, 1999.
Talbert, C. H. *Reading the Sermon on the Mount. Character Formation and Ethical Decision Making in Matthew 5–7.* Grand Rapids: Baker Academic, 2004.

Chapter 5: The Resurrection of Jesus

Nickelsburg, G. W. E. *Resurrection, Immortality and Eternal Life in Intertestamental Judaism and Early Christianity.* Expanded edition. Cambridge, MA: Harvard Theological Studies, 2006.
Perkins, P. *Resurrection. New Testament Witness and Contemporary Reflection.* New York: Doubleday, 1984.
Segal, A. *Life after Death. A History of the Afterlife in Western Religion.* New York: Doubleday, 2004.

Wright, N. T. *The Resurrection of the Son of God*. Minneapolis: Fortress, 2003.

Chapter 6: The Beginnings of Christology

Dunn, J. D. G. *Christology in the Making*. 2nd edition. Grand Rapids: Eerdmans, 1989.
Hurtado, L. W. *How on Earth Did Jesus Become a God? Historical Questions about Earliest Devotion to Jesus*. Grand Rapids: Eerdmans, 2005.
———. *Lord, Jesus Christ. Devotion to Jesus in Earliest Christianity*. Grand Rapids: Eerdmans, 2003.

Chapter 7: The World of Paul

Lieu, J. M. *Christian Identity in the Jewish and Graeco-Roman World*. Oxford: Oxford University, 2004.
Meeks, W. A. *The First Urban Christians. The Social World of the Apostle Paul*. New Haven: Yale University, 1983.
Sampley, J. P., ed. *Paul in the Greco-Roman World*. Harrisburg, PA: Trinity Press International, 2003.

Religious and philosophical movements

Beard, M., North, J., and Price, S. *The Religions of Rome*. Cambridge: Cambridge University, 1998.
Klauck, H.-J. *The Religious Context of Early Christianity*. Edinburgh: T. & T. Clark, 2000.
Reydams-Schils, G. *The Roman Stoics. Self, Responsibility, and Affection*. Chicago: University of Chicago, 2005.
Tripolitis, A. *Religions of the Hellenistic-Roman Age*. Grand Rapids: Eerdmans, 2002.
Turcan, R. *The Gods of Ancient Rome*. New York: Routledge, 2000.
Warrior, V. M. *Roman Religion*. Cambridge: Cambridge University, 2006.

Special topics

Beard, M. *The Fires of Vesuvius. Pompeii Lost and Found*. Cambridge, MA: Harvard University, 2008.
Glancy, J. A. *Slavery in Early Christianity*. New York: Oxford University, 2002.
Horn, C. B., and Martens, J. W. *"Let the Little Children Come to Me." Childhood and Children in Early Christianity*. Washington, DC: Catholic University, 2009.

Klauck, H.-J. *Ancient Letters and the New Testament*. Waco, TX: Baylor University, 2006.

Lefkowitz, M. R., and Fant, M. B. *Women's Life in Greece and Rome*. 3rd edition. Baltimore: Johns Hopkins University, 2005.

Smith, D. E. *From Symposium to Eucharist. The Banquet in the Early Christian World*. Minneapolis: Fortress, 2003.

Toner, J. *Popular Culture in Ancient Rome*. Cambridge: Polity Press, 2009.

Chapter 8: The Life of Paul

Meeks, W. A., and Fitzgerald, J. T., eds. *The Writings of St. Paul. Annotated Texts, Reception and Criticism*. 2nd edition. New York: W. W. Norton, 2007.

Murphy-O'Connor, J. *Paul. A Critical Life*. Oxford: Clarendon, 1996.

Schnelle, U. *Apostle Paul. His Life and Theology*. Grand Rapids: Baker Academic, 2005.

Pauline theology

Dunn, J. D. G. *The Theology of Paul the Apostle*. Grand Rapids: Eerdmans, 1998.

Fee, G. *Pauline Christology. An Exegetical-Theological Study*. Peabody, MA: Hendrickson, 2007.

Furnish, V. *The Moral Teaching of Paul*. 3rd edition. Nashville: Abingdon, 2009.

1 and 2 Thessalonians

Ascough, R. *Paul's Macedonian Associations. The Social Context of Philippians and 1 Thessalonians*. Tübingen: Mohr, 2003.

Malherbe, A. *The Letters to the Thessalonians*. New York: Doubleday, 2000.

Philippians and Philemon

Fitzmyer, J. *The Letter to Philemon*. New York: Doubleday, 2001.

Reumann, J. *The Letter to the Philippians*. New Haven: Yale University, 2008.

Thurston, B. B. *Philippians and Philemon*. Collegeville, MN: Liturgical Press, 2005.

Chapter 9: Christians: Jew and Gentile

Donaldson, T. L. *Paul and the Gentiles. Remapping the Apostle's Convictional World*. Minneapolis: Fortress, 1997.

Stendahl, K. *Final Account. Paul's Letter to the Romans*. Minneapolis: Fortress, 1995.

Galatians

Dunn, J. D. G. *The Theology of Paul's Letter to the Galatians*. Cambridge: Cambridge University, 1993.
Martyn, J. L. *The Letter to the Galatians*. New York: Doubleday, 1998.
Matera, F. J. *Galatians*. Collegeville, MN: Liturgical Press, 1993.

Romans

Byrne, B. *Romans*. Collegeville, MN: Liturgical Press, 1996.
Fitzmyer, J. A. *The Letter to the Romans*. New York: Doubleday, 1993.
Haacker, K. *The Theology of Paul's Letter to the Romans*. Cambridge: Cambridge University, 2003.

Special topics

Esler, P. F. *Conflict and Identity in Romans. The Social Setting of Paul's Letter*. Minneapolis: Fortress, 2003.
Fitzmyer, J. A. *Spiritual Exercises Based on Paul's Letter to the Romans*. Grand Rapids: Eerdmans, 2004.

Chapter 10: Divisions in Corinth

Ancient Corinth

Murphy-O'Connor, J. *St. Paul's Corinth. Texts and Archaeology*. 3rd edition. Collegeville, MN: Liturgical Press, 2002.

First Corinthians

Collins, R. F. *First Corinthians*. Collegeville, MN: Liturgical Press, 1999.
Fitzmyer, J. A. *First Corinthians*. New Haven: Yale University, 2008.
Furnish, V. P. *The Theology of the First Letter to the Corinthians*. Cambridge: Cambridge University, 1999.
Murphy-O'Connor, J. *Keys to First Corinthians*. Oxford: Oxford University, 2009.
Perkins, P. *1 Corinthians*. Grand Rapids, MI: Baker Academic, 2012.

Second Corinthians

Lambrecht, J. *Second Corinthians*. Collegeville, MN: Liturgical Press, 1999.
Matera, J. *II Corinthians*. Louisville: Westminster, 2003.
Murphy-O'Connor, J. *The Theology of the Second Letter to the Corinthians*. Cambridge: Cambridge University, 1991.

Chapter 11: Universalizing Paul's Message

Dunn, J. D. G. *Epistles to the Colossians and Philemon*. Grand Rapids, MI: Eerdmans, 1999.

Lincoln, A. T. *Ephesians*. Dallas: Word, 1990.

Lincoln, A. T., and Wedderburn, A. J. M. *The Theology of the Later Pauline Letters*. Cambridge: Cambridge University, 1993.

MacDonald, M. Y. *Colossians and Ephesians*. Collegeville, MN: Liturgical Press, 2000.

Chapter 12: Mark: Jesus, Suffering Messiah

Boring, M. E. *Mark*. Louisville: Westminster, 2006.

Donahue, J. R., and Harrington, D. J. *The Gospel of Mark*. Collegeville, MN: Liturgical Press, 2002.

Moloney, F. J. *The Gospel of Mark*. Peabody, MA: Hendrickson, 2002.

Special topics

Bockmuehl, M., and Hagner, D. A. *The Written Gospel*. Cambridge: Cambridge University, 2005.

Malbon, E. S. *In the Company of Jesus. Characters in Mark's Gospel*. Louisville: Westminster, 2000.

Perkins, P. *Introduction to the Synoptic Gospels*. Grand Rapids, MI: Eerdmans, 2007.

Telford, W. R. *The Theology of the Gospel of Mark*. Cambridge: Cambridge University, 1999.

Chapter 13: Matthew: Jesus, Teacher of Israel

Harrington, D. J. *The Gospel of Matthew*. Collegeville, MN: Liturgical Press, 2007.

Luz, U. *Matthew 1–7*. Minneapolis: Fortress, 1992.

———. *Matthew 8-20*. Minneapolis: Fortress, 2001.

———. *Matthew 21–28*. Minneapolis: Fortress, 2005.

Special topics

Luz, U. *The Theology of the Gospel of Matthew*. Cambridge: Cambridge University, 1995.

Luz, U., and Lapide, P. *Jesus in Two Perspectives. A Jewish-Christian Dialog.* Minneapolis: Augsburg, 1985.

Saldarini, A. J. *Matthew's Christian-Jewish Community.* Chicago: University of Chicago, 1994.

Chapter 14: Luke: Jesus, the Lord

Fitzmyer, J. A. *The Gospel According to Luke I–IX.* New York: Doubleday, 1981.

——. *The Gospel According to Luke X–XXIV.* 1985.

Johnson, L. T. *The Gospel of Luke.* Collegeville, MN: Liturgical Press, 1991.

Special topics

Darr, J. A. *On Character Building: The Reader and the Rhetoric of Characterization in Luke-Acts.* Louisville: Westminster, 1992.

Green, J. *Body, Soul and Human Life. The Nature of Humanity in the Bible.* Grand Rapids, MI: Baker, 2008.

——. *The Theology of the Gospel of Luke.* Cambridge: Cambridge University, 1995.

Chapter 15: John: Jesus, the Divine Son

Brown, R. E. *The Gospel According to John I–XII.* New York: Doubleday, 1966.

——. *The Gospel According to John XIII–XXI.* 1970.

Lincoln, A. T. *The Gospel According to Saint John.* Peabody, MA: Hendrickson, 2005.

Moloney, F. J. *The Gospel of John.* Collegeville, MN: Liturgical Press, 1998.

Neyrey, J. *The Gospel of John.* New York: Cambridge University, 2007.

Special topics

Koester, C. *The Word of Life. A Theology of John's Gospel.* Grand Rapids, MI: Eerdmans, 2008.

——. *Symbolism in the Fourth Gospel. Meaning, Mystery, Community.* 2nd edition. Minneapolis: Fortress, 2003.

Moody Smith, D. *The Theology of the Gospel of John.* Cambridge: Cambridge University, 1995.

Reinhartz, A. *Befriending the Beloved Disciple. A Jewish Reading of the Gospel of John.* New York: Continuum, 2001.

Thompson, M. M. *The God of the Gospel of God*. Grand Rapids, MI: Eerdmans, 2001.

Chapter 16: Acts: The Gospel to the Nations

Fitzmyer, J. A. *The Acts of the Apostles*. New York: Doubleday, 1998.
Johnson, L. T. *The Acts of the Apostles*. Collegeville, MN: Liturgical Press, 1992.
Pervo, R. *Acts*. Minneapolis: Fortress, 2009.

Special topics

Alexander, L. *Acts in its Ancient Literary Context. A Classicist Looks at the Acts of the Apostles*. New York: T. & T. Clark, 2005.
Johnson, L. T. *Septuagintal Midrash in the Speeches of Acts*. Milwaukee, WI: Marquette University, 2002.
———. *Among the Gentiles. Greco-Roman Religion and Christianity*. New Haven: Yale University, 2009.
Tannehill, R. *The Shape of Luke's Story. Essays on Luke–Acts*. Eugene, OR: Cascade, 2005.

Chapter 17: Hebrews: The Heavenly High Priest

Johnson, L. T. *Hebrews*. Louisville: Westminster, 2006.
Koester, C. *Hebrews*. New York: Doubleday, 2001.
Lindars, B. *The Theology of the Letter to the Hebrews*. Cambridge: Cambridge University, 1991.

Chapter 18: The Pastoral Epistles: A Pauline Tradition

Collins, R. F. *1 and 2 Timothy and Titus*. Louisville: Westminster, 2002.
Marshall, I. H. *A Critical and Exegetical Commentary on the Pastoral Epistles*. Edinburgh: T. & T. Clark, 1999.

Special topics

Collins, R. F. *The Many Faces of the Church. A Study in New Testament Ecclesiology*. New York: Crossroad, 2003.
Young, F. *The Theology of the Pastoral Letters*. Cambridge: Cambridge University, 1994.

Chapter 19: The Catholic Epistles: An Apostolic Heritage

Elliott, J. H. *1 Peter*. New York: Doubleday, 2000.
Hartin, P. J. *James*. Collegeville, MN: Liturgical Press, 2003.
Perkins, P. *First and Second Peter, James, and Jude*. Louisville: John Knox, 1995.
Senior, D., and Harrington, D. J. *1 Peter, Jude and 2 Peter*. Collegeville, MN: Liturgical Press, 2008.

Special topics

Painter, J. *Just James. The Brother of Jesus in History and Tradition*. 2nd edition. Columbia: University of South Carolina, 2004.
Perkins, P. *Peter. Apostle for the Whole Church*. Columbia: University of South Carolina, 1994.

Chapter 20: The Johannine Epistles: A Church Divided

Brown, R. *The Epistles of John*. New York: Doubleday, 1982.
Lieu, J. *I, II, and III John*. Louisville: Westminster, 2009.
Painter, J. *1, 2 and 3 John*. Collegeville, MN: Liturgical Press, 2003.

Special topics

Lieu, J. *The Theology of the Johannine Epistles*. Cambridge: Cambridge University, 1991.

Chapter 21: Revelation: Christianity and the Empire

Blount, B. K. *Revelation*. Louisville: Westminster, 2009.
Harrington, W. J. *Revelation*. Collegeville, MN: Liturgical Press, 2008.

Special topics

Bauckham, R. *The Theology of the Book of Revelation*. Cambridge: Cambridge University, 1993.
Blount, B. K. *Can I Get a Witness? Reading Revelation through African American Culture*. Louisville: Westminster, 2005.
Schüssler Fiorenza, E. *The Power of the Word. Scripture and the Rhetoric of Empire*. Minneapolis: Fortress, 2007.

INDEX OF MAPS, CHARTS, ILLUSTRATIONS, AND SUPPLEMENTAL TEXTS

SCRIPTURE AND
ANCIENT TEXTS INDEX

Pseudepigrapha, Dead Sea Scrolls, and Works of Ancient Authors

SUBJECT INDEX

Abba. *See* God
Abraham, 153, 157, 159
Acts, Book of, 5, 236–48
Adam: and Christ, 104, 154, 156
Antioch, 24, 113
Apocalyptic, 41–44, 274–75, 280, 287–88, 291, 294–96
Apollos, 166–67
Apostles, 68, 126, 264, 281
Apuleius, 116
Aramaic, 13, 100, 102
Archaeology, 15–18
Ascension, 136
Astrology, 114–15
Augustus, 189, 219, 297–98

Baptism, 103, 157, 184, 237; of Jesus, 199–200
Barnabas, 155
Bible: as literature, 11, 135
Bishops, 124, 263
Burial, 17, 66, 123

Caesar, Julius, 112, 296–97
Caesarea Maritima, 26–27
Calendar, 16, 40
Caligula, 297–98
Canon, 9–11, 275, 288
Capernaum, 18, 28, 201
Christology, 95–108, 210, 225, 280
Church, 125, 166, 179; as "body of Christ," 120, 170–71, 181–85; cultural models for, 19, 123–25, 265; house church, 124–25; leadership in, 208–9, 260, 263–64

Claudius, 17, 113, 131
Colossians, Letter to, 7, 178–85
Corinth, 121, 164–65
Corinthians, First Letter to, 5, 93, 121–23, 166, 170–72
Corinthians, Second Letter to, 5–6, 14, 167–70, 173–75
Covenant, 1–2; new covenant, 1–2, 37, 254–55
Creation, new, 157, 175; God as creator, 104–6
Crucifixion, 70, 99, 180, 216

Daniel, Book of, 42–44
Deacons, 264
Dead Sea Scrolls. *See* Qumran
Diaspora, 20
Disciples: the Beloved, 228, 279, 281; the Twelve, 67
Discipleship: in Acts, 245–47; in Hebrews, 254–55; in John, 232–34; in Luke, 221–22; in Mark, 107, 196–97; in Matthew, 60, 108, 208–10; in Revelations, 299–300
Divorce, 61, 170
Domitian, 298
Dualism: apocalyptic, 37, 40–42, 182; Johannine, 230, 280; philosophical, 251

Ecumenism: Bible and, 19–21
Emperor: veneration of, 112, 296–98
Empire, Roman, 111, 242, 295–96; Christian views of, 161, 299
Epaphras, 178